The Routledge
International Busir

An effective coach can help the business leader make sense of the challenges and complexities of modern international business, unlocking the potential of both leader and organization. This important new handbook offers the first comprehensive and detailed introduction to the theory and practice of international business coaching, drawing on the very latest academic research, as well as real-world examples of international best practice.

This book provides practitioners and students with an innovative theoretical framework, which extends existing coaching models to place coaching within cultural, organizational and group-team contexts. Contributors from around the world explore different perspectives and practices and offer practical tools to apply the theories and models to the real-life business context.

The Routledge Companion to International Business Coaching is essential reading for all business coaches, all students of coaching theory and method, and for business leaders looking to understand better the role of the modern business coach.

Michel C. Moral PhD is an executive coach, author, lecturer, coach-trainer and coach-supervisor. He teaches coaching and intercultural management at University of Paris VIII, France. He also has his own consulting and coaching practice.

Geoffrey Abbott PhD is an educator and consultant in international business coaching and leadership. Geoff runs public and corporate seminars in international business coaching as Director of the Centre for International Business Coaching (his consulting business). His executive experience is in corporate strategy. He is based in Brisbane, Australia with the Business School of the Queensland University of Technology where he teaches various programs relating to leadership, coaching and systems thinking.

The Routledge Companion to International Business Coaching

Edited by
Michel C. Moral and Geoffrey Abbott

LONDON AND NEW YORK

First published in hardback 2009
by Routledge
2 Park Square, Milton Park, Abingdon, Oxon OX14 4RN

Paperback edition published 2011
by Routledge
27 Church Road, Hove, East Sussex BN3 2FA

Simultaneously published in the USA and Canada
by Routledge
270 Madison Avenue, New York NY 10016

Routledge is an imprint of the Taylor & Francis Group, an Informa business

Typeset in Bembo by RefineCatch Ltd, Bungay, Suffolk
Printed and bound in Great Britain by
MPG Books Ltd, Bodmin, Cornwall

British Library Cataloguing in Publication Data
A catalogue record for this book is available from the British Library

Library of Congress Cataloging-in-Publication Data
The Routledge companion to international business coaching / edited by Michel Moral and
Geoffrey Abbott.
    p. cm.
Includes bibliographical references and index.
1. Executive coaching.   I. Moral, Michel.   II. Abbott, Geoffrey.
HD30.4.R684 2009
658.3′124—dc22
2008023493

ISBN: 978–0–415–45875–7 (hbk)
ISBN: 978–0–415–66941–2 (pbk)
ISBN: 978–0–203–88679–3 (ebk)

Contents

Section 1: International coaching frameworks and tools

List of Illustrations

Figures

Tables

About the Editors

Michel C. Moral is an executive coach, author, lecturer and coach-trainer. He has spent most of his career in an international environment. After several years at IBM France in sales, he joined IBM Eurocoordination where he was involved in the operations of different business units dealing with products, industries and finally emerging markets such as Central and Eastern Europe, Middle East and Africa. In these organizations, he managed teams in many different countries. He lived for several years in the USA and Germany.

In 2003 he created his own consulting and coaching practice and currently teaches coaching and intercultural management at University of Paris VIII and Business Schools. As an executive coach, Michel Moral works with senior-level executives, managing teams and international organizations and also supervises coaches. Michel Moral holds a Masters degree in Science & Technology, and a PhD in Psychology. He has written several books on intercultural management (*Le manager global*, Dunod, 2004), coaching (*Coaching, outils et pratiques*, Armand Colin, 2006; *Coaching d'équipe, outils et pratiques*, Armand Colin, 2007; *Coaching d'organisation, outils et pratiques*, Armand Colin, 2008) and family dynamics (*Belle-mère ou marâtre, quel rôle pour la femme du père*, L'Archipel, 2008).

Geoffrey Abbott is an educator and consultant in the field of international business coaching and leadership. As Director of the Centre for International Business Coaching (his consulting business), Geoff delivers international business coaching seminars in Europe, the Americas and Australasia, coaches and consults to global leaders and provides coach mentoring. Geoff's international coaching work is based on his ground breaking doctoral research with expatriate managers which he conducted in Central America from 2003 to 2006. He has coached senior international executives from across multinational corporations, regional companies, government, universities and development organizations. Geoff's academic background is in organizational psychology and international management. He has a PhD in Business from the Australian National University. Geoff has written book chapters and academic journal articles on a range of issues relevant to international coaching and has developed a 360-degree tool specifically for international managers. Geoff has extensive executive experience in corporate strategy with the Special Broadcasting Service (Australia), a national multicultural radio and television broadcaster. He is based in Brisbane, Australia with the Business School of the Queensland University of Technology where he teaches various programs relating to leadership, coaching and systems thinking.

Contributors

Hilary Armstrong is the Director of Research and Training at the Institute of Executive Coaching and oversees the IEC Community of Practice. She is a master coach and a skilled presenter and facilitator with significant experience in building people's capacity to reach their potential in today's challenging workplace environments. Hilary holds a PhD in critical social sciences with a speciality in critical psychology. She specializes in integral and narrative coaching, ethical conversations, and reflective practice. She is on the advisory panel of the *International Coaching Psychology Review* and has published works in the field of qualitative and evaluation research, executive coaching, ethical conversations, and narrative forms of practice. Hilary directs and oversees the development of the Institute of Executive Coaching (Asia Pacific) through curriculum design, training, research and publications as well as overseeing the growing Community of Practice.

Geetu Bharwaney is Founder and Managing Director of Ei World Limited and a thought leader in the application of Emotional Intelligence in business. She has built Emotional Intelligence interventions and has proven measurable results from her work. She leads global projects involving leadership development, Emotional Intelligence and coaching in a cross-cultural context. As an external coach, she provides coaching services for high achievers where Emotional Intelligence is the foundation across a global context. She has assessed the Emotional Intelligence of some 5,000 people including through her own research on the role of health, Emotional Intelligence and management performance as part of leadership success. Geetu is a Member of the Ei Consortium whose mission is to advance research and practice of emotional and social intelligence in organizations. She has a strong record of accomplishment as both an applied researcher and a practitioner in the field of emotional intelligence development.

Marie-Brigitte Bissen is the Managing Director of Evolution^PLUS, a personal development company providing executive coaching, team-coaching, talent and succession planning programs, Europe-wide. She is the President of the European Association of Coaching/EMCC of Luxembourg. Prior to launching her company, Marie-Brigitte was Vice-President Human Resources and member of the Executive Committee of Nationwide Global Headquarters, in Luxembourg. Her prior experience includes 18 years with the European chemical branch of the former Mobil Oil (now Exxon Mobil) where she held various Human Resource positions with increasing responsibility. Marie-Brigitte holds a BA in economics and a degree in labor and social law and was trained as a sophrologist. She is also a Master-Practitioner in Neuro Linguistic Programming, a certified MBTI coach and she holds a Master's degree in coaching from the University of Paris.

Katrina Burrus is the founder of MKB Conseil & Coaching, providing executive coaching to global nomadic leaders and consulting to their organizations worldwide. She holds three Masters and a PhD in human and organizational systems from The Fielding Graduate University. She was the first Master Certified Coach in Switzerland from the International Coaching Federation. A global nomad herself, she grew up in Italy, Germany, Switzerland and Spain. In her professional practice, she draws on her experience throughout her adult life of working for multinationals in over thirty countries. Her experience spans a who's who of multinational firms in food, clothing, telecommunications, banking, education, chemicals, pharmaceuticals, luxury goods, tobacco, healthcare, nutrition, nonprofit, biotechnology, information technology, research, academia, cosmetics/fragrances. She is writing her first book, following numerous published articles and presentations at various international forums. Katrina specializes in Executive Coaching for Leadership Development, Global Nomadic Leaders, and Abrasive Executives. She has been coaching global C-suite executives for more than ten years. www.mkbconseil.ch

Judith Chapman is an Associate Professor of Management in the College of Business, University of Western Sydney, Australia. She has a PhD in organizational change and has published widely in this area. Her knowledge and interests span the range of workplace issues from individual work behavior and group dynamics to organizational design, culture and strategy. Judith has extensive experience in the human resource development field in a career spanning 30 years during which she has worked as an organizational psychologist, HR professional, academic and organization development consultant. She is currently collaborating on a project investigating leadership and strategy in global business enterprises and networks. As a practicing coach, her focus is on talented managers in transition to the next level and those seeking a position in the boardroom. She also works with organizations in developing their succession plans.

Grace Cheng is the Country Manager for Russell Reynolds Associates in Greater China. Working across Beijing, Shanghai and Hong Kong, she also conducts industrial/natural resources searches in China, with emphasis on general management and cross-border assignments for multinational companies at both the market entry and consolidated growth phases. She has eleven years of executive search experience. Before joining the executive search industry, she was Head of Human Resources for TNT's China joint venture, where she played a key role in the company's initial growth and later expansion strategies. She has lived in the United Kingdom, while she was a Research Fellow at the London-based think-tank, Policy Studies Institute (PSI), where her focus was work, employment and organizational behavior. Grace serves on the advisory board of the Chinese Returnee Association of Entrepreneurs. Grace received her BA in English from Beijing Foreign Studies University, her MA in sociology from the University of Massachusetts and her D Phil from the University of Oxford.

Danièle Darmouni has led International Mozaik, a company which specializes in research, coaching and training in the Arts & Crafts of Change, since 1992. Her approach aims to co-create vivid learning processes with clients that are grounded in real work and which help the clients develop new ways of thinking, feeling and acting over time. She is a member of a versatile, multicultural network of experienced coaches and international trainers and is the learning leader of the Master Business of Coaching (MBC) programs, the first European coaching training to be accredited by the ICF. After having begun her career as finance consultant, she currently coaches executives, teams and organizations, across the world. Danièle is a Vice-President of the International Coaching Federation – ICF – and a member of the ICF International Assessment Team. She holds a Master's degree in Economics and Psychology and is an active member of SoL France.

David B. Drake is Director of the Center for Narrative Coaching in California where he currently lives. He works globally with organizations to improve their coaching capabilities, develop integrated coaching strategies, and foster agile coaching cultures. As part of his work, he has taught coaching skills to over 3,000 professionals, managers and leaders. He also teaches advanced narrative and coaching skills to coaches and others around the world (www. narrativecoaching.com). David has a doctorate from Fielding Graduate University and he has taught coaching at several universities, including Melbourne Business School. He has written over twenty publications on narratives, evidence, and coaching, and he was the lead editor for *The Philosophy and Practice of Coaching: Insights and Issues for a New Era* published by Jossey-Bass in 2008 (www.practiceofcoaching.com). His next two books will be out in 2009: a primer on narrative coaching and an introduction to narrative approaches to building coaching cultures.

Michelle Duval is a master coach, speaker, trainer and founder of Equilibrio International, a global executive and personal coaching firm. As a pioneer in the field of developmental and transformational coaching, Michelle has co-developed The Axes of Change Model, Neuro-Semantic Benchmarking Model and co-developed the international Meta-Coach Training System®, educating professional coaches in more than 35 countries. She has co-authored two international handbooks on coaching and been featured in a book entitled *Secrets of Great Success Coaches Exposed*. Michelle co-founded the Meta-Coach Foundation, a global organization for research into developmental coaching. She was a founding committee chair for the ICF Australasia and has spoken at many ICF international conferences. Michelle currently specializes with entrepreneurs, CEOs and senior managers in both small businesses and multinational corporations in Australia, USA, UK and Asia.

L. Michael Hall is a researcher/modeler and trainer in Self-Actualization Psychology. His doctorate is in the Cognitive-Behavioral sciences from Union Institute University. For years he worked as a psychotherapist; he wrote several books for Richard Bandler in the field of Neuro-Linguistic Programming. In 1996 Michael co-developed the field of Neuro-Semantics with Bob Bodemhamer. He has written more than forty books related to communication, psychology, and coaching. Michael both co-developed Meta-Coaching and co-founded the Meta-Coach Foundation with Michelle Duval.

Sabine K. Henrichfreise is an inspiring and successful business coach and a recognized expert in collective creative intelligence, leading-edge management and transcultural executive coaching. She intervenes in three languages for her client base, which extends throughout Europe and includes CAC 40 and Fortune 500 companies. She created Philena, her own coaching and consulting company, dedicated to developing multicultural organizations, teams and international executives by strengthening their capacity for creating significant breakthroughs and succeeding collectively. Sabine is co-founder of the innovative concept of Tandem Coaching™, co-designer of the Elusis Solution Tanks™, where peers coach peers to create new solutions to real business challenges in real time, and co-created the 2007 International ICF Coaching Conference (Long Beach). She has a PhD in law, is a former practicing attorney and has prior business experience as Legal Director and Director for Top Executives and Diversity in a worldwide automobile company. She is the French partner of the European Institute for Managing Diversity based in Barcelona and is member of EPWN (European Paris Professional Women's Network). She actively contributes to the European Movement 'Art and Business' and participates in different leaning networks, where she explores the fields of collective intelligence, creative leading and masterful dialogue. She is a featured speaker, dynamic facilitator of large-group interventions and seminar trainer for various European Business and Coaching Schools. She is co-author of the book *Coaching d'organisation* (Paris: Armand Colin, May 2008).

Ari Jokilaakso is a senior HR professional with a technical background. He has worked within a large corporation and part of his success has involved implementing Emotional Intelligence frameworks and providing coaching for key people within the leadership development programs of Outotec, a company which specializes in providing technology for the mining and metals sector. Outotec is a high growth company which has experienced the value of focusing on Emotional Intelligence as a set of performance tools in a fast-paced and demanding business environment where engineering is the key discipline and the key profession represented, not an environment that many people would associate traditionally with the term 'Emotional Intelligence'.

Rita Knott is Founder and Managing Partner of Coaching Mentoring Consulting, a company specialized in executive, team and organizational development in Luxembourg. One of her particular fields of interests is a Cross-Mentoring Program for Women in Leading Positions in different cultural environments. She is also member of the Board of the European Association of Coaching/EMCC Luxembourg holding the Marketing and PR function. Before building up her own company, Rita worked with an Israeli Bank in Luxembourg for 26 years and for the last 10 years as a member of the Board of Management. She has extended her Management, Human Resources Management and Organizational Development skills by studying Coaching and Supervision (2003–2006) at the University of Applied Sciences in Frankfurt, Germany. She holds a diploma as certified Coach and Supervisor.

Margaret A. Krigbaum transitioned to coaching in late 1994, after 11 years in private law practice. Her coaching assignments are typically in the areas of increasing leadership skills, change management, strategic planning, business development, organizational and team productivity, and executing breakthrough projects. Her clients include Fortune 500 companies, senior executives, and professionals and her client base extends throughout the United States and to Europe and Asia. She currently coaches individual and team clients in 12 countries and is also a leader in the coaching industry. She currently sits on the board of the International Consortium for Coaching in Organizations (ICCO) and has received the Master Certified Coach designation from the International Coach Federation (ICF). Margaret is a recent chair of the ICF Research and Education Committee and the Education Steering Committee and for the ICF 2007 International Conference, which served 1,700 coaches. In addition, she is former vice president of EFCF, past chair of the ICF's Application Review Committee and past Chair of its Credentialing and Continuing Education Committee. She is the recipient of the ICF's

Jennifer White Award for Outstanding Contribution to the Coaching Profession. In addition, Margaret is a featured author in the books, *Working Wisdom* and *The Law and Ethics of Coaching*.

Leon Laulusa advises French firms doing business in China with Chinese companies. He also advises Chinese firms on doing business in France. Leon is French with Chinese origins and has more than twelve years' experience in Multicultural environment, particularly in South East Asia. He holds an MBA from Paris Pantheon Sorbonne University, is a French Chartered Accountant and holds a PhD in Management Science from Paris-Dauphine University. The topic of his doctoral dissertation is the influence of Confucianist values on the management in Chinese firms in Mainland China, Taiwan and Singapore. He is currently a partner at Deloitte's Paris office and assistant professor at the European School of Management, ESCP EAP, where he teaches financial accounting, management control and Chinese management. Previously, he was part-time lecturer at HEC business school, Paris-Dauphine University and the Institut National des Telecommunications (INT). He was also a partner at BDO Marque & Gendrot, where he led various projects and consulting missions in accounting, financial and organizational audit at both national and international levels, and more specifically in Asian countries on behalf of large listed firms and governmental organizations.

Ho Law is Founder Director of Empsy® Ltd & Morph Group Ltd, a Chartered Occupational Psychologist, Chartered Scientist, and an international practitioner in psychology, coaching, mentoring and psychotherapy (www.empsy.com). He is an honorary lecturer at Liverpool John Moores University (2006–), and International Advisory Board Member, Coaching Psychology Unit, City University, London (since 2006). He has had over twenty years' experience in providing advice and consultancy for both public and private sectors. He was one of the first equality advisors to the Assistant Permanent Under Secretary of State in the UK's Home Office. Ho is the President of Empsy® Network for coaching, a founding member of the Society for Coaching Psychology, the founding editor of *The Cutting Edge* journal, a consulting editor of *The Coaching Psychologist* and an international editor of *Coaching – an International Journal of Theory, Research and Practice*. He has published over 40 papers and delivered over 100 workshops and conference seminars in the UK and abroad including Australia, Barcelona, Brussels, Christmas Island, Hong Kong, Paris, Singapore, Stockholm, and Zurich. He was the former Head of the Professional Forum for the Association for Coaching, and was selected as one of the top 20 European coaches to participate in the 2005 international coaching program at Rice University, in Houston. He received numerous outstanding achievement awards including the Local Promoters for Cultural Diversity Project in 2003, the Positive Image (Business Category) in 2004, and Management Essentials Participating Company 2005.

Eddie Lievrouw is managing partner of the European Institute for Intervention and Prevention on Burn Out. His career has followed an unconventional path. Graduating from the Royal Military Academy as a master in aeronautical sciences, he continued his academic education to become a business engineer. In parallel, he started training to become a combat survival instructor for fighter pilots and Special Forces. As a senior-ranking officer, he specializes in coaching managers in suddenly changing environments. Eddie is coordinator of the education program of International Mozaik in Belgium, the Netherlands and Luxembourg, and he also teaches at the ICHEC Business School.

Jean-Marc Loeser has worked for 20 years in small and large international businesses, where he was involved in new ventures (subsidiaries; buy-outs; corporate alliances and acquisitions) as well as cross-cultural management, primarily in Europe and the US. He spent the first half of his career in sales and marketing positions for Schlumberger in China and Eastern Europe, and for Trophy – a medical imaging start-up recently acquired by Kodak – mainly in Germany, the USA and Japan. During the next ten years he was Managing Director for Southern Europe and Africa at Invensys, where he participated in the transformation of fourteen national entities into a single pan-European marketing and supply-chain organization. He is now Managing Partner of Kairos, a consulting and coaching firm specializing in change management, which he founded in 2004. A Graduate Engineer educated in France and the UK, Jean-Marc Loeser holds Masters Degrees in Change Management from HEC (Paris) and Templeton College (Oxford), as well as in Business and Coaching from the University of Paris.

Chip McFarlane grew up in New York City and has coached internationally, in the US, London, Singapore, Paris, Hong Kong and Australia in industries such as banking and financial services, pharmaceutical companies and professional service firms. His experience ranges over a number of areas of leadership development including training and coaching the elements of inspirational leadership and skill development. He works with CEOs and senior executives who need a sense of direction and someone outside their company or their board to help them with business strategy or to challenge their ideas. Chip has over 11,000 hours' coaching experience at the executive level and the nature of his assignments have included coaching senior individuals around business skills, interpersonal skills and the full spectrum covered by leadership and management competency. During the last several years Chip has worked with senior leadership teams across Asia, helping them to succeed in leading culturally diverse organizations. His intercultural and wide-ranging background adds diversity and depth to his executive coaching practice. His management experience includes the position of Regional Director of Operations for a French-based multinational company covering 27 sites in 14 countries. He is a senior fellow of the Professional and Personal Coaches Association (PPCA). Chip has lived in Australia since 1989 and is an Australian citizen. He is a Director of the Institute of Executive Coaching, Australia.

Andrew L. Miser is President of Elysian Enterprises, a coaching and consulting firm. He has worked as a psychologist with the State of Connecticut, as Executive Director for a consulting firm; and from 1991 to 2002, as a psychologist and marriage and family therapist in private practice in Hartford, Connecticut. Andrew is a member of the American Psychological Association and a Clinical Member of the American Association of Marriage and Family Therapy. He is currently a Certified Professional Co-Active Coach, through the Coaches Training Institute in California, and is a member of the International Coach Federation. From 2002 to 2006, Andrew lived with his wife and children in Amsterdam, the Netherlands, where he designed an innovative couples' coaching curriculum and provided coaching for expatriate couples. During his career, he has held senior positions that have called for initiative, creativity, and leadership in private, public, and non-profit agencies. He holds a BA from Colgate University, 1972; an MA in educational psychology from the University of Nebraska in 1974; and a PhD in developmental psychology from the University of Connecticut in 1985. Andrew currently lives with his family in Brookline, Massachusetts.

Martha F. Miser is President of Aduro Consulting which provides consulting, education and coaching on leading and enabling organizational change in the US and Europe. Martha has extensive experience as a practitioner in organization and leadership development, team-coaching, and education design and delivery. Martha began her career in the field of City

Management, after completing her MA in Public Administration from the Maxwell School of Citizenship and Public Affairs in Syracuse, NY. Martha worked with Aetna Financial Services, in Hartford, in a variety of leadership education and internal consulting positions, including Head of Organization Effectiveness and Leadership Development for the US businesses. During four years as an expatriate with ING, Martha created and led a global Leadership and Change initiative, with the objective of building a high performance culture across ING. Martha is currently pursuing a PhD in Leadership and Change, at Antioch University.

Julio Olalla Julio is founder and president of **the Newfield Community**, an international education and consulting company. Newfield is committed to developing and providing powerful, new, integrative learning systems to individuals and organizations in the United States, Latin America, and Europe. For over a decade, Julio and his team of master coaches and facilitators have worked with people in the US, Canada, the United Kingdom, Spain, Argentina, Brazil, Chile, Mexico, Venezuela, and Australia. Julio recently ran a coaching seminar with the new cabinet of Chile. Julio generates learning environments that establish the trust, safety, respect, and well-being that accelerate learning potential. He has trained over 50,000 individuals worldwide and worked with more than 300 organizations to develop increased integration, productivity, strength, and well-being of individuals, teams, and leaders. Julio has addressed large audiences in London, Argentina, Canada, Switzerland, and the US on the topics of leadership, organizational learning, education, and coaching. Newfield's thriving, dynamic, worldwide alumni community is committed to being of service and living from gratitude, as taught in Newfield's programs. The community consists of leaders, managers, and individuals in organizations, executive coaches, personal coaches, and individuals committed to personal development. Newfield's alumni community extends from North and South America to Europe and Asia.

Philippe Rosinski is a world expert in executive coaching, team coaching, and global leadership development. He is the author of *Coaching across Cultures* (Nicholas Brealey Publishing/ Intercultural Press, 2003) and his pioneering work in bringing the crucial intercultural dimension into the practice of coaching has won him worldwide acclaim. He is principal of Rosinski & Company, a global consulting firm that helps leaders, teams and organizations unleash their human potential to achieve high performance together with high fulfillment. He is a Professor in the MBA in Globalization at the Kenichi Ohmae Graduate School of Business in Tokyo, Japan. Philippe is the first European to have been designated Master Certified Coach by the International Coach Federation. He spent six years in the engineering field as a software engineer in the Silicon Valley, California, and as a project manager in Brussels. He received an Electrical and Mechanical Engineering degree from the École Polytechnique in Brussels. He holds a Master of Science degree in Electrical Engineering from Stanford University and the Cepac post-graduate business degree from the Solvay Business School in Brussels.

Omar Salom is a very well recognized executive coach in all Latin America and is mainly focused on the applications of Neurosemantics and cognitive psychology to the field of executive development. As a director of Salom Change dynamics he has coached presidents and directors from different companies like Monsanto, Cadbury, City Bank, Scotia Bank, Schneider, etc. He also designs and implements programs that integrate assessment, cultural transformation, team building and leadership development. His integrity, clarity and creativity have been a source for many companies and executives in the Latin American World.

Paul-Michael Schonenberg is the Chairman and CEO of the American Chamber of Commerce in Luxembourg. A senior level international executive with 40 years of leadership experience in Government, business and non-governmental organizations; he was elected the Luxembourg Human Resources Manager of the Year in 2004. He has a Masters Degree in Counseling Psychology, a Masters Degree in Management and is currently studying for a PhD in Organizational Leadership.

Rebecca Sprengel is a cross-cultural trainer and executive coach. Her clients are multinational corporations and SMEs. Originally from London and now based in Germany, she has lived and worked in various countries. She founded International Communication, a cross-cultural management training consultancy in 1993. Rebecca's activities have included: corporate coaching, train the trainer, communication and intercultural training and language consultancy. She has published a number of books, training material and articles. She has introduced and pioneered the concept of Cross-Cultural Coaching in German industry. Rebecca has degrees in Science of Education and Applied Modern Languages from the University of Paris X, as well as a Postgraduate Certificate in Coaching and Mentoring Practice from Oxford Brookes University. She has been a board member of various professional associations.

Bruce W. Stening is a professor in the Vlerick Leuven Gent Management School. He is based at the China Center for Economic Research at Peking University where he is the International Dean of the BiMBA Program. For over thirteen years he was a professor in the Australian National University in Canberra where he was the Executive Director of the National Graduate School of Management. He has published a large number of books and papers, principally in journals of management and psychology. Most of his research has focussed on organizational behavior and human resource management in the context of international business in East Asia. He has consulted widely to firms around the world, but most particularly in Asia. He has also taught extensively on executive programs for leading business schools and has been a visiting professor at many top-ranked universities. His teaching expertise lies broadly in organizational behavior and management and more particularly in cross-cultural management and the development of managerial skills.

Monika Verhulst is a trilingual coach and consultant for interpersonal an intercultural relations, with ten years experience in a multicultural environment. Over the last twenty years, she has lived and worked in Switzerland, France, Belgium, Germany and the USA. As an expatriate with her family, she has also spent two years in Australia and two years in India. Monika is presently in charge of the European Development of the France-based Association Européenne de Coaching. She is cooperating with different coaching professionals from all over Europe. Her special interests are the field of research on coaching in general, and the definition of Life Coaching standards in particular. Monika holds a degree of the 'Institut d'Études Politiques' in Paris, and is a Master of International Studies of the Sydney University. She holds a Life Coaching degree from the Paris VIII University.

Chapter Summaries

CHAPTER 1: CONSIDERATIONS ON THE EMERGENCE OF ORGANIZATIONAL COACHING

After individual coaching and team coaching, a new concept emerges: organizational coaching where a team of coaches helps an organization to change. In the past, different approaches have been invented to force a collective change of behavior or a modification of the corporate culture. This chapter examines change processes through shifts from traditional organizational structures, to matrix, and finally to 'cyborg' organizations which are characterized by fluidity, constant change and uncertainty. Organizational coaching is presented as an ideal intervention to energize change processes within the new dynamic organizational environments of international business.

CHAPTER 2: INTEGRAL COACHING

There has been much written about the value of coaching in the development of personal insight. This chapter proposes that insight is not enough, especially when working in global environments. What is also required is 'outsight' encompassing a cultural sensibility. A cultural sensibility is the mental and emotional understanding of, and response to, the influence of the tacit, essential ethical frames of meaning constructed by a culture that are expressed through social roles, race, class and gender differences. This chapter uses practice narratives to draw out aspects of a cultural sensibility and how it can be enhanced by integral executive coaching.

CHAPTER 3: COACHING TO HIDDEN FRAMES

While we all know that culture is a human construct, the specific ways that we so construct it in our minds, live in it, and carry it with us as we move in and out of other cultures are still somewhat of a mystery. The chapter describes the theory and practice of 'meta-coaching' which has a primary focus on coaching the processes, structures, and contexts of a person's thinking and understanding – the meta-levels. From a cultural perspective, the authors use the concept of 'hidden frames' to encourage coaches to work beneath the surface to examine deeply embedded cultural influences on thinking and behavior. The models help to de-mystify culture so that it is not seen and felt as a 'thing', but as a process that we all engage in and can re-construct to increase effectiveness and reduce conflict.

CHAPTER 4: IDENTITY, LIMINALITY AND DEVELOPMENT

This chapter draws on Milton Bennett's (1986, 1993) six-stage model of intercultural sensitivity as a frame for the author's contention that the key dynamics which play out when people relate to other cultures in the external world also play out as people navigate the cultures they have been internalized as narratives in their inner world. The chapter draws on the author's research on rites of passage to explore some of the liminal tensions clients experience as they develop and adapt their responses to these cultural demands. A case study outlines the ways in which Bennett's model can be applied at an intrapersonal level in coaching and how a narrative approach can assist in using the model to assess and foster development in coaches. Narrative skills enable coaches to be more effective in helping clients to face increasingly complex cultural demands *while* maintaining a coherent narrative and sense of identity in the process.

CHAPTER 5: ONTOLOGICAL COACHING

This chapter applies the foundations of Ontological Coaching™ to the field of international business coaching. Ontological Coaching™ is a powerful, integral and interdisciplinary model for working with others to transform their capacity for effective, meaningful action. Onto-logical Coaching™ is based on the understanding that human beings are essentially linguistic beings and as such language is indispensable to knowing and learning. Language and culture are viewed as inseparable. The approach integrates transactional and transformational coaching and applies both to professional and personal contexts. The construct of trust and how it operates as an essential element for successful cross-cultural interactions in the coaching context are explored.

CHAPTER 6: COACHING FOR EMOTIONAL INTELLIGENCE IN INTERNATIONAL BUSINESS ENVIRONMENTS

Emotional Intelligence appeared more than a decade ago in the psychology literature across the applications of counseling, psychiatry, coaching and leadership development. This chapter explores the opportunities and challenges for coaches using Emotional Intelligence tools and frameworks in an international business environment. Some implications for practice are high-lighted. Emotional Intelligence is useful for peeling the layers of cultures, a person's own culture, working culture and ultimately national culture. Emotional Intelligence development as a subset of coaching can provide coaches with tools applicable in a cross-cultural context for deepening self-awareness, promoting greater personal clarity and achieving client progress more rapidly.

CHAPTER 7: COACHING INTERNATIONAL LEADERS TO SUCCEED COLLECTIVELY

The author introduces the concept of collective intelligence as a valuable concept to assist in the development and implementation of coaching programs in international business contexts. Collective intelligence is defined as the genuine capacity of a group to think, learn and create collectively. To be effectively mobilized in organizations, the author proposes that collective intelligence needs a vehicle which she terms 'collective leading'. The chapter addresses four crucial questions:

1   What is the business context generating the need for promoting collective intelligence?
2   How can we define collective intelligence?
3   How can we nurture the emergence of collective intelligence?
4   What do we have to change in the way we coach?

The latter question is given particular attention in the case study, which demonstrates how coaches might apply collective intelligence in the way they work.

CHAPTER 8: THE HEART OF CROSS-CULTURAL CREATION

This chapter gives attention to the heart and spirit of coaching. In our current vernacular, the term cross-cultural is used frequently to define a desired business end. While much time is spent discussing how to be cross-cultural and why that is good for the business, little time is spent discussing why real cross-culturalism works or what it does for the people in a corporation. Without understanding the heart and spirit, any cross-cultural initiative will eventually crack at its foundation. The authors illustrate this principle through the building of the International Coach Federation multicultural assessment team.

CHAPTER 9: STIMULATING ADVERSARIAL GROWTH IN CULTURAL UNCERTAINTY

The author is a military survival instructor – and an executive coach: in this chapter, he links the two. Based upon research in worldwide real life survival situations it appears that only 20 per cent of people are able to assess appropriately the traumatic situation they are experiencing. The rest have their reasoning significantly impaired. Similar dysfunctions occur in the turbulent and diverse world of international business. This chapter examines the transposition of disaster survival theory and practice to complex international business situations (both the dramatic and the mundane). The main point is that coaches armed with knowledge of survival techniques that work can assist their executive clients to cope and thrive in situations, which, while on the surface are not life-threatening, in reality and over time can be just that.

CHAPTER 10: FOSTERING INDIVIDUAL AND COLLECTIVE DEVELOPMENT USING THE CULTURAL ORIENTATIONS FRAMEWORK ASSESSMENT

Multidisciplinary research has found that there are differences between people based on their cultural backgrounds. These differences can be measured using various scales, including those based on the work of Geert Hofstede, Fon Trompenaars and others. These tools are widely used in cross-cultural management and are of increasing interest in global coaching. This chapter examines how differences between people can be leveraged for advantage in the international business context. The chapter provides a tool – the Cultural Orientations Framework – and explains how it can be used to leverage differences and unleash client potential. The case study provides evidence of the efficacy of the tool in coach-training and in dealing with diversity generally.

CHAPTER 11: INTERCULTURAL COACHING TOOLS

Most of the tools used by executive coaches have been designed in Esalen or Palo Alto in the USA and carry many assumptions of Western culture and business. The global coach who is working across cultures has to make judgments about which tool to use in which context, or how to customize tools to meet client needs. Adopting a constructivist approach in the selection of specific coaching tools, the coach and the clients alike are led to examine their own underlying assumptions about their own and other cultures. It is this understanding of an individual process of reality construction that helps internationally active professionals to effectively deal with very different cultural contexts. This chapter examines some of the major constructivist tools that are available and what choices might be open to the global coach in applying them.

CHAPTER 12: COACHING EXPATRIATE EXECUTIVES

The chapter gives some attention to how extensive research on different aspects of the expatriate manager experience can be applied to design and enhance coaching interventions for sojourners and their families. The authors stress the importance of coaches working interactively with their clients across the cognitive, emotional and behavioral dimensions, while paying attention to cultural and situational factors. They refer to some of the major research on cultural dimensions by Geert Hofstede and others, at the same time noting the need for caution in applying such research findings in the coaching situation, particularly the need to avoid cultural stereotyping. Guidance is provided to coaches on different phases of the expatriate experience and how they might maximize impact.

CHAPTER 13: COUPLES COACHING FOR EXPATRIATE COUPLES

The high cost of failed expatriate assignments and the role that spousal and family adjustment problems have in those failures are well documented. In addition to the services already offered to expatriates and their families, the authors propose that multinationals could benefit greatly from offering couples coaching as an available support service. A coaching relationship, if made available to and requested by the expatriate, can focus on the satisfactory adjustment and fulfillment of the expatriate couple and their family, areas that traditionally have been outside the control of the company. Ultimately, coaching for expatriate couples represents a sound investment for international businesses.

CHAPTER 14: COACHING WOMEN MANAGERS IN MULTINATIONAL COMPANIES

Executive success in multinationals relies on leadership skill, expatriate experience, and intercultural competence. Yet, despite strong numbers of women ready for key international posts, few women are chosen for overseas assignments. Both global and indigenous prejudices and misunderstandings about women in international roles might be responsible. This chapter explores the myths, paradoxes, and realities of women as expatriates in multinational companies; outlines the specific issues they face; and details keys to coaching women in multinational companies.

CHAPTER 15: COACHING MANAGERS IN MULTINATIONAL COMPANIES

Various types of multinational executive are defined, including the expatriate, the immigrant, and the global nomadic leader. Executive nomadic leaders are described: those internationally mobile executives who have been exposed to multiple cultures while growing up and have a multicultural 'third culture' reference. The author suggests that the qualities and experiences of global nomadic leaders position them well for high-impact leadership roles in global businesses. The characteristics, multicultural talents, and challenges of the global nomadic leader are detailed. Scenarios and tips for coaching the global nomad are discussed.

CHAPTER 16: WHEN FAR EAST MEETS WEST

Many models of coaching come from Western cultural frameworks. The authors propose that other models are required for non-Western business contexts, and where possible alternative models should be synthesized to generate high-impact coaching interventions. For Westerners applying coaching models in the Eastern cultures, it is crucial for them to understand their cultures and be sensitive about their values and how these values manifest in their behaviors and interactions. For example, the value 'respect' is translated in Chinese language as to 'save face'. In behavioral terms, this may mean one does not openly criticize others in public. The cultural learning and synthesis process is two-way with many opportunities for cultural differences to be combined to make a superior third way.

CHAPTER 17: EXECUTIVE TEAM COACHING IN MULTINATIONAL COMPANIES

Team coaching is becoming increasingly common in organizations. The addition of group dynamics to the coaching relationship offers new challenges and possibilities. In an international context, team coaching takes on other dimensions as culture and distance add greater degrees of complexity. This chapter provides some guidance of how to navigate the territory and discusses some of the central challenges for coaches and executives who undertake team coaching projects with international frameworks.

CHAPTER 18: COACHING WITH GLOBAL VIRTUAL TEAMS

Virtual business is a hot topic in management literature. In particular, global virtual teams (GVTs) are getting attention. This virtual world of work is complex, uncertain and ambiguous. All the challenges of locally bound work are there – and then some. Leading such teams has added complexity but also the possibility of great reward. In the pace and pressure, there is a risk of individuals and teams becoming alienated and disconnected from each other and also their organizations and even societies. By taking GVTs through solution-focused discussion and action planning exercises related to the themes discussed above, leaders and coaches may be able to set the stage for a new GVT, or lift engagement levels and add cohesion in environments where the virtual teaming exercise may be struggling. A case study and powerful model are provided from a successful GVT action learning coaching intervention in Orange telecommunications.

CHAPTER 19: INTERACTIVE COACHING WITH CORPORATE VENTURES

Mergers and acquisitions are strong catalysts of cultural change: coaching the 'corporate venturers' who lead such operations in a global environment implies facilitating the cultural and human processes by which the required aptitudes for the new venture can emerge. The author cautions that these emerging skills are also vulnerable to the inertia of the pre-existing structures on the very momentum they have created. The chapter suggests strategies for corporate venturers and their coaches for maintaining momentum and for maximizing value to the host organization. The main advice is that in today's matrix-shaped and multicultural international organizations, the leaders of these new ventures need to rely on building strong alliances rather than on traditional managerial coordination.

CHAPTER 20: EXECUTIVE COACHING THROUGH CROSS-BORDER MERGERS AND ACQUISITIONS

There is an international trend towards consolidation in virtually all industries – airlines, steel, computing, etc. The consequences are that mergers and acquisitions (M&As) are becoming the norm rather than the exception. Also, new players are entering the market – from India, China, Brazil, etc. The cultural frameworks involved in the consolidation of companies are therefore becoming more complex. Many M&As do not meet pre-deal expectations. This chapter suggests that coaches can add value at various points. The authors explore the reality of how coaches might best approach assignments in the sometimes (but not always) hostile and difficult environments of organizational mergers across boundaries, noting the potential for coaches to add value at the often-neglected integration phase. A case study is provided of an Australian–Chinese alliance that went wrong. The example is provided in the style of a business school case study, along with suggested activities for coaches and managers who may be engaged in the volatile M&A field.

CHAPTER 21: INTERNATIONAL COACHING

This chapter provides to both human resources (HR) professionals and coaches some ideas and feedback from experience in order to better 'bridge the worlds' and meet in a true common area of interest. It will assist executive coaches to better understand the variety of HR realities within international organizations. It will then provide tools and techniques to HR professionals in order to select professional coaches who can make a difference and several perspectives which will help them use coaching in the most efficient and effective way. A four-frame model is provided that encourages HR professionals and coaches to examine structural, political, psycho-social, and cultural factors – and their interrelationships – as they design and implement coaching programs in international organizations.

CHAPTER 22: CHOOSING COACHES FOR INTERNATIONAL BUSINESS LEADERS?

Recent research has suggested that successful global leaders and senior executives require intellectual grunt, energy and resilience, cultural adaptation skills, emotional intelligence, and an inquisitiveness to explore. The authors propose that if coaches are to have an impact with global executives, it is reasonable to ask that they have similar characteristics – and more. This chapter examines the characteristics of a global coach, giving particular attention to the fact that different cultural business contexts are likely to require different qualities in a coach. The chapter includes guidance on how companies might go about choosing a global coach in the form of a set of suggested interview questions.

Acknowledgements

We would like to thank the authors for their extremely rich contributions. Many new ideas came out of this project and the understanding of international coaching made great progress through all the discussions, questions and interactions we had with the community of authors. We also want to thank the editorial staff at Routledge, particularly Sharon Golan for her support during the production phase of the book. We are grateful for the outstanding work done by Deborah Ford and for all the work done 'behind the scenes' that was necessary to put the book together. Finally, we have to thank our partners and relatives for their patience and support during this long process, Geoffrey especially to Eduardo Batres, Alexandra Kate Ford and Jocelyn Abbott and Michel especially to Florence Lamy.

INTRODUCTION

A new paradigm for coaching in the global business environment

Michel C. Moral, Geoffrey Abbott and Danièle Darmouni

We now live in a global economy. Much has been written about this and the evidence is clear for all to see, yet resistance to the new reality is still strong and continues to appear in sometimes frightening forms, most notably through terrorist attacks directed at symbols and major players in the global marketplace. This *Companion* is based on the premise that there is an emerging paradigm in international business with which professional coaching is closely aligned and which positions coaching at the forefront of interventions to assist individuals and organizations to fulfill their potential in the face of ongoing change and complexity.

Some challenges and features of this new reality, which we believe coaching is well suited to address, include:

- Powerful multinational companies whose budgets and influence often outstrip those of governments;
- The increasing economic influence of emerging countries, particularly through Asian business interests;
- Increasing numbers of mergers and acquisitions (many of which flounder);
- Unpredictable and rapidly evolving international business strategies;
- Growing cross-border trade;
- Disassociation between national and organizational loyalties;
- Complex government–business negotiations and relationships;
- The roll-out of globally distributed technologies;
- Greater concerns about safety;
- Resource scarcity;
- Volatile political, religious and social climates; and
- Huge environmental challenges.

The result is complexity at every level of business – large-scale and small. Change is a constant. Little wonder that global executives are often overwhelmed, stressed and confused!

Expansive, fast-paced global media and communications mean that a lot is known about the international business environment yet there are few effective strategies for harnessing the emerging forces and trends in positive ways. The *Companion* demonstrates how coaching –

1

done from a perspective that views difference as opportunity – can assist companies to thrive in the complexity of the global marketplace. The *Companion* provides valuable knowledge, tools and approaches to coaches and human resource professionals whose roles are to facilitate change and success in hugely challenging environments. The fundamental philosophy of global coaching seeks to go beyond the profit motive to deal with the ethical, cultural, social, political and environmental dilemmas of our time.

The growth and maturity of professional coaching over the past ten to fifteen years has been immense. The model of the executive coach working one-to-one with a senior leader has proven powerful. However, like business itself, professional coaching needs to constantly reinvent itself to keep pace with the new reality of the changing global environment. Increasingly, coaching is being drawn into the life of organizations in different and expanding ways. This *Companion* offers a contemporary approach to coaching that embraces the new paradigm and provides practical approaches and ideas for coaches, consultants, leaders and managers to meet the challenges that are emerging.

ARCELOR MITTAL: LESSONS FOR THE FUTURE

Early in 2006, the steel manufacturer Mittal, owned by an Indian family, made a public offer to absorb its major rival Arcelor, an international company with French heritage. Arcelor executives were sharply dismissive of Mittal's initial offer and vowed that it would never go through. Former Arcelor CEO Guy Dolle at one point reportedly described the offer as having been made with 'Monopoly money' and later denigrated Mittal's products: 'They make eau de Cologne, we make perfume.' The French media gave a very negative representation of an 'emerging far-eastern raider' stealing the best of occidental industry. The French government was clearly against the deal. The initial reaction from the broader European business community was attentive. French unions and left-wing politicians were stunned to discover that the government had virtually no control of such a business tsunami.

In the end and after a bitter fight, pragmatic shareholder interests won out and the merger proceeded. Arcelor-Mittal is now the world's leading steel company and operates 61 plants across 27 countries. Mittal founder Lakshmi Mittal was made president of the company. His son Aditya became chief financial officer. Roland Junck, senior vice president of Arcelor since 2002 and a native of Luxembourg, was appointed CEO (but was later replaced as CEO by Lakshmi Mittal). Arcelor-Mittal is looking to strengthen relations with Japan's Nippon Steel, the world's second-largest steel maker. The two companies already have connections, including an automotive sheet steel venture in the US. This example illustrates several trends which are the focus of this introduction and explored from various perspectives through the *Companion*.

Limited protection of local enterprises

First, locally owned enterprises in most countries have limited protection from foreign mergers and takeovers. This situation contrasts with two or three decades ago when governments tended to give preference to locally owned enterprises. There are still exceptions in some parts of the world, particularly for small enterprises. However, the ongoing march of globalization has resulted in big corporations facing the reality of choosing between going worldwide or extinction. Governments have had to accept the same reality in designing regulatory regimes for foreign investment.

A paradox: companies must be agile and flexible but also robust and consolidated

Second, modern companies wishing to remain viable are being forced to be agile and flexible and to be constantly prepared for rapid transformation. However, at the same time they are being required to optimize and consolidate their existing strengths and assets through more robust structures and systems. This is one paradox of the modern industrial world: attack and defense must be simultaneous.

There are significant differences between Eastern and Western business practices

Third, the Arcelor-Mittal story highlights a broad difference in the structure of multinational companies in the West compared with those based in Asia. Shareholders in Western companies are traditionally enterprises or pension funds, while Eastern companies are usually owned by governments or families. One implication is that Western concepts which have dominated the global marketplace for decades will not necessarily apply in all of the new conglomerates, or if they do remain they will do so in a substantially modified form. Consequently, business coaching and organizational consulting practices will need to be aligned with the nature of the business cultures that are emerging. For example, most coaching techniques have been invented in Esalen or Palo Alto with the basic assumption that an individual human being owns its destiny. This contrasts with an Asian perspective which assumes that a person always has a higher loyalty to some collective entity. This picture is of course a bit oversimplified. Many of the leading Asian businesspeople are well schooled in Western business practices. Many coaches use techniques that have drawn from Eastern religions, philosophy and thinking. However, the intent is to show that:

- The way of doing business is often quite different between East and West; and
- If coaches want to be of value in the global business environment they need to take account of the differences and – crucially – assist clients to make use of them.

Takeovers can come from any direction

Fourth, other recent examples show that the raids originate anywhere. In 2005, the Chinese National Offshore Oil Company tried to acquire the American petroleum group Unocal but failed because the Congress was strongly against this deal. The fact that a Chinese petroleum company could make a serious bid for a US company – and come close to success – shows how much the global marketplace has changed. A company located in Dubaï, controlling six American harbors, was asked to transfer the headquarters to an American entity. The French energy group Suez was the subject of a takeover bid from its Italian rival Enel. The Russian energy company Gazprom is clearly looking at absorbing some European energy distributors. In 2006, Mexican building material company Cemex announced a hostile takeover bid of Australian rival Rinker, sending shockwaves through Australian company boardrooms. Older deals are already forgotten: in 2003, the virtually unknown Chinese company TCL bought the TV division of Thomson, and in 2004 Lenovo bought the PC division from IBM. Both deals pushed China as the prime producer of these products.

The mergers of large groups in the steel, airline and other industries mean that during the next ten years every major industry sector (for instance airline and steel) is likely to be represented by no more than five global companies.

The merging of sometimes radically different corporate cultures is a critical and ongoing challenge

Fifthly, if 'external development' will represent effectively the main source of growth for the global companies, then merging corporate cultures will be a critical issue these companies will have to cope with. The experience of many mergers and acquisitions is that underlying cultural differences and tensions still linger many years after the structural and financial work has been done. Looking ahead for Arcelor-Mittal, it seems very unlikely given the bitterness of the takeover that differences in organizational cultures – undoubtedly linked to differences in national cultures – will magically disappear. Companies will need to look to interventions that assist in cultural synthesis – most notably coaching.

Managing unpredictability is another critical and ongoing challenge

Sixthly, the second critical issue will probably be the management of unpredictability. The initial reaction to the Mittal move on Arcelor was incredulity. No one saw it coming, and even when it came, few within Arcelor believed it would succeed.

The combination of these trends illustrates very clearly that the global environment is complex and is becoming incredibly more complex. The globalization of business is raising a number of unexpected and unpredictable issues, even beyond those raised so far. The alternative to dealing with mind-boggling complexity is to be blinded by it and to risk receiving a metaphorical bullet from one's global competitors! The question facing company executives who are under increasing pressure to perform is: 'How do we manage the seemingly unmanageable?'

The main point we want to make here is that professional business coaching is emerging as a powerful tool for individual executives, teams and organizations to try to make some sense of the complexity and to find satisfying and productive ways of moving ahead. Not only that, coaching is one of the few tools available that has been shown to be effective in the new global climate of change.

Organizational consultants have traditionally offered solutions to common business problems. Consultants have typically worked with companies to implement solutions that have been found to be effective across similar situations – a little like administering a new drug. The diagnosis process, dose, packaging and bedside manner might vary but the chemicals are the same. However, this approach is no longer effective because the world is now changing faster than the capacity of such consultancy service providers to find new solutions that work. The traditional approach reflects a problem–solution paradigm that does not fit the current global environment. There is no 'disease'; instead there is an ongoing environmental pressure that requires organizations to be constantly vigilant, and ever ready to be both reactive and proactive at the same time.

The example of Mittal illustrates perfectly this assertion: despite several early warnings, the raid was a complete surprise and initial reactions from Arcelor were inadequate. Part of this was cultural. Western culture is convinced that any issue can be fixed by providing enough resources. The community of occidental consultants does not believe that long-term anticipation is mandatory. The problem can always be 'fixed'. For the same reason, the community of occidental coaches is not yet convinced that coaching of organizations is really its future. Organizational consultants are finding, however, that to remain in the game they are being required to take on the skills and characteristics of professional coaches. We are proposing that professional coaching provides an effective lead intervention which can facilitate experts within companies to find their own unique solutions to their own unique issues. Much of the coaching work being done now is in 'mopping up' operations after the mergers have been done. Coaches are brought in when the 'pain meter' enters the red zone! There is scope for coaching to assist executives earlier in the process in examining the cultural and other consequences of mergers and to engage in preventive medicine.

AN ANALOGY: THE CHANGING FAMILY UNIT

An analogy is useful here to make the point: the traditional family has existed since the beginning of civilization. Millennium after millennium, different cultures have elaborated solid sets of rules to regulate the behavior of parents and children in a given social environment. Then, suddenly, starting at the end of the 1960s, the rate of divorce increased significantly in the occidental world. These single parents soon married again and the number of stepfamilies rose rapidly, reaching presently 10–15 per cent of the total number of families. The change was so sudden (a few decades) that the society was unable to establish new rules and, despite the existence of books, groups, consultants, each new stepfamily has to create its own rules to survive. One of the reasons for this is that the typology of stepfamilies, compared to families, is so diverse that the social scientists were unable to identify general laws. Adding to the complexity was that once a set of rules was established, another change in the family made it redundant.

It is exactly the same with organizations: twenty years ago, most companies were essentially hierarchical, with a management system which, from a pyramidal shape thirty years ago, evolved slowly to some kind of 'staff and line' structure and, later on, to a matrix organization which allows much more flexibility and a greater ability to react quickly to an external threat. But facts are demonstrating that this is not enough. In international business, the shift of concentrated economic power away from traditional occidental centers is like the explosion of divorce in our family analogy: a new paradigm appears suddenly while there are no rules to manage the unexpected situations. Each enterprise has to create its own set of values and rules, as does each stepfamily.

Being successful requires dealing with the paradox of having firm values and rules while at the same time knowing that they are subject to change as major and often unpredictable shifts occur in the economic, social, political and technological contexts of the business.

COACHING FOR CONTINUOUS AND SUSTAINABLE CHANGE

If there are no general rules, no universal management system, then individuals and organizations (including governments) are being required to accept permanent change as a reality and take advantage of it just instead of managing the budget, flowchart and balance sheet. In other words, everyone has to learn how to survive in a perpetually changing environment. Being able to change continuously is the answer to this challenge. Coaching has emerged in response to the new paradigm, not just in international business but across the range of human endeavors.

There are life coaches, family coaches, business coaches, career coaches, sales coaches, political coaches, and so on. The common thread is the environment of continual change.

The Introduction to the *Evidence Based Coaching Handbook* begins as follows, 'Change is a constant. So, too, is the search for better, more effective ways to create and sustain change' (Grant and Stober 2006: 1). Note that the authors are suggesting that we *create and sustain* change, rather than resist or tolerate it as a necessary evil. In this *Companion* we take up this theme. Each author looks at how change, supported by coaching, can be generated in productive ways and how executives and organizations can legitimately create futures of ongoing success within a constantly changing environment.

COACHING OF ORGANIZATIONS

A major theme of the *Companion* is that coaching in the new paradigm of international business needs to be done at the level of the organization. The new paradigm presents the organization with the challenge of finding contextual solutions to highly complex issues that are situationally unique. It is hard to imagine that any off-the-shelf approach would have helped the executives of Arcelor to find a smooth passage through the events of 2006! Additionally, the paradigm dictates that not only are the challenges unique, but to add to the complexity they are constantly changing. Already, Arcelor-Mittal is looking to new horizons. The objects of their interest are in for interesting times. Coaching is well suited to this organizational reality. Our contention is that to provide high impact in international business, coaching must be delivered systematically within organizational systems, while understanding that those organizational systems are not closed and are going to be subject to ongoing and often radical renewal.

There is no easy fit between current organizational change interventions and coaching. Organizational development is a relatively mature field, but it is fair to say that it has been slow to embrace coaching. Similarly, organizational psychology has not warmed particularly to coaching, even though business coaching relies heavily on proven approaches from psychology and the other behavioral sciences. Coaching has been viewed as a separate activity, and one that can be threatening to existing providers of organizational change services and to human resource departments (to the latter because executive coaches have direct access to the top decision makers in companies, and considerable influence).

Professional coaching has developed from occidental cultural frameworks which have given prominence to the role of the individual. Executive coaching is often akin to a kind of business psychotherapy where the executive meets offsite with his or her executive coach and there is little or no connection between the coach and the organization other than through the impact on the behavior of the executive. The model has proven very powerful. If nothing else, individual coaching gives executives regular opportunities to step out of their situations and to reflect on:

- What is going on in their organizations and the environment;
- How they are operating; and
- Ways of implementing strategies that will make them more effective and more satisfied.

More recently, coaching has extended to executive teams. What generally happens is that the CEO sees the power of individual coaching and realizes the potential for the coach to work with his or her executive team (often as a way of offloading some responsibility for dealing with performance, personality, relationship or communication problems within the team, though this motive might not be made explicit!). It is now clear that coaching a management team has obvious positive and significant effects. However, those effects are limited in time if nothing is done through the entire organization.

We are now seeing the next phase where organizations are realizing the power of coaching almost as an organizational leadership philosophy. American leadership consultant, researcher and theorist Daniel Goleman has found that effective leaders use multiple leadership strategies depending on the context. He listed coaching as one of the more powerful but least-used of six leadership styles (Goleman 2000). Coaching is now beginning to make an organizational impact. Manager-as-coach training programs are becoming commonplace. Internal coaching units are being set up and external coaches are increasingly viewed as agents of organizational change. Of course, the one-to-one model still works and it is now commonplace for senior business and even government leaders to have coaches.

We suggest that coaching will be best placed to make a strong and positive impact in international organizations if it is viewed as a multidimensional organizational intervention that can assist people at all levels to embrace change. Ideally, external and internal coaches will work in partnership with manager-coaches to focus on developing individual and organizational potential in ways that do not rely on static structures and processes. In other words, coaching can provide a pathway to personal and collective growth even while the environmental changes alluded to above continue to play out.

THE INFLUENCE OF CULTURE: COMPLEXITY, UNPREDICTABILITY AND POSSIBILITY

At the end of the 2006 football World Cup, the French captain Zinedine Zidane received insults from an Italian player and – seemingly oblivious to the importance of the game and the moment, and the global visibility of his actions – reacted brutally. The referee applied the normal penalty and Zidane was banished. France lost.

This event is illustrative of the kinds of cultural undercurrents that run through intercultural management and gives some insight into why individuals might behave in unpredictable ways when under pressure. Zidane was part of the French football team and therefore belonged to this 'us' when playing. He also belonged to his family and cultural roots, another 'us'. Finally, he has his own 'I'. When he reacted to the insults, at the exact instant he attacked the Italian player, he was supposed to be giving priority to the 'French team us' but instead he obeyed his 'I', or maybe to the 'family and cultural roots us'.

We can conclude from this short story that time is playing a role in the intercultural team dynamics. Zidane was under high pressure and, at the very first millisecond, the prevalent mechanism had been to react according to the 'I' needs and not be loyal to the 'French team us' – despite all the team building efforts and the fact that half of the planet was watching him. This is not a general rule as we know that, for instance, the 'team us' is often prevalent in high-risk military operations. The other factor to be considered is that Zidane was stretched between the 'French team us' and the 'family and cultural roots us'. What was the exact role of that second 'us' in the dynamics of the very first millisecond when he let the 'I' act? We know that once the 'coping' processes have started, usually after a few seconds, the prevalent factor is one of the 'us' attractions. But we do not know exactly how it works.

The implication for global management is that we cannot predict how executives will react under intense pressure. How will, for example, the bicultural CEO of a global company react at the announcement of an offshore raid against the enterprise? How will an expatriate manager perform in a new assignment in culturally unfamiliar territory? Coaching can introduce opportunities for individuals to explore their cultural contexts and their individual identities and to mentally prepare for the inevitable surprises that the new global landscape brings up.

Coaching at an organizational level must have a cultural dimension. When an organization is changing and expanding, the question of corporate culture is critical, especially in a global environment where certainties and knowledge are disrupted or no longer adequate for the global business environment. The variety of geographical locations for employees in global companies has led to an increased contact between individuals of diverse backgrounds and cultural beliefs. These cultural differences introduce an additional level of complexity in the arena of management in the global marketplace: use of power, importance of hierarchy, performance and outcome evaluations, gender and ethnicity. Even the way that people communicate has cultural implications. Virtual management teams rely on internet communications services that remain very low-context. That is, managers who are more comfortable in face-to-face situations and do business through strong interpersonal skills and relationships are being asked to operate outside of their comfort zones.

The global nature of business and change requires a new and more profound awareness of cultural differences and corresponding innovative organizational structures and communications systems as they influence both the global workplace and managers in a multicultural work environment. Such awareness can be the key that leads to success or failure in the multicultural business context and mastering culturally relevant coaching skills may be an essential component of executive and team coaching in the future. Coaching individualizes the influence of culture and equips executives to take advantage of their individual cultural repertoires.

Cultural differences play a leading role in the complexity of the global business environment. Cultural influences impact in many ways. There are obvious influences – such as the stark cultural contrasts between Mittal, representing a relatively new Indian family business culture, and Arcelor whose culture was inextricably linked with the traditions of French and European business. Other influences are more subtle and are often underestimated. There are culture differences in multinational companies between:

- 'Head office' and the operations in different cultures, often influenced by national culture;
- Various country operations;
- Departments in head office where powerful cultural silos generally exist;
- Functional areas in country operations, delineated by functional areas;
- Country operations between expatriate and local staff; and
- Former smaller companies taken over by multinationals, and so on.

The complex nature of multinationals leaves open the possibility that not just one or two of these but all of them exist as potential points of tension – or of advantage. For example, in El Salvador, London-based multinational SAB Miller controls the former family beer company La Constancia, the bottled water distributor Cristal, and Coca Cola. Part of its regional management is in Colombia. SAB Miller is a merger of South African beverage giant South African Breweries and Miller in the US. Its interests are expanding daily, as is the cultural complexity of its operations. For managers who have to navigate across different operational or geographical units, the challenges are obvious.

Individual coaches who have been coaching within multinationals have been working with culture for many years. However, the coaching literature on culture has been sparse and coaches have been forced to design approaches through trial and error. Relatively recently, a specific cultural perspective has begun to emerge in coaching. Rosinski (2003), Chapman, Best, and

Casteren (2003), Moral and Warnock (2005), and Rosinski and Abbott (2006) are examples of how the profession has begun to recognize the role of culture in coaching and also to view it as a positive source of leverage with corporate clients.

CULTURAL DICHOTOMIES AND MEASUREMENT

Culture is often measured through dichotomies. The work of Geert Hofstede is well known in international management. Hofstede (1980) identified four dimensions along which culture can be measured, and more recently added a fifth (Hofstede 2001). The work of Hofstede and others has been immensely useful in helping to identify issues that are culturally related and for devising strategies to work with them to advantage. However, the complexity of the global business reality is that the measurement of culture through such relatively static and linear methods is becoming less useful. It can only go so far in making sense of the environment. This is another paradox of coaching in the international business field; it is necessary to be informed about cultural dimensions and the preferences of different individuals, departments, countries, and so on, but at the same time it is important not to fall into the trap of what Osland, Bird, Delano and Jacob (2000) term 'sophisticated stereotyping' through the overuse or misuse of such tools and knowledge.

MULTICULTURALISM

Many countries and certainly many organizations and work teams are genuinely multicultural. Coaching needs to work with diversity within open organizational systems, not just across them. To use the example of SAB Miller, the company now has a mobile and multicultural team of expatriate managers who do not reflect one cultural background or one set of dimensions. Also, as the managers move from country to country they undergo transformational shifts in identity and perspective that take them a long way from their cultural origins.

The idea of the typical expatriate manager has been challenged. The image of a white married man in his late forties with a 'trailing spouse' and children, all of whom come from the home country of the multinational, is no longer universally recognizable. Expatriates come from everywhere. They sometimes marry locals and then shift to a culture that is alien to both partners. More women are taking on expatriate roles.

MULTIPLE LEARNING STRATEGIES: EXPERIENTIAL, NON-LINEAR, HOLISTIC

In order to help global companies to survive in a continuously changing environment, we need to define new and creative ways of teaching. Experiential teaching techniques, combining the best of science with the best of coaching, have been developed out of knowledge of Systems Theory, Cognitive Psychology, Action Learning, Constructivism and Emotional Intelligence as well as masterful coaching tools, including intuition.

Comprehensive learning comes from an alignment of head, heart and body. True understanding is the result of experiential learning in which we are intellectually connected, emotionally engaged and physically involved. Learning to change is a place in which the joy and chaos of exploration and inquiry are always present.

The brain in the occident is a pattern-seeking organ (Nisbett 2003). Every learner's brain is a uniquely organized system which is highly self-generating. The search for meaning is innate and occurs through the continuing search by the brain for patterns and relevance to the learner. Emotions are a fundamental part of learning because the brain 'down-shifts' whenever there is a perceived threat or emotional upset, diminishing its capacity for engaging in higher-level thinking. And the brain 'up-shifts' whenever there is a perceived hope or emotional reward, enhancing its capacity for engaging in higher-level thinking.

According to Constructivism, learning is a process of creating personal meaning from new information by tying it to prior knowledge and experience. Learning is not linear; rather, it is recursive, iterative, and tied to particular situations. We transfer information from one context to another only if we construct bridges to higher levels of learning.

Above all, learning is strategic. It is goal-oriented and involves the learner's assimilation of strategies associated with meta-cognition (thinking about thinking) and knowing when to use knowledge, how to adapt it, and how to manage one's own learning process. Coaches as well as executives need to adopt multiple learning strategies. We add a related note of caution that the trend towards the development of private coaching training institutions – as good as some might be – carries a risk. Some schools promote proprietary models of coaching that carry an assumption there is one approach to coaching which is superior to others. How coaches operate with executives partly reflects their training. How executives operate in their organizations reflects to some extent their coaching. In the international environment, coaches cannot afford to be limited. Their agility and flexibility must be at similar levels to those required of their organizational clients.

CASE STUDY AND ACTION LEARNING METHODOLOGIES

We ascribe to evidence-based coaching which refers to the intelligent and conscientious use of the best current knowledge in making decisions about how to deliver coaching to clients, and in designing and teaching coach-training programs (Grant 2005: 7). Accordingly, each chapter provides case studies to support the theories and coaching approaches that are discussed. Our assumption is that all evidence-based coaching methodologies that are developed with rigor and supported by research in the field have something to offer. The more of these approaches that coaches can incorporate in their repertoire, the more likely they are to have success in the evolving international business environment.

The favored methodologies in most of the chapters are related to action learning and research (e.g. Kolb 1984; Lewin 1946). That is, the coaching approach is to work in partnership with clients to generate actions and solutions to their challenges. Action research methodologies encourage perspectives beyond the individuals to their teams, organizations, communities, countries and to the impact on global society in general. The coaching works through cycles of exploration, awareness, action, reflection, and so on. External or 'expert' knowledge has no sacred position – it is only valuable if it can be applied in context. Similarly the carriers of such external knowledge – coaches – have no assumed status.

Various related images and metaphors of the external coach are explored – consistent with the social constructivist position of international coaching which assumes multiple realities and thus multiple roles for a coach. The coach can operate in the role of the 'friendly outsider', and as a 'zhengyou' – a true friend or partner who sees beyond immediate benefit (Chapter 18). The coach can be a 'bricoleur' – a pragmatic 'jack-of-all-trades' who works within and across the stories of each situation (Chapter 20). Through the action learning and action research lenses, the coach is a bridge between theory and practice – one who is both inside and outside at the same time.

The emphasis on case studies gives readers an insight into the complex reality of coaching in international business. It also reflects the nature of coaching as a contextual experience that relies on narratives of real people operating in real situations for which there are no packaged or formula responses.

Readers can traverse the different chapters and case studies that appear relevant to their contexts and do their own research and analysis to inform their coaching and organizational practice. This exploration will generate new insights and generate informed action that is appropriate to the external reality. Then after reflection on what happened as a result of their new actions, readers explore further and try new approaches, and so on. We are therefore putting the book forward as an action learning resource. The application of case studies to different situations puts a degree of responsibility on the readers to make their own judgments about what will work and what won't – termed in case study research as 'analytic' or 'natural-istic' generalization (Yin 2003; Stake 2000). Similarly in coaching the assumption is that clients (working in partnership with coaches) have the knowledge and capacity to determine whether or not approaches drawn from somewhere or someone else will be useful.

COACHING TOOLS

Each chapter concludes with a practical tool or model which coaches and managers can use and adapt. An evidence-based coaching approach is based on the application of sound theory and research. Fundamentally though, its effectiveness is based on results. The tools and models are aimed to increase the impact of coaching – to assist practitioners to bridge the gap between the science and the practice. From the various chapters, readers can be pragmatic in selecting tools that will enhance their own practices.

CONCLUSION

We are putting forward themes, strategies, case studies and approaches that we believe offer models for coaching in the new paradigm of international business. Yet, we know that the reality of coaching in each organization and within each sub-unit within each organization is going to be different. The influence of culture ensures a lack of predictability and the need for executives to explore their own cultural backgrounds and how they are situated within their international and organizational contexts. There are no recipes that will bring success in all situations. The organizational context must drive the coaching process. International business coaching therefore requires the same acceptance of constant change that is required by execu-tives who are working in international business generally. Exploration, awareness, curiosity, flexibility and adaptability are vital ingredients for successful coaching relationships. The idea is for global coaches and executives who are using coaching approaches to become equipped with a variety of techniques and methodologies that they can use depending on the context. Coach-ing in international organizations in the new paradigm needs to be multidimensional and multifaceted.

The *Companion* is divided into three sections. The first section contains alternative and complementary frameworks and models that can be applied in coaching interventions in inter-national business. Each has a body of evidence to support its efficacy. The art of international business coaching practice is to 'mix and match', i.e. to synthesize different approaches into an intervention that works for the client in the context. The second and third sections examine specific challenges and opportunities – individual and collective – and provide guidance and strategies from the field that can be used by coaches and organizations to meet these challenges and take advantage of the opportunities.

Bibliography

Chapman, T., Best, B. and Casteren, P. V. (2003) *Executive Coaching: Exploding the Myths*, New York: Palgrave Macmillan.

Goleman, D. (2000) 'Leadership that gets results', *Harvard Business Review*, March–April 2000: 78–90.

Grant, A. M. (2005) 'What is evidence-based executive, workplace and life coaching?', in M. J. Cavanagh, A. M. Grant and T. Kemp (eds), *Evidence-Based Coaching: Theory, Research and Practice from the Behavioural Sciences* (Vol. 1), Bowen Hills: Australian Academic Press.

Grant, A. M. and Stober, D. R. (2006) 'Introduction', in D. R. Stober and A. M. Grant (eds), *Evidence Based Coaching Handbook: Putting Best Practices to Work for Your Clients*, Hoboken: John Wiley & Sons.

Hofstede, G. (1980) *Culture's Consequences: Comparing Values, Behaviors, Institutions and Organizations across Nations*, Beverly Hills: Sage.

Hofstede, G. (2001) *Culture's Consequences: Comparing Values, Behaviors, Institutions and Organizations across Nations* (2nd edn), Thousand Oaks, CA: Sage.

Kolb, D. A. (1984) *Experiential Learning: Experience as the Source of Learning and Development*, Englewood Cliffs, NJ: Prentice-Hall.

Lewin, K. (1946) 'Action research and minority problems', *Journal of Social Issues*, 2(4): 34–46.

Moral, M. and Warnock, P. (2005) 'Coaching and culture: Towards the global coach', in M. Goldsmith and L. Lyons (eds), *Coaching for Leadership: The Practice of Leadership Coaching from the World's Greatest Coaches* (2nd edn), New York: Pfeiffer.

Nisbett, R. E. (2003) *The Geography of Thought: How Asians and Westerners Think Differently . . . and Why*, New York: The Free Press.

Osland, J. S., Bird, A., Delano, J. and Jacob, M. (2000) 'Beyond sophisticated stereotyping: Cultural sense-making in context', *Academy of Management Executive*, 14 (1): 65–79.

Rosinski, P. (2003) *Coaching across Cultures: New Tools for Leveraging National, Corporate and Professional Differences*, London: Nicholas Brealey Publishing.

Rosinski, P. and Abbott, G. N. (2006) 'Coaching from a cultural perspective', in D. R. Stober and A. M. Grant (eds), *Evidence Based Coaching Handbook: Putting Best Practices to Work for Your Clients*, Hoboken: John Wiley & Sons.

Stake, R. E. (2000) 'Case studies', in N. K. Denzin and Y. S. Lincoln (eds) *Handbook of Qualitative Research* (2nd edn), Thousand Oaks, CA: Sage.

Yin, R. K. (2003) *Case Study Research: Design and Methods* (Vol. 5; 3rd edn), Thousand Oaks, CA: Sage.

Section 1

International coaching frameworks and tools

CONSIDERATIONS ON THE EMERGENCE OF ORGANIZATIONAL COACHING

International perspectives

Michel C. Moral and Sabine K. Henrichfreise

INTRODUCTION

If many books have been written addressing organizational change, very few mention organizational coaching. None provides frameworks and perspectives that can assist coaches working in multinational companies or on cross-border challenges. Most approaches rely on either the Organization Development (OD) paradigm (Lewin 1947; McGregor 1971) or the Corporate Culture Change methods (Schein 1985). Models were either 'commitment based', trying to convince employees and middle management by showing positive images of the future, or 'compliance based', changing behaviours by imperatives. These models only go so far in providing guidance and clarity for coaches immersed in the complexity of global business. The two authors have published a book on this subject in France (Moral and Henrichfreise 2008). This chapter summarizes its key ideas and includes new international experiences from their organizational coaching activities.

Coaching for executives and high potential managers developed in the USA and in Europe during the 1980s. Team coaching for executive boards or for project leading teams started to be a reality at the beginning of the 1990s. Logically, organizational coaching should have emerged early in the millennium. In fact, its development has been slowed down by the existence of several strong 'compliance based' methodologies like, for instance, business process re-engineering (BPR) (Stewart 1993) and performance management. These methodologies assume a top-down approach with an 'external expert' or 'guru' role for highly paid consultants. They give token attention to inclusive, action-learning approaches which position organizational players at all levels and locations with shared responsibilities for change. It is in this latter kind of organizational change paradigm that executive coaching is starting to have an impact and which is the focus of this chapter.

CHANGES IN THE ENVIRONMENT

The organizational challenges face top level management and the executive coaches who they are increasingly engaging to assist them. Invariably, these challenges have strong international dimensions, often related to shifting labour markets. With the rapid development of Chindia (China-India) during the last decade, Western countries are facing a situation where one billion new workers are potentially available all over the planet at a very low salary rate. In order to cut production and administrative costs, the occidental multinational companies are moving their workloads to countries where infrastructure and personnel costs are low. More and more plants, call centres and administrative tasks are implemented in Eastern Europe, Asia, Africa or Latin America. Market changes are now very fast, and competition between enterprises is looking more like a kayak race in the rapids, rather than a rowing contest on the Thames. If they want to be effective, coaches need to be informed about such trends. Plus, they need to be professionally and personally equipped to deal with international and organizational 'white water'. The concepts and examples that follow may be of assistance.

RECENT APPROACHES TO ORGANIZATIONAL CHANGE

If we consider the many theories of organization, from the very beginning, with Frederick Taylor and Henri Fayol, to the most recent ones, we eventually come to representing an organization as a system interacting with its environment. Within this system, four subsystems are possible entry points when one considers triggering a change:

1 The corporate culture. Many authors have considered changing the organization by changing its culture: Edgar Schein, of course, but also Ronald Burt (1999), John Kotter and James Heskett (1992), Gareth Morgan (1989), Millward (2003), Weick and Quinn (1999), Giroux and Marroquin (2005), etc.;

2 The corporate structure, which is more or less represented by a combination of the organization flowchart and the corporate processes, both being implicit or explicit depending on the country and the activity;

3 The information technology, which is providing new opportunities not only in terms of communication between people, but also in terms of managing data, to extract from it information and perhaps knowledge. Originally, the Socio-technical System Theory (STS) (Trist and Bamford 1951) considered the tight relationship between the social and the technical systems. Recent technology development makes it possible to have organization patterns that were beyond our imagination a few years ago. Not only is the functional structure, designed by Frederick Taylor in 1911, finally possible to implement, but also, since then, a multitude of other organizational layouts have been created. Enterprises are more and more like cyborgs, half human, and half cybernetics; and

4 The decision system, which carries objectives to execution, usually from top to bottom.

This four-subsystem representation is similar to how Dr Tony Grant at the University of Sydney (Grant and Greene 2003) identifies four elements in the coaching process:

• behaviours (equivalent of the decision system above);
• emotions (corporate culture);
• situation (structure); and
• cognition (technology).

There are tight interactions between the four subsystems. Acting on one of them usually strongly impacts on the three others. Any change process that takes account of only one

16

subsystem is doomed to fail because resistance will be overwhelming. The message is that while there are four potential entry points, it is necessary to traverse all four subsystems to facilitate sustainable change. Let's look at an international example.

A medium-sized European company, specializing in telecommunication systems, decided to develop its business in the Americas and in Asia. A group of consultants recommended working on their corporate culture (i.e. subsystem 1 above), and a number of seminars were held with the different divisions – run by outside consultants. The objective was to develop a new set of values and behaviours. Resistance was high. The process did not work and the enterprise pursued its development unchanged. Later on, an organization manager was hired. He immediately noticed that the prevalent forces were the executives in charge of product lines. Also he noticed that the distribution managers, organized per geography, had limited power. He proposed shifting a number of key responsibilities from the product lines to the distribution lines. For instance, the decision to promote and increase the salary of the marketing groups was transferred to the distribution executives. The executive in charge of developing business in the Americas and in Asia became a king in an instant, and his first-year achievements far surpassed business objectives. The initiative was done in tandem with further and related virtual seminars on corporate culture and structure. These were run by managers with the assistance of executive coaches. The power of the intervention came from the fact that it interactively worked across subsystems 1, 2, 3 and 4.

RESISTANCE AS AN OPPORTUNITY

According to Tannenbaum and Hanna (1985) resistance is due to the lack of closure which prevents organizational members letting the past go. Another view is that change may create a threat to self-esteem (Jetten, O'Brien and Trindall 2002). Also, the analysis of potential gain and loss by people has been considered by Prochaska, Redding and Evers (1997) as a good predictor of resistance. But, the research on resistance and organizational inertia is insufficient overall and urgent attention is needed from the community of researchers.

What we know for sure is that resistance to change is inevitable, but not unhealthy. In the outside expert model, those who resist are often viewed as 'not getting it' and either demonized or excluded from the processes of change. In the complex international systems which make up large contemporary corporations, such approaches make little sense. Executive coaches who are savvy in such systems use resistance as information and as energy to accelerate the transformation. Coaches expect resistance and their sole concern is how to use it. Those who initially resist are engaged within the system (although some may need to leave the organization if they will not or cannot work with the transformation).

AN ANALOGY WITH PHYSICS

Physicist Louis de Broglie had the idea of 'matter as wave' and a consequence of this concept is what is called the 'tunnel effect'. Unlike the classical mechanics of particles, quantum mechanics allows light as well as particles (such as electrons and protons) to appear even where the 'wall' of potential should prevent them from appearing. The analogy of tennis balls being bounced over a brick wall illustrates the effect of particles tunnelling through walls of potential (see Figure 1.1). Imagine thousands of tennis balls (representing particles) being simultaneously thrown to the ground with a given energy in each ball of, say, 100 units. The maximum bounce

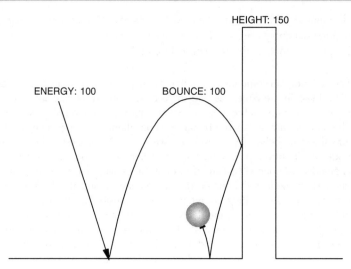

Figure 1.1 Tennis ball analogy of the tunnel effect

of each ball is 100 units. If the wall is 150 units high, logically no tennis ball will bounce over the wall. But, quantum mechanics demonstrates that particles with energy lower than the wall of potential can go through it. More precisely, some of them, not all of them, will appear on the other side. This is called the 'tunnel effect' because it is as though there were a hole or a tunnel in the wall of potential, allowing some of the particles to pass through it. According to quantum mechanics, matter with appropriate energy can go through the wall, since particles, as well as light, have particle–wave duality. Waves, according to Schroedinger's equation, can do what particles, according to Bohr's laws, cannot.

In our tennis ball illustration, the scenario would be that a bunch of some 10,000 tennis balls is thrown on the ground with energy of 100, and that some of them would reach the other side of the wall. Tennis balls are not dual and therefore remain as matter. But, there are interactions between the balls inside this chaos of 10,000 tennis balls bouncing around everywhere. Some energy can be transferred by several balls to others, which then have enough impulse to fly over the wall.

However, it is our purpose to discuss organizational coaching, not physics or tennis. The tunnel effect is potentially a very useful concept for coaches working with executive clients who are facing very high and solid walls of resistance to vital change processes.

LOOKING FOR A TUNNEL IN THE PROCESS OF ORGANIZATIONAL COACHING

There are walls of potential – in the form of resistance – in all coaching, as shown in Figure 1.2, and it is much higher when we deal with international organizations. (As noted earlier, high-impact coaching views resistance as potential.)

Coaching helps a client change. Systems Theory considers that there are two levels of change. The first level of change (change 1, in Figure 1.2) is limited to do more of the same, for instance automate the processes to increase productivity and make more money. The second level of change (change 2, in Figure 1.2) is a shift of paradigm, for instance re-engineering the processes to access totally new areas of business and to double income.

18

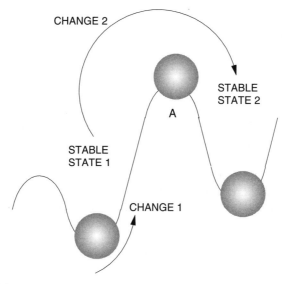

Figure 1.2 Levels of change

To achieve a second-level change, the client has to reach a point (shown as A, in Figure 1.2) where everything becomes uncertain. A change of this nature requires considerable energy. For instance, a married couple may be in a stable state (state 1) in their relationship. Before they decide to have a baby (state 2), there are often months of discussion, contemplation and hesitation.

In international organizations, high and solid walls of resistance/potential exist between state 1 and state 2, i.e., between the current state and the desired state. In individual and team coaching, it is not a big issue because the height of the wall is usually not that intimidating and we have now developed sophisticated coaching tools to jump over or remove most of them. In organizational coaching, the walls are high, very high – and solid. The challenge for coaches is to find and utilize methodologies to work with organizations to harness energy and produce a tunnel effect which would allow change processes to proceed through the various walls (see Figure 1.3). The alternative of trying to knock down the walls requires enormous resources

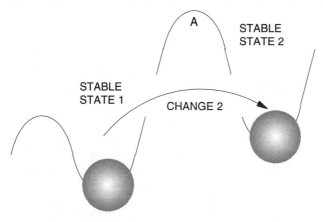

Figure 1.3 Tunnelling from state 1 to state 2

and saps organizational energy. Plus, it is unlikely to work – primarily because the resulting conflict will generate further resistance and higher walls. (Some conflict is, of course, a necessary part of any change process.)

THE TUNNEL

Our experience with enterprises demonstrates that we need to distinguish three categories of situations. The first one, illustrated in Figure 1.4, is the purely hierarchical organization: each person has only one manager.

Such organizations still exist. They are quite happy with normative change methods, as the vertical descending flow from objectives to execution usually works well. Bottom-up approaches are problematic because of the resistance factor, and pilot approaches are not very successful, due to the 'not invented here' syndrome. Probably the good old OD is still the best to trigger a change 2, to a matrix organization.

The second category of organization is the matrix, as shown in Figure 1.5. In these organizations, the main concern is reactivity to market changes. It is like a rowboat trying to react like a kayak in the rapids. Frequently, the decision system generates so many layers of control and such a level of uncertainty and frustration within middle management that this type of organization tends to give prevalence to only one of the dimensions of the matrix. The real functioning is more similar to a pure hierarchical system, where there is little chance of finding a 'tunnel'. Wise executives have understood that frequently switching prevalence, from one dimension to another, is a way of adapting to the fluctuations of the environment. For these organizations, change 2 consists in moving towards the third category of organization. This is the hypermodern organization, also called 'cyborg' (cybernetic–organic) type of organization as shown in Figure 1.6.

In science-fiction literature, a cyborg is a human being part of whose body is made of electromechanical devices, and who therefore is a (cyb)ernetic (org)anism. Very advanced organizations spend more than $US50,000 per employee to have an extremely sophisticated internal information system which allows management and sharing of all data, information and knowledge of the enterprise. Cyborg organizations are even more advanced as the information system is flexible enough to cope with frequent changes of structure. In Figure 1.6, teams (business entities like a branch office in a country) A and B are assembled in January to form a business unit. Later the same year, in June, a new business unit is created with

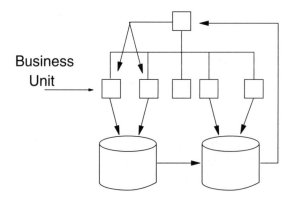

Figure 1.4 Hierarchical structures

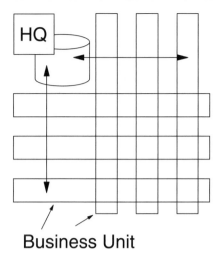

Business Unit

Figure 1.5 Matrix structures

B and C. Such organizations have been designed to face rapid changes in the business environment.

Cyborg organizations are more and more common because of two major trends. The first is the decrease in the size of the teams functioning as a small enterprise within large organizations. For instance, in the 1980s, when IBM was still hierarchical, only a country subsidiary had control over the profit, thus a unit of tens of thousands of people. When the matrix layout was put into place in the 1990s, the IBM European business units (the product divisions for example) had control of the profit. Their size was several thousand people. Over time, the size of the unit functioning 'as a business' dropped to several hundred people. The second trend is that the information system now provides the glue that holds these small units together. More

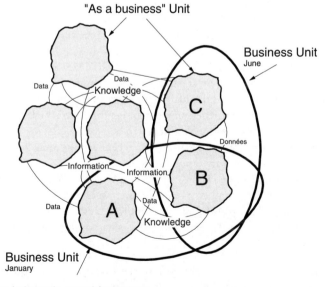

Figure 1.6 Cyborg (cybernetic–organic) structures

21

precisely, it is supposed to provide the glue by managing the data and by helping transform these data into information and eventually into knowledge to be shared not only with the members of the organization, but also with customers and subcontractors. This intellectual capital is now more widely considered as an asset.

In the organizations represented in Figure 1.6, a Business Unit, the entity in charge of a business segment on the market, is a sub-organization, obtained by assembling several units functioning as a small enterprise, say A and B. If the market is changing, it is possible to create a new Business Unit, by assembling B and C. Adaptability is at its maximum level compared to the hierarchical (Figure 1.4) and matrix (Figure 1.5) organizations where a complete reorganization is needed to cope with a change of the market structure.

In fact, we need to consider two different situations when we are trying to initiate a change 2 through a 'tunnel':

- move a matrix organization to a cyborg organization;
- move a cyborg organization to some kind of cyborg+ organization.

MOVE A MATRIX TO A CYBORG

Matrix organizations are not uniform. Some of them have already implemented an information system, which provides more or less the flexibility of a cyborg, except that the organizational flowchart is still rigid. The executives are not used to reigning over a kingdom whose borders change continuously and they hesitate to reshape their business unit with market fluctuations. Sometimes the corporate culture is the cause of the rigidity. For instance, in the field of imagery, enterprises involved in the 'argentic' technology, such as Kodak or Fuji, were too slow when the wave of 'binary' technologies appeared. Exactly like a tsunami, the wave caused devastation, forcing the whole 'argentic' supply chain to adapt or die. This was also true for all industries in the West where the cost of personnel is high: production has been displaced to countries where salaries are ten to twenty times less than in Europe or America. The automotive industry, clothing industry, etc. had to react quickly to declining margins. Currently, the balance between the euro and the dollar is forcing the European aircraft industry, especially Airbus and Dassault, to rapidly move production to the dollar zone. In these examples, the market change was sudden and all these organizations had difficulties implementing appropriate and timely responses.

Many matrix organizations are busy extending their business from the European and American regions to Eastern Europe, Latin America and Asia. Deeply involved in this challenge, they have no time to think about a new, creative way to higher levels of success, i.e., becoming a cyborg. Instead, they remain fixed in the matrix paradigm and concerned with doing more of the same. Coaches can be willing partners in maintaining this state which appears at the time – from the perspective of the organizational players – to be healthy.

An illustration of this situation comes from our recent involvement in the organizational coaching of a medium-sized company, specializing in financial services. The objective was to expand its international operations in order to become global. Due to the prudence of the executive team and to the very rigid corporate culture, we had to go through a very cautious process, working just with the top 200 managers. Our role as coaches was to work with them in groups of twenty through a two-day seminar. We facilitated discussion on a number of key issues, such as:

- Creating an above-country structure, for instance a worldwide headquarters;
- Having local persons as general managers of the subsidiaries;

- Including Asian or African cultures in the executive committee, which is still very European;
- Forcing the subsidiaries to use the same processes;
- Putting into effect a unique working language.

The process followed a predictable pattern. There was initial resistance to changing the status quo. The group coaching medium was useful in allowing a sharing of concerns and a building of trust and commonality among top-level managers. The company made progress on each of the key issues and people were generally satisfied. As coaches, we felt we had added value and we received very positive feedback. However, looking at this from the helicopter view, there was little substantial change. The result was a move from a matrix to a more sophisticated matrix. It was a first-level change process and the organization was still in state 1.

A second-level change would be to move such a matrix to a cyborg. Such a change would imply, in addition to the awareness and strong will of the executive committee, having access to many more than just the 200 top managers. Approaches, like World Café (Brown et al. 2005) described later, are then mandatory. That is, the process needs to harness more energy from more organizational 'tennis balls' in order to achieve a tunnel effect and thus navigate the walls.

MOVE A CYBORG TO A CYBORG+

Cyborg organizations are in continuous change and it is difficult to identify a 'stable state 1' and a 'stable state 2' as in Figure 1.2. Most organizational change theories (Lewin, 1946, 1951; Argyris, 1971; Porras and Silvers 1991; Srivastva and Cooperrider 1990; Schein, 1999; etc.) assume that the initial state is so solid that a phase of organizational destabilization or an 'unfreezing' is needed, followed by change and then a 'refreezing' to a new state (Lewin, 1947). For an achieved cyborg organization, a single, linear organizational process such as this is meaningless. Responding to environmental fluctuations is a permanent process and change happens through multiple interrelated processes that tap into all of the organizational sub-systems. As shown in Figure 1.6, the change occurs by redistributing the small units functioning as a business into a business unit able to cope with a new market challenge. The timeframes might be quite short and new structures are in a constant state of forming and reforming in response to or anticipation of market and environmental demands – all with global associations.

One-to-one executive coaching traditionally saw a coach working with an executive on a relatively stable set of goals over say a six- or twelve-month period. In the cyborg model, the coaching challenge is to assist executives to deal with rapid changes in responsibilities where predictable chains of command and stable goals are the exception rather than the rule. Flexibility, open-mindedness, creativity and a capacity for trust-building and collaboration are essential qualities. Coaches will increasingly be asked to assist clients to work developmentally on building up these kinds of skills and qualities.

Cyborg organizations require a pool of executives who are immediately ready to leave established business units and accept, in a flash, new responsibilities in a newly formed entity which combines elements of one or more business units. The goals of the new entity will not necessarily be clear, neither will the power and decision-making processes. It also means that the senior executive team has to acquire sufficient experience and wisdom to manage the managerial resources in this way. In this kind of fluid and dynamic environment there is a role for coaches in assisting executives to find some kind of clarity and focus.

This kind of change and highly volatile organizational model is still unusual, and we have limited experience in how to add high coaching value. However, the aim here is to raise awareness of the trends and challenges so that coaches can – like the executives they coach – avoid paralysis and work in-the-moment to design strategies that will be appropriate to the context.

In the next section, we describe a case study where the coaching interventions were constructed with the cyborg organizational paradigm. It is presented not as 'best practice', nor something that could be transplanted in a new context. It aims to illustrate the complexity of coaching in the international business environment and to stimulate reflection by coaches on how they might approach their current challenges in different ways.

CASE STUDY

In 2006, a French business was being acquired by a company based in Switzerland. The Swiss company was a technical leader in its field, operated worldwide, and was organized in a 'three-dimensional matrix' (functions, business operations and cross regions), had about 3,600 employees, managed a network of 40 representations and affiliates in the world and had presented a turnover of €520 million in 2006. The managing director of the French business – now a subsidiary – contacted an international business coach to help them succeed in their post-merger integration process.

Two weeks after the first phone conversation, the business coach was contacted by the human resources director (HRD) of the Swiss headquarters asking for support to reawaken the pioneering spirit of their leaders, to implement a culture of human innovation (and not only technical innovation), to prevent their leaders from becoming 'control freaks' and 'useless globetrotters' and to promote values like collective improvisation and creative relationships. In addition, they wanted to preserve their strong image of an ambitious, fast-growing, highly innovative company.

At the first meeting between the coach, the managing director and the HRD the different requests and their connections were explored. Included were items or themes such as, 'How much time are you are willing to invest?', 'Do we need success indicators?' and 'How can the coach model the pioneering spirit when intervening?' The discussion was fluid, different points of views were creatively analyzed and all participants agreed that a standard culture change process in 'three steps' would be the 'security path', attracting the group of 'control freaks' and disappointing the tribe of pioneers looking for something more unique, innovative and organic.

The 'control community' was searching for 'managed' change, the others for chaotic transformation. The subsidiary was interested in becoming a part of the overall organization, the 'brain' of the organization wanted culture change. Both were compatible in the sense that there was a need for developing a common spirit, innovative cooperation and shared values.

ORGANIC REQUEST, COACH COMMUNITY AND THE TUNNEL POSSIBILITY

When coaching a globally acting organization, we have to look at three different levels of interaction: the dynamics of the client system, the agility of the coaching system and the interaction of both. In addition to this, however, we must first find a set of answers to three core questions:

1   What requests are being made of the coach(es) by the organization, and from where did they emerge?
2   Can a single person coach an organization effectively?
3   How can we, as coaches, create the possibility of a tunnel effect when coaching an organization so as to support the client in his or her desire for transformation?

THE EMERGENCE OF THE ORGANIZATIONAL COACHING REQUEST

The coaching request of an organization can emerge from everywhere. As coaches, we are generally used to receiving these requests from the company's top representatives, i.e., its managing director, its board of directors, its HRD. As it is, we might question the fact that top representatives have developed their own analyses and identified their own demand. Instead, let us imagine that they are somehow expressing a hidden request of the living system as a whole. In that case, we can furthermore imagine that the 'organizational living system' is already engaged in a sort of unconscious transformation process and that we, as coaches, can rely on its energy.

In this perspective we can also assume that an organizational coaching request could emerge from alternative sources – say through a subsidiary or from any other cell of the organizational periphery. In addition, this organizational request can emerge – simultaneously or not – in its different 'phenotypes': a desire for post-merger integration, a wish for cultural change (as expressed by headquarters), a request for developing leadership, a proposal to foster creative collaborative work, and so on. It is even possible to imagine that one specific request could change its phenotype when travelling throughout the organisation: a desire for post-merger integration finally becomes a request for culture change when approaching the centre, i.e., the headquarters of the organization.

After consideration, we decided to respect the original request as expressed by the managing director of the French subsidiary, to consider it as one face of the hidden, overall request of the organization and to honour the request for culture change, expressed by the executive committee. Furthermore we thought it possible to invite our clients to create meaningful connections between these phenotypes so that they would get a whole new picture of what was at stake and sense the overall hidden organizational request which wanted to emerge – much like putting the pieces of a puzzle together. To initiate that 'connection creating', we proposed a 'wave of interviews' with the intention of sensing the different phenotypes of the overall organizational request expressed in its various forms throughout the company.

A COACHING COMMUNITY TO MIRROR THE CLIENT'S ORGANIZATION

When we come to realize that an organizational coaching request can be expressed throughout the organization in terms of its different forms – training, individual coaching, leadership seminars, reorganization projects, mergers and acquisitions – we have to accept that even the most brilliant person cannot coach a profound organizational request alone. There is not only a need to combine various competencies, such as consulting, facilitation, coaching, creativity and intercultural sensitivity, but we also must take into account that coaching an organization means managing different interventions, at different places, at the same time, through different people in more than one language. Hence it follows that we have to create a 'mirror image' of the client organization by creating a coaching organization, meaning a community of coaches able to connect, create and contribute in a unique way.

A 'standard' network of connected individual coaches, as is regularly found, will not be sufficient. Instead, we need a community of coaches who are individually able to let go of their personal approaches in order to give way to some sort of collective creation. The community has to be capable of using their system as a 'mirror image' of the client's system so as to sense the emergent opportunities and risks, to co-create appropriate interventions, to explore collective coaching and leadership and all questions which may arise during the coaching process.

Finally, these coaches have to be willing to take the risk of being part of this community today and of being excluded tomorrow, not because it is their own decision, but because the client system rejects a specific coach or because there will inevitably be 'victims along the way' in organizational coaching done through this kind of engagement. With respect to financial remuneration, innovative ways of 'getting paid' are needed because such a community cannot live with the traditional idea that one coach 'claims' the client and is therefore able to ask peers for a 'perpetual annuity' in terms of a fee percentage.

We decided to create such a coaching community by grouping together five different coaches who represented four different nationalities, were of different educational backgrounds, each speaking two or three languages and, as a whole, presenting various kinds of expertise in terms of facilitation and coaching skills. A previous successful, common coaching experience was an additional criterion for at least two of us. Furthermore, the coach who had been contacted by the client decided to experience the role of the 'meta' coach, meaning his role was to stay in the meta-position, interconnecting the different interventions, acting as the client's contact point and choosing his or her direct system interventions very carefully. The coaching community met via phone conference calls and regular face-to-face meetings to ensure more thought-provoking conversations, to clarify possible interrelational cultural viruses and to allow space for co-creation, learning and exploring.

ORCHESTRATING A TUNNEL EFFECT

To instigate the possibility of creating a tunnel effect, we discussed various solutions:

a   The possibility of setting up a linear intervention map that would be deployed simultaneously throughout the whole system and that would hence create different energy disturbances at different levels and locations at the same time;

b   The option of accepting the various subsystem requests without any further discussion but of connecting them in terms of purpose, emergence and change through permanent conversations, both within the coach system and between the coach system and the client system at the top level;

c   The option of working with the executive committee to help them change the visible structure of the system (the organizational structure) and nurture the invisible living part of the system (i.e., its information, knowledge and communication flow) in addition to helping them change their collective leadership style through team coaching; and

d   The last option we discussed was to combine all these options 'into one spirit' and to add events of some overall connecting and emergence value, creating large group interventions such as Open Space events and World Cafés.

In addition, we discussed whether it would be necessary to start our intervention with work at the top level before dealing with the other 'phenotypes'. Some of us found it difficult to accept that an organization can be coached without starting at the top level; others were convinced that this would be the best way to go. By exploiting our passionate and fruitful discussions as a possible mirror behaviour of our client organization, we started to gain awareness of the amount of energy required for the client system to accept and adopt our proposed approach of 'orderly chaos', wherein we consider an organization as a living and evolving system that accounts for the phenomena of emergence, evolution, bifurcation, hesitation and flow.

Coaching this organization by instigating a sort of creative chaos and maintaining the just-necessary order through regular conversations and specific schedules with the managers of the different units seemed, to us, to be the most effective approach to creating the possibility for generating sufficient energy to 'pass through' the tunnel of resistance and to stabilize the system on a new higher level.

We asked the client for a second meeting at which we presented them with our idea of using a community of international business coaches rather than the 'one coach fits all' methodology. We shared with them our different 'intervention designs', linking them to their specific objectives of reawakening the pioneering spirit and of looking for organizational innovation. To honour their search for an innovative approach to organizational coaching, and to assist their leaders to abandon their current 'control trip', we proposed our last option (d), the option of creative chaos, based on the idea of 'letting go of control' so that collective intelligence and system capabilities for self-organization could emerge. To our surprise, our proposal was accepted, as well as our recommendation to conduct a wave of interviews throughout the organization with the intention of sensing the unifying source for organizational coaching.

TUNNEL INTERVENTION, TRIPLE POINT AND TIPPING MOMENT

We conducted our 'wave of interviews' throughout the organization by talking to 30 people in different countries, representing the diversity of the organization. It turned out that the desire for optimized integration was a common 'song' expressed not only by the companies which had recently joined the group, but also by headquarters. Implicit in this request was the need for creating a common basis of understanding, the desire to be part of a real community and the need for acceptance as a high-value contributor. In other 'cells of the organism' we heard the need for more space to connect with others and to exchange, others asked for team coaching, and again others argued for a failure culture as a basis for innovation. We heard complaints about missing regulations, shadow management and the total absence of an inspiring and federating vision.

Designing the 'tunnel intervention'

When combining these different 'phenotypes', the client started to realize that the source for organizational transformation was an overall implicit request for deeper, creative connections, a search for shared meaning and identity, and a need for freedom to explore. On this basis, we proposed to coach a two-and-a-half day event with about one hundred key players from different countries and functions. The purpose of this first event, as coordinated with head-quarters, was to bring people together, make them exchange their respective successes and launch the platform to instigate a federating vision. With our support, the Executive Committee worked out an overall inspiring theme, implicitly referring to the organizational transformation request: 'Integration and connection, a never ending source for creating our future.'

The event was conducted as a World Café (Brown et al. 2005) for the first day, with the objective of having people connect through meaningful conversations. On the second day it was conducted as an Open Space Conference (Owen 1997; 2004), to enable the group to work out concrete actions, projects and initiatives. Combining both methodologies was important to create sufficient energy to pass through the tunnel a first time, to make collective intelligence emerge and to motivate different emerging leaders to take action and responsibility for launching future actions.

Generating a momentary 'triple point'

In addition, we decided to provoke a momentary organizational 'triple point'. In physics and chemistry, the triple point of a substance is the *temperature* and *pressure* at which three *phases* (*gas, liquid* and *solid*) of that substance may coexist in *thermodynamic equilibrium*. There is a moment where pure *water*, pure *ice*, and pure *water vapour* can coexist in a stable equilibrium. What is important to know is that at that point, it is possible to change all of the substance to ice, water or vapour by making infinitely small changes in pressure and temperature.

To use this triple point as a metaphor for our coaching process, we wanted to create a combination of time and pressure, enabling the one hundred people to achieve a state where they could collectively appreciate the value of the past, sense the emergence of the new, and feel the freedom of choice. Then, they could experience simultaneously the world of chaos, protection and emergence. At this point, little interventions like encouragement, a speech from a member of the board of directors (or an outside speaker) or a specific language can cause a group to 'collapse' to one of the three possible states: remaining in the past, embracing the future or getting stuck in the process of choice. Since our client's values were those of pioneering and innovating, it was relatively simple to make the system collapse into the future state, even if there was a small group of 'past promoters', which is quite normal in such a coaching process.

However, even if this event was a tremendous success in terms of connecting, exploring the future and sharing feelings of being an integral part of a larger community, one intervention like this is not sufficient to stabilize the system at the new level and to trigger different daily behaviour, management or leadership patterns. Not only was it important to launch specific projects on cooperation and integration, but it was also crucial that the company's formal structure nurtured this new way of thinking and connecting, and hence be adjusted to adapt. The various ongoing integration processes should be managed consciously so as to integrate the human dimension. In the new adaptive structure, new behaviour, such as risk taking, would be rewarded, whereas former behaviour, such as 'control mania', was to be ignored (which is more effective than being punished).

Leveraging the 'tipping moment'

We therefore helped the company and its various leaders regularly fuel the 'tipping moment'. As Gladwell (2002) expresses in his book, the word 'tipping point or moment' comes from the world of epidemiology. It's the name given to that moment in an epidemic when a virus reaches critical mass. It's the boiling point, and as he explains, 'The virtue of an epidemic, after all, is that just a little input is enough to get it started, and it can spread very, very quickly'. Inspired by this metaphor, we invited our client to identify their seven per cent of pioneering leaders, those willing to take risks and to bet on collective intelligence more than on the well-spread managerial, 'I know what to do approach'. Simultaneously, we also enabled the system to maintain the necessary speed to get the new philosophy spread very, very quickly through different interventions launched simultaneously.

COACHING THE INITIAL REQUEST OF THE FRENCH SUBSIDIARY

One of us was appointed to coach the French subsidiary's merger integration phase, but not as a huge step-by-step integration project. Instead the coach helped the various teams identify so-called 'leverage projects', such as 'making a common offer', 'orchestrating visits and meetings' and 'optimizing the installation of a new and innovative test facility'. For all these projects, the human dimension was part of the agenda, as was cultural awareness. Also, gaining effectiveness as an international team was a strategic objective. After six months, we organized a World Café with 20 highly involved people to guarantee an exchange of experience, new ideas and ways of propagating this newly acquired knowledge throughout the organization. At the same time, one of our coaches helped the subsidiary's Managing Director structure his team. The coach also assisted in developing their management skills and their way of working and taking decisions together.

FOSTERING PERIPHERAL ALLIANCES

Another coach was asked to encourage a cooperation between the French subsidiary and the German subsidiary in order to leverage 'periphery collaboration'. The possibility of demon-strating intelligent and effective cooperation between sub-cells on the basis of individual initia-tives impressed the executive committee. Consequently, their members started discussing and exchanging on processes of collaboration, integration and co-creativity when visiting the various subsidiaries, offices and factories. After nine months, these people were perceived as bridge-builders and challengers instead of useless globetrotters and headquarters control freaks. Some of these managers were even integrated, in some way, into the subsidiaries. Integration can indeed work in both directions.

NURTURE INTERCULTURAL SENSITIVITY

Another coach agreed to organize and facilitate cultural awareness seminars to increase under-standing of the different cultures, businesses and ways of doing things. Since they were connected to 'Integration and connection, a never-ending source for creating our future', these seminars were not launched as separate training activities. As an integrated initiative, they helped increase connections between people and to spread a common spirit.

CULTIVATE THE DIVERSITY OF COACHING

Individual coaching was carried out in various forms and in different locations, including in headquarters. Interdisciplinary and cross-regional co-development groups were launched and peers helped peers create new solutions and share individual challenges. Coached by a few of us, these groups made it possible to maintain the network of conversations and collective learning, hence combining the development of individual skills and promoting collective intelligence on an ongoing basis.

HUBS, TRIBES AND VIBES

After 28 months, the company culture leveraged the idea of the organization as a living system of hubs, tribes and vibes. Initiatives taken to organize 'living hubs', i.e., creative events of exchange, connection and conversation, spread naturally without being over-exaggerated.

'Living tribes', such as subsidiaries, functions, project groups and cooperation teams, developed an important sense of community for the duration of their existence. When a project was over, new tribes emerged to take the next step or to explore something new. One tribe (a commercial project team) even suggested organizing a World Café with clients and suppliers to extend their objectives and to get a bigger picture.

Finally, the company experienced the power of thinking in energetic 'vibes' (from the word vibration), rather than controlling the effects of particles working together. In quantum physics, an object is both a wave and a particle and it depends on the observer and his or her focus of attention as to which of these two dimensions finally take form. The company's internal language integrated words and expressions, such as 'communication wave', 'wave of rumours', 'negative vibes' and 'energetic vibes'.

In addition, some leaders developed tools, such as 'energy barometers' and 'cooperation indicators'. This company's workforce included an impressive number of engineers and especially chemists, quantum physicists and other creative people coming from 40 locations around the world. It thus represented the necessary diversity; the wave aspect of the business was clearly going to be easier to leverage than with a population of mono-cultural mechanical engineers. Nurturing this idea of living hubs, tribes and vibes is a strategic task when an organization wants to maintain its organizational energy at a level high enough to maintain the system on the edge of sensitive disequilibrium, the state where ongoing creation, learning and agility is possible without falling into counterproductive chaos.

THE TRIPLE RESULT

The living culture changed. The so-called initial post-merger integration became a major lever of organizational transformation. By the way, this form of post-merger integration, as conducted by an intercultural coach, became the reference and business case for future integrations. Open Spaces and World Cafés were integrated as the 'normal' way of meeting and were described as a regular 'living hub' for connecting ideas, sensing future opportunities and asking those questions that no one asks individually. The value of technical innovation was strengthened and connected to the value of human innovation, which created more inspiring relationships with the customers and hence an even better image and – new business.

The organization structure evolved and continued to adjust with the synergy of the living system. The matrix organization was maintained as a reference, but 'improvisational cooperation of tribes beyond borders' was highly encouraged. Individual mobility from one unit to another was facilitated, and the group started to create a pool of executives who were ready to immediately leave their current tribe, i.e., a business unit, to create, connect or integrate a newly formed or existing tribe. In the beginning, there was little interest, but later the interest grew.

The leadership style was renewed. Through coaching and training, current and future leaders learned to think together, to assimilate the idea of an organization as a living system and to develop other leaders. They recognized that diversity was the fuel for creativity, that living systems strive for identity and meaning and that if you want to keep a soulful company, employees need to express their soul in that business. They acknowledged that they had to combine the world of measurement with the realm of emergence, to create a breakthrough by creating and leveraging connections instead of analyzing parts and controlling indicators. They understood the possibility of simultaneously striving for individual excellence and for collective improvisation, to combine objectives and goals with the duo of intention and identity. They finally dared to ask the question: 'Do we have to abandon the idea of permanent re-engineering and focus instead on regular organizational re-energizing?'

WHAT OUTCOME FOR THE COACHING COMMUNITY?

The coaching community turned out to be a permanent collective resource for perceiving the client's system, its future opportunities, and its possible resistances and failures. Three coaches completed the entire 28-month coaching process, one was 'rejected by the client system' and one decided to leave the coaching community after nine months. Two new coaches were integrated, thus enabling the coaching community to itself experience and explore the issue of inspiring and effective integration. The community kept abreast through regular phone conversations and three face-to-face meetings. Emotional viruses were eliminated and the discussion of options was encouraged. At the end of this experience, this 'coaching tribe' was dissolved. Several coaches regrouped for new projects, others went their own way and reconnected later. Even others stayed together to create a learning community where each member had the possibility to ask their peers for advice, to show their vulnerability and to create new ways of coaching individuals, teams and organizations.

In this way, this 'coaching tribe' perhaps became a model for the new emerging reality for coaches, meaning getting connected for one project, then continuing one's own way, then reconnecting differently for the next time, thus demonstrating that the art and mastery of creating living hubs, tribes and vibes is not only important for global businesses to leverage, but also for globally acting coaching communities. The tunnel effect is not only of major interest when working with a globally acting organization, but also for inspiring coaches to get to the next level of collective intelligence, creativity and wisdom.

CONCLUSION

As analyzed by Christopher Langton (1989; Langton et al. 1992) complex systems show four categories of behaviour; steady, periodic, 'edge of chaos' and chaotic. The fourth category is a permanent mess while the first two are inflexible. The third one is potentially truly adaptable and living systems behave this way, combining preservation forces with transformation forces, to make homeostasis and adaptation coexist.

Provoking tunnel effects to help organizations pass the walls of resistance invites us as coaches to shift our reference frames and to see organisations as living systems with its dilemmas, unpredictable bifurcation, and phenomena of emergence, hesitation and flow. Globally acting organisations represent a *terrain propice* for this kind of transformation since the genuine diversity of people, cultural patterns and notions of speed can be leveraged for creating the necessary amount of transformative energy. Theoretical studies (Kaneko and Suzuki 1994) suggest that evolution, itself driven by a changing environment, leads the system to this 'edge of chaos'. This is our ambition, as organizational coaches, to help locate this exact point where adaptation becomes possible without ruining the organization's heritage or 'genotype'.

The role of the coach is to find the most appropriate entry to the tunnel of change. The first step consists in analyzing the four subsystems (culture, structure, technology, decision process) and encourage clients to consider all of them – instead of focusing only on the one familiar to the HR community (culture) or to the management (decision process). Rather similar is the Ken Wilber (2000) Integral Model of four quadrants, or the Bolman and Deal (1997) Four Frames Model (structural/systemic, cultural/symbolic, psychosocial, and political).

Coaching is in fact a flexible process where the route is not to force resistance but either to use it or to stay away from it. Compared to other approaches, it needs to be ready to quit the rigid frame of a methodology. On a sailing boat, the rudder blade is useful not for maintaining a direction but for understanding what the boat wants. Once the skipper has gained this understanding, he or she can change the sheets of the sails to keep the heading. Listening to what the organization wants is the key to this type of coaching.

Bibliography

Argyris, C. (1971) *Management and Organizational Development: The Path from Xa to Yb*, New York: McGraw-Hill.

Bolman, L. G. and Deal, T.E. (1997) *Reframing Organizations: Artistry, Choice, and Leadership*, San Francisco: Jossey-Bass.

Brown, J., Isaacs, D. and the World Café Community (2005) *The World Café, Shaping Our Future through Conversations that Matter*, San Francisco: Berret-Koehler Publishers Inc.

Burt, R. (1999) *Quand la culture d'entreprise est-elle un atout stratégique?* Paris: Echos.

Giroux, N. and Marroquin, L. (2005) 'L'approche narrative des organisations', *Revue française de Gestion*, 159: 15–42.

Gladwell, M. (2002) *The Tipping Point: How Little Things Can Make a Big Difference*, Boston, MA: Back Bay/Little, Brown and Company.

Grant, A.M. and Greene, J. (2003) *Solution-Focused Coaching: A Manager's Guide to Getting the Best from People*, London: Pearson Education Ltd.

Jetten, J., O'Brien, A. and Trindall, N. (2002) 'Changing identity: Predicting adjustment to organizational restructure as a function of subgroup and superordinate identification', *British Journal of Social Psychology*, 41: 281–97.

Kaneko, K. and Suzuki, J. (1994) 'Imitation games', *Physica D*, 75: 328–42

Kotter, J. and Heskett, J. (1992) *Corporate Culture and Performance*, New York: Free Press.

Langton, C.G. (1989) 'Artificial life', in C.G. Langton (ed.), *Artificial Life: Santa Fe Institute Studies in the Sciences of Complexity* (Vol. VI), Redwood City, CA: Addison-Wesley.

Langton, C.G., Taylor, C. Farmer, J.D. and Rasmussen, S. (1992) 'Preface' in C.G. Langton (ed.), *Artificial Life: Santa Fe Institute Studies in the Sciences of Complexity* (Vol. VI), Redwood City: Addison-Wesley.

Lewin, K. (1946) 'Action research and minority problems', in *Resolving Social Conflict*, London: Harper & Row.

Lewin, K. (1947) 'Frontiers in group dynamics', in K. Lewin (ed.), *Field Theory in Social Science: Selected Theoretical Papers*, London: Social Science.

Lewin, K. (1951) *Field Theory in Social Science*, London: Tavistock.

McGregor, D. (1971) 'Theory X and theory Y', in D.S. Pugh (ed.), *Organization Theory*, New York: Penguin.

Millward, L. (2003) *Managing Diversity in Multinational Teams* (report under contract), Farnborough: Quinatec.

Moral, M. and Henrichfreise, S. (2008) *Coaching d'organisation: Outils et pratiques*, Paris: Armand Colin.

Morgan, G. (1989) *Images of Organization*, Thousand Oaks, CA: Sage.

Owen, H. (1997) *Open Space Technology: A User's Guide*, San Francisco: Berrett-Koehler.

Owen, H. (2004) *The Practice of Peace*, New York: Human Systems Dynamics Institute.

Porras, J. and Silvers, R. (1991) 'Organizational development and transformation', *Annual Review of Psychology*, 42: 51–78.

Prochaska, J. O., Redding, C. A. and Evers, K. E. (1997) 'The transtheoretical model and stages of change', in K. Glanz, F. M. Lewis and B. K. Rimer (eds), *Health Behaviour and Health Education: Theory, Research, and Practice* (2nd edn), San Francisco: Jossey-Bass.

Schein, E. (1985) *Organisational Culture and Leadership*, New York: Jossey-Bass.

Schein, E. (1999) *Process Consultation Revisited: Building the Helping Relationship*, Reading, MA: Addison-Wesley.

Srivastva, S. and Cooperrider, D. (1990) *Appreciative Management and Leadership: The Power of Positive Thought and Action in Organisations*, San Francisco: Jossey-Bass.

Stewart, T. (1993) 'Re-engineering: The hot new management tool', *Fortune*, 127 (23): 41–8.

Tannenbaum, R. and Hanna, R.W. (1985) 'Holding on, letting go, and moving on: Understanding a neglected perspective on change', in R. Tannenbaum, N. Margulies, F. Massarik and Associates (eds), *Human Systems Development*, San Francisco: Jossey-Bass.

Trist, E. and Bamford, K. (1951) 'Some social and psychological consequences of the Longwall method of coal-getting', *Human Relations*, 4: 3–38.

Weick, K. and Quinn, R. (1999) 'Organisational change and development', *Annual Review of Psychology*, 50: 361–86.

Wilber, K. (2000) *Integral Psychology: Consciousness, Spirit, Psychology, Therapy*, Boston, MA: Shambhala.

2

INTEGRAL COACHING

Cultivating a cultural sensibility through executive coaching

Hilary Armstrong

> . . . but if the wind of thinking . . . has shaken you from sleep and made you fully awake and alive, then you will see that you have nothing in your grasp but perplexities, and the best we can do with them is share them with each other . . .
>
> (Hannah Arendt 1978: 175)

There has been much written about the value of coaching in the development of personal insight. This chapter proposes that insight is not enough, especially when working in global environments. What is also required is a cultural sensibility. A cultural sensibility is the mental and emotional understanding of, and response to, the influence of the tacit, essential ethical frames of meaning constructed by a culture that are expressed through social roles, race, class and gender differences. This chapter uses practice narratives to draw out aspects of a cultural sensibility and how integral executive coaching enhances it.

INTRODUCTION

Previously I have written about executive coaching as a cultural phenomenon that is fulfilling an archetypal need in work life today: that of a quiet, reflective space – a sanctuary – in which to chew the fat, be challenged in one's assumptions and asked reflective questions to get one to think differently. This proposal emerged from the results of an ongoing coaching effectiveness study conducted by the Institute of Executive Coaching, Sydney, Australia. In the study we ask coachees how they think that coaching worked to produce its benefits. Their descriptions suggest the ancient archetype of the Greek goddess Hestia. In ancient times, Hestia represented the centre of the home or city – the hearth – which was a place a visitor or family member was required to visit before doing any other business. This was seen as essential to the ongoing well-being of the city and its citizens. Thinking about coaching in this way helped us understand why 90 per cent of coachees, across the board, are highly satisfied with the coaching experience. In organizations today there are few opportunities to reflect, talk through personal issues or work together on solutions. Executive coaching then could be thought of as the 'hearth' in an organization – a sanctuary in which people can take time to focus on themselves and gain insight into behaviours and actions.

In this chapter, I want to shape coaching not only as a sanctuary for personal insight and behaviour change, but also as a space for the development of a cultural sensibility. With a cultural sensibility one has the flexibility to think and act in ways that demonstrate not only insight, but also 'outsight'[1] – the ability to take into account the complexity of any situation shaped as it is by power hierarchies in terms of ethnicity, gender, positional power, etc., and that the cultural narratives – roles, relationships, opinions and stories – that ensue, influence in-the-moment human interactions.

Integral coaching[2] broadens the scope of executive coaching to include outsight. It recognizes that gaining personal awareness of our individual subjectivity is only a part of the story. There are social structures and cultural narratives as well as psychological and biological processes which shape individuals' behaviour. Coaching that focuses primarily on insight, as in psychologically driven forms, is problematic especially in terms of culture. Social structures construct and mould who we are as much as our biology does. Integral coaching therefore includes a double loop of reflection; reflection on one's own psychological process and actions (insight), and outsight, reflection on social structures and roles in a situation – knowing that the latter is also shaping what is happening. It is by taking into account both aspects of lived experience that a cultural sensibility is promoted and enhanced.

A CULTURAL SENSIBILITY AND GLOBAL MANAGEMENT

In a study done by Development Dimension International (DDI) in which executives in multinational companies were interviewed about working in cross-cultural environments, researchers identified five characteristics that separated successful global executives from their less successful colleagues (Tandukar 2006). They are: intellectual grunt (analytic skills to deal with significant levels of complexity and ambiguity), emotional intelligence (the ability to reflect on our self-narratives), curiosity/openness (the drive to understand the dynamics of culture), cultural adaptation (the ability to read cultural nuances and adjust their style accordingly) and resilience (the capacity to function in often challenging environments while maintaining a consistent, positive demeanour). All these characteristics together make up to a cultural sensibility, a refined mental and emotional response to the tacit, essentially social and cultural frames of meaning that shape conduct and relationships.

What is interesting about these characteristics is that while insight and mindfulness are vital to cultivate in working in complex environments, there is a tendency in the individualism of Western cultures to presume that with well-developed personal insight and behaviour flexibility, people will operate successfully. This chapter takes the view that personal insight is important but, as this research reflects, it is only a part of the picture. Global executives need outsight – or as Arendt vividly termed a 'visiting imagination' (1978), the ability to observe and read others, and imagine stepping into their shoes. In other words to tune into the phenomenon called culture, the pervasive, yet largely tacit set of collective practices and stories that form and perpetuate individual relating and social reality. Executive coaching for global management must involve tools and skills that enable the development of outsight. This is important particularly in Western cultures where the focus of insight practices can simply feed the existing propensity for narcissism. Without including tools that will encourage outsight, executive coaches are at risk of perpetuating the very thing they are trying to influence, the ethnocentricity that prevents many individuals from being successful in global environments.

35

Integral coaching, while focusing on insight, also works to recognize that this is only half the picture. Our work is to guide coachees to observe outwards, and take into account that social and cultural realities are shaping their responses. For example, one coachee talked about finding himself silenced in a global meeting when he knew the answers and solutions, because every time he offered an opinion or solution, his boss would agree and the regional chief executive officer (CEO) would throw an obstacle in his path. His goal was to present confidently, but because he was not picking up the signals of competition between his boss and the regional CEO he was unable to. Another coachee was frustrated with being surrounded by 'yes men'. His goal was to develop better interpersonal skills but he was unaware of the cultural signals of respect for the 'absolute authority' that in the particular culture, his role contained. A female member of a senior financial team was continually angry about meeting behaviours because when she put forward an opinion it was rejected, only to be later spoken by a male colleague and accepted. She was giving herself a hard time for being angry but she was not aware of the signals of a culture of sexism. These are all examples of cultural signals (whether a national culture or a local, group culture) that can place people in roles/positions/opinions that may not (or may) be helpful.

The coachees would have been able to make more informed decisions about their responses if they had been (also) alert to local cultural nuances.

CULTURE AND INTEGRAL COACHING

Culture is defined in many ways. It is made up of the myriad of everyday stories and practices embedded in shared values and experiences of any group, big or small. We live it, we contribute to it, we shape it and it shapes who we are, how we relate and how we live. At a simple level it is a system of shared symbols, values and practices that shape lived experience and give it meaning and identity. Culture is pervasive – it does not only operate across national boundaries. There are transnational cultures and national cultures, and also regional cultures, local cultures, workplace cultures, family cultures, group cultures and many more, making culture an ever-present influence at all levels of lived experience.

Integral coaching takes a 'storied' view of culture,[3] i.e., that in the life of communities, organizations and groups there are 'stories' – patterns of lived experience that are passed along as we interrelate. These patterns are viewed as cultural narratives that emerge, produce and grow to keep alive a group's collective structure and identity. They convey shared meaning in a variety of ways. There are symbolic stories (such as about a company brand, a national flag, or a mascot), myths (narrated stories that are passed through organizations (the 'good old days')), hero stories (as in the Hestia archetype mentioned earlier), everyday conversation such as work-place gossip (the juicy stories shared around the water-cooler), ritualized practices ('the way we do things around here') such as the manner in which birthdays are celebrated, meeting and greeting habits or the conventions around recognition effort. The stories are always held together by implicit shared values – a collective and tacit preference or inclination for what is considered by the group, organization, family or nation as worthy.

Cultural stories shape our daily interactions with each other. They are always present, largely imperceptible inhabiting the space between the individual and the social organization. Different cultural stories lead to differently cultivated behaviours and we notice their influence only if something interrupts our usual patterns of relating, disturbing us with its difference (e.g., visiting unfamiliar cultures, or a job in a new organization alerts us to this process as we begin to notice difference and make comparisons with our habitual ways of relating). Unless we can notice, be curious about the difference and open to its worthiness (it has worked for others) as well as take it into account in our reactions and responses, we will be unable to build dialogue and effective working relationships.

People with a cultural sensibility are aware that culture is an invisible shaper of relationships. They have self-understanding (insight). They also have outsight in that they observe and notice difference because they are curious and they do not judge it immediately as inferior/superior. They are open and engaged. They value dialogue (in the sense of keeping the communication channels open) as the most important task and have the courage to keep trying new behaviours and resilience and make mistakes to enable this.

The following case studies describe the different aspects of a cultural sensibility. The first one relates the story of a newly appointed global executive who struggled to develop a cultural sensibility; the second, the story of different personal reactions to cultural pressure; and the last, the story of a global executive who successfully found the middle ground in his adaptation to a different culture.

A senior executive working in a multinational company was told that some of his virtual team members and customers had complained to his immediate superior on exit interviews that he was a micromanager and that he did not understand the business. They gave this as the reason why they were leaving. The executive was a self-involved and anxious man on his first global assignment. The culture he was promoting in his new job was process-driven and highly conventional, a style that was also manifest in his relationships. His worldview was that correct processes and procedures were all that was required in management. He worked hard to enforce this focus and neglected anything that was less pragmatic (soft skills), believing them unnecessary. He pushed hard when someone opposed him and was considered a bully by his reports. He took no responsibility for mistakes, believing them to be due to inadequate processes or people not following process.

While there had been a lot of rumbling in the company about his behaviours, it was not until a large customer bluntly refused to deal with him on one of his trips overseas that the organization took action. The CEO recommended executive coaching with a view to its assisting this person to improve his relationships with his teams and customers in other countries. The executive took the suggestion of coaching as an example of lack of support and people out to 'get him'.

After a three-way meeting between the CEO, coach and coachee, coaching began with the coach eliciting the coachee's version of the story. As the coachee told the story there was no sign that he was taking any responsibility for any of the problems. The exploration of the coachee's actions and the approach he was taking was elicited through a reflection about his role, its global context and all the 'external' factors that influenced it. This provided the coach with the background (through the coachee's self-narrative) and the opportunity to build trust through demonstrating active listening and empathy. As the coachee relaxed he began to open up about the anxiety which led to his micromanagement – which he also continued to justify on the grounds that he had no effective staff. Over subsequent sessions, with careful questioning and patience from the coach, the coachee began to develop some awareness, and relationships with his team at home improved somewhat. However, his relationships with his overseas teams deteriorated.

The coachee's blind spot was his ethnocentricity. He maintained throughout coaching that his role with his overseas reports was to enforce the Western standards of the company and he would countenance no other way (because all other ways to him were inefficient, time-wasting and unethical). He was adamant that his overseas reports do things his way even though budgets and targets were healthy. The coachee talked about his overseas staff as though they were 'naughty children' whose behaviour needed correcting. His belief in the superiority of his Western identity and his own self-importance remained unshaken. This affected his ability to think beyond simple ideas of right and wrong, black and white, reducing his ability to deal with the complexity required to work in global environments. Although he had gained some degree of insight, he had hit a wall. He lacked the ability to recognize the necessity of understanding the 'other' and walking in their shoes in order to understand their world – in other words, 'outsight', and therefore a cultural sensibility.

The central character of this story is not unusual. He is taking a stance that is prevalent in Western organizations. People who rise to the top are often egocentric (self-superiority) and this feeds ethnocentricity (cultural superiority). His egocentricity was demonstrated in his self-centred belief that his way was the best – if not the only way. His changes through coaching were minimal, and by recognizing that anxiety was his main driver he was able to see that others were capable of doing things and if the outcomes were successful how they did it was less important. He also began to practise small changes, greetings, leaving his door open for easier access, asking for more regular updates, delegating. But this only worked with people who worked closely with him – and my sense was that they had learnt to manage his anxiety as well. When it came to his virtual teams, his mindset was intractable. He was capable of some insight, but he lacked a cultural sensibility: i.e., he could not think beyond his own ethnocentricity.

When working with people operating in global environments, executive coaching must address ethnocentricity (something not exclusive to the West but endemic). Added to this is the egocentricity that is common in Western senior executives and this goes hand in hand with ethnocentricity – people regarding their own culture (as well as themselves) as superior. This superiority is expressed in the belief that any processes and procedures that work 'at home' are necessary in other cultural contexts to upgrade the perceived inferiority. Ethnocentric managers, like the executive above, cultivate an attitude of entitlement. With this they fail to notice 'difference' or recognize that diversity of any form is essential to the enrichment and survival of systems and species. 'Others' are simply a warped version of themselves and their entitlement gives them the right to correct them. Furthermore, the more self-centred a person is, the more likely they are to revert to simplistic 'us/them', linear, 'black and white' thinking and this polarizes people and foments hatred, 'isms' and divisions.

Our coaching was successful to the extent that the coachee's negative self-talk reduced and he modified his management style. But coaching also had a limit – the manager's ethnocentricity. If he had expressed curiosity about his team members' behaviours, about the CEO's feedback, about why a customer would not deal with him, about his own cultural embeddedness and difference (rather than assuming superiority) he may have been able to conduct himself differently. Instead he was irritated by the coach's curiosity about these things. His ethnocentricity (along with other things of course) got in the way.

In our experience, many coaches are not trained in recognizing how power structures social reality through hierarchies of culture, type of work, class, age, gender, roles and responsibilities. Yet, in coaching, issues that reflect these dynamics are often present: the inability to influence colleagues or teams in other areas, the demonization of different departments, such as risk and compliance, the view of top management, of people on the shop floor. Stereotyping is everywhere and what produces it is an informal pecking order of class, gender, work styles and work content, which makes up the culture of a group. Integral coaching emphasizes this aspect of coaching practice as vital because it is always present, whether it is across national boundaries or particular workplace cultures.

The next scenario illustrates the effects of different organizational cultures, and the way different people respond. In this example, the process of outsight brought personal insights that changed the situation as well as the person.

A highly accomplished senior academic and researcher with an international reputation accepted a role of associate director (AD) in a government department to head and assist with policy in her field of research. Within three months, she was asked to accept coaching because the 'cultural' fit between her and the organization was not good – which on briefing seemed a euphemism for her lack of people management skills and the dissatisfaction of her team and others in the department. The stakes were high. Unless she 'changed her ways', her contract would be dissolved. She was shocked and surprised when told her contract might not be renewed.

The AD (coachee) was oblivious to culture and its effects. She was familiar with achievement-oriented, autonomous university environments. In these, academic freedom is vital, and, although always reconciled against broader university goals, opinions can be at odds with them. In government and corporate environments this freedom of speech is less encouraged, especially if it is at odds politically or culturally. At a systemic level the AD was excellent in terms of political and cultural savvy, but in terms of the department and her team, savvy was not present.

With her team she was curious and then annoyed at the seeming lack of cooperation. She challenged them and was ignored – people kept doing what they had always done, and she was kept out of the loop. Her frustration grew. She counteracted by ascertaining that one of her staff was inadequate for the job and two others were engaged in a competitive relationship that was not productive. Being used to academic environments that were based on merit and autonomy, she thought directness was the best policy. She therefore told the team her problems with them in no uncertain terms and she laid down her new expectations. The reaction was immediate. One woman went straight to the chief policy officer and the director and complained. The others were less obvious and began covertly working against her more. There was a stalemate. She was stunned therefore to be informed that her presence was causing difficulties and people were demanding her resignation.

Culturally the department was a very different place from the university and it was staffed by people who had worked together in different areas in the public service for many years. In addition, there was a political appointment on the AD's team and a sensitive one in terms of the survival of the department. Two other team members were engaged in a sort of sibling rivalry and when something went wrong they reported it to another senior woman. The coach asked what a metaphor for the culture might be. The AD immediately said a 'family'. When the AD was questioned further she recognized that there was a local 'mother' and 'father' – the father with the positional power and the mother with the informal power. Anything that occurred, any decisions that were made, any complaints, gossip, outputs were put through the department head and his informal deputy – the local mother and father. She was an outsider who did not fit.

When faced with cultural perplexity people respond differently and in many cases a usually empowered person can quickly become frustrated and depressed. The reaction leads to more rudimentary communication styles and this amplifies the negativity, leading to a vicious cycle in which differences are amplified out of proportion and perpetuate the story (early coaching was filled with stories of complaint and protest). In this case the AD moved to the safety of task orientation and rationality (she decided to keep her head down and just do the job and forget about the team). Sadly, in the face of cultural perplexity such responses as this are counterproductive. When people miss or misread cultural symbols, the ability to relate to others becomes even more important. If, as the AD did, one becomes more introverted and isolated, the problems tend to amplify. In the AD's case there was even difficulty in everyday meeting and greeting (she dreaded going to work) and the responses from her team did not help.

Much of the early coaching sessions were aimed at the development of relationality. The first steps began with her curiosity about the 'family culture'. This led to an inquiry into how the local culture developed historically from certain events that were built into the fabric of its interactions. She found a number of people in other parts of the department who were friendly and she was able to build confidence. Talking with her new friends, she realized there was an existing joke about the department as a family. She began to look at the role she was playing within it and she reflected that it mirrored the role she had taken up in her family. This was the pivotal moment for her, as the understanding gave her choices as to when (and whether or not) she would adopt this role.

She then tackled her main relationship challenges. She forced herself to be less isolated. A good opportunity came to test this when one day the department head requested that she, the AD, 'loosen up' at work. She managed to hide her distress at the comment and asked what he meant. He suggested she chat more and perhaps have a social drink after work with him and others. She was able to recognize her seriousness as part of her family story. Although, in the face of this comment, she found 'loosening up' extremely difficult, she showed enormous courage to adapt and join others socially through project work, social events and conference visits. Her other challenge, the Department 'mother', remained a challenge in every way. After several failed attempts, after our coaching she took on the task of asking a trusted colleague how he managed 'mother'. He was very helpful, first normalizing the AD's difficulties (he and others had similar experiences of the 'mother') then sharing with her his strategies of how he bypassed this person.

Over the year she was coached, her situation markedly improved and there was no question about renewal of contracts.

Executive coaching in this case was about encouraging insight and behaviours, but this process was meaningful for the coachee only when outsight was encouraged. Outsight provided the awareness of what symbolically was sculpting the relationships in the environment and once she recognized this she was able to choose and adapt with awareness. Any situation that we enter has a history of action and events which have built up its culture and we cannot ignore this history. Understanding this belongs to a cultural sensibility.

Culture needs always to be taken into account. Any organization, by its very nature, is conflictual as it is arranged both by a formal hierarchy that shapes communication and an informal set of networks that aim to level people through open conversations and affiliations. Different cultures lie at different points along a continuum between these two sets of relationships. With a cultural sensibility a new appointee bides their time and observes the informal networks. Often people think in generic terms when it comes to culture, but what is really required is awareness of one's own perplexity in the face of cultural difference, because once one can pick this up, relevant response is possible.

My last scenario is a success story about a cultural sensibility in a global environment.

A newly appointed CEO in a takeover of an offshore manufacturing company decided to begin his term by introducing the management practices that had made him successful in Australia. One of these practices was to hold relatively short, action-oriented Monday morning meetings with his direct reports. He saw this as a necessary catch-up at the beginning of a week to energize his people and to plan and strategize decisions for the week ahead. He was an experienced leader and enjoyed different environments, and he was quickly accepted by his staff. He considered himself sensitive to cultural difference, and after several rather brief, too efficient, Monday mornings, he began to notice a pattern of conduct that aroused his curiosity. Each Monday he and his direct reports gathered, chatted, and then got down to business and agreed with everything he said. At first he found this fine, but then he began to realize that there was no dialogue or discussion. His frustration was further amplified because, after each meeting, the rest of his morning was spent with his team, one at a time, filing in and out of his office to tell him what they really thought. He was finding this time-consuming. Nothing helped and finally his increasing frustration and bewilderment led him to engage an executive coach.

In coaching he presented his problem as a behavioural issue on the part of his direct reports that needed 'fixing' and he wanted advice on how to do this. The coach resisted, and, using externalizing questions, assisted him to use outsight. He began to realize that external factors might also be shaping the interactions. As part of this he examined his assumptions and the cultural narrative and values that were driving them. Through the process of 'other-oriented' questions he developed a 'visiting' imagination, placed himself in the shoes of his direct reports and then imagined, from his knowledge of the culture, what assumptions and cultural values they might be bringing to the meeting. In the course of this process, he began to recognize that his role as CEO might be differently perceived by his team. With this new understanding, he tried new ways of meeting. Initially he shortened his meetings to 15 minutes and then put aside the rest of the meeting time for 'post-meeting' meetings. Everybody was very happy with this arrangement.

If we interpret this story through a narrative view of culture we can see the CEO's cultural narrative is different from his team's. Their narrative regards his role as supreme authority who should not be challenged in public (respect him so he does not lose face). This was a different cultural narrative from the CEO's and from these different narratives, different sets of values and behaviours were being expressed. Neither narrative is superior, they are simply different.

The CEO expressed a cultural sensibility. He was open and curious about the behaviours and, with questioning, reflected on it objectively. He developed a keen ability to observe what was going on, to read the signs and symbols around him, to sometimes name them, and at others to work them out and strategize around them. He moved away from being ethnocentric to outsight and to the enjoyment and acknowledgement of difference.

THE PRACTICE – INTEGRAL EXECUTIVE COACHING FRAMEWORK

The Institute has shaped its training and practice in executive coaching to reflect an integrated and holistic approach that addresses the 'whole' person within a context. This means taking into account that people both influence and are influenced by personal, organizational, social and cultural demands. Integral coaching is a transformational process that regards the coachee as a participant in a whole system that includes the culture, systems and social context of their situation. There are three domains of coaching outcomes identified as leading to sustained change: the intrapersonal, interpersonal and instrumental domains. Cumulatively the three domains of integration incorporate outcomes for the person and the organization (see Figure 2.1).

In integral coaching the mindset is one in which human beings 'story' the world and through self- and collective narratives construct and contour it. Coaching therefore must exam-ine the ways that people structure their worldview. The ability of outsight requires ways of thinking that enable us to imagine we can stand outside ourselves and witness our actions and behaviours. To do this, integral coaching employs an 'externalizing' conversation.

People are not problems, problems are problems, and people get captured by them, as the social constructionist maxim says. The statement means that although problems or obstacles exist, it is the way of thinking or construct that we employ to approach the problem that is the important thing. If we can think of the problem as an object which can be thought about in a

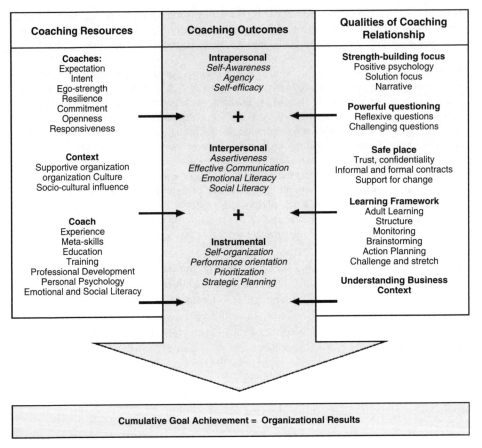

Coaching Resources	Coaching Outcomes	Qualities of Coaching Relationship
Coaches: Expectation Intent Ego-strength Resilience Commitment Openness Responsiveness	**Intrapersonal** *Self-Awareness* *Agency* *Self-efficacy* **+**	**Strength-building focus** Positive psychology Solution focus Narrative **Powerful questioning** Reflexive questions Challenging questions
Context Supportive organization organization Culture Socio-cultural influence	**Interpersonal** *Assertiveness* *Effective Communication* *Emotional Literacy* *Social Literacy* **+**	**Safe place** Trust, confidentiality Informal and formal contracts Support for change **Learning Framework** Adult Learning Structure Monitoring
Coach Experience Meta-skills Education Training Professional Development Personal Psychology Emotional and Social Literacy	**Instrumental** *Self-organization* *Performance orientation* *Prioritization* *Strategic Planning*	Brainstorming Action Planning Challenge and stretch **Understanding Business Context**

Cumulative Goal Achievement = Organizational Results

Figure 2.1 Coaching outcomes

variety of ways, we have externalized it. By externalizing it we can then examine and begin to understand how our thinking is getting in the way. The coach employs externalizing questions to draw out storylines that are shaping a person's acting and thinking and, in a collaborative dialogue, the coach and coachee ascertain the different storylines and listen for the preferred ones (those that fit a person's goals). Integral coaching therefore is solution-focused, valuing and giving more airtime to more helpful and proactive patterns of thinking and action.

People live multi-storied lives. Stories are never coherent or complete and there are myriads of them. We get drawn into some and not others. Sometimes this is helpful and at other times it is not. However, there are always snippets and echoes of other narratives present and the role of the coach is to listen for what does not fit the existing cognitive frameworks – news of difference. In all problem stories there are exceptions to the storyline and these often provide the seed of the solution. An integral coach listens for the exceptions and uses them as the springboard for new stories, actions and outcomes.

In the final scenario the CEO realized his implicit and dominant self-narrative was ethno-centric and he had been blind to the cultural nuances that were also present. He lacked outsight. With the use of reflexive questions, he started thinking in terms of outsight and he realized very quickly that taking it personally was an unhelpful storyline in his present circumstances. His actions changed and he and his team found a middle ground in which all were satisfied.

In the second scenario, once the coachee recognized that the department was a different culture, she was able to free herself from her self-blame to the extent that she strategized different ways to fit in and she was able to make more choices about how she responded and acted.

A powerful questioning method that elicits outsight is the use of other-directed questions (Epston 1993). Examples are: 'If you gave me some advice in this situation, what would it be?' or 'What would your colleague have said about that?' The CEO was asked: 'If you were in your team's shoes and had grown up in their culture, how might you be thinking, acting?' He was open to the question and employed a 'visiting imagination' (Arendt 1978) to answer it. The coachee in the first scenario, on the other hand, when asked other-directed questions struggled and replied: 'Because I am not the other person I would not have a clue, and anyway anything I say is me saying it and I cannot speak for another!' Unfortunately he was speaking and doing for the others most of his time and that is what they were objecting to!

So how does one develop or teach outsight? Below (Figure 2.2) is a four-quadrant landscape adapted from Wilbur (1996, 2000) which maps a selection of questions to elicit insight and outsight.

In conclusion, this chapter has explicated a cultural sensibility as an important meta-skill for global executives. Executive coaches in global environments therefore need to be aware of it. It has been drawn out as a process of insight and outsight, the ability to observe, read and understand the significance of social and cultural influences on human interaction. My purpose for doing it is to try and understand more fully the characteristics that the DDI research

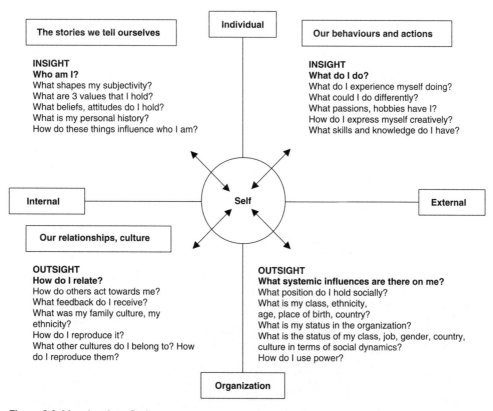

Figure 2.2 Mapping the reflexive process

identifies as being important for working in the current global markets. As an executive coach the concept of a cultural sensibility belongs to an ethical stance about our work. Unless the rampant ethnocentricity and egotism of many powerful individuals is challenged and new models of being and relating encouraged, dialogue between peoples will not be possible and in a global world this would be a recipe for disaster. We, as a profession, have a responsibility to be aware and open to not only internal influences on behaviour but also how the social realities we all dwell in, and perpetuate, are important creators of our beings in the world.

Notes

1 'Outsight' is not in the dictionary. I first heard it used by David Epston, a narrative therapist from Auckland, New Zealand during a conversation.
2 Within the field of executive and business coaching there are different approaches and emphases. Some organizations and clients focus specifically on tools and skills directly related to work task performance and coaching is viewed as an individual development process achieved through a semi-prescriptive program of skills or behaviour development. The Institute has shaped its training and practice in executive coaching to reflect an integrated approach that addresses the whole person within a context. Using Wilber's (1996, 2000) Integral Model as a landscape for the coaching process, the Institute takes into account that people both influence and are influenced by personal, organizational, social and cultural demands. Executive coaching, for the Institute, is a transformational process that regards the coachee as an actor in a whole system that includes the culture, systems and social context of their situation.
    The IEC coaching framework identifies three domains of outcomes/cumulative goal realization from coaching; the intrapersonal, interpersonal and instrumental domains. These outcomes are shaped by factors that include resource factors brought to the coaching, including factors requiring 'outsight' for the development of cultural sensibility, as well as relationship quality factors, which cumulatively produce outcomes. The outcomes/goal realizations are not cumulative in a linear sense but build on each other, often in a circular fashion to produce outcomes (see Figure 2.2).
3 There is a considerable tradition of narrative psychology, sparked by people like Jerome Bruner (1986), and taken into practice by the narrative therapy practice of Michael White (1992) and David Epston (White and Epston, 1992). Information about this tradition is readily available on the web, e.g., the Virtual Faculty at Massey University in New Zealand and the Dulwich Centre, Adelaide.

Bibliography

Arendt, H. (1978) *The Life of the Mind*, New York: Harcourt Brace & Company.
Bruner, J. (1986) *Actual Minds, Possible Worlds*, Cambridge, MA: Harvard University Press.
Development Dimension International, <www.ddiworld.com>.
Epston, D. (1993) 'Internalised other questioning with couples', in S. Gilligan and T. Price (eds), *Therapeutic Conversations*, New York: Norton.
Tandukar, A. (2006) 'Global powers', *Business Review Weekly*, 2–8 Nov: 36–8.
White, M. (1992) 'Deconstruction and therapy' in D. Epston and M. White (eds), *Experience, Contradiction, Narrative and Imagination*, Adelaide, Australia: Dulwich Centre Publications.
White, M. and Epston, D. (1991) *Literate Means to Therapeutic Ends*, Adelaide, Australia: Dulwich Centre Publications.
Wilber, K. (2000) *A Theory of Everything*, New York: Shambhala.
Wilber, K. (1996) *A Brief History of Everything*, New York: Shambhala.

COACHING TO HIDDEN FRAMES

Facilitating transformational change in complex environments

L. Michael Hall, Michelle Duval and Omar Salom

EXECUTIVE SUMMARY

Meta-Coaching offers a systematic approach to coaching, using cognitive-behavioral, developmental, and self-actualization psychology as formulated in Neuro-Semantics. This grounds the Meta-Coaching approach in these psychologies as well as in the theoretical frameworks of Gregory Bateson, Alfred Korzybski, Timothy Gallwey, etc. From this come numerous practical tools for coaching which are ideally suited to the international business context with its inherent high levels of complexity – meta-questioning, matrix framing, and stepping back for quality control.

META-COACHING THEORY

Our approach in coaching is called Meta-Coaching. That's because we view the distinguishing factor in coaching as its meta-discipline nature so that it does not require expertise in the client's content (Grant and Greene 2003), but expertise in the process of facilitating generative change for actualizing one's highest and best (Hall and Duval 2003). In calling it Meta-Coaching our primary focus is to coach the processes, structures, and contexts of a person's thinking and understanding – the meta-levels (Hall 2000).

Theoretically, these higher levels arise from our unique form of human consciousness and its working as self-reflexive consciousness. The factor of reflexivity within the human way of thinking and reasoning means that after we have constructed our first awareness, idea, understanding, belief, etc., we inevitably then think about our first thoughts, we then layer a third level of thoughts-and-feelings upon the second, and so on. In fact, this process is not only inevitable, but inescapable and infinite.

As a result, we never just have 'a thought', we have layers upon layers of embedded thought (and emotion) that make up a whole 'thought system' or 'belief system' which, in Neuro-Semantics, we call a Matrix. Because we human beings operate from a Matrix of beliefs, frames of references, meaning frames, etc., effective coaching has to enter into that Matrix of meaning and address it. For coaches who are working in the international business arena, the

45

Matrix construct takes on even greater relevance because there are multiple and highly diverse individual and collective matrices of meanings. The coaching task, guided by meta-coaching theory, is to assist individuals, teams and organizations to make sense of situations where multiple beliefs and frames of reference are constantly interrelating. Also, coaches need to be particularly cognizant of cultural influences in multinational, multicultural and cross-border coaching contexts.

META-COACHING THEORY ABOUT CULTURE

This theory informs our understanding of culture. For us, a 'culture' is a set of meaning frames. We also recognize culture as an evolving and dynamic process of collectively recognized rules, rights, responsibilities, duties, obligations, rituals, and powers that arise within a community. This system operates as the group's shared reality. The problem with the term 'culture' is that it is often conceptualized as a 'thing', empirical, fixed and external. It is not. Conceptualized as a set of meaning frames, it is constantly changing and open to challenge and renewal. Conceptualized as process, culture encompasses the group processes, which cultivate the minds, hearts, and habits of those within a community or organization. The meaning frames and processes are constructed as layers of thinking-reasoning-feelings. Consequently, we coach to 'culture' by addressing these layers.

'Culture' has a hidden verb inside it (cultivate). Culture therefore arises from the way we are cultivated. A culture cultivates within us a certain way of thinking, feeling, relating, and acting. These meanings and their quality have powerful influences on our relationships and life experiences. Our culture becomes embedded in our individual identities. We incorporate within us the meaning frames of our culture. Now we can take our culture with us everywhere we go. We carry it with us in our mind as our hidden frames about what things are and what they mean. Meta-Coaching raises clients' awareness of their hidden frames, and – where appropriate – to challenge and change them. It also raises clients' awareness of alternative individual and collective hidden frames that others might hold and how creative synergies might be created between contrasting frames.

We move out into the world with hundreds of cultural frames that we assume are real. These deal with our understandings about roles, wealth, business, career, productivity, achievement, accomplishment, respect, etc. Our belief frames may create within us a strong work ethic enabling us to achieve a lot and fill our hours with productive work. Or our cultural frames may focus more on family and connection with others, more on respect and honor. Whatever the frame, we assume it to be 'the way it is' about life, business, work, gender, etc.

Similarly, an organizational culture is made up of meanings that have been reinforced to such an extent that they are now habituated into our processes of relating, performing, working, deciding, and the way we go about doing business in performing the functions of the organization. These meanings include what is considered 'right' or 'wrong' behavior or speech in specific contexts, from one specific division or branch of an organization to being habituated norms enterprise-wide.

These hidden frames of meaning are then reflected in the organization's branding, advertising, recruiting, induction, incentive and bonus programs, performance reviews, internal communications, office layout, uniforms, work flow and systems, etc.

Within one organization there are many hidden frames – i.e., many assumptions and beliefs. This complexity of hidden cultural frames is even greater where there has been a merger with a distinctly different corporate entity. International business is a landscape of constant mergers and acquisitions, meaning that the world of an international executive is likely to be bewildering in its complexity. Meta-Coaching provides a means by which executives can find clarity and ways of achieving their potential amidst the chaos.

CULTURAL META-LEVELS THEORY

This meta-structure of cultural belief frames lies at the heart of Meta-Coaching and comes from work by Michael Hall (2000) on Meta-States, which integrates the brilliant analysis of the social construct of reality by John Searle. Searle (1995) had created a formula to describe how we construct social realities that involves meta-levels of ideas: X counts as Y in C.

In this formula, X is any brute fact, any empirical, see-hear-feel referent in life: paper, metal coins, a field marked with white chalk lines and two poles with a net stretched between, etc. Y stands as a meta-term, a conceptual or non-empirical abstraction: money, game, point, winner, championship, etc. C stands for context, the when and where; the X term counts as a Y term. I diagram this formula in our work on cultural modeling (Hall 2001a) as set out in Figure 3.1.

Searle has also enumerated numerous processes by which we construct social reality. For example, we do so by 'speech acts'. This is language which is not about representing reality; it is not a map about something. Instead it is a speech act that actually creates what it refers to. For example, in saying the following we create the experience:

The meeting is called to order.
I pronounce you husband and wife.
The proposal is accepted.

Speech acts are actions. In so speaking we actually construct the social reality. The function of so speaking goes to the person or people with the status to so speak for a social group. Group leaders will have a strong influence in creating the social reality of the group. A board hires a CEO, a president is elected, a soldier rises through promotion to General, and so on. The person acquires – in whatever way – a functional role that gives him or her the status to speak for the group and therefore have a strong influence on the construction of the group's reality. Meta-Coaching of organizational leaders is therefore intimately connected with construction of the organizational reality. The outcomes of coaching are heightened awareness of and capacity to shape hidden frames of meaning. Then, the consequential behavior is in the form of speech acts.

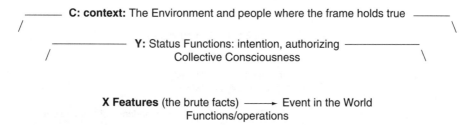

Figure 3.1 Meta-levels

CONTEXTS WITHIN CONTEXTS

Meta-Coaching works within a layered series of frames in the mind. This framework can be represented as levels of contexts within contexts within contexts (see Figure 3.2). The frames at each level contain social constructs *about* the self and others. As a structure of meta-levels, this applies to not only large national groups, but also groups of all sizes.

LEVELS OF DEVELOPMENT AND CHANGE

Meta-Coaching distinguishes three different levels of generative learning and change (Bateson 1972) which lead to three forms of coaching interventions (Hall and Duval 2004):

1   Performance Coaching: incremental change to skills and behaviors;
2   Developmental Coaching: evolutionary change to beliefs, values, rules, identity, etc.; and
3   Transformational Coaching: revolutionary change to direction, purpose, etc.

The context of the coaching engagement will determine the nature of the intervention. In the international business context, Developmental Coaching will often be appropriate since it directly engages with cultural frames with embedded values, rules, beliefs, and identity. However, there are times when Transformational Coaching is required, particularly when organizations have lost their way and have lost relevance or traction. Performance Coaching has relevance when individuals are building capacity following raised awareness of new skills and behaviors that are necessary if they are to utilize their potential in the context.

EVIDENCE FOR META-COACHING

Many change models in the field of coaching originated from therapy (Hall and Duval 2004). This is true of the TTM (the Trans-Theoretical Model), the Cognitive models (Grant and Greene 2003), etc. Meta-Coaching is primarily a constructivist framework enriched by three psychologies: Developmental Psychology, Cognitive-Behavioral Psychology, and Self-Actualizing Psychology.[1] Self-Actualizing Psychology (Maslow 1954/1970; Hall 2000) focuses on the way that psychologically healthy people change, consistent with recent developments in Positive Psychology (Seligman and Csikszentmihayli 2000).

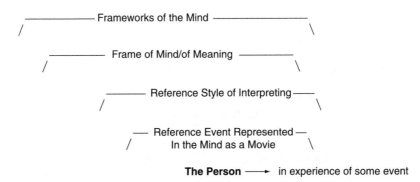

Figure 3.2 Contexts within contexts

As we work with clients, we assume that their sense of self, sense of reality, and sense of others arise from how they have mentally and emotionally mapped things. This allows for another assumption, one that combines Abraham Maslow (1954/1970) and Alfred Korzybski (1933/1994), i.e., people are not broken or sick: they simply operate from the maps that they have created and do the best they can given their maps.

By focusing on generative change, rather than remedial, Meta-Coaching does not center on problems, but on what a person wants that brings out his or her best. This enables us to distinguish coaching from therapy, consulting, mentoring, and training. Believing in a person's potentials, we believe they have the capability of creating all the necessary resources. This means they do not need to be taught, told, or trained so much as they need a facilitation to optimize their innate powers.

In coaching, we initiate an exploration conversation to understand a client's inner world of understandings. When we then come upon a 'problem' in the person's understandings, emotions, skills, lifestyle, response patterns, or social context, our operating premise is singular: 'The person is never the problem; the frame is always the problem.'[2]

All executive coaching clients present to coaching with a matrix of frames developed through their lifetimes, including cultural frames that define and influence their environments and contexts. Their meaning of things – the meaning of life, of self, of organizations, of leadership, of others, etc. – are already constructed in their experiences. Each executive over time absorbs the meanings inherent in language, in rituals, in injunctions and prohibitions, in understandings, in religious beliefs, philosophical beliefs, etc. Executives with multiple sojourns in different locations, and across different companies, will present with a multi-layered and complex matrix that contains inherent tensions, contradictions and paradoxes.

A Meta-Coaching intervention will coach to these frames. Attention will be given in the coaching program to the client's understandings, beliefs, intentions, permissions and prohibitions, decisions, etc. The coaching operates at a higher (or meta) level beyond the person's immediate experience. Whatever the immediate experience is (e.g., delegating, communicating, working through a conflict, adjusting to a new country, creating a product, servicing a client, or planning for a new project), above and beyond that experience are all of the person's interpretative frames about the experience.

The bottom line is that all of us live inside multiple layers of meanings that we have learned and absorbed from the cultures in which we live. We inherited many of these meanings from our family, religion, race, and educational cultures. We inherited frames of meaning about a thousand different things – respect, honor, communication, people, emotions, etc. We live inside these multiple layers of frames as we live within the atmosphere. We breathe these meanings often without awareness that they are frames. Yet they powerfully influence and govern our perceptions, understandings, emotions, responses, style, and personality. In the international context, Meta-Coaching provides an invaluable way of teasing out the confusions, contradictions and complexities that are inherent in any executive experiences.

Meta-Coaching can bring to the consciousness of the executives their hidden frames and provide some awareness of how and why they are responding to their immediate circumstances and experiences. The way is then open for them to revisit the frames with the new awareness, reshape them, and also to develop alternative responses to presenting situations. For example, Meta-Coaching with a talented executive – let's call him Herman – may reveal hidden frames regarding working with virtual teams. Herman's past negative experiences may have embedded (hidden) beliefs around virtual teams that limit his capacity to fulfill his considerable potential in managing virtual situations. Herman's new level of consciousness of his frames may enable him to change his responses by, for example, adopting a new belief that virtual teams are excellent vehicles for rapidly progressing global projects. Awareness of our layers of frames enables us to move to a choice point for selecting better frames. This allows us to run a quality control on our cultural frames so that we have them rather than they have us. Herman now has choice. He can, if he wishes, continue to close down virtual opportunities – or not.

FROM CULTURAL FRAMES TO CULTURAL FRAMES

In this kind of coaching, coaches operate from the matrix of their own frames including the cultural frames. Coaches work from an awareness of how their frames intersect with the frames of the client as they are revealed during the coaching. This enables them to predict and work with resistance and potential situations where a coach's frames get in the way of developing client potential. Where there are marked differences in the backgrounds of coach and executive (e.g., in cultural orientations, religion, racial background, education, communication style), it is even more important that the coach be aware of his or her frames and how they are impacting on the coaching here and now. Coaches cannot afford to wait until conflicts occur before exploring their own frames. Ideally, coach-training will provide self-development opportunities for this kind of preparatory work. This type of preparation can assist them to facilitate their clients' development work in uncovering frames and exploring old and new meanings related to current experiences.

Coaches and clients need to be aware of cues that reveal differences in their embedded, hidden frames and those that might be operating in the coaching or business context. When we encounter another culture the different reality feels 'weird' as we experience a cultural gap. The strangeness of the other's reality, meanings, and responses signals that we are interrelating with assumed frames different from our own. Depending on how different the other's reality orientation, we may have the feeling of strangeness, unfamiliarity, confusion, or even wrongness.

Coaching to a client's frames requires that we first detect the client's frames and then address their meaning frames. This allows us to 'get to the heart of things' in the coaching conversation and identify the leverage frames to increase awareness and choice.

CASE STUDIES

Four case studies follow giving illustration of how Meta-Coaching works in real-life experiences in the international business context.

Case study 1: coaching respect

The case study centers around different meanings, expectations and behaviors associated with respect. Culturally, respect is a high value that everybody wants. But what is respect? How do you know you're respected? Hardly any concept activates our cultural frames more intimately than does the idea of respect. Yet what are the empirical facts underlying respect? There are different realities, depending on the cultural frames in operation. Is respect displayed from:

- looking away and *not* looking the person in the eye when speaking to them?
- *not* crossing your legs so that the bottom of your shoe points at them?

- using a kind and soft voice when communicating instructions?
- being direct?
- being indirect?
- taking polite turns in conversation?
- being so engaged and involved that you're talking over each other?

In the end, respect is a personal evaluation based on cultural beliefs, ideas, associations, memories, and values. From inside these frames, it is easy to know what signifies respect. Those operating with shared frames related to respect will quickly recognize it when they see, hear, and feel it. Disrespect and absence of respect will be obvious. Yet when asked to make respect specific or to explain why certain behaviors are 'respectful' and others are not, that's when individuals begin to become conscious of their own cultural frames that are constantly with them. Meta–Coaching can create opportunities for just those kinds of conversations.

> While coaching senior managers in the First Rand Bank in South Africa, we (L. Michael Hall and Michelle Duval) found that most of the high-level managers who were blacks, and not of British or Dutch origin, did not like the Western way of 'looking people in the eye' when speaking. Rather than a sign of respect, as in our culture, they interpreted constant eye contact as 'disrespectful'. They did not like looking in the eyes of their reports.
>
> Now while most of them had adapted to this to get by in the corporate context, most still had cultural frames that made the experience feel disrespectful. We carried into that context our experiences of coaching which were associated with building and showing respect through direct eye contact. However, the Meta-Coaching framework encouraged us to examine our cultural frames and check to see if alternative approaches might be necessary regarding respect in this context. We discovered that we were more effective with them when we gently glanced at them without holding eye contact. That made them feel accepted on their own terms, respected, and so made it feel that they did not have to come to the 'Western world' to be understood.

Case study 2: coaching self-identity in a corporate culture

Brian,[3] a 47-year-old respected male director of an investment bank in Australia, had been overlooked for the next level of promotion on two occasions. While he possessed the skills, reputation, commercial results and the respect of his team, feedback from more senior management and from a peer review indicated he did not 'self promote'. That is, he did not speak about his personal achievements and accomplishments to senior management or peers. The feedback also indicated that he resisted (i.e., openly criticized) the internal politics within the organization (i.e., actively influencing other people's opinions).

The following transcript is from one coaching conversation that I (Michelle Duvall) had with him which demonstrates the use of meta-questions. These are used to tease out the meaning frames that he assumed were in the organization and that he was managing from.

Michelle: What do you believe about self promoting yourself? [Meta-question about belief.]
Brian: Where I come from, results speak for themselves. You should not have to sing your own praises.
Michelle: And where do you come from?
Brian: Well, we all know I am Irish, and we do not ever put ourselves above others. It is conceited to speak about yourself.
Michelle: You said '*should* not have to sing your own praises.' Is that a rule? [Meta-questioning challenging rules.]

Brian: Well I guess when you ask it that way, yes, it is an unspoken rule.

Michelle: Who sets this rule? Where does this rule come from? (Meta-question challenging authority index.)

Brian: (long pause) I don't know, it is just the way it is. It has always been this way. It is a given. Just ask all my friends from university, many of them now work in other parts of the world too. We pride ourselves on not being like those who will do anything to get ahead. It is part of our culture, our heritage.

Michelle: What do you believe about this rule and your Irish culture? (Meta-question about a belief.)

Brian: If I speak about what I do and attempt to get others to see me in a certain way, I am putting myself above others. It is dishonest. People should be able to see my work and that should be enough. If they cannot see my results – that is their problem.

Michelle: That is their problem? (Meta-question challenging the personal index.)

Brian: Well, okay, it is my problem. But it is just the way I am. It is who I am.

Michelle: It is just the way you are, it is who you are?

Brian: Yes.

Michelle: As you step back from what you have just said, what do you become aware of regarding your 'culture' as you call it, your 'identity', and working in this organization? (Layered meta-question.)

Brian: In the culture of this organization if you do not seek to influence others, your ideas are not given air time or received. And from what that review says, it is the very thing that is preventing others from seeing my potential at the next level.

Michelle: What are you now discovering?

Brian: My personal culture is different to the culture here. The culture here (this organization) demands influencing and self promoting. And if I want to succeed in this culture I will have to change my own culture.

Michelle: If this is true, what do you believe about changing your own culture? (Meta-question about belief.)

Brian: Well it is who I am. I do not know if it is possible.

Michelle: As you again state 'it is who I am,' what do you understand about culture and your self identity – of who you are? (Meta-question about identity.)

Brian: I think of them as the same thing; my culture is how I relate and respect others and my identity is who I am.

Michelle: And are they the same thing? (Meta-question challenging distortion.)

Brian: (pause) Well, maybe not . . . Maybe one is about how I relate to others and what I think of as the 'norms' and the other is who I actually am. Maybe they are actually two different things . . . Okay, what I am now seeing is that if I self promote I would not be true to my culture.

Michelle: (extended pause) What is important to you about being true to your culture? (Meta-question about intentionality and values.)

Brian: I have never thought about that before . . . (long pause). It means that I act from those values . . . (eyes looking away).

Michelle: What did you just become aware of?

Brian: Well, my culture is not only my Irish background or values, but all the different places I have worked in and also my culture or values with my children and my family.

Michelle: And what does that now open up to you?

Brian: There is no one definitive set of values or way of acting . . . yes, that is very interesting . . .

Michelle: Okay, as you hear that distinction, 'There is no one definitive way of acting,' how do you now think and feel about self promoting and influencing other people's perceptions of you and your ideas? (Layered meta-question.)

Brian: I don't know how to do it yet, but as long as I can do it and remain honest it will be okay to add it into my own personal culture and values.

Michelle: Is there any reason that you should not add this into your own personal culture and values? (Meta-question checking ecology.)

Brian: (pause) I can't see any reason not to, as it just becomes a choice and not right or wrong, it just becomes dependent on where I am and who I am working with . . .

Michelle: So is that a decision? Would you like to now develop that skill while maintaining your honesty? (Meta-question about decision.)

Brian: Yes, surprisingly I do!

This case study demonstrates how Meta–Coaching dialogue and questioning around frames can result in clients choosing new behavioral and belief options that will allow them to develop their potential in new environments. As an illustration of the complexity of cross–cultural hidden frames, Australian executives often find the same issue as Brian when dealing with executives from North America. The Australians tend – by comparison – to undersell themselves.

Case study 3: gender expectations

While I (Omar Salom) was engaged in Executive Coaching in a large Mexican corporation, the company engaged Maria Lupita (not her real name), a Colombian-American female executive. At the time she was the human resources director for an American multinational company and an expatriate to Mexico. She had dual American and Colombian citizenship and shared a mixture of frames of both cultures regarding her identity as a female executive. In coaching, she presented this as her 'problem'.

As a Colombian woman, Lupita believed that it was desirable for a successful woman to go for higher positions in an organization. Women have difficulty being promoted to senior positions in Latin American countries, yet she had always felt proud of her achievement of being an executive for over six years. Lupita had been promoted several times into new and challenging positions, in three different countries.

Leadership came easily to Lupita. It was part of her natural frames to seek senior roles with management responsibility. She enjoyed and was well received in giving instructions and guidance to both men and women. Lupita and her husband had two children and employed domestic help. In the USA, Lupita had formed friendships with women with similar profiles, i.e., high-level executives with families who enjoyed overseas assignments. Lupita and her husband both enjoyed the excitement of taking on assignments in new environments.

Lupita expected success to continue in her new position in Mexico. However, she met considerable resistance early in the sojourn. Within elements of the Mexican culture (mainly the upper class), her life as an international senior executive was viewed as unnatural or inappropriate. She was getting negative comments as someone 'who did not have good feelings' as a woman, particularly from some of the wives of her businesses associates. She reported to me that other women considered her 'inferior because she was a working woman'. Mexican women would ask, 'Doesn't your husband earn enough money?' and, 'The poor woman! She needs to work'. This obviously created considerable social pressure for her. She felt isolated and somehow had begun to feel as if she was 'a loser' (her words). This negative pressure was new to Lupita, whose frames around promotion had been built on different experiences. In the past she had received praise and admiration from other women. The clash between her frames and those of many of the women around her made it very hard for her to socialize in this new culture.

There were some other problems. Within her new company she reported that some of the

Mexican men perceived her as 'less than feminine', bossy, and someone that was 'occupying the place of a man'. They did not seem to know how to relate to her as a leader and as a woman.

When I started my coaching conversations with Lupita, she was feeling overwhelmed and confused. She did not know how to handle the pressure that she was experiencing from the way the people from this new culture perceived her. She was feeling insecure and angry with some of the people as she attempted to deal with them as well as with her own attitudes.

In response to meta-questioning techniques, Lupita started to unveil the frames of mind responsible for these feelings. She began to realize that the pressure she was feeling and the associated behaviors and attitudes (e.g., a slight coldness towards the host nationals, social withdrawal) were the consequence of her frames of mind. She realized that there were conflicting cultural frames in the new situation which she had not experienced before. She began to realize that none of the conflict was personal or about her specifically.

Little-by-little she started to understand that people were not the problem. The problem rested entirely in the cultural frames that she brought to the situation. It was the conflicting frames – not the Mexican people – that were at the core of her feelings of discomfort. I explored in depth the nature of her frames. She responded with comments such as, 'There must be something wrong with me as a woman. Maybe I have been wrong my whole life.' This enabled her to realize that she had been confusing her cultural frames with reality.

As a result of her reflections, and the realization of those personal and cultural frames, her level of tension and stress began to ease. Gradually, she began to respond differently to her new situation. Her behavior became less hostile and more appropriate to the context. Consequently, she reported that her peers began to treat her differently. Her approach to the male Mexican executives was to hold her ground as a senior executive and to be respectful yet assertive, and to allow them time to get used to the fact that there was a competent senior woman in their midst. Similarly, with her new understandings, she accepted that her role was very confronting for the Mexican women, whose experiences and frames contrasted starkly with her own. Again, she gave them time to accept her. Lupita took every opportunity to socialize with the wives of her business associates and took every opportunity to share with them stories that demonstrated her commitment to her husband and family. She no longer felt the need to take their attitudes as personally affronting, but simply recognition of different cultural frames.

At times, there were still tense situations with both men and women. Lupita realized that many Mexican women are today redefining the way they see themselves and the traditional frames still predominate in many ways, especially in the middle and upper classes. She took some pride in the fact that her role in a Mexican corporation as a senior female executive from a Latin American background would provide a model to others. Lupita saw that she could model new experiences that may shape new cultural and gender frames in others.

Case study 4: coaching to the hidden frames about making money

Recently while in New Zealand, I (L. Michael Hall) had the privilege of coaching with many Maori people to actualize their entrepreneurial and leadership potentials. Common challenges being presented to me in coaching sessions were mostly centered around money, such as budgeting and working in wealth creation. Meta-questioning revealed that they shared common cultural frames in which focusing on money was viewed as 'a lesser way of life'. To make lots of money meant 'putting oneself above the community', as 'not fully embracing our culture', and as 'choosing a less than spiritual path of life'.

All of the Maori coaching clients seemed to believe that these attitudes towards money were unique to their culture. They were surprised to discover that *not* everyone in the West focuses on money or views money-making as 'the purpose of life'. The frames of these men and woman also contained associations between 'the Western way of capitalism' and the 'Christian way'. Accordingly, they feared becoming a Christian if they became financially successful. Those I worked with were adult men and women in their forties and fifties who had grown up in families of seven to thirteen brothers and sisters, which meant that they had experienced severe need and poverty. So money, plenty, abundance, business, business acumen, etc. had *not* been a part of their original family experience. Presumably, their past experiences of Westerners had almost exclusively been of people focused on money, who had less apparent commitment to family, and were Christians.

Having framed 'money' and 'wealth' as Western and Christian values, they believed these were antagonistic values to their culture and religion. This created their inner conflict about money. I shared the cultural frame of some Christians who view money as 'the root of all evil' and the frame that many in America actually view money as an undesirable 'competitive dog-eat-dog capitalism'. In so doing, I was revealing and challenging their cultural and religious frames.

For most, this was generally a surprising, even shocking, realization. For some individuals it helped to loosen the all-or-nothing nature of their frames that was preventing them from stepping up to be the businessmen and women that they wanted to be. Progress towards an improved financial situation generally followed through the subsequent coaching process. With others, the cultural frames were seemingly more entrenched and less open to modification or challenge. They continued as before and did not release their potentials for financial independence.

Exploring further into how the Maori frame-of-mind worked about money, I discovered that those with the most fully developed beliefs lived their lives in a spiritual world. For them, the world of material things and the world of spirit co-existed. They viewed life as moving through this dual reality, seeing the spirits of their fathers and grandfathers and the spiritual world as solidly as the physical world.

Not knowing precisely what this meant in terms of their relationship to money, and for the activities of budgeting, billing, asking for money, negotiating, etc., I inquired from a respectful 'know-nothing' frame of mind. What I discovered was that they had to link any financial success in the creation of wealth as a direct and immediate benefit to their community. They had to believe that it would increase the overall resourcefulness of their people, would leave a richer legacy for their children, and so on. Success in making money had to do with their whole community, only then would they permit themselves the right to become financially independent. With this spiritual frame they could then view the making of money positively. Asking for money, talking about it, planning, budgeting, etc., could now be viewed as a contribution, an enrichment of others, a gift to children and grandchildren for ages to come.

META-COACHING TOOLS

We have derived several tools in Meta-Coaching that have strong application in international business contexts. These include Meta-Questions, Matrix Questions, the Step-back Skill for Quality Controlling one's reasoning and meaning, and Benchmarking intangibles.

Meta-questions

We coach to the constructed human reality of frames-within-frames, and therefore we coach to what is invisible to the eye and ear. To 'see' and 'hear' such *invisible frames* requires specific tools and a framework for detecting and discerning levels. In Meta-Coaching we tease out the meaning frames by asking meta-questions that expose the frameworks of the person's mental and organizational matrix.[4]

While there are more than 70 different Meta-Questions, the following are some general examples that can be adapted within various coaching conversations and contexts:

- What do you *believe* about X?
- What does this *mean* to you?
- What do you understand about X?
- What *decision* have you made or will you make about it?
- How does X impact your *identity* or sense of self?
- What's your highest *intention* with X?
- What could be your highest *outcome and expectation*?
- What is X like? What *metaphor* activates X for you?
- What *inspiration* does this create for you?
- As you think about all of this, what do you now *realize*?
- What else *opens up* for you with this?
- What does this X now *mean* to you?
- What else can you *ascribe* to it?

The following are examples of Meta-Questions in-action in coaching international business:

- What does this division *value*? Why is that *important* to you?
- What do you *believe* are the new unspoken rules since the merger occurred?
- What are the *consequences* of speaking that way in this country?
- What do you *understand* about this culture and the changes that you are experiencing?
- What is this *like* for you? What is this *like* for your team?
- What do you *believe* is the highest *intention* of the parent company's *decision*?
- What *assumptions* have you made that prevent you from being authentic in this culture?
- How does off-shore *decision* making cause you to feel powerless?
- How would you *think about 'time'* to make full use of all the time zones you are working within?
- What have you not *accepted* about living and doing business in this way?
- What are your unspoken *concerns or fears* for you and your family in this move?
- How do these *impact* your day-to-day in business?
- If you were to embrace and fully *accept* the guilt you feel about your *decision* on your team and your family, what *opens up* for you?
- What *customs, beliefs, routines and habits* no longer serve you doing business here?
- What are the leadership *opportunities* for you among this continuous feeling of chaos?
- What are you *learning* about business, culture and your own leadership in this environment?
- What adaptability and flexibility are you now *discovering*?
- That is one meaning it could have; what else could you ascribe to that?

Matrix questions

Meaning matrix

- What does it mean? What is its significance?
- What do you believe about X (whatever the subject)?

- What do you believe about that belief?
- What inspires you and makes you feel most alive?

In the international business context:

- What do you believe about culture in this division? Company? Country?
- What do these customs or rituals mean about how you do business?
- What do you understand is being asked of you? What do you believe about this?

Intention matrix

- What do you want? What's important to you?
- What's your ideal outcome? Why go for that?
- When you get that, what does that do for you?

In the international business context:

- What is most important in this situation?
- What is most important to you as you make this decision?
- What do you think is most important for each stakeholder as you negotiate?

State matrix

- What state are you in? How are you feeling?
- How intense is the state? What triggers the state?
- How do you access the state? What do you call the state?
- What new states do you want to develop and experience?

In the international business context:

- What are the feelings associated with this change for you? Your team? The company?
- How do people express (or not) their feelings in this culture? What are the cues?
- What states would you need to be in to negotiate in this situation?

Self and identity matrix

- Who are you? Who else? What are you like?
- How do you define yourself? Who do you want to become?
- Is your value and worth as a person unconditional?
- If not, what do you condition it upon?

In the international business context:

- How do you define yourself in this company? In this role? In this culture?
- What self definitions have you brought into this role that no longer serve you?
- How are you valuing yourself with the difficulties that you are facing?

Power matrix

- What other powers and capacities do you have?
- Your *modus operandi*. What can you do? What else?
- What do you dream about doing?

In the international business context:

- What is your current skill level? What resources do you need?
- What resources do you have from other situations that can support you during this transition?
- What are the skills and capabilities that you will draw on during this phase?
- What additional abilities or expertise do you to bring in to support you and your team?

Others matrix

- How do you think about other people?
- What are they like? Are they friendly or unfriendly?
- What do you believe about human nature, good or bad?
- What social skills do you have? Which do you not have?

In the international business context:

- How do you think about the people in this company? Country?
- How do these beliefs serve your connection and relating with them?
- How could you think about your team and management that would create more trust?

Time matrix

- What do you think about 'time?' Is it a friend or enemy?
- How much of your mental-emotional time do you live in the past, present or the future?
- How do you experience time? As the eternal now? Sequentially?
- Are you able to get lost in time when you so choose?

In the international business context:

- How is time experienced in this culture? What are their and your expectations about time?
- Is this culture present, past, or future orientated? How does this serve you and the team?
- How do you need to adjust your expectations of 'time' for each of the time zones and cultures you work within?

World matrix

- What worlds of meaning exist for you?
- What universes would you like to visit or excel in?

- How well are you adapted to external reality?

In the international business context:

- What assumptions have you made about doing business internationally?
- What rules do you have from the cultures you come from that impact business here?
- What do you associate with this merger?

SUMMARY

In Meta-Coaching it is all about frames and framing. It is about finding and respectfully calling attention to the frames that a person operates from and recognizing our own operating frames as well. This enables us to facilitate the kind of development or change that enables people to create new frames to enhance their lives and empower them as persons. One of the particular challenges for people working in international business contexts is that it is virtually inevitable that the frames of others will contrast with their own – at many levels. Meta-Coaching can explore the depth and breadth of executives' hidden frames, where they might differ from or connect to the frames of others, and how to generate creative synergies that will facilitate the use of potential.

Meta-Coaching starts from the premise that the person is never the problem, thus removing a potential barrier to change that many change processes never cross. The problem can only be some frame of meaning or reference. One of the most powerful tools is to use meta-questions to get to the higher-level structures and facilitate a conversation that gets to the heart of things. In international business 'things' perpetuated in organizational and individual frames are highly complex. There are multiple frames at multiple levels carrying attitudes, beliefs and behaviors related to race, religion, leadership, money, gender, communication, love, play, and so on. The kind of dialogue encouraged by Meta-Coaching gets down into the complexity and creates leverage for transformational change at individual and organizational levels.

Notes

1 The Meta-Coaching system is a systematic approach based on the distinction between map and territory (Alfred Korzybski, General Semantics), Neuro-Linguistic Programming (NLP), Rational-Emotive Therapy (RET), and the pioneering work of Abraham Maslow. For more see the Meta-Coach series of books, the first volumes being: *Coaching Change* (Hall and Duval 2004) and *Coaching Conversations* (Hall and Duval 2003).
2 For more about this premise, see *Winning the Inner Game* (Hall 2006). This has led to a series of books on the inner and outer games, *Games Business Experts Play* (Hall 2002b), *Games Great Lovers Play* (Hall 2004), and *Games for Mastering Fear* (Hall 2001b).
3 This and names in subsequent case studies are fictitious to protect anonymity.
4 Meta-questions are questions about the higher levels of our experience, our meta-states of beliefs, values, identity, etc. For a list of 26 meta-questions, see 'Coaching Change' in (Hall and Duval 2005).

Bibliography

Bateson, G. (1972) *Steps to an Ecology of Mind*, New York: Ballantine.

Grant, A. and Greene, J. (2003) *Solution-Focused Coaching: Managing People in a Complex World*, Harlow, UK: Pearson Education Limited.

Hall, L. M. (1999) *Secrets of Personal Mastery: Advanced Techniques for Accessing Your Higher Levels of Consciousness*, Camarthen, Wales: Crown House Publications.

Hall, L. M. (2000) *Meta-States: Managing the Higher Levels of the Mind*, Clifton, CO: Neuro-Semantic Publications.

Hall, L. M. (2001a) *Training Manual for Cultural Modeling*, Clifton: Neuro-Semantic Publications.

Hall, L.M. (2001b) *Games for Mastering Fear: How to Play the Game of Life with a Calm Confidence*, Clifton: Neuro-Semantic Publications.

Hall, L. M. (2002a) *The Matrix Model*, Clifton: Neuro-Semantic Publications.

Hall, L.M. (2002b) *Games Business Experts Play*, Bancyfelin: Crown House Publishing.

Hall, L.M. (2006) *Winning the Inner Game: Mastering the Inner Game for Peak Performance*, Clifton: Neuro-Semantic Publications.

Hall, L. M. and Duval, M. (2003) *Coaching Conversations: Robust Conversations that Coach for Excellence*, Clifton: Neuro-Semantic Publications.

Hall, L. M. and Duval, M. (2004) *Coaching Change for Higher Levels of Success and Transformation*, Clifton: Neuro-Semantic Publications.

Hall, L. M. and Duval, M. (2005), *Meta-Coaching, Volume I: For Higher Levels of Success and Transformation*, Clifton: Neuro-Semantic Publications.

Korzybski, A. (1933/1994) *Science and Sanity: An Introduction to Non-Aristotelian Systems and General Semantics* (5th edn), Lakeville, CT: International Non-Aristotelian Library Publishing Co.

Maslow, A. (1954/1970) *Motivation and Personality*, New York: Harper and Row.

Searle, J. R. (1995) *The Construction of Social Reality*, New York: Simon and Schuster.

Seligman, M. E. P. and Csikszentmihayli, M. (2000) 'Positive psychology: An introduction', *American Psychologist*, 55 (1): 5–14.

IDENTITY, LIMINALITY AND DEVELOPMENT

An intrapersonal view of intercultural sensitivity

David B. Drake

INTRODUCTION

In this chapter, I draw on Milton Bennett's (1986, 1993) work on intercultural sensitivity as a frame for my contention that the key dynamics that play out between cultures in the external world also play out between cultures as they've been internalized as narrative within individuals. I will use elements from my research on rites of passage to outline some of the liminal tensions clients experience as they develop responses to these cultural demands. I will outline the way in which the six stages in Bennett's model can be applied more explicitly at an intrapersonal level and offer a case to demonstrate a narrative approach to this work in coaching. I do so with humility as I would not claim to have mastered all six stages within my own development. Perhaps the gift of writing this chapter is the opportunity to assess where I am on this journey and to share some of what I am learning along the way.

Rebecca[1] was the executive director for a human services program funded by the US federal government. One of the key roles she played in this position was to help the organization continuously adapt to the ever-shifting political and financial landscape. She had developed an agile and savvy leadership style in order to sustain a high level of morale and service in the face of constant change. In doing so, she often mediated between the demands of the employees, the clients and the government while balancing limited budgets, complex guidelines and increasing demands. Rebecca sought coaching when she began to feel, as she put it, 'stretched way too thin' as a result of the significant changes thrust on her program by the new Administration. Of particular concern for her was how to retain a sufficient level of authority and autonomy given these new demands.

In coaching her, it would have been easy to stay at the surface level in dealing with her frustrations around the ideological clashes with her new federal bosses. In addition to being less than productive it would have meant skipping over deeper issues at play for her. Knowing that she had devoted her career to being a public servant on behalf of children and families, I invited her to 'tell me more about what loyalty means for you right now'. Was it loyalty to the internalized stories of her grandparents about how others had helped them – and how she should continue to repay that 'debt'? Was it to the stories of her ethnic culture about doing whatever it took to get things done in the face of power? Was it to the stories of the women on her staff about being polite and not 'rocking the boat'? As a leader, she had developed each of these aspects of herself in order to fit and thrive in each of these cultures. Now it was time to recognize the conflicts she experienced as a result of her divided loyalties in order to create a more authentic and effective response to feeling stretched too thin.

In working with Rebecca, it was clear that the dilemmas she faced as a leader could be understood, in part, as clashes between the narratives of the cultures with which she identified and in which she worked each day. In looking at her situation this way, she recognized the disconnections between the liberating culture in which she had been raised in the 1960s and the stifling culture in which she was now asked to work. It was through coaching her that I began to think more earnestly of coaching across cultures as an *intra*personal phenomenon in addition to an *inter*personal and collective one. While good work has been done on coaching *across* cultures, insufficient attention has been paid to how clients navigate cultures *within* themselves. In part this requires coaches to adopt a more critical pedagogy and nuanced understanding of culture so as to move away from the binary systems of thought (McLaren 1993) at the core of Western epistemology toward one more fitting for the demands of the twenty-first century.

As part of this shift, authors who live in border worlds between cultures (Anzaldua 1987) have helped us think about a dynamic, fluid and identity-based view of cultures as they play out in us in any given situation. As Kenneth Gergen observed, 'Our "self" becomes situationally-defined to a greater degree than ever before. . . . All the selves lie dormant, and under the right conditions may spring to life' (Gergen 1991: 71). Therefore, coaches can ask 'how are clients handling the "selves" that make up their ongoing sense of identity, and the loyalties and roles inherent in each one'? In this sense, it seems important for clients to become aware of their positional patterns relative to these cultural narratives and how these *identity performances* (Mishler 1999) play out for them at work.

Culture is defined here as 'a set of basic tacit assumptions about how the world is and ought to be . . . that determines [a person's] perceptions, thoughts, feelings, and, to some degree, their overt behavior' (Schein 1996: 12). In looking at how clients internalize cultural narratives, I pay particular attention to how they *position* themselves in the cultural stories that are central to their identity and life (Davies and Harré 1990). This is key because clients tend to see the world from the vantage point of the positions they have taken and in terms of the 'particular images, metaphors, story lines and concepts which are made relevant within the particular discursive practice in which they are positioned' (Davies and Harré 1990: 46). Clients' stories shed light on the vantage points they've chosen; coaching can open up new possibilities for framing these formative narratives, their ongoing identity, and their responses in current situations. However, this can be challenging for clients if they have internalized positions that conflict with one another. Coaching can help clients increase their positional repertoire so they are more able to move flexibly from one position to another (Hermans 2004; Polkinghorne 2004) in order to achieve their goals.

The notion of 'narrative identity' is central to this pursuit. While there is a drive for continuity, to keep a particular narrative going (Giddens 1991), our identity is also kaleidoscopic in nature as varying cultural 'colors' move in and out of focus as we live out our life story. For example, in my own life I've watched as elements from a previous career have moved in and out of salience in my life and sense of self. I have come to integrate some of these elements, now distinct from the original role, in my identity and my coaching/consulting practice. In this time of accelerated change, it is difficult to sustain a sense of continuity or an ability to embody (let alone evolve) all of the ways in which we are asked to position our 'selves'. Coaches can create holding environments in which they can attend to clients' stories, their narrative construction of identity, and any ways in which they experience internal cultural discordance. This is particularly useful when the roots of this discordance are in stories that have been carried forward from other generations or on behalf of others.

> For example, Maria, a third-generation Mexican woman running a program for first-generation Mexican laborers became increasingly aware of her internal struggles around gender and power differences, levels of acculturation between the generations, and her competing desires to be successful in the eyes of her Caucasian supervisors so she would be promoted and successful in the eyes of her 'brothers' so she would be loyal to the cultural norms around 'la familia'. I helped her create a Venn diagram with four circles representing her key cultures (ethnicity, gender, immigrant status, and management) and then asked her: 'Tell me about what it is like for you in the middle.' We worked with stories from her past in getting to this job, her present in terms of daily decisions she faced, and her future in terms of her aspirations for herself and others. From this coaching conversation she was able to develop ways to artfully educate her supervisors on the nuances of her culture and establish a hybrid style that was effective within the system yet respectful of the ways of her culture.

NARRATIVE IDENTITY

> 'My wife and I met in English.' With these words, Peter, an American client who had become reasonably fluent in Japanese, came to understand why he had difficulty relating with his Japanese wife in her native tongue. The language in which they had built the relationship and formed the stories of their early years was shaped by the parameters of the English language and the American culture. He found the relationship challenging because they could not bridge some significant cultural differences in making several important life decisions. In a sense, they had met in one language and culture but needed now to make decisions in another. This realization was prompted through my invitation for him to consider the space between both sets of stories as represented by my two outstretched hands. He recognized that his role in the marriage made sense within an American narrative and the stories of how they met in English, but seemed much less so when told within a Japanese narrative and discourse – as when they went to visit her parents in Japan.

Stories bring together and shed light on the connections between the boundaries of discourse and the nature of identity.

A key assumption in this approach is the postmodern belief in the dynamic, relational and multifaceted nature of identity. This approach can be seen in Stevens-Long's (2000) notion of the *prism self* and Bakhtin's (1984) view of the self as a *carnival* in describing efforts to retain a coherent narrative identity and yet be continuously adaptive 'at the threshold between interior and exterior, between self and other' (Rutherford 1990: 24). As such, identity can be seen as a dynamic and relational process of continual negotiation as people interact with their environment through conversations and relationships. Identity is a *situated* (Ochs and Capps 1996) and *psychosocial* process (McAdams, Diamond, de St Aubin and Mansfield 1997) in which people navigate between presenting identities that are acceptable and functional in their social contexts (as experienced and internalized) and embodying identities that are authentic and meaningful in their personal context.

I find William James' (1927) distinction between 'I' and 'Me' helpful for clients in surfacing their navigational patterns as evidenced in their stories. For example, I might ask a client: 'What

63

did you want to do at that moment?' then follow with: 'What held you back?' and: 'What might this say about whom others expect you to be?' Their identity, for better or worse, is situated in the space between these answers. In this way, it may be more fitting to think of identity as a verb than as a noun and for coaches to engage in the narrative processes by which clients identify themselves.

We narrate our identity in large part based on unspoken, implicit cultural models of what selfhood should be, could be, and should not be (Bruner 2002). As a result, certain stories are readily available to us in defining and maintaining our identity, while others are not. We often do not recognize the contours and limitations of our available narratives until we try to cross their normative boundaries or seek to narrate our experiences or selves outside of them. The stories that clients share in coaching provide powerful material through which they can better understand their available plot lines (Polkinghorne 1998) and narrative habits – and renegotiate them as so desired. Rather than just taking a client's story at face value or, worse yet, imposing their own values on a story, coaches can help the client contextualize the story within the internalized cultural norms and narratives that shaped its form and by which it is measured. It is here we see the value of stewardship in working with the narrative material of clients at these critical junctures where the building blocks of their identities are in play.

We narrate our experiences so as to *accommodate*, to confirm and sustain our identity (the stories we tell about ourselves, others, and the world), or to *assimilate* anomalous events into our identity (and our stories) and restore equilibrium (Block 1982). Our narrative identity evolves over time and is defined in large part by our choices in terms of accommodation and assimilation relative to the cultural narratives in which we are embedded. Many of the tasks in coaching have to do with helping clients surface the choices they have made along these lines, candidly assess the consequences of these choices, and shift these patterns in order to be more effective in achieving their desired way of being and/or results.

However, one of the challenges in working with people and their stories is that the dominant narratives in their life tend to blind them to the possibilities that other narratives exist (Drake 2007). Therefore, coaches can help clients understand the tacit cultural forces that shape their views of the world and themselves, their language and behavioral choices, and more. As people recognize limitations inherent in the available narratives in which they are embedded, they can create a sense of distance from these narratives, see them more clearly, and surface the submerged voices of their selves (Polkinghorne 2001). A major step in this process is to help clients identify additional narrative data from their lives that support an alternative view of who they are and how they will be in the world.

Taking this step often creates tension for clients in areas where they closely identify with more than one culture in defining who they are and how they are to act.

> For example, a client who has been taught within his ethnic culture to always look after his mother as her oldest son experiences difficulty when he is promoted to a leadership role and is expected to have tough performance conversations with women who work for him. He is torn between pleasing his new boss to honor the cultural norms around status as a man and deferring to the needs of others to honor the cultural norms around service as a son. The initial task for him was to surface the internalized narratives (and their implicit norms) and to sit with the tension of the two competing expectations. I worked with him to reframe them from polarized opposites created by others to parallel qualities within himself. He was able to take who he was at his best in each position and use it to inform the other such that, for example, he was able to give feedback with respect. I knew that any new behavior had to be grounded in a more integrated narrative about himself. As we shall see, it is from within this tension that the richest development can occur in terms of integrating cultural and narrative complexity.

AN INTRAPERSONAL VIEW OF CULTURE AND DEVELOPMENT: THE DEVELOPMENTAL MODEL OF INTERCULTURAL SENSITIVITY

This model by Milton Bennett (Bennett 1986, 1993; Bennett and Hammer 1998) is based on the premise that as people are able to make more complex and sophisticated distinctions relative to their experience of cultural difference they become more competent in relating with others across cultures. The cognitive patterns characteristic of each stage are correlated with patterns in the person's level of awareness, attitudes and behaviors; changes in the former lead to shifts in the latter. I will make the case that changes in cognitive orientation, seen here as both ways of thinking and levels of mindfulness, also help people clarify and evolve their own identity. The goal is not just an increased ability to handle greater cultural complexity in relating to others but also an increased ability to handle greater cultural complexity within oneself. In doing so, clients become more resilient, agile and effective across a wider range of experiences and with a larger repertoire of potential responses.

The first three stages are classified as *ethnocentric* because they revolve around the experience of one's own culture as central to reality. The second three stages are classified as *ethnorelative* because they revolve around the experience of one's culture in the context of others (Bennett and Hammer 1998). I have chosen in this chapter to focus on the intrapersonal aspects of this development process. The six stages can be characterized as follows:

1 Denial: Unable to recognize cultural differences; assumes that one's own culture (inherited or adopted) is the only real one; separates from cultural differences through isolation, indifference and/or aggression;
2 Defense: Can recognize cultural differences but evaluates one's own culture as the only good one; organizes the world into us/them, we/they, good/bad; feels threatened by cultural difference and responds with judgment and projection.
3 Minimization: Recognizes cultural differences but assumes that the familiar elements of one's own culture are universal because 'people are people'; cultural differences are either minimized or romanticized;
4 Acceptance: Enjoys cultural differences and recognizes that one's own culture is just one of many equally valid ways of being in and viewing the world; other cultures may still be judged negatively, but there is an underlying sense of respect and curiosity;
5 Adaptation: Expands worldview to incorporate other constructs and see the world through another's eyes; experiences another culture in ways that result in perceptions, communication and behaviors appropriate for and effective in that culture; and
6 Integration: Expands one's experience of 'self' to include movement in and out of different cultural worldviews; may be best suited for people dealing with their own cultural marginality rather than being seen as the highest level of intercultural competence (Bennett and Hammer 1998).

I propose that these six stages inform not only the development of clients' intercultural sensitivity but also their *intra*cultural sensitivity – the ability to integrate diverse cultural narratives within themselves and to channel the results to achieve their goals. This is critical in this time when many of our clients live what Kenneth Gergen (1991: 109) called the 'pastiche life' with its proliferation of roles and identities. I use the rites of passage model to articulate and explore how my clients and workshop participants move through these stages as part of their development and maturation. In particular, I work with them in the liminal dimensions in between the cultural narratives they have internalized as central to their identity, as seen in this example.

65

For example, I am working with a client who is making the transition from a long career in the engineering culture into the executive culture. Since his new role will place him in charge of the engineering function, we are talking about how he wants to position himself relative to his former peers and to his need to remain fluent enough in his old world while taking on a new one. One way I supported this shift for him was to enlarge the scale of my questions each week. What began as, 'What do you need most right now?' became, 'What does your group need most from you?' became, 'What does the CEO need most from you?' to, finally, 'What does the business need most from you?

IN BETWEEN CULTURES: A RITES OF PASSAGE PERSPECTIVE ON DEVELOPMENT

One of the ways to view the progress through these six stages is analogous to many Eastern philosophies in which the beginner sees no duality, the student sees only the duality, and the master comes to recognize, albeit at a higher level, that there really is no duality. By developing a greater ability to resolve and integrate intercultural tensions within themselves, clients free up energy previously spent either avoiding full awareness (being unconscious of the duality) or rigidly clinging to one side of the dynamic (being attached to part of the duality). As a result, they are more able to see the whole picture and integrate the cultural elements once seen as separate from one another. Their stories often signal where they are relative to the six stages and their development, and they frequently provide a rich source of material for coaches.

Some would contend that this middle way involves the idea of a 'third' (Evanoff 2000; Lefebvre 1980; Schwartz-Salant 1998). Paul Tillich (1965) contended that the development of a multicultural personality involved the creation of a 'third area' beyond the bounded territories, an area where one can stand for a time without being enclosed in something tightly bounded. Coaching seems like a natural opportunity to 'unbind' our clients and their stories so they can breathe again and create new options for themselves. To do so requires what Freud (1912: 111) called 'evenly suspended attention' so that the tension is allowed to rise without judgment or bias. As Jung repeatedly suggested, the tension of opposites must be held until its meaning, the unknown third, appears as part of an individual's development process (Hollis 2004). There is a clear sense that development first requires the naming of the opposites so they can then be separated and dissolved in order to create the 'third' out of this union. It is difficult to travel this road with clients if coaches have not done the work themselves. Fortunately for coaches there are centuries of experience in a number of cultures on how to support individuals – and themselves – to move through this 'rite of passage'.

Van Gennep (1960) distinguished three major phases in a rite of passage: separation (séparation), transition (marge), and incorporation (agrégation). As Turner noted, 'the first phase detaches the ritual subjects from their old places in society; the last installs them, inwardly transformed and outwardly changed, in a new place in society' (Turner 1979: 149). Eliade defined the threshold that separates these two places as 'the limit, the boundary, the frontier that distinguishes and opposes two worlds – and at the same time the paradoxical place where these worlds communicate' (Eliade 1959: 24). The move from one place to the next involves external changes (e.g., states, roles, statuses) and internal transitions (e.g., identities, beliefs, attitudes) at both personal and social levels. This inner/outer, personal/social dynamic also plays out in the formation, narration, and interpretation of people's stories as part of the ongoing emplotment and enactment of their identity. The rights of passage model is a core element of narrative coaching work (see Drake 2003, 2004, 2005) as a way to help clients to more openly recognize how they have tended to position themselves, internally and externally, relative to key cultural narratives. The process helps clients take up new positions relative to these narratives such that they experience a greater sense of coherence, peace, and efficacy. For example, I worked with a client who, through her stories, traced her migration from a 'youngest' to 'in the middle' to becoming an 'oldest'.

While it is important for coaches to manage the processes of separation and incorporation to help clients become change-ready and complete their transitions, respectively, most break-throughs emerge in the liminal phase. It is here that the attachments to the ordinary and familiar plane have been released (or severed) but the new plane and form have not yet been reached. As a result, there is a lot of energy in play that can be channeled in new directions once the way becomes clear. One of the first steps in narrative coaching is to help clients reach this level of clarity where they can finally see both the road they've taken and the one not taken (or at least not owned) as well as the fact that these paths, once polarized as opposites, could come together in some new third way. An important step in this process is for clients to become more fully aware of the cultural narratives that have shaped them so they are more able to reframe and renegotiate the role, meaning and impact of their narratives.

Moving into, through and out of in-between space between the old story and the new one exposes the basic building blocks of a culture and its norms, values and axioms in ways that are not available through a client's everyday experience (Turner 1969). By surfacing these cultural norms, liminality creates a frame within which clients can experiment with the familiar categories of culture – isolating their elements and recombining them in a variety of patterns and unprecedented combinations (Turner 1967, 1974, 1982). Transformation often occurs in the liminal realm as the internal structures of clients' identities are dissolved and surrendered, and new ones are constellated (Alexander 1991; Stein and Stein 1987). It is a place where expectations are challenged, unspeakable subjects discussed, and new roles tested. In the process, clients are not only attaining a new status, role, or identity in relation to their social systems, but there is also a change of being itself, an ontological passage (Carson 1997). Coaches can help clients integrate energies they have split off into unhealthy dualities that represent conflicting cultural norms and narratives. In doing so, coaches touch on what Jung (1964: 35) described as the 'transcendent function' in which a hybrid inclusive of, yet beyond, the original dualism is discovered and enacted.

> I saw this in coaching a project management team whose members seemed entrenched in what I came to see as a parent–child dynamic with the leadership team to which they reported. I was initially caught up in the same dynamic as I shuttled back and forth coaching the two teams in a multi-million dollar project. I colluded with the system to a degree, operating as a 'wise uncle' or 'eldest son' who would intercede on their behalf. Once I moved out of my own denial, defenses and minimization, I intervened with the management team, mirrored the dynamic that I had observed and my role in it, helped them to reconfigure their function and identity as a team, and change how they communicated with the leaders. We worked through the binds and sense of powerlessness they felt to help them define and enact a role as 'adults'. They were able to have a significant impact on both the leadership team and the project as a result of following Gandhi's famous maxim to 'be the changes they wanted to see'.

As the coach, I took a large step forward in being able to handle cultural complexity within myself as I sorted through the cultural narratives that had shaped my original role with them and how the internalized framing of my role changed through this work with them. In general, coaches can use this transcendent dynamic to help clients move out of polarized fixations (and the resulting behavioral ruts) and create openings to renegotiate identity, power, and choice in their lives (Drake 2005). We see here the value of bringing into the foreground the often submerged and conflicted cultural narratives that have shaped the client's identity in order to create a new relationship among them and story about them. As English observed, 'Third space is where we negotiate identity and become neither this nor that but our own' (English 2002: 109).

So, what would Bennett's model of intercultural sensitivity reveal if we focused more explicitly on the intrapersonal dimensions – the ways in which a person's identity and stories evolve as her relationships with the larger cultural narratives mature? I have mapped the six stages of his model onto a traditional rites of passage framework in which the 'self' as it is currently constructed and presented (*persona*) is contrasted with the construct of the 'other' as it is projected onto others or introjected from others (*shadow*). At the earliest level of development (Denial), the client is far away from any recognition of the 'other' either outside or inside themselves. It is in these early stages that the 'other' becomes the reified 'Other' and identity is dependent on maintaining this separation. The arrows trace the path through the six stages as the person passes through an in-between space and into the ethnorelative stages. Working in the 'third space', clients can see beyond the dualities and the accompanying narrative patterns, as they have internalized them, to reconcile and integrate them in a more generative fashion.

The following case illustrates the journey of one client as he moved through each of these stages within himself around some key issues in his life. While there was clearly more work to be done, he left coaching a changed man; he had reconciled some conflicted stories within himself about who he and others thought he should be. I make no claim for his movement in terms of his intercultural sensitivity in relation to others – though I observed changes there – but I can attest to changes in terms of his sensitivity within himself and the results of doing so.

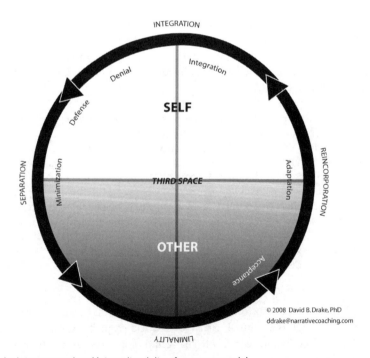

Figure 4.1 An intrapersonal and intercultural rite of passage model

In doing this, I will undoubtedly streamline the nuances of his character. It does not do him full justice, but it enables me to articulate some important points using the intrapersonal and intercultural models.

Denial

In the first session, Don, a department manager for a mid-sized city, talked about the union, his team, the HR director, the mayor and the city council as the sources of the problems he was experiencing. Even as he expressed his interest in being coached, he seemed more interested in complaining about everyone else. He seemed inclined to stay in denial through isolation in overwork and some aggression when people didn't live up to his high standards. He was unable to see at first that (a) much was wrong at all and (b) that there were any other views of the world than his own. What contributed to an opening beyond lots of deep listening was to ask him to talk about some of the other characters in his stories. It was here that he mentioned his family for the first time and created an initial foundation for what was to become a pivotal part of our work together. It was also the one topic about which he was willing to show even the slightest hint of a feeling.

Defense

Over the next couple of weeks we coupled more coaching with opportunities to walk around and talk with people – on my own and with him. Some of the challenges he faced with his family began to surface as I followed my hunch that this was an important vehicle for change. As the perspectives of others began to creep their way into his stories and his awareness in our work together, the denial began to be unsustainable. However, he still saw the world very much as a 'lone ranger' positioned paradoxically in service to others and against the others. As he slowly allowed himself to become aware of his tendencies to work at the exclusion of everything else and admit the consequences of this pattern for his team, his employees and himself, he became more open to the possibility that there were other ways of working. A big part of this shift for clients, as it was for Don, is the recognition of the consequences of one's choices. Defenses kick in to buffer us from full consciousness of this recognition; coaching helped Don slowly release the need to defend himself.

Minimization

At first he didn't think all this fuss was that big a deal. He passed the problems off as the same as others in his position were facing in the city. Three actions on my part seemed to help him shake out of his trance and become aware of his 'competing commitments' (Kegan and Lahey 2001) and move through his 'refusal strategies' (Bennett and Hammer 1998). One was attention to his health. I chose to focus on homework assignments around eating as a way for him to become much more conscious of his actions during the day and to eat in ways that were much healthier. These simple tasks became significant eye-openers for him as he realized how out of touch he truly was with himself and others. Two, I began to gather formal and informal 360-degree feedback for Don. When I presented the findings with him he began to realize that others (a) cared about him and (b) thought that his issues were more significant than he had allowed himself to see. Third, it became apparent that more direct and heartfelt action might be necessary. At one point in the conversation when the timing felt right, I leaned across his desk, looked him straight in the eye, and said, 'If you don't change your work habits SOON, you will end up dying long before your time . . . and that feels like a great loss to me'. At this point the threshold was breached and we began a very different caliber of conversation.

Acceptance

He acknowledged the way that others saw him in his current state and began to make some adjustments in his work habits such as remembering to eat three meals and taking a walk over his lunch break. Like most everything else he did, he did it without fanfare. We began to examine his stories about his role as a leader, a boss, a husband, a father, a son, and a person. In doing so, we didn't throw out any of them for the sake of the others; instead, I worked with him on his internal conflicts so he could establish a different sensitivity and relationship among them. For example, he was obsessive about work in order to avoid, in both consciousness and behavior, dealing with his difficult family situations. As he grew in his respect for himself, he began to admit the costs of trying to appease too many people in his immediate and extended family and he made some hard choices in confronting them as a prelude to renegotiating those relationships. The weight that lifted from him in doing so was palpable. He no longer had to force the 'other' in them or in himself to remain cut off from how he operated each day. As a result, he started to do more 'management by walking around' instead of commanding from his office. His expectations were still high but they were at least *his* now – and not a result of the expectations others had placed on him about how he was supposed to be for them.

Adaptation

By learning to deal with these issues more effectively, he freed himself to adopt a healthier middle way that included a balanced approach to work. The complaints about others had diminished significantly as he continued to focus on his own health, well-being and leadership. While he retained some rough edges, morale went up while his weight and stress went down. He began to shift his perceptions, communication and behaviors to match what his department actually needed from him in a time of rising requirements and shrinking budgets. He had sorted out all but the hardest choice *vis-à-vis* his family but he had come to a greater sense of peace about the latter for now. At work, there were a variety of responses to the shifts he was making. Some people seemed to have difficulty adjusting and they continued trying to act the old stories back into existence. A lot of my work at this stage was to help Don solidify and stabilize his gains in order to sustain the change. As part of that process, I did some work with his leadership team and a couple of key contributors to help Don be successful. My contract ran out at this time but it seemed like Don was ready to take it from there.

Integration

I learned some months later from the human resources director that Don had repeatedly talked about the coaching work as a turning point in his life. He had decided to take early retirement – now that he had his health and life back – and move to another city to be closer to his young adult children. The director said I would have been proud of the big smile he had on his face as he walked out of the door after nearly thirty years in the same department. I've lost track of him since then but trust that he has found the integration he had been looking for in our work. It had been a lot of work, but he had made it to the other side and back. He had completed this rite of passage.

CONCLUSION

Passed beyond the pairs . . .
For he that is freed from the pairs
Is easily freed from conflict.

(Bhagavad Gita)

We tell stories to find out who we were, who we are, and who we are becoming. These stories are formed out of material from larger narratives that existed before we were born and will continue on in some form after we die. The work of coaching is, in part, to help clients make adjustments in their relationship to the primal human drives for continuity *and* change, love *and* liberation, individuation *and* belonging. While none are mutually exclusive and, in fact enrich the other, tensions often emerge when these drives are undefined, undifferentiated, and/or 'unintegrated' within a person. When that is the case, the client is less able to handle the cultural and narrative complexities in their environment and in themselves. The result is a client who is less agile, less resilient, and less productive as they remain captive to the plot lines of others and to the tensions they create.

It is my contention that the development of intercultural sensitivity in relating to others mirrors the development of sensitivity around the cultures within ourselves as seen through the stories we tell. As Earley and Mosakowski remind us, the people who are 'socially the most successful among their peers often have the greatest difficulty making sense of, and being accepted by, cultural strangers' (Earley and Mosakowski 2004: 140). The rites of passage model is so useful in coaching because it supports people to let go of their attachments and defenses around their current story of themselves and others in order to befriend the strangers within themselves. By guiding clients through this process, particularly attending to the liminal phase, coaches can help clients reframe their understanding of and relation to the cultural narratives that once defined them. As a result, clients are actually more able to see the 'Other' and develop a healthier relationship to the projected and introjected characteristics as needed for their own development.

Clients' stories provide valuable material for coaches. Rather than focus on what the story means, coaches should ask: what does this story do? This was one of Freud's strategies: he considered not just what the client said but also what the client was doing with, and through, her story (Sarup 1996). As I've demonstrated in an earlier work (Drake 2008), stories have seven primary functions, each of which is useful to understand in coaching clients in support of their intercultural and identity development. They are: (1) claim and navigate our formal and informal memberships; (2) establish and sustain social identities; (3) discern influential cultural/contextual norms; (4) observe ourselves from other vantage points; (5) negotiate our identity performances in key environments; (6) test and rehearse new selves; (7) situate ourselves in a meaningful larger narrative. It is important for coaches to understand these functions as they listen to their clients' stories and actively engage with them.

Among the narrative skills that are useful in working with client stories along these lines are:

1 Understand change and development as taking place at the boundaries/borders in clients' narratives and identity and in the intermediate realms (Schwartz-Salant 1998)

71

between and beyond the coach–client dyad. This will involve better abilities to track 'markers' (Strauss 1997: 14) in coaching conversations indicative of, and openings to, the liminal boundaries in clients' stories. These can be seen as points where a narrator is on the edge of entering new (and often unknown and/or unconscious) territory in her narration and approaching a new aspect of her identity;

2   Develop a more critical stance on the stories within coaching conversations. This means looking at personal narratives for both coaches and clients in terms of their cultures' dominant narratives. It also entails recognizing that not all narratives share a similar status; some exist, highly devalued, within society's rifts and margins (McLaren 1993). If coaches want to support clients to change, they must be more conscious of the larger narratives in which their clients' identities are situated. Coaches must be willing to ask questions such as: 'Who decides what are the normative narratives against which client stories should be measured?' and 'What stories are not allowed to be lived or told – by coaches and clients?'; and

3   Develop a greater respect for the needs of the whole person in coaching and a greater ability to move into liminal and third spaces with clients. This requires coaches to be able to stay with clients during the hard work of narrative reconstruction and, in particular, to remain aware of behaviors on their part that perpetuate dualistic thinking and undermine the use of third spaces for their development (Drake 2005). A big part of this process is to balance the transactional, behavioral focus on intercultural relations with a transformational, intrapersonal focus on intercultural identity.

In the end, these narrative skills will help coaches be more effective with clients in facing increasingly complex cultural demands and maintaining a coherent narrative and sense of identity in the process. As we saw with Rebecca, Don and the others, the stories clients tell in coaching are a powerful tool in helping them to move through the six stages in developing greater intercultural sensitivity and integration at an intrapersonal level. Our role in the process is to be stewards and midwives who help clients bring new, more integrated, stories to life.

Note

1   Client names and some case details have been changed to preserve anonymity.

Bibliography

Alexander, B. C. (1991) *Victor Turner Revisited: Ritual as Social Change* (Vol. 74), Atlanta: Scholars Press.

Anzaldua, G. (1987) *Borderlands/La Frontera: The New Mestiza*, San Francisco: Aunt Lute Books.

Bakhtin, M. (1984) *Problems of Dostoevsky's Poetics*, trans. C. Emerson, Minneapolis: University of Minnesota Press.

Bennett, J. M. and Bennett, M. J. (2004) *Developing Intercultural Competence: A Reader*, Portland, OR: Intercultural Communication Institute.

Bennett, M. J. (1986) 'A developmental approach to training for intercultural sensitivity', *International Journal of Intercultural Relations*, 10 (2): 179–95.

Bennett, M. J. (1993) 'Towards ethnorelativism: A developmental model of intercultural sensitivity', in M. Paige (ed.), *Education for Intercultural Experience*, Yarmouth, ME: Intercultural Press.

Bennett, M. J. and Hammer, M. (1998) '*The developmental model of intercultural sensitivity*'. Available online at <www.intercultural.org/pdf/dmis.pdf> (accessed 14 March 2008).

Block, J. (1982) 'Assimilation, accommodation, and the dynamics of personality development', *Child Development*, 53: 281–95.

Bruner, J. (2002) *Making Stories: Law, Literature, Life*, Cambridge, MA: Harvard University Press.

Carson, T. L. (1997) *Liminal Reality and Transformational Power*, Lanham, MD: University Press of America.

Davies, B. and Harré, R. (1990) 'Positioning: The discursive production of selves', *Journal for the Theory of Social Behavior*, 20 (1): 43–63.

Drake, D. B. (2003) 'How stories change: A narrative analysis of liminal experiences and transitions in identity', unpublished dissertation, Fielding Graduate Institute: Santa Barbara.

Drake, D. B. (2004) 'Creating third space: The use of narrative liminality in coaching', in I. Stein, F. Campone and L. Page (eds), *Proceedings of the Second ICF Coaching Research Symposium*, Quebec City: International Coach Federation.

Drake, D. B. (2005) 'Narrative coaching: A psychosocial method for working with clients' stories to support transformative results', paper presented at the Second Australia Conference on Evidence-Based Coaching.

Drake, D. B. (2007) 'The art of thinking narratively: Implications for coaching psychology and practice', *Australian Psychologist*, 42 (4): 283–94.

Drake, D. B. (2008) 'Thrice upon a time: The contributions of narrative psychology to coaching', in D. B. Drake, K. Gortz and D. Brennan (eds), *The Philosophy and Practice of Coaching: Insights and Issues for a New Era*, San Francisco: Jossey-Bass.

Earley, P. C. and Mosakowski, E. (2004) 'Cultural intelligence', *Harvard Business Review*, October 2004: 139–46.

Eliade, M. (1959) *The Sacred and Profane: The Nature of Religion*, New York: Harcourt.

English, L. (2002) 'Third space: Contested space, identity, and international adult education', *Proceedings of the CASAE/ACEEA 21st Annual Conference: Adult Education and the Contested Terrain of Public Policy*, Toronto: CASAE/ACEEA.

Evanoff, R. (2000) 'The concept of "third cultures" in intercultural ethics', *Eubios Journal of Asian and International Bioethics*, 10: 126–9.

Freud, S. (1912) 'Recommendations to physicians practising psychoanalysis', in J. Strachey (ed.), *The Standard Edition of the Complete Psychological Works of Sigmund Freud* (Vol. 12), London: Hogarth Press.

Gergen, K. J. (1991) *The Saturated Self*, New York: Basic Books.

Giddens, A. (1991) *Modernity and Self-Identity: Self and Society in the Late Modern Age*, Stanford, CA: Stanford University Press.

Hermans, H. J. M. (2004) 'The innovation of self-narratives: A dialogical approach', in L. E. Angus and J. McLeod (eds), *Handbook of Narrative and Psychotherapy: Practice, Theory, and Research*, Thousand Oaks, CA: Sage Publications.

Hollis, J. (2004) *Mythologems: Incarnations of the Invisible World*, Toronto: Inner City Books.

James, W. (1927) *Psychology: Briefer Course*, New York: Henry Holt and Company.

Jung, C. G. (1964) *Mysterium Coniunctionis*, trans. R. F. C. Hull (Vol. 14), Princeton: Princeton University Press.

Kegan, R. and Lahey, L. L. (2001) *How the Way We Talk Can Change the Way We Work*, San Francisco: Jossey-Bass.

Lefebvre, H. (1980) *La Presence et l'absence*, Paris: Casterman.

McAdams, D. P., Diamond, A., de St Aubin, E. and Mansfield, E. (1997) 'Stories of commitment: The psychosocial construction of generative lives', *Journal of Personality and Social Psychology*, 72: 678–94.

McLaren, P. (1993) 'Border disputes: Multicultural narrative, identity formation, and critical pedagogy in postmodern America', in D. McLaughlin and W. G. Tierney (eds), *Naming Silenced Lives: Personal Narratives and Processes of Educational Change*, New York: Routledge.

Mishler, E. G. (1999) *Storylines: Craftartists' Narratives of Identity*, Cambridge, MA: Harvard University Press.

Ochs, E. and Capps, L. (1996) 'Narrating the self', *Annual Review of Anthropology*, 25: 19–43.

Polkinghorne, D. E. (1988) *Narrative Knowing and the Human Sciences*, Albany: State University of New York Press.

Polkinghorne, D. E. (2001) 'The self and humanistic psychology', in K. J. Schneider, J. F. T. Bugental and J. F. Pierson (eds), *The Handbook of Humanistic Psychology*, Thousand Oaks, CA: Sage Publications.

Polkinghorne, D. E. (2004) 'Narrative therapy and postmodernism', in L. E. Angus and J. McLeod (eds), *Handbook of Narrative and Psychotherapy: Practice, Theory, and Research*, Thousand Oaks, CA: Sage.

Rutherford, J. (1990) 'A place called home: Identity and the cultural politics of difference', in J. Rutherford (ed.), *Identity: Community, Culture and Difference*, London: Lawrence and Wishart.

Sarup, M. (1996) *Identity, Culture, and the Postmodern World*, Athens: The University of Georgia Press.

Schein, E. (1996) 'Three cultures of management: The key to organizational learning', *Sloan Management Review*, 38 (1): 9–21.

Schwartz-Salant, N. (1998) *The Mystery of Human Relationship: Alchemy and the Transformation of the Self*, New York: Routledge.

Stein, J. O., and Stein, M. (1987) 'Psychotherapy, initiation and the midlife transition', in L. C. Mahdi, S. Foster and M. Little (eds), *Betwixt and Between: Patterns of Masculine and Feminine Initiation*, La Salle, IL: Open Court.

Stevens-Long, J. (2000) 'The prism self: Multiplicity on the path to transcendence', in P. Young-Eisendrath and M. E. Miller (eds), *The Psychology of Mature Spirituality: Integrity, Wisdom, Transcendence*, Philadelphia: Routledge.

Strauss, A. L. (1997) *Mirrors and Masks: The Search for Identity*, (2nd edn), New Brunswick, CT: Transaction Publishers.

Tillich, P. (1965) 'Frontiers', *Journal of the American Academy of Religion*, 33 (1): 17–23.

Turner, V. (1967) *The Forest of Symbols: Aspects of Ndembu Ritual*, Ithaca, NY: Cornell University Press.

Turner, V. (1969) *The Ritual Process: Structure and Anti-Structure*, New York: Aldine Publishing.

Turner, V. (1974) *Dramas, Fields and Metaphors*, Ithaca, NY: Cornell University Press.

Turner, V. (1979) *Process, Performance and Pilgrimage: A Study in Comparative Symbology*, New Delhi: Concept Publishing.

Turner, V. (1982) 'Liminality and the performative genres', in F. A. Hanson (ed.), *Studies in Symbolism and Cultural Communication*, Lawrence: University of Kansas.

Van Gennep, A. (1960) *The Rites of Passage*, London: Routledge and Kegan Paul.

ONTOLOGICAL COACHING

Intercultural coaching and trust

Julio Olalla and the Newfield Community

THEORETICAL FRAMEWORK

The particular approach to coaching this chapter addresses is ontological coaching. We will begin with a theoretical framework, explore the application of this framework within the context of intercultural coaching and trust and conclude with tools to assist the coach in exploring this territory. Sound theory and practice are essential in any professional practice, like coaching, that provides valuable and beneficial service to individuals and organizations.

Communities do not invent new approaches unless needed for an emerging concern. Either intuitively or rationally we know that many of our existing practices no longer meet emerging concerns of individuals, leaders, organizations or communities at large. We believe that people at large and the coaching community more specifically are looking for practices that give rise to deeper discussion and thought concerning a more substantial and sustainable understanding of age-old questions. Society revolutionists are reexamining and challenging traditional notions such as:

- The nature of knowledge (epistemology) – what one believes about the nature of knowledge, in particular what is the foundation, the scope and the validity of knowing. Informing this area in their interdisciplinary work are Humberto Maturana (1988), John Austin (1959), John Searle (2004) and Elaine Hatfield (Hatfield, Cacioppo and Rapson 1993);
- The nature of the universe (cosmology) – what one believes about the origin and structure of the universe as it directly impacts our human actions in the world. Interdisciplinary conversation by Richard Tarnas (1991), Brian Swimme (1996), Fritjof Capra (1975/ 1999) and David Bohm (1980) are challenging traditional notions; and
- The nature of being (ontology) – what one believes about the nature of being or self. Thinkers and writers such as Mihaly Csikszenthmihalyi (2004), R.D. Laing (1982) and Martin Heidegger (Farrell Krell 1993) provide valuable insight.

These emerge as concerns because we are at a major historical transition point in the history of Western culture, characterized by continual rapid change in technology, values and key social institutions, which can have a deeply unsettling, even turbulent, impact on how we live and relate. This profound historical shift demands fundamentally different ways of thinking and perceiving, of learning and relating (including how we do business). The recurrent concerns or breakdowns we see in the world are not being addressed by current practices of thinking, perceiving, learning and relating. Substantial shifts are required to effectively navigate the recurrently turbulent waters of everyday living. Approaching coaching as shifting how we observe provides a basis for generating these substantial shifts in how we live and relate in the world.

ONTOLOGICAL COACHING: DEFINED

Ontological coaching offers interventions that allow shifts in the observer we are, thus creating the means for individuals to navigate through the ever-changing environment of life. Specifically ontological coaching is based on the understanding that human beings are essentially linguistic beings and as such language is indispensable to knowing and learning. This approach to coaching is distinctive because it draws a direct correlation between language and action. In other words, language functions as more than just a description of reality; it generates reality, predisposes us to action and carries an historical discourse of meaning. This approach to coaching allows for an external intervention that potentially expands the coachee's space for possibilities in their external world by allowing them to create an observer's lens that opens an individual to view themselves within this larger context of meaning making. For example, every decision that we make and every action that we take is done within a particular historical discourse. That discourse is generated by a reality that often has limited options. Opening the observer's lens to new possibilities and options thereby expanding the consciousness of a given historical discourse can be life-shifting for an individual.

ONTOLOGICAL COACHING: PRINCIPLES

The ontological approach to coaching is often classified as transformational coaching because learning happens at a meta-level. Entering into this process is a conscious choice for both the coach and coachee designed to create ontological shifts – shifts in the fundamental lens of perception. The choice is the acceptance of the proposition that we can observe, question and change basic principles of coherence that we define as our personal and historical discourse in life. This involves accessing multiple learning pathways such as language, emotion-mood and body-soma on a meta-learning level. The most remarkable consequences of admitting that we live viewing the world through an interpretive lens are that:

1 The type of world we live in reveals the type of being we are;
2 Everything we do or say reveals a piece of our interpretive lens as a person in the world; and
3 Supporting this is a complex coherence among our body, emotions-moods and language.

Therefore as we are engaging with the world – interacting with objects, individuals and surroundings whose very meaning, value and existence are connected to us and through this process – we truly invent ourselves. These principles are at the essence of ontological coaching, providing a means for contextualization across cultures, as the examples further on will demonstrate (Brothers 2005).

76

Ontological coaching touches people at a very personal, intimate level. Permission to work at this meta-level of the change process must be established through a relationship of trust. Trust lives in many domains; it is linguistic and it is emotion and is held in the physical soma of an individual. Trust is our assessment (judgment), based on past experience, of the likelihood we will get the results we believe we have been promised. Exploring, creating, maintaining and repairing trust is the territory that makes ontological coaching possible. Ultimately the coachee trusts the coach to evaluate, observe, provide feedback, challenge, and question and explore within his or her individualized historical context. The assessment of trust is based on the sincerity, competence and reliability of another to deliver what has been promised with specific conditions of agreed upon satisfaction (Solomon and Flores 2001). In the coaching relationship, the coachee must assess that the coach is 'sincere', 'competent' and 'reliable' in a process that will produce an ontological shift.

When we talk about sincerity in the coaching relationship, it is the belief that another person's intention is not to deceive but to be genuine or authentic. Are our private conversations and public conversations consistent? Is there congruency with what we say and our behavior and presence in all of life?

Competence in the coaching relationship is the assessment that this individual has the experience, knowledge and keen observation skill to deliver on a promise made. Ontological coaches must be competent observers of other people as well as have the ability to design and manage the coaching conversation to create actions and practices that can lead to effective ontological shifts. The coach must perform at the highest standards, which makes it possible for conversations that are candid, honest, not based on pleasing, comforting or protecting the coachee.

Reliability in the coaching relationship is a consistency in the capacity of the coach to create a dependable open environment for conversation and observation to take place. The aim of ontological coaching is to create the context that allows for the transformation of the coachee, in essence creating a consistent powerful space, free from distractions.

When we talk about trust in this way we are talking about 'nurtured' trust, as distinct from simple trust or blind trust. Blind trust is a trust that comes without questions or prudence. Simple trust is trust that is untested, unfiltered and innocent. In ontological coaching, the trust the coachee places in a coach and vice versa (nurtured), is a trust of choice, in permissioned awareness, and this trust over the course of the relationship is dynamic and an evolving part of a relationship commitment to another. This is particularly important to understand in the coaching relationship, but is also powerful when using the distinctions in addressing trust in business and organizations (Solomon and Flores 2001).

ONTOLOGICAL COACHING: INTERCULTURAL INTERVENTION

It is important for coaches and organizational change initiators operating across cultures to note that, even with this expanded understanding of trust, it would be naïve to believe that issues of trust could be simply addressed. There are many complex forces at work. Although we have mentioned trust in the coach and coachee relationship specifically, the forces at play in the intercultural historical discourse of trust are multi-layered with emotion, mood, and language that predisposed contextual action. Consider as an example the impact on individuals that live within the context of a cultural drift where economic insecurity exists in a society built on trade, commerce and competition. Legitimate fears and constraints can trigger one's instinct to hoard resources at critical times. Implementation of rules and regulations to control behavior is not necessarily effective in long-term conditions and entrenched systems of accepted behavior and practices. Cultural distrust can exist in environments where the assessment of distrust was made a long time ago and persists until today. In such situations people do not make the assessment for themselves; the judgment has already been made for them.

When you enter this territory through cultural exchanges, differences can lead to huge misunderstandings and generally a lack of a foundation of mutual understanding of the specifics of nurtured trust in intercultural environments. It is essential to create the conditions constitutive to nurtured trust. The nature of promises made and the way they are communicated are central to the way trust is developed. Clear, precise communication is necessary to develop nurtured trust. For example, a promise must be clearly distinguished from an expectation; yet most people see the two as indistinguishable. Expectations are often requests that are couched in the hope that the other person will guess what you want and understand your conditions of satisfaction. Promises, by contrast, carry clearly communicated understandings and conditions. It is our experience most individuals operate on expectations that are unvoiced and which live in the background of conversations and cultural histories. These expectations usually carry an assumption that things will continue the 'way they have always been done'.

So how exactly do these principles of ontological coaching work in intercultural environments? In the following case study we will examine an ontological coaching relationship in a multinational business context.

CASE STUDY

When we speak about 'multinational businesses' or 'intercultural environments' we should be careful to consider that this describes an enormous number of entities in today's world both large and small. A sushi restaurant in the Netherlands that employs a Japanese chef is an intercultural environment. A Chinese electronics manufacturer that employs a Chilean to head its operations in Latin America is intercultural and multinational. A small engineering company based in the central states of the US that sells directly to customers in Europe and South America is multinational. In fact it is the transparence of the fact that these companies are multinational and trans-cultural that makes this such a relevant area to explore.

> The client we chose for our example is a firm engaged in the design, engineering and manufacture of high precision sensors and measuring tools used in the packaging, automotive and medical manufacturing sectors. The leader we coached is one of the founders and owners and has been a leader in the company for 25 years, overseeing the growth of the organization from 3 employees to 25 in two US locations. The organization has engaged reps in Asia, Europe and South America as part of its extended sales force and provides technical advice from its US offices. The firm has in the past three years undertaken a deliberate effort to revitalize its mission and direction resulting in a clear organization-wide commitment to (1) being in partnership with its customers, and (2) focusing on providing clients with systemic solutions rather than individual products. Due to the nature of its business one of the organization's continuous challenges is working at the limits of current engineering technology and materials.
>
> Imagine this small US engineering company, a multinational by our examined definition. Due to the ease and rapidity of travel and communication at the opening of the twenty-first century, most parts of the world are markets for their highly specialized products. Consider the cultures the leader of this organization swims in: there is his native culture (US, Northern European, Protestant, Caucasian, baby boomer, male, educated, economically privileged by global standards), the varied culture of his workers (including US, Northern European and

Hispanic, Protestant and Catholic, male and female, varied levels of education and awareness, various levels of economic security, and differing generations), the culture of his customers in Asia, Europe, and South America (which also include variety of age, gender, economic security, language, history, etc.). In our example vast cultural variety and multinational elements are contained even within the forty or so business relationships identified.

It is impossible for any person to be in continual awareness of the nearly unlimited variety of cultural norms represented even by this relatively small number of people. One could easily despair at the impossibility of the task. How would we ontologically coach to empower the observer in and action taking of this leader, particularly in regard to trust? How could we support this leader to learn the tools that will increase his ability to navigate these waters?

Imagine that this leader's breakdown is an inability to trust three specific people in his group of business relations. One is inside his company, one is a representative of a supplier and one is part of a client organization. His success as a leader to some degree depends on his ability to trust and be trusted by these three people.

Here was our approach:

1   Have the coachee declare his own cultural and historical background articulating as many facets as possible. Create the awareness of the place from which the leader is leading. Declare the observer he is;

2   Challenge the coachee to declare that his culture is a particular culture and that the world is full of other cultures of equal value. Declarations by definition lead to breakdowns that the coachee must then resolve. In this case there was a transparent belief (which most of us carry) that the culture the leader knew was the 'best' or 'right' way to be in the world (this is the self-preservation mechanism of culture that ensures its continuation. Without this mechanism we would simply and easily overthrow any cultural element that 'got in our way' and the culture would dissipate);

3   Have the coachee articulate his breakdowns in this declaration and explore whether his beliefs in this area are chosen or inherited. Most of what we claim to know of life is inherited from those we were surrounded by early in life. Often when a coachee realizes that a particular belief is not one he or she chose but rather one that was 'assumed', there is an opening to become a new observer;

4   Returning to consider the three people the coachee is challenged with in the area of trust, explore what the connection is between the three in terms of the trust model previously presented: sincerity, competence and reliability. It could be that each of the three individuals had broken trust with or betrayed the coachee. If so, specific actions might be called for with each individual relationship; and

5   Having established 'reliability' as the area of challenge, have the coachee search for the cultural connection among the three which might underpin a standard for reliability that differs from that of the coachee.

The discovery of the coachee was that the breakdown was between cultural norms held by his generation and another. In this example we could speak of the ontology of trust being true across all of the cultures considered, while the standards in the various domains of trust varied. For instance, in the coachee's generational standards, reliability was closely linked to promptness and the element of time. In the younger generation's standard, reliability was connected with task accomplishment and quality while promptness was considered of minor importance.

Having uncovered the ontological aspects of the breakdown, our client could consider choosing a new 'multicultural' standard for reliability; one that allowed him to design a conversation with his younger colleagues that promoted trusting and being trusted. In effect our client shifted the observer he was, which allowed for an expanded range of actions and the opportunity for new results to emerge.

TOOLS

What practices around trust can ontological coaches use to generate purposeful, meaningful, and powerful shifts in their clients' language, body, and emotion – and, ultimately, the interpretive lens from which they see and interact in the world?

This naturally raises the question whether there are absolutes, practices, and behaviors for human interaction in today's international business world that transcend intercultural differences and promote personal and organizational well-being (increased creativity and a fully engaged workforce), productivity (improved products and services and organizational resiliency), and reputation (delivering on commitments and enhancing leadership capability).

INDIVIDUAL AND ORGANIZATIONAL TRUST

Ultimately, trust is at the heart of effective relationships and is the glue that binds individuals and organizations together. High trust supports creative, innovative, and productive outcomes. Low trust stifles productivity and creates an environment where people are reluctant to bring themselves fully to work.

As individuals and in organizations, we often generate 'unintended and undesirable' effects on trust. These show up when we fail to thank colleagues for meeting their commitments or keep our own promises. They are present when we don't provide the opportunity for complaint and when we avoid complaining when promises to us are not fulfilled. And, trust is undermined when we practice 'cordial hypocrisy', a term coined by Solomon and Flores (2001: 58) to mean that we act as if everything is fine, but underneath there are important issues that aren't being addressed.

The results of such behaviors include missed deadlines, ineffective leadership, employee disengagement, costly and redundant processes, rules and procedures, lack of commitment, minimal or no opportunities to learn from experience, and persistent moods of resentment and resignation among employees. When clients raise issues such as these in coaching, distrust may be the primary cause and building trust the primary solution.

Practices and behaviors that model and build personal and organizational trust include setting and clearly communicating direction, creating a climate of collaboration, allowing for the opportunity to learn from failure, acknowledging mistakes and missed commitments, following up on promises, embracing and valuing change, and having and practicing clear and consistent organizational values and norms of behavior. These apply in cross–cultural settings and positively impact key organizational outcomes, leading to stronger business alliances, better execution of decisions, heightened loyalty, enhanced innovation, improved collaboration, and highly engaged and motivated employees.

TOOLS FOR COACHING: FIVE PRIMARY STEPS FOR CONVERSATIONS OF TRUST

There are five primary steps we recommend for engaging in conversations of trust with individual and organizational clients:

1 Explore the costs of the current state of trust;
2 Identify where there is passion, energy, and commitment to address issues of trust;

3 Review the current trust-based behaviors and practices of the individual leader or teams and together develop new practices that the leader and team can commit to;

4 Translate the insights into specific actions designed to strengthen trust; and

5 Provide for ongoing coaching.

There are many ways coaches can raise and address trust issues with their clients. We recommend approaches built upon the ontological distinctions of trust and survey assessment tools referenced earlier in this article:

- Use the behavioral-based trust statements from the Triscendance LLC Organizational Trust Survey (OTS)[1] and the Leadership Team Trust Survey (LTS) as sources for deeper coaching inquiry;
- Introduce your client to the distinctions of trust (e.g., reliability, sincerity, competence, building, maintaining, and restoring trust, and attentiveness to trust). Help the client assess how well he or she practices trust-based behaviors on a daily basis. Explore the role the client and others play in building trust throughout the organization;
- Introduce the importance of working with language, emotions/moods, body-soma, in the workplace and how to harness that power. Create awareness of the role that language plays, practice conversations for action based on the client's concerns, and challenge the client to have these conversations with others to model the behaviors that build trust;
- When working with organizations, address how the 'body' and 'energy' (i.e., the 'embodiment') of the organization shows up (e.g., by using the 'Culture' statements and 'Mood' questions from the Organizational Trust Survey). 'Connect the dots' by including an action plan that the organization is committed to and can move forward with;
- When working with leadership teams, consider that the art of the coach is to assess what the leaders are ready for and to balance that with where the opportunities are. For example, it may be appropriate to have the leadership team take small steps with an easier issue, in order to build confidence and success in moving forward;
- Help leadership teams address critical aspects of team performance including developing trust, handling conflict, building commitment, taking accountability, and delivering results;
- Have conversations with your individual clients about trust-building actions and how they assess themselves (e.g., in keeping confidences, speaking and acting authentically, making clear offers and requests, fulfilling promises or renegotiating, making complaints when promises have been broken, generating pockets of trust in one's domain of influence, and identifying areas in which one can be more trustworthy);
- Have conversations with organizational leaders about trust-building actions and how they assess themselves (e.g., calling distrust by its name, role modeling and practicing trust, allowing mistakes and using them for learning, allowing people to say no to requests or renegotiate, creating a mood that supports trust, creating a culture where a complaint follows lack of fulfillment of a promise, distinguishing authentic/nurtured trust from blind or simple trust, generating pockets of trust starting with top management, and keeping confidences);
- Convey 'embodiment of trust' as the individual and organizational capability derived from continually practicing and being attentive to trust behaviors; and
- Model trust with your clients by practicing and pointing out behaviors that engender and mitigate trust in your coaching relationship and encourage your client to hold you equally accountable.

TOOLS FOR ORGANIZATIONS

Trust assessment tools designed around an ontological framework will have universal appeal, significance and apply well in multicultural and international business settings. Effective assessment tools are those that enable respondents in an organization to reflect on a variety of behaviors familiar to anyone working in the organization. What is particularly powerful is to look at behavioral statements through the lens of the ontological distinctions of trust introduced earlier. Leaders and others can then see the specific behaviors that contribute to varying levels of trust throughout the organization or on the leadership team and the competencies of those involved in strengthening trust. Assessment tools that measure levels of trust in the hierarchies of the organization (e.g., peers, managers, and senior leaders) and also balance the responses to specific survey statements provide the coach, in partnership with the leader and his or her team, with a strong idea of where problems may exist and where to start designing and taking action.

One such diagnostic tool is the Organizational Trust Survey (OTS) developed and published by Triscendance LLC in consultation with Newfield Network, Inc. This on-line, confidential survey identifies where there are issues of trust (and distrust) in the organization. OTS results show the coach and the leader where and how issues show up, and identify areas requiring attention. The OTS breaks organizational 'transparencies' such as those described above in ways the organization can understand. The particular stories of the organization can then be viewed through this lens. This provides the coach with a 'jumping off' place and/or places to look and dive deeper into conversations with clients about key trust issues.

Another trust survey tool available for intact leadership teams is the Leadership Team Trust Survey (LTS) developed by Triscendance LLC. This survey can be administered either web-based or by interview and is designed to help teams enhance their levels of mutual trust and thereby deliver excellent results for themselves and their organization. Behavioral-based statements relate to the team leader, team members, and the overall team and are based on characteristics of high-performing teams.

The link between behaviors and levels of trust is often not clear to those involved in organizational situations, particularly where there is an added variable of cultural complexity. A key role of the coach is to help surface what is going on in relation to trust and to identify places and areas where more or different knowledge is required to enable new actions to serve transformational change. The use of a variety of assessments – including formal assessment tools as described above or in structured conversations – offers an efficient method of collecting different kinds of information. The knowledge can then be used by the client, assisted by the coaching relationship and process, to undertake deeper examinations and explorations that may be required before the client is able to progress. In the case of a leader, even when a leader is aware of serious issues relating to trust that need attention, he or she may not have the tools or the will necessary to generate lasting shifts.

As coaches, we help our clients to untangle the personal, organizational and cultural complexity that surrounds them, to recognize trustful and distrustful behaviors and to take action. Creating new awareness and helping the client to build the required new competencies are the key roles of the ontological coach.

Without trust there is no relationship and without relationship there is no coaching.

(Julio Olalla)

Note

1 Organizational Trust Survey and Leadership Team Trust Survey, contact Bill Benner, Triscendance LLC, at (804) 306–3177 or <bill@triscendance.com>.

Bibliography

Austin, J. L. (1959) *Sense and Sensibilia*, Oxford: Oxford University Press.
Bohm, D. (1980) *Wholeness and the Implicate Order*, London: Routledge.
Brothers, C. (2005) *Language and the Pursuit of Happiness*, Naples, FA: New Possibilities Press.
Capra, F. (1975/1999) *The Tao of Physics*, Boston, MA: Shambhala.
Csikszenthmihalyi, M. (2004) *Good Business: Leadership, Flow, and the Making of Meaning*, London: Penguin.
Farrell Krell, D. (ed.) (1993) *Martin Heidegger: Basic Writings*, San Francisco: Harper.
Hatfield, E., Cacioppo, J.T., and Rapson, R.L. (1993) *Emotional Contagion*, New York: Cambridge University Press.
Laing, R.D. (1982) *The Voice of Experience: Experience, Science and Psychiatry*, Harmondsworth: Penguin.
Maturana, H. (1988) 'REALITY: The search for objectivity or the quest for a compelling argument', *The Irish Journal of Psychology*, 9: 25–82.
Searle, J. (2004) *Mind: A Brief Introduction*, Oxford: Oxford University Press.
Solomon, R. and Flores, F. (2001) *Building Trust in Business, Politics, Relationships and Life*, New York: Oxford University Press.
Swimme, B. (1996) *The Hidden Heart of the Cosmos: Humanity and the New Story*, Maryknoll, NY: Orbis Books.
Tarnas, R. (1991) *The Passion of the Western Mind*, New York: Ballantine.

6

COACHING FOR EMOTIONAL INTELLIGENCE IN INTERNATIONAL BUSINESS ENVIRONMENTS
Challenges and opportunities

Geetu Bharwaney and Ari Jokilaakso

INTRODUCTION

Emotional Intelligence appeared more than a decade ago in the psychology literature (across the applications of counseling, psychiatry, coaching and leadership development). Today there are several tools for measuring Emotional Intelligence and this specialization within psychology has been growing at a pace (in 1999, there were 3 hits on the internet for the term 'Emotional Intelligence', today there are over 1,800,000 hits on the internet using Google and over 23,000 on Google Scholar). Through this time professional coaching has been increasing in popularity as an organizational intervention to support executive development and performance. The two fields are increasingly intersecting; with most coaches starting to pay some attention to Emotional Intelligence in their work with clients (though the way this is done, the rigor and the use of best practices dramatically varies between coaches). As coaching based on Emotional Intelligence can be considered to be a contemporary approach to coaching, this chapter is designed to serve as a helpful introduction to its challenges and controversies.

Despite the growing interest in Emotional Intelligence (and other forms of intelligence such as Cultural Intelligence and Social Intelligence), little has been written to date about the practical aspects of using Emotional Intelligence in coaching work in an international business environment. This chapter focuses on the practice of using Emotional Intelligence tools, strategies and frameworks specifically in coaching in an international business context. Three dimensions will be considered and interwoven – Emotional Intelligence as a coaching methodology; coaching using Emotional Intelligence; and the influence of an international business context on both these activities. As little evidence exists connecting these three variables – coaching, Emotional Intelligence and international business – theoretical arguments will be put forward as to why these combined should result in positive outcomes for executives and businesses. Four case studies will be used to demonstrate Emotional Intelligence coaching in action. Coaching has been much more open to qualitative case study research and is not necessarily supported by questionnaire or assessment data; many coaching interventions are considered to be highly contextual and beyond measurement. From their own experiences in international business contexts, the authors advocate that coaching based on Emotional Intelligence has the potential to overcome the somewhat personal and subjective nature of coaching.

This chapter explores questions that have not been asked before and which influence the way in which Emotional Intelligence frameworks can be used in an international business coaching context. For example:

- Is it possible to make generalizations about 'success' in an international arena, in other words, is the way to high achievement the same for a Finnish person as it is for an American or Chinese executive, etc.?
- If these are vastly different, can you use Emotional Intelligence frameworks and assessment tools for all international clients in a business context and introduce them into coaching programs?
- If so, how can you ensure that you are not biasing the outcomes through the selection of tools, etc.?
- How would one start to understand the use of Emotional Intelligence frameworks available for coaching and how can this contribute to coaching impact in an international business context?
- Is there a universal definition of 'success' in coaching when it is conducted in an international business context using Emotional Intelligence frameworks?

These and other dimensions of coaching will be explored. In Section 1 the theoretical framework is explored including definitions. In Section 2, evidence and case studies are put forward to inform coaching practice in an international business context.

SECTION 1 – THEORETICAL FRAMEWORK

Emotional Intelligence is defined as 'the essential mix of emotional, personal and social competencies that influences our ability to be personally effective and professionally productive' (Bharwaney 2007: 184). These skills are needed more in today's society and they distinguish high performers in a variety of contexts.

Coaching interventions based on Emotional Intelligence in international business settings typically involve either coaching alone or coaching combined with group work (but rarely group work alone). Bharwaney (2007: 184) refers to this form of coaching as 'a process designed to help improve Emotional Intelligence so that people can be more personally effective or organizationally productive'. Such interventions are more thoughtfully implemented when 22 guidelines for long-term change are built into the design (Ei Consortium 2003). Bharwaney, Bar-On and MacKinlay (2007) selected 10 of the original guidelines and documented the features of interventions that had the most impact with coaching clients. Coaches who work in an international business environment are encouraged to consult these guidelines for the purpose of self-assessment against established best practices for coaching based on Emotional Intelligence. Bharwaney (2007) documented a 12-hour coaching process for creating measurable impact from global executive coaching. Further, Bharwaney (2008 in press) documented a process for coaching high achievers either individually or in groups, based on four pillars of support found to be necessary in the design of coaching programs to effect concrete behavioral change.

The international business environment described here refers to cases where the client's business environment and context are different from that of the national culture and home territory of the coach, producing a level of complexity which is higher compared to coaching taking place in one's own context. When the word 'culture' is used, it covers a number of different types of culture. The client has his or her own culture, which is referred to here as 'the way they do things in their home context'. Their 'working culture' is their team or organizational culture which is in the background of their own culture and may involve a separate culture in itself. Beyond this, national culture comes into play and all these 'circles' of culture are present in the coaching relationship. It is as if the coach is on an athletic track of multiple lanes with the client in the middle, and the coach's task is to get through the hordes of runners crowding the track, in order to reach the client at the centre of the action. The coach has to unpick the culture of the client in order to be directly helpful with the client's own goals, challenges and aspirations. In this chapter, the use of Emotional Intelligence in coaching to help unpick these layers of culture will be explored further. The three concentric circles of 'culture' which can be gleaned from an Emotional Intelligence instrument are illustrated in Figure 6.1.

Data as a starting point for international business coaching

Coaching in an international business context is complex. One of the distinguishing factors of a coaching approach based on Emotional Intelligence is the use of specific data about the client, gained from individual assessments of Emotional Intelligence, to inform both the initial needs analysis and also the style of coaching. These themes will be expanded within the case study section of this chapter. Where groups of managers or executives are being coached at the same time as part of a leadership intervention, such data can include collective as well as individual data. With this in mind, case studies have been selected to illustrate in a practical way how information about a person can yield insights about a client and specifically their own 'culture' – defined here as 'the way they do things'. Note the use of the word 'they'. The use of Emotional Intelligence assessments involves the coach putting him- or herself into the heart of the client's world and using assessments to take a '2nd perspective' (to borrow a term from Neuro Linguistic Programming), rather than relying primarily on questioning and their own insight into the client from a '1st perspective'. The insight of a coach is limited by their field of vision and the coach's field of vision can be expanded to include objective assessments like Emotional Intelligence.

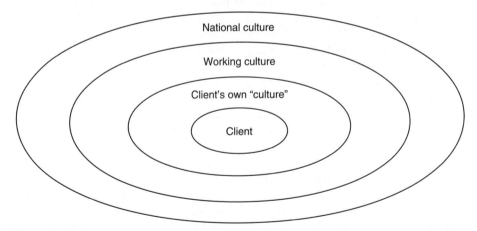

Figure 6.1 The running track of the client's world: circles of culture revealed by Emotional Intelligence assessments

Source: G. Bharwaney (2008)

SECTION 2: EVIDENCE

This section includes a discussion on why/how theoretically Emotional Intelligence would be valuable as a coaching tool in international business contexts. First evidence is considered about the validity of Emotional Intelligence frameworks as a valuable part of a coaching intervention in a cross-cultural context. Then selected case studies are used to illustrate the inclusion of Emotional Intelligence frameworks as a valuable part of a coaching intervention in an international business context. In other words, the value of not Emotional Intelligence per se but *Coaching* with Emotional Intelligence will be explored.

Validity of Emotional Intelligence frameworks as a valuable part of a coaching intervention in a cross-cultural context

Emotional intelligence is regularly acknowledged as a significant variable in executive coaching programs. For example, leading exponents of evidence-based coaching, Anthony Grant and Jane Greene list Emotional Intelligence as an essential quality of a great manager-coach. They also refer to recent work with Emotional Intelligence and coaching, indicating that long-term success requires much more than sheer rational thinking power (Greene and Grant 2003: 2).

The validation of Emotional Intelligence as a construct continues to be somewhat controversial with a number of different schools of thought. It is beyond the scope of this chapter to do justice to the current debate on what is Emotional Intelligence so the definition used earlier in this chapter will be used as the theoretical framework. The authors have used a variety of frameworks but have found the Bar-On Emotional Quotient Inventory™ (Bar-On EQ-i® for short) to be the most popular and well validated tool for use in cross-cultural groups. A short summary of the scales is included in Table 6.1.

The availability of cross-cultural norms based on age and gender considerations within this specific psychometric tool is an important feature as a client's scores are not calculated in isolation. They are compared with their supposed peer group of people of a similar age and gender so that the client gets a measure of where they are in relation to their current phase in life compared to people of a similar gender in their own national culture. We know that Emotional Intelligence rises to a peak in the 40s so you would expect a client in her 50s to have higher levels of functioning compared to someone in her 30s, for example. This makes intuitive sense. Contrary to what might be thought, few cross-cultural differences on Emotional Intelligence have been found from research data. Research data on culture and Emotional Intelligence are growing, however, and once differences have been thoroughly researched in a variety of contexts, one could in the future be more confident about moving beyond the anecdotal differences between country managers mentioned later. One Emotional Intelligence tool has been translated into a total of 10 different languages (Trait Emotional Intelligence Research program – <www.teique.com>). The Bar-On EQ-i®, which has more than two decades of underpinning research, was available in at least 17 languages at the time of publication, including Czech, Danish, Dutch, English, Finnish, French, German, Italian, Japanese, Lithuanian, Mandarin, Norwegian, Swedish, Russian and Turkish. As these languages cover a considerable proportion of the world's population, the use of Emotional Intelligence as a tool for coaching becomes a more concrete reality in the context of international businesses. A short summary of the development of the Bar-On EQ-i® is included below.

Table 6.1 Bar-On EQ-i® competencies and subscales

The EQ-i® is a self-report measure of emotionally and socially intelligent behavior, which provides an estimate of one's underlying emotional-social intelligence. The EQ-i® was developed over a period of 17 years and normed on close to 4000 adults in North America. A more detailed description of the psychometric properties of this measure and how it was developed can be found in the *EQ-i Technical Manual* and in the *Burros Mental Measurement Yearbook*. The tool is published by Multi Health Systems, Toronto (www.mhs.com)

1) **Intrapersonal competencies** (self-awareness and self-expression):
   These competencies include the following sub-components that govern our ability to be aware of ourselves, to understand our strengths and weaknesses, and to express our thoughts and feelings non-destructively:
   • **Self-regard (SR):** The ability to be aware of, understand and accept ourselves.
   • **Emotional self-awareness (ES):** The ability to be aware of and understand our emotions.
   • **Assertiveness (AS):** The ability to express our feelings and ourselves non-destructively.
   • **Independence (IN):** The ability to be emotionally self-reliant.
   • **Self-actualization (SA):** The ability to set and achieve our goals and actualize our potential.

2) **Interpersonal competencies** (social awareness and interpersonal relationship):
   These competencies include the following sub-components that govern our ability to be aware of others' feelings, concerns and needs, and to be able to establish and maintain cooperative, constructive and mutually satisfying relationships:
   • **Empathy (EM):** The ability to be aware of and understand how others feel.
   • **Social responsibility (RE):** The ability to identify with and feel part of our social group.
   • **Interpersonal relationship (IR):** The ability to establish and maintain mutually satisfying relationships with others.

3) **Stress management competencies** (emotional management and regulation):
   These competencies include the following sub-components that govern our ability to manage emotions so that they work for us and not against us:
   • **Stress tolerance (ST):** The ability to effectively and constructively manage our emotions.
   • **Impulse control (IC):** The ability to effectively and constructively control our emotions.

4) **Adaptability competencies** (change management):
   These competencies include the following sub-components that govern our ability to manage change, by realistically and flexibly coping with the immediate situation and effectively solving problems as they arise:
   • **Reality-testing (RT):** The ability to validate our feelings and thinking with external reality, and to keep things in their correct perspective.
   • **Flexibility (FL):** The ability to cope with and adapt to change in our daily life.
   • **Problem-solving (PS):** The ability to generate effective solutions to problems of a personal and social nature.

5) **General mood** (self-motivation):
   General mood is a facilitator of emotionally and socially intelligent behavior and includes the following sub-components that govern our ability to generate positive effect, be optimistic and sufficiently self-motivated to set and pursue our goals:
   • **Optimism (OP):** The ability to have a positive outlook and look at the brighter side of life.
   • **Happiness (HA):** The ability to feel content with ourselves, others and life in general.

Source: adapted from *Bar-On EQ-i Technical Manual* and Ei World Workshop Materials, Advanced EQ-i® Workshop Materials May 2007.

Development of the EQ-i® by Dr Reuven Bar-On, clinical psychologist

- Development of a theory of human effectiveness (1980).
- Construction of an inventory to examine the theory (1983).
- Data collection and validation across cultures (from 1984).
- Translated into more than 30 languages (from 1985).
- The first Emotional Intelligence measure to be published by a psychological test publisher (1997).

- The first and only Emotional Intelligence assessment referred to in a US Congressional Report (1998).
- The first Emotional Intelligence measure to be reviewed (in 1999) in the *Mental Measurement Yearbook* (MMY, an annual book of peer-reviewed psychometric tests published by the Burros Institute).
- The most widely used Emotional Intelligence measure – the EQ-i® passed the 1,000,000 mark worldwide in the first five years after its publication in 1997.

In recent times, a few Emotional Intelligence tools have met international standards of validity and reliability for psychometric tests and been featured in the Mental Measurement Yearbooks (see Geisinger et al., 2007). At the time of writing, three Emotional Intelligence measures have met this 'gold standard' for psychometric tests.

Three ways to measure Emotional Intelligence have been noted: (1) self-report, (2) 360-degree (or multi-rater) assessment, and, (3) an ability test. Norms have been created in various cultures where these assessment tools have been used. It is likely that Emotional Intelligence tools have the potential now to measure 'national' culture even though this is not the primary application for Emotional Intelligence tools in the world today. Work is needed to bring the disparate studies on culture and Emotional Intelligence from a variety of universities and academic institutions to a world stage. More research is needed and this chapter is designed to point towards future areas of enquiry.

In the paper 'EQ and the Bottom Line', Bharwaney, Bar-On and MacKinlay (2007) summarized research from a variety of contexts on the role of Emotional Intelligence for business success. A variety of key research questions have already been posed within the Emotional Intelligence field – such as,

- Does Emotional Intelligence matter?
- If it does, how much does it matter? and,
- How does Emotional Intelligence link with success?

Most of the answers have been affirmative, pointing to the importance of this construct. For example, a number of writers have reported the links between Emotional Intelligence and leadership performance (Bharwaney 2005).

While test publishers have been busy translating their tools into a variety of languages, and while we can theoretically propose the use of Emotional Intelligence frameworks for international coaching as the acceptance of evidence-based coaching grows, there is a big gap in the literature. Our coaching practices using Emotional Intelligence tools in an international arena suggest that national culture, and culture generally, can have subtle yet sometimes strong influences on a client's emotional intelligence in organizational contexts. As with any psychometric tool, the challenge when working across cultures is to be mindful of the possible influence of culture while at the same time avoiding making stereotypical assumptions based on cultural background. Some of the differences we found from the limited samples with which we worked are noted in the following paragraphs. The point of listing them is not to suggest that these differences somehow represent a cultural norm, but to highlight that coaches working across cultures need to be constantly vigilant about what is happening in each context. In our work, we found, for example, that Australians were more 'independent' compared with their British peers; Germans tended to have higher 'reality testing' compared with their Finnish peers. We noticed that the Spanish Managers tended to score lower than others on 'reality testing' but were, nonetheless, highly effective managers compared with their western European peers with higher 'reality testing'. This might (or might not) have been because of their generally greater strengths in the 'interpersonal' arena (see Table 6.1 for descriptions of these components of the EQ-i®). We observed that the Indian managers tended to have lower 'independence' (this was also found in the original data collection for the EQ-i®, see Bar-On 2005). Swedish managers tended to have much lower levels of 'optimism' but not lower levels of 'happiness'. Cultural differences of various kinds, revealed by Emotional Intelligence assessments, can provide coaches with useful insights – provided that findings in one context are not used as predictors of behavior or assumptions for coaching in other contexts.

The second author has found some interesting and contrasting characteristics among Germans, Finns and Australians, the three dominant national cultures in his company. As an HR manager, Jokilaakso has used his experiences as an internal coach (especially with the employment of Emotional Intelligence), to increase the value he adds to his company. His early work as an HR professional involved purchasing external coaching services. Today he is an HR person trained in tools and involved in assessments, feedback, training and coaching within the company such that he adds value and is a major influencer of innovative people development processes. The use of Emotional Intelligence tools has been an important feature of this work over the last six years. As an HR professional, he is in frequent contact with managers around the company. He has grown to know some managers very well, for example through their participation in internal training programs over the years. As his own background is in the heart of a highly technical business (as a manager in product development and process engineering), he understands the work and challenges that managers in his company face on a daily basis. As part of his desire to serve them better, he became equipped to administer Emotional Intelligence assessments and give feedback (using the Bar-On EQ-i®). Today, he works as an internal coach, and identifies coaching needs and solutions for managers and leaders. His experience is that people are very similar in every country, when it comes to their very basic individual values and Emotional Intelligence skills. However, having an eye to culture can provide opportunities for coaches to add further value to their work.

Global business requires certain characteristic Emotional Intelligence skills. In fact, the authors have found these to be more important than cultural differences. For example, successful senior managers from Finland, Germany and Australia have something in common. Their *Independence, Assertiveness* and *Reality Testing* are very high, and *Emotional Self-awareness* is relatively lower. In other words, they are typically self-reliant, self-expressive and practical yet somewhat tuned out of their own emotions. They may be on 'auto pilot' as they go about their daily work, almost routinely coping with everything that comes up but with little emotional engagement with what they are doing. Surprisingly, middle managers from South America in this company seem to have a similar combination of strengths and weaknesses. When this is combined with lower interpersonal scores, for example, there can be challenges in collaborative projects, and careful planning is needed before communicating about such projects with these managers. There is a big difference if, instead, the *Interpersonal* cluster is high. This is an example of the 'working culture' that is depicted in Figure 6.1 and is part of what an Emotional Intelligence assessment can provide, thus equipping an international business coach with insights beyond those that can be gleaned from a productive conversation. This will be illustrated in the next section with the help of case studies.

Using Emotional Intelligence as a coaching methodology in an international business context

In this section, three coaching case studies are used to illustrate how Emotional Intelligence insights from Emotional Intelligence assessments can be useful in coaching in an international business context. Each case study is drawn from a multicultural context and within the section that follows the introduction to each case study, we include the actual Emotional Intelligence profile of the person and a brief description of the expressed need, the real need based on the client's own 'culture' as measured by Emotional Intelligence, the 'working culture' of the team or organization which influences the territory of change that the coach is working in (including the ideal format of coaching help), the challenges in coaching this particular person and some possible solutions and strategies.

In presenting these case studies there are three key assumptions to keep in mind:

1 There is a real business need that is being addressed through an Emotional Intelligence coaching intervention;
2 There is senior sponsorship (without this, the impact of the coaching will be limited); and
3 Emotional Intelligence is understood by the client as a serious weighty leadership topic (i.e., there has been some prior communication or information provided to the client which has resulted in a commitment to start the coaching based on *a solid understanding of the value of Emotional Intelligence as a component in leadership development*).

There are various frameworks and tools for assessing Emotional Intelligence and these can be used to better understand the client's own culture. This chapter is not going to regurgitate details that can be found on test publishers' websites. Instead, through the use of four case studies, we explain how an Emotional Intelligence tool can be used for tackling three specific behaviors that are difficult to coach. Each case study is presented together with the actual Emotional Intelligence data, the way in which the coaching proceeded, and the style of feedback that worked for the client. The studies are as follows:

1 A hard-of-hearing leader – a leader who repeatedly did not hear feedback;
2 A very quiet and introverted middle manager;
3 A highly task-orientated senior manager who has interpersonal challenges; and
4 A leader whose career has stuck.

CASE STUDY 1: HARD-OF-HEARING LEADER – A LEADER WHO REPEATEDLY DID NOT HEAR FEEDBACK

Situation

This leader is highly intelligent and quick in his area of technical specialization. He is suffering from a very high workload (he does everything himself, as he regards others as slow and inept) and frustration results, because people around him do not listen to the solutions to daily problems that he regularly offers. Many of his meetings are unproductive as he is speaking most of the time in monologue. Following this leader's failure in being accepted for a senior leadership development program, he was offered an opportunity to complete an

Emotional Intelligence test (the online Bar-On EQ-i®) as the first step in a coaching intervention. The profile is in Figure 6.2.

Own culture

Most striking in the profile is the pair of EQ components – relatively high *Assertiveness* coupled with relatively lower *Flexibility* alongside relatively low *Interpersonal* skills. In other words, he is someone who is able to express what he thinks but will have his own way of doing things and may not unduly care about what others think or feel ('It's my way or the highway . . .!'). His 'winning formula' (or combination of key strengths) is *Assertiveness, Stress Tolerance, Reality Testing,* and *Impulse Control.* In other words, he is extremely convincing in his area of expertise, resilient and strong. He seems to keep everything in strict and neat order in both his professional and personal life. The Overall Health cluster (a combination of four scores which describe the individual's current state of emotional well-being – *Self-Regard, Self-Actualization, Optimism* and *Happiness*) indicates effective functioning as they are all in the middle band of scores known as 'effective functioning'.

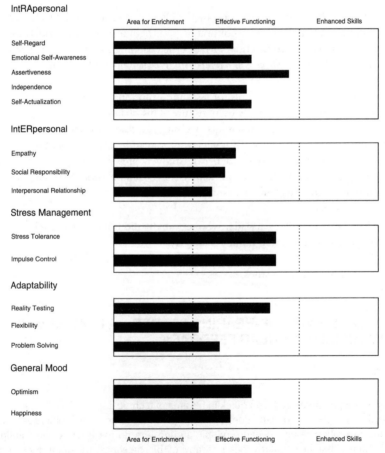

Figure 6.2 Case study 1 – extract from EQ-i® Report

Source: Sub-scales of the EQ-i, using data from the BarOn EQ-i®, copyright MHS

Working culture

This is assessed by looking at *radars* (the combination of *Emotional Self-Awareness* (an internal radar), combined with *Empathy* (a social radar) and *Reality Testing* (an external radar). An effective person needs all three to be effective in working with others). This leader is more tuned into the reality around him (*Reality Testing* – i.e., external radar) than how he is relating to himself and his inner world (*Emotional Self Awareness* – i.e., internal radar) or his reading of other people (*Empathy* – i.e., social radar). This way of working combined with high *Assertiveness* drives him gradually to stalemate, because he tries to put the world in order, and when this does not succeed, he ends up in the behavior described above. His focus is the world outside him, and he is rather blind to others and his inner self.

Challenges in coaching this person

In the two-hour feedback session with the coach, he did most of the talking. Eventually the coach stopped the session and asked the leader to go away and think about his next steps. The individual's non-acceptance of the results was true to his profile (see the section above under 'Own Culture'). During the subsequent meeting the coach focused on next steps. Again, the individual talked most of the time. The coach asked him: 'Who is doing all the talking now?', and, 'How is this conversation similar to the other conversations you have at work?' He tried to justify why he needed to talk. Eventually he continued with a different coach.

Solutions and strategies for providing coaching and/or feedback to this person

The key here is to notice how the combination of high *Assertiveness* with the three radars indicates a low desire on the part of the client to be coached and strategies need to be thought of at the outset. In this instance, the first coach was not able to find a way through to help the client (the coach's own Emotional Intelligence profile was the complete opposite of the client's). Perhaps with clients with this Emotional Intelligence profile, an effective strategy would be to match their profile – to be highly direct.

The second coach took a direct approach while working through a coaching program for developing personal skills, based on 'practicing values'. The coaching continued over several months. One key value the leader worked on with the coach was happiness (both a value and a component in the EQ-i®). Today, the leader makes a much more balanced contribution; he only takes the floor in meetings when he has something relevant to say. His colleagues are thrilled – his subordinates have more responsibility and can concentrate on their own tasks. He still has high *Assertiveness* and low *Flexibility*, but what is most important is that he is now aware of it and its importance for his effectiveness and success, and has learned to 'work with himself'.

CASE STUDY 2: VERY QUIET AND INTROVERTED MIDDLE MANAGER

Situation

This middle manager has worked in a number of different countries and participated in an internal leadership training program which included EQ-i® assessment.

93

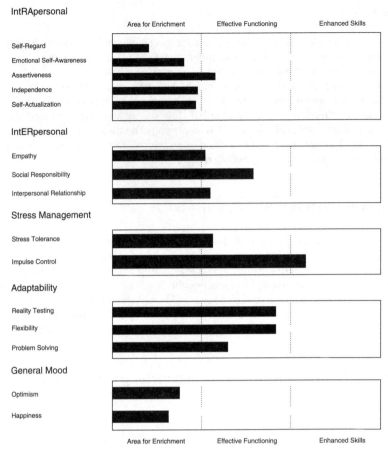

Figure 6.3 Case study 2 – extract from EQ-i® Report

Source: Sub-scales of the EQ-i, using data from the BarOn EQ-i®, copyright MHS

Own culture

His EQ-i® profile revealed a very controlled person with low *Intrapersonal* skills and general mood. His 'winning formula' is *Impulse Control, Reality Testing, Flexibility,* and *Social Responsibility*. This means that he takes time to stop and think, is able to change/adjust when necessary and is pragmatic and persistent. He maintains focus and is persistent, considerate and puts others' needs first, and is helpful and loyal. The Overall Health cluster suggests that his self-confidence needs a boost; he might want more out of his life or may be uncertain of his direction and purpose; he may get depressed from time-to-time.

Working culture

The radars suggest that he is more concerned about the world around him; he is realistic and practical, maintains focus, but he may not trust his own feelings and is not very tuned into how he is feeling nor how others might be feeling. He appears very quiet, calm and a little shy, and also as someone who is not enjoying life too much. This reflects also in his work performance and relatively low self-actualization.

Challenges in coaching this person

The challenge here is how to find a development approach that supports his aspirations and creates energy, and only after that, to find ways to help him improve his *Self Regard*.

Solutions and strategies for providing coaching and/or feedback to this person

During a one-week intensive leadership program the coach suggested that he work on the *Intrapersonal* (self) components as well as *General Mood*; for example, 'Avoid comparing yourself to others, be as forgiving to yourself as you are of others, learn the difference between thoughts and feelings, learn what gives you joy and try and have more of it in your life'. During the first day he created a development plan based on 'practicing values', and started to apply it directly. By the end of the week, the difference was visible: he looked happier, was more determined and more outgoing.

In this case, the Emotional Intelligence and the tool offered an objective way to address those issues that he could focus on in order to make his life more meaningful and enjoyable. He made a personal commitment to spend more time with his daughters, which had an immediate positive effect on his life.

Emotional intelligence can be a language that can be used to highlight where to start work. The Overall Health cluster provides a very elegant way of pinpointing the pain of a client and provides some signposts for the coach to question the client about areas of dissatisfaction. Within this cluster, where low scores appear (in this instance, on *Self-Actualization* and *Self-Regard*), is usually the place to start work with a client. Another suggestion arises from the presence of relatively high *Impulse Control* in a client's EQ-i® profile. This usually indicates that they are able to tolerate their pain for longer without changing anything. It can also be a signal that solutions and development suggestions need to be well reasoned and considered, and the client needs to be given plenty of time to absorb them. These themes can influence the style of coaching that is ideal for this client.

CASE STUDY 3: HIGHLY TASK-ORIENTATED SENIOR MANAGER WHO HAS INTERPERSONAL CHALLENGES

Situation

The person works globally and relies on single conversation impact, has few interpersonal skills and lacks followership. This client is a pace-setting senior manager who is very fast (in an impulsive way) and demands high performance from his colleagues. As a part of the company's management development approach, Emotional Intelligence was introduced to top management. As part of this initiative, the client is offered the possibility to complete the EQ-i® and receive coaching.

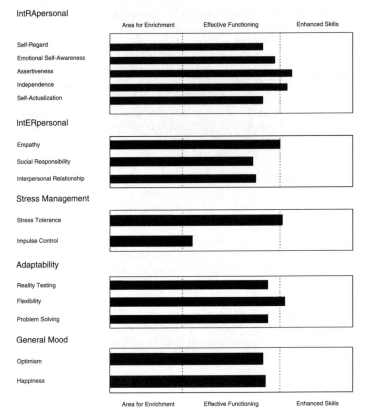

IntRApersonal

| | Area for Enrichment | Effective Functioning | Enhanced Skills |

Self-Regard
Emotional Self-Awareness
Assertiveness
Independence
Self-Actualization

IntERpersonal

Empathy
Social Responsibility
Interpersonal Relationship

Stress Management

Stress Tolerance
Impulse Control

Adaptability

Reality Testing
Flexibility
Problem Solving

General Mood

Optimism
Happiness

| Area for Enrichment | Effective Functioning | Enhanced Skills |

Figure 6.4 Case study 3 – extract from EQ-i® Report

Source: Sub-scales of the EQ-i, using data from the BarOn EQ-i®, copyright MHS

Own culture

This senior business manager has an enhanced EQ-i® profile, but his *Impulse Control* is very low compared to the other EQ components. Also noteworthy are the three high components, namely *Assertiveness, Independence* and *Flexibility*. His 'winning formula' is *Assertiveness, Independence, Flexibility, Stress Tolerance* and *Empathy*. This suggests someone who is strong, supple, resilient, and can read emotions in others. The Overall Health cluster is fine and the radars suggest a person who is equally tuned in to the outside world, others around him and his inner self.

Working culture

His low *Impulse Control* (compared with other components) results in impulsive behavior. He jumps into everything, changes his opinion according to the situation or the most recent person in front of him (through his high *Empathy*) and displays frustrated body language in discussions if he disagrees or has to wait his turn. He sees threats, not opportunities, in his daily life (even though his *Optimism* is high). He is very fast and demands the same from others, but takes control very quickly. This appears as micromanaging in many situations, for example resulting in excessive travel to due to over-involvement in local issues around the globe.

Challenges in coaching this person

This kind of a person is difficult to coach, because the two components in the *Intrapersonal* area (*Assertiveness* and *Independence*) are so dominating. He does his own thing and does not have patience to listen to anyone who suggests another way. In an international business context, this appears as 'cooperation' in issues that are aligned with his ideas and that benefit his business, and as 'resistance' or 'disagreement' on issues that would mean changes or inconvenience to him or his business. It took a long while for the coach to encourage this individual to take up a development focus. The real challenge with this profile, especially very high *Assertiveness* and *Reality Testing*, is how to convince the client that the Emotional Intelligence framework has scientific and organizational validity and can be used as a basis for development.

Solutions and strategies for providing coaching and/or feedback to this person

Low *Impulse Control* has challenges as the individual makes decisions quickly. For example, they may have already made a decision about whether or not to be involved in follow-up coaching. In these instances, it is very useful to have up to four development options already lined up (and not restrict the options to executive coaching) and to provide prompt follow-up within hours or days of the initial session. Additionally, as he holds in high regard those he considers more 'powerful', the coach may suggest the support of a more senior executive in the company who is respected by the client and who could act as a mentor or sponsor. Also, any benchmark results or examples of successful development programs from other companies that he respects would be beneficial.

CASE STUDY 4: SENIOR LEADER WHOSE CAREER HAS STUCK

Situation

As a part of a management review process, business area management team members completed their EQ-is®. One of the leaders is a highly intelligent female who has global responsibility for her area. She was stuck in her current position, which was not satisfying and she did not have enough influence in her area. Also, she was not able to identify how she would like to change her situation.

Own culture

The EQ-i® profile indicates a comparatively low *Intrapersonal* area, especially *Assertiveness* and *Independence*, which may be contributing to the client's difficulties. We can see the possible consequences of the situation she is in: low *Optimism* and *Self-Actualization*. The client might be reticent to speak up yet at the same time may be somewhat down in her mood and feeling, and somewhat disengaged from what she is doing. Her 'winning formula'

97

Figure 6.5 Case study 4 – extract from EQ-i® Report

Source: Sub-scales of the EQ-i, using data from the BarOn EQ-i®, copyright MHS

is *Empathy, Social Responsibility* and *Problem Solving*, which shows in her actions. She is good at identifying how to help others and as a leader is well liked by team members.

Working culture

The Overall Health cluster shows up a central problem in her daily life: low *Optimism* and comparatively low *Self-Actualization* and *Happiness* point towards the fact that she is not happy with her current situation at work. Considering the radars, she is a very focused and tuned-in person (*Reality Testing*), but more focused on others (*Empathy*) than on herself (*Emotional Self-Awareness*). She is a very pleasant person to work with, because she can be trusted and will offer help and support (*Empathy, Social Responsibility* and *Impulse Control*). She understands and takes into account how others feel in a dignified or cultivated way, she is very responsible and accountable person who takes care of quality and goals, and acts in a considerate way. Her profile reveals some of the costs to her of being this way: She is the person who makes sure that those things that 'somebody should do' are taken care of. Some others may feel that she is the self-appointed 'office policewoman'!

Challenges in coaching this person

It was clear that she would benefit from being coached, and she was happy to take up this development opportunity. The agreed theme of coaching was career development, but the coach and the client experienced some difficulties defining and clarifying exactly what she wanted to do. This was partly due to her low *Flexibility*, low *Optimism* and comparatively low *Emotional Self-Awareness* together with low *Stress Tolerance*. On the basis of the profile, it appears likely that the client (1) cannot easily see how to change, (2) doubts her own ability to change, (3) and is somewhat on 'auto pilot' – tuned out of her own emotions yet feeling the knocks of the stress in her daily life. (This latter observation sounds like a contradiction but is common in senior leadership EQ-i® profiles.)

Solutions and strategies for providing coaching and/or feedback to this person

As *Problem Solving* and *Social Responsibility* are her strengths, the solution was to work systematically with as much information as possible, including other test results indicating her personality type and learning style. The aligned strategy was to encourage her towards an understanding of how she could best benefit the organization (*Social Responsibility*). It was important for her to figure out the solutions so this leader needed especially to be coached with 'intelligent' questions. One such question was, 'Which of these relatively higher EQ scores and relatively lower EQ scores has the greatest cost to you?' The end result was excellent; she defined her new responsibilities and organizational strategy; she found her own goals and direction. A follow-up assessment was being arranged later in the year.

SECTION 3: CONCLUSION

An international business coach cannot always spare the luxury of spending four to five hours getting to know a new client. Assessment and measurement are valuable strings to the bow of an insightful coach. Emotional Intelligence is an intelligence that has a bearing on the effectiveness of coaching as the client's own culture may influence outcomes. An Emotional Intelligence assessment helps a coach to know the territory of a person's functioning and can make the job of coaching much easier and less open to the unknown. Coaching based on Emotional Intelligence may be a useful part of the coaching toolkit for coaches who work in international business contexts.

When embarking on a new coaching program, the use of data makes the coaching more specific and targeted to needs. The use of Emotional Intelligence is consistent with Milton Bennett's (1998) advocacy of a 'platinum rule' of empathy rather than just the 'golden rule' of sympathy. That is, instead of coaches treating a client *as the coach would wish to be treated if placed in the same situation*, the use of Emotional Intelligence assessment involves the coach using imagination and empathy to treat each client *as the client would wish to be treated, if he or she was in the driving seat of the decision*.

This chapter has explored the opportunities and challenges for coaches using Emotional Intelligence tools and frameworks in an international business environment. Some implications for practice have been highlighted. Emotional intelligence is perhaps useful for peeling the layers of culture, starting with a person's 'own culture', examining their 'working culture' and ultimately where possible their national culture – and how all of these relate. Emotional

Intelligence development as a subset of coaching can provide coaches with tools applicable in a cross-cultural context for increasing self-awareness and promoting greater personal clarity. Emotional intelligence tools and constructs are valuable in achieving client progress more rapidly and are consistent with business pressures in the global business arena today.

This challenging business context of the case studies is a useful testing ground for the use of Emotional Intelligence in coaching. The coaching stories shared in this chapter are of engineers from diverse backgrounds in organizational and industry cultures that are not natural locations for 'high empathy' coaching. Most are people with high *Reality Testing* – they are scientists who need to be convinced by hard facts before accepting that their behavior should and could be changed. This is not untypical of international business executives more generally who operate in fast-paced, difficult situations and are required to get results. With the engineers, the challenge for the coach in working with Emotional Intelligence was to have the relevant facts and arguments right and ready; to earn their clients' respect with intelligence and knowledge. Once trust and respect was established, they listened to the coach. They were polite and cooperative, but even so there was no commitment to action without associated evidence that change would bring better outcomes.

High-performance international organizations will generally want to calculate the return of investment (time or money) of any planned external intervention such as coaching. When coaching from an Emotional Intelligence framework, this has its own challenges – there are so many variables at play in the development of clients. We generally recommend the use of a rigorous Emotional Intelligence test which can provide strong and convincing data: 'the evidence' – along with comprehensive feedback and a structured coaching approach. A coaching approach based on a scientifically proven method/test puts more emphasis on the robustness of the test and the skill of the coach. That said, evidence comes in different forms – not only through quantitative data. The nature of convincing and useful evidence is determined by the context. Coaching that involves Emotional Intelligence concepts in cross-cultural situations may be just as (or even more) powerful without test data. The very act of 'testing' in some cultural and business contexts may derail learning processes. A further challenge is that many executives are both time-poor and over-evaluated. It may be that the client is better served by the introduction of Emotional Intelligence concepts through dialogue rather than quantitative data. The coach's challenge is to gauge the context and the culture before determining an appropriate coaching program.

Done well, coaching based on Emotional Intelligence has the potential to appeal to a highly discerning group of customers in the international business context because it can 'get under the skin' of organizational culture. Emotional Intelligence may provide the framework for coaches to develop the 'thinking', 'motivational' and 'behavioral' components that make up 'Cultural Intelligence' (Earley, Ang and Tan 2006):

1   The thinking component is *understanding* the value of Emotional Intelligence in coaching and *in theory* knowing how to appropriately apply it in different contexts;
2   The motivational is *wanting to* use Emotional Intelligence; and
3   The behavioral is *being able to* conduct high impact and culturally/contextually appropriate coaching programs.

This chapter has touched on all three components. We invite coaches to reflect on their own practice and ask themselves the question: 'to what extent can I work with Emotional Intelligence with my clients on *their* terms and in *their* territory and in *their* interests?' Executives can ask themselves a similar question: 'to what extent am I and my organization utilizing Emotional

Intelligence potential to advance individual and collective interests?' These are challenges around the implementation of Emotional Intelligence in coaching in international business contexts. However, working with evidence and structure – and their high Emotional and Cultural Intelligences – coaches can work at deep levels and with high impact in the most demanding, volatile, and diverse of organizational contexts.

Bibliography

Bar-On, R. (2005) Bar-On EQ-i® *Technical Manual*, Toronto: Multi-Health Systems.

Bennett, M.J. (1998) *Basic Concepts of Intercultural Communication*, Maine: Intercultural Press.

Bharwaney, G. (2007) 'Coaching executives to enhance Emotional Intelligence and increase productivity', in R. Bar-On, J. G. Maree and M. J. Elias (eds), *Educating People to be Emotionally Intelligent*, Johannesburg: Heinemann Educational Publishers.

Bharwaney, G. (2008) 'Notes on Culture from Ei World's recent interventions based on Emotional Intelligence', unpublished.

Bharwaney, G. (2005) 'Health, Emotional Intelligence and schools leadership: A study of Boarding Schools Association heads', unpublished dissertation, City University, London.

Bharwaney, G. (2008, in press) 'Developing high achievers through Emotional Intelligence: More intelligent than emotional', in M. Hughes, J. Terrell and D. Thompson (eds), *The Handbook of Developing Emotional and Social Intelligence: Best Practices, Case Studies & Tools*, San Francisco: Jossey-Bass.

Bharwaney, G., Bar-On, R. and MacKinlay, A. (2007) 'EQ and the bottom line', Pamphlet, Unpublished, 1 June 2007.

Earley, P.C., Ang, S. and Tan, J.S. (2006) *CQ: Developing Cultural Intelligence at Work*, Stanford: Stanford Business Books.

Ei Consortium (2003) *Technical Paper on Training Guidelines*. Available online at <http://www.eiconsortium.org/reports/guidelines.html> (accessed 21 April 2008).

Geisinger, K.F., Spies, R.A., Carlson, J.F. and Plake, B.S. (2007) *The Seventeenth Mental Measurements Yearbook*, Lincoln: Burros Institute of Mental Measurements. Available online at <http://www.unl.edu/buros> (accessed 21 April 2008).

Greene, J. and Grant, A. M. (2003) *Solution-Focused Coaching: Managing People in a Complex World*, Harlow: Pearson Education.

7

COACHING INTERNATIONAL LEADERS TO SUCCEED COLLECTIVELY

The re-genesis of collective intelligence, our genuine capacity for collectively creating our future

Sabine K. Henrichfreise

What if by acceding only to our collective intelligence can we create a desirable future? What if through only meaningful conversations can we creatively discover new emergent possibilities? What if through only collective leading can we create and implement the necessary variety of actions we need to cope with the diversity of challenges we face? These questions emerge as some of the challenging features of today's world of business coaching. Individual solutions, even if brilliant, seem no longer sufficient to cope with today's complex business environment. Instead, we could make the 'law of requisite variety' one of our guiding principles of innovation and intervention. In 1956 Ross Ashby stipulated, 'when the variety or complexity of the environment exceeds the capacity of a system (like an organization) to create the corresponding variety of answers, the environment will dominate and ultimately destroy that system' (Ashby 1956: 202). Hence it follows that an organization or a group without requisite variety will fail whenever it encounters the unexpected and . . . die. We get a glimpse of the application of this law in business when leaders operate with a limited set of individual success strategies thus being unable to succeed within a different cultural environment or when they use previously fruitful 'business solutions' to manage today's complex collective challenges. In order to help our clients to create that requisite variety of answers they need, we need to develop their 'collective intelligence'.

THE SCOPE OF QUESTIONS

In order to set a frame for appreciative investigation on collective intelligence in the business environment, there is a first set of four crucial questions:

1 What is the business context generating the need for promoting collective intelligence?
2 How can we define collective intelligence?
3 How can we nurture the emergence of collective intelligence?

4   What do we have to change in the way we coach?

What is the business context generating the need for promoting collective intelligence?

The origin of the word 'intelligence' is its Latin expression 'intellegere', combining 'inter' (between), and 'legere' (choose, cueillir) or 'ligare' (link), hence suggesting the capacity of connecting elements which without connection would remain separated. Intelligence is hence connected to the notion of 'space between the elements'. For a long time researchers focused on how this phenomenon of intelligence emerges within individuals. The scientific community ended up in creating the concept of individual multiple intelligences (Gardner 1993/ 2006). The business world has since been deeply connected to this idea. Executive coaches are regularly invited to help clients to develop their various intelligences – emotional, relational, intuitive, creative, moral, spiritual, cultural, situational, and so on. Leadership seminars promote this individual approach when focusing on how to develop individual capacities and intelligences. However, negative consequences are emerging from this mainstream focus on individual performance. These include e-mail overload, burn out, taskforces that go nowhere, pointless meetings, never-ending decision-making processes, too much data, not enough focused information, frustration of not getting the knowledge people need because of organizational walls and silos.

There is a general feeling that an enormous amount of the energy that leaders and organizational followers put into the system is wasted. Additionally, we can observe an increasing number of 'relationship autistics' in the business world who get promoted as 'single champions of ideas' but are desperately searching for some meaningful food for their 'empty soul' (Aburdene 2005: 66, 115; Ridderstrale and Nordström 2008: xxi). It may be that the business world has over-valued individual excellence while neglecting the need for collective intelligence. Maybe today there are too many leaders who are successful individually but collectively approaching the edge of failure because they have not learnt to leverage their intelligences together (Bryan, Joyce and Claudia 2007: 24). Advanced business leaders, coaches and researchers therefore decided to open the gateway for making collective behavior and collective intelligence an emerging field for exploring new ways of leading, learning and operating (Surowiecki 2004; Noubel 2004/2006; Lovelock 1990; Scharmer 2007).

In parallel, today's business world is an interconnected economy – people are always connected, the web will answer their queries and colleagues are just 'a few clicks away' (Ganascia 2007; Bloch and Whiteley 2007). A new generation of connective technologies invites people to participate in collective projects such as Second Life, Google, Wikipedia, Facebook, MySpace, etc. The common and underlying pattern of success of these connective experiences via internet/technology seems to be a sort of enhanced collaborative work where people agree to combine their so-called 'tacit' or 'intangible' assets such as knowledge, relationships and reputation in order to collectively create innovative applications and products (Linux).

An English futurologist therefore promoted during a conference the idea of 'overwhelming artificial connection being the next state in humanity' (Ray Hammond 2007). We may disagree with that impression, that the destination of our humanity and the business world is to become a cyber brain, a worldwide-connected knowledge machine or a fully intertwined computer. Nevertheless, this new technological field of space and possibility generates a specific type of 'collective intelligence' which connects people beyond boundaries, space, beliefs, cultures and time. Since technology and humanity are deeply interconnected (Scharmer 2007; Capra 2004) we have to leverage both, the technology and the human web, in order to help our clients in creating a different future.

Finally, leaders of global organizations face new levels of complexity and disruptive change. Monolithic corporations are replaced by a complex network of alliances, such as joint ventures, outsourcing relationships, and global sourcing partnerships. Leaders have to find innovative ways to direct multicultural, multi-continent and multifunctional teams across organizational boundaries to create the necessary variety of responses they need in reaction to the new era of complexity. They have to deal with the dilemma generated by their desire for structural leanness and the need for high levels of commitment, the desire for a flat hierarchy and the reality of impermanent project teams (see Scharmer 2007: 59; Capra 2004: 121).

Complexity and unpredictable challenges make it impossible for even the most self-directed, brilliant modern business leader to individually lead a global acting organization. Some of them start to recognize that the experiences and solutions of the past do not necessarily help when dealing with these emergent challenges of today and tomorrow. But knowing what does not work anymore does not necessarily mean that people ask for new perspectives and different solutions. However, Ilya Prigogine, winner of the Nobel Prize in 1977, proposed a different model when demonstrating that any open system – such as an organization – has the capacity to respond to change and disorder by reorganizing itself at a higher level of organization (Prigogine and Stengers 1984; Stacey 2005). There is a caveat. The elements of the system must have the freedom to take initiatives and develop the ability to create a repertoire of responses that can match or exceed the number of different stimuli it may encounter in its environment.

In order to create this repertoire of responses, we need to promote and strengthen the capacity of business leaders to think, learn and create their future collectively without exactly knowing what the future will be.

How can we define collective intelligence?

When investigating the idea of collective intelligence within international teams and multicultural organizations, there is a surprising variety of answers and controversial understandings. Whereas leaders are supposed to be driven by individual motivation, personal intention, bonuses, vision and clear objectives, they regularly mention collective experiences as their most important business experience with comments such as, 'Only as a team were we able to challenge our company's culture balance patterns', 'Because we were deeply linked by a shared intention, we were capable of overcoming the strong resistance we faced', and 'Individually I was lost, collectively we were able to make sense of it'.

It also becomes clear, when working with multicultural teams, that some cultures are more driven by collective success and collaborative efficiency (Northern Europe, Japan) whereas other communities are striving for individual excellence and inspiring competition (France, Italy, US) (see Trompenaars and Hampden-Turner 2004; Théry 2002). Most Asians seem at ease with thinking collectively, while Western cultures prize and practice individual thinking (Lewis, 2007: 137). Most Anglo-Saxon management books focus on individual success and personal development strategies. You find less on how to generate and develop collective intelligence and collective leading, at least in the western part of the globe.

Additionally, the meaning of collective intelligence varies from one person to the other. Some business people use the idea of collective intelligence to 'uplift' standard concepts of teamwork, brainstorming and project management. Some replace 'team spirit' with collective intelligence; others consider that having organized an effective meeting is the result of collective intelligence. Again others associate it with the way people connect and create through the web. For some experts collective intelligence and knowledge management mean more or less the same or are at least deeply connected (Zara 2005).

But we also might listen to people who argue that collective intelligence motivates people to freely interact with everyone else in the company, to choose their working associations based on the nature of the work that needs to be done, to combine their knowledge, networks and approaches in order to create new responses which one person alone never could imagine. We also might agree with the statement of one top executive who closed a recent team brainstorming session (which I was facilitating) with, 'In the beginning of humanity there was collective intelligence . . ., our genuine capacity of collectively creating our future. We have probably lost it during our human evolution and we now are looking to rediscover its genius again.'

A common definition of creative collective intelligence is missing. Olivier Zara (2005: 13) defines collective intelligence as the capacity of an organization or group to (1) ask itself the right question and (2) find – collectively – the appropriate answer(s). François Noubel (2004/ 2006: 2) defines it as 'the capacity of a group of people to collaborate in order to formulate their future and to realize it within a complex context'. Others speak about enhanced collaboration enabling people to create wealth through a twenty-first-century organization (Bryan, Joyce and Claudia 2007).

When working with global organizations and international leaders, I discovered the 'triple point' of collective intelligence. In physics and chemistry, the triple point of a substance is the *temperature* and *pressure* at which three states (*gas, liquid*, and *solid*) of that substance may coexist in *thermodynamic equilibrium*. Applied to the notion of collective intelligence, the three states that coexist are collective intelligence as an experience, a mindset and a whole interconnected process of emergence. To generate collective intelligence, people have to engage in a process of transformational conversations and meaningful experience where they can connect information, knowledge and experience in creative ways (Cholle 2007; Stacey 2005; Naisbitt 2006). This process of connecting people 'fills the space between them' and generates different fields of connectivity, energy and exchange which I term 'collective fields'. These collective fields influence people's experience of collective intelligence which I define as the 'genuine capacity of a group to think, learn and create collectively'. In order to transfer the 'creative outcome' of this experience into daily business life, collective intelligence needs a vehicle which I term 'collective leading'. Finally, we need to invent an organizational design and a new set of indicators which nurture the need to create relationships and promote collective intelligence. This overall process can be visually summarized as in the figure below and it goes in both ways (Figure 7.1).

Applied to the business context in which international leaders operate and global organizations thrive, the whole process of collective intelligence could be summarized as 'the creative process of connecting people enabling them to generate fields of interpersonal connectedness, energy and exchange where they experience their genuine capacity to collectively think, learn, and create their future'. Collective intelligence under this perspective means both a re-genesis of our genuine capacity to create together and a significant shift of collective attention. Instead of focusing only on exchanging content and checking whether results are produced, people learn to focus their attention on their process of relating, to identify from which source they operate (past or future) and to listen to what the future calls them to do. It is the leap from collectively leveraging individual intelligences to collective thinking, learning and creating. It is the tipping point where a group accepts the risk of entering the field of the unknown where control is replaced by guidance, expertise by tacit knowledge and evidence of the known by emergence of the new.

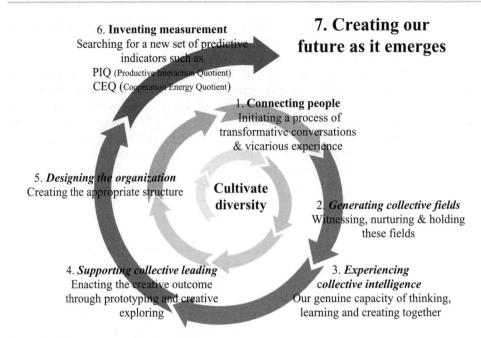

Figure 7.1 The process of collective intelligence

How can we nurture the emergence of collective intelligence?

Promoting diversity

For collective intelligence to emerge, the first ingredient we have to promote is diversity, defined as a mixture of differences, similarities and tensions (Sepheri and Wagner 2002: 123; Thomas 1996: 5). Working with others who are different from us and doing so in creative ways is a key element for requisite variety and hence a key ingredient for future collective success. However, individual differences and contradictions in collective cultural patterns turn out to be a major source for individual frustration, nasty climates of distrust and collective failure, hence preventing teams and organizations from generating meaningful conversations and experiencing collective intelligence (Zohar 1994: 182, 328). To overcome these genuine consequences of diversity, business leaders tend to highlight similarities – 'we all are humans' – and to promote their 'identity creating company culture'. However, in over-emphasizing the collective aspect, diversity can become an undefined soap of similarities with no identity and no genuine force. As Danah Zohar (Zohar and Marshall 1994: 200) puts it, 'the one gives us the Tower of Babel the other a sort of "non inspiring melting pot of individuals" '. In fact we need both to generate collective intelligence – the 'particle' and the 'wave' aspect of diversity (Klein 2004: 113; Wheatley 1999: 66). That is, we need the virtue of individual differences (the particle aspect) and, at the same time, the collective spirit and common understanding (the wave aspect). As in quantum physics, particles and waves coexist as potentialities, so do these two aspects of diversity. It depends on the focus of attention we choose as coaches which of these genuine states of existence collapse into reality at which moment.

Searching for collective intentionality

Collective intentionality or the 'We-Intentionality' represents the second ingredient for collective intelligence to emerge. The etymological sense of the word intention means 'direct attention' (from the Latin 'intendere', to direct attention). Individual intentions shape individual actions but they will not generate collective intentionality and creating. When a team focuses its attention on sensing a possible underlying collective intentionality, team members start a process of conversation and interacting which provides the necessary structure for diversity to express itself through the uniqueness of each group member (Shaw 2002; Isaacs 1999; Zohar and Marshall 1994). Collective intentionality is both the result of a process of meaningful connecting and its beginning. It is more than a collective objective or a shared vision. Instead, it is the process of directing attention on patterns of interaction, common understanding and individual uniqueness.

Mastering the art of conversations

Diversity and collective intentionality are not sufficient for collective intelligence to emerge. In addition, we need a creative process of connecting people and their ideas on a deeper level. The most appropriate process of creative connecting is to promote, nurture and cultivate multiple networks of transformational conversations (Shaw 2002). In its etymological sense conversation means the 'act of living with or keeping company with'. Combined with meaningful vicarious experience, inspiring conversations become the human matrix for creating, transforming and learning. Mastering the art of gathering and holding meaningful conversations is becoming one of the key competences of today's business leaders. Indeed, leaders testify that whenever there is a significant leap in the way their team works together, an organization embraces permanent leaning and change or a highly emotional breakthrough is achieved, it generally flows from their investment of time in initiating and participating in purposeful and transformative conversations. Even so-called individual inventions are often the intermediate result of ongoing conversations (Zeldin 1998: 74).

In summary, a winning formula for collective intelligence to emerge could be as follows:

$$(\text{Diversity} + \text{Collective Intention}) \times (\text{meaningful conversations})$$
$$= \text{Emergence of Collective intelligence}$$
$$\textbf{Or: (D + CInt)} \times \textbf{MC} = \textbf{ECI}$$

What do we have to change in the way we coach?

Choosing our focus

First, we have to accept that the concepts of collective intelligence and collective leading are somehow provocative in today's business environment. Individual leadership, with its inherent limitations, remains the day-to-day activity for many who lead diverse teams and global organizations. The collective form it seems is emerging as a powerful metaphor, and as desire and food for imagination rather than as daily business practice. We therefore have to help our clients to choose a different focus and to look at their organizations with new lenses, to consider their organizations as living systems and 'thinking creatures' and to see the web of relationships as a major underlying pattern of influence and identity (Zohar 1990: 27; Capra 2004: 12; Wheatley 1999: 14; Parikh 1999/2005; Brafman and Beckström 2007).

International business organizations are systems of complex and ever-changing interconnections. People working in these organizations have to create and navigate within these networks of complex human relationships all the time. They do it by phone, video-conference and meetings and they do it within constantly changing groups, alliances and communities. They create official ways of communication and hidden channels of communicating. As coaches we have to encourage meaningful connections and conversations, beyond existing silos, cultures and habits. We have to enable groups of leaders in creating the most innovative organizational design for allowing these conversations to happen. And we can help to enhance people's individual skills to initiate the process of collective intelligence in their business environment. Consequently, our common challenge consists in inventing possibilities for initiating and nurturing creative human interconnections while reducing unproductive interactions such as useless meetings, interface battles and information hiding. By inviting our clients to create innovative predictive indicators such as a dynamic 'productive interaction quotient' (Bryan, Joyce and Claudia 2007: 47) we can help them to invest in both the living and dynamic web of relationships, the value of intangible assets and creative collaborative processes as well as in organizational structure, tangible results and concrete solutions. As Prigogine and Stengers remind us: 'Whatever we call reality, it is revealed to us only through an active construction in which we participate' (1984: 293).

Leveraging dilemmas and emotional fields

Second, when coaching global companies, we have to take into account collective dilemmas. One of these consists of the fact that our elementary human attitudes, needs, ideas, and emotions seem to be the essence of diversity and thus the essence for collective intelligence. And they also are exactly those factors which jeopardize the process of meaningful conversation and creative connecting, thus preventing organizations and their leaders from leveraging their collective intelligence to create their future.

Another collective dilemma emerges when clients experience conflicting emotions during this process of connecting conversations. Sometimes it is enlivening, sometimes deadening, sometimes annoying or anxiety-provoking, and on other occasions just useless. Indeed, the underlying emotional field for collective learning is often that of despair, frustration, irritation, polarization of thoughts and a sense of wasting valuable time. Emotions are contingent and if the collective emotional barometer goes down, we need to create space for these emotions to 'leave the field'. Otherwise a group of people may get stuck in the negative conversation and fall back into habitual discussion patterns. If we can hold and nurture that space and energy field for the necessary time, the team will take the initiative to go beyond it to generate the collective sensitive field where creative chaos becomes possible (Isaacs 1999: 253). There, they can collectively experience collective intelligence, feel what is at stake and sense what the emerging future might be for them.

Being capable of transforming negative fields of emotions, aggressiveness and distrust into positive collective sensitive fields and holding these various sensitive fields for the necessary amount of time without trying to 'fix things' is one of the most important prerequisites to be mastered when coaching the emergence of collective intelligence.

Developing cultural sensitivity

Third, we need to broaden our own cultural sensitivity. Cultural patterns influence individual strategies. Common business words such as 'strategy', 'concept', 'performance', 'efficiency', and so on, carry whole worlds of different meanings depending on context and perspective. We need to be able to leverage cultural patterns, to go beyond our own prejudgments, to integrate stereotypes when working internationally, learning to coach in different languages and in silence. We have to learn how to leverage the underlying field of permanent misunderstandings as the essential 'fuel for meaningful conversations'. We have to feel that cultural intelligence is a key ingredient for creating a sustainable business future.

Re-composing our mindset

To help our clients to leverage collective dynamics, intelligence, intentionality and fields, we need to integrate recent discoveries in science, and challenge our own assumptions. We need to 'unlearn' approaches, concepts, methods we are used to applying. The most important challenge is to let go of our past fruitful strategies of success and to replace them with new questions and an intention to explore the unknown. We have to become masters in creating collective trans-formative conversations, artists in moving a group through different collective fields, and experts in combining individual learning, collective thinking and organizational design. Approaches such as world cafés, open space conferences and collective storytelling (Frenzel 2004, 2006) have to become part of our way of coaching collective intelligence. We have to learn to let go of our obsession for achieving smart objectives in order to open up new possibilities for creating outstanding results. If we start to think that collectively we have access to all the wisdom, variety, agility and resources we need to cope with the variety of challenges we face, we can create new ways to facilitate the emergence of collective intelligence. Hence we can support our clients in exploring new territories of performance and creating innovative agile business cultures.

AN INTERNATIONAL BUSINESS CASE STUDY

The company is in the industrial equipment manufacturing sector. It is has 4,000 employees who are constructing and operating three plants in Europe. In 8 years operations will be expanded and there will be 11,000 employees in 30 plants all over the world. The coaching engagement described below was with a team of 15 people established by the executive management group to create significant breakthroughs in terms of engineering, commercial relationships and financial results. All members were qualified in terms of technical expertise, some of them had managed cross-organizational projects and 10 had international experi-ence. The team was multinational and communicates in English. At the time a coach was engaged, top management was increasing pressure and regularly requesting significant action plans and reports. Individual team members reported in preliminary conversations with the coach that they had never had the opportunity to reflect on the future they were supposed to create, the various fields of resistance and alliances they faced and their strategy of creating breakthrough. They all felt individually competent but they sensed that the sum of their indi-vidual excellences would not be sufficient to make things happen under the current circum-stances. Additionally, their underlying field of emotions was full of 'negative vibes' generated by feelings of frustration, distrust, competition and cultural misunderstandings. The coach's brief was to help the team achieve its objectives through an ongoing process of support.

Conversations to leverage diversity

A first team meeting was organized to articulate a common mission. Instead of facilitating a process of visioning or brainstorming the coach invited all 15 to take part in a process of meaningful inquiring conversations, thus creating the container for creative collective intelligence to emerge. Participants were asked to gather in groups of five and to discuss what their common mission might be. The coach did not give a precise set of rules, understanding that the concept of rules differs from culture to culture. During the first 20 minutes of exchange the group faced the phenomenon of its diversity, which included a strong diversity of opinions concerning their mission. There was competition and conflict over deciding 'the best definition'. Team members reacted to arguments, opinions and ideas like handball goal keepers in a training session desperately trying to protect their goal. Instead of exploring a possible common intention, these 15 individual leaders used this first conversation as an arena for searching out the best scapegoat, trading the best information and point-scoring. Their only focus on listening was a search for 'conclusive evidence' – i.e., they only listened to arguments which confirmed their respective opinions. The whole conversation ended in emotional manipulation, polarized clans, virtual 'cultural slaps' and common frustration. It was a perfect example of a group working from an underlying negative collective field of destructive emotions, also called the 'battle field' (see tool 'The field of fields').

When debriefing the process, members expressed their difficulties in understanding the meaning of what colleagues were saying because of the diversity of backgrounds both in terms of national cultures and of professional disciplines. They worked out that their communicative interaction pattern was formed by power relations, cultural misunderstandings and consequent feelings of inclusion and exclusion. They shared the perception that various degrees of individual internal resignation popped up over time and that a common desire to leverage differences with an intention of creating something collectively was completely missing. One participant summarized the first round of conversation: 'I am impressed by our capacity of maintaining a highly sophisticated battle of arguments fuelled by a nice "I am right you are wrong" mentality'. One participant added, 'Our heads were at work, our hearts were asleep'. When asking them for options to listen differently, they proposed to engage in 'listen for difference and surprise' instead of 'excelling in listen-less listening'.

Misunderstandings are the rule more than the exception

With a new approach agreed, the coach asked every member to define his or her meaning of the word 'mission'. Listening to each definition, the team recognized that this word opened a whole world of differences. They better understood why the earlier attempt to clarify the meaning of the word and to propose a common definition had ended up in confusion and conversational pathways leading to dead-ends. They realized that the English language they used as common business language was working as an open source of misunderstandings rather than a bridge for understanding. During this conversation round, the group experienced 'productive resignation' and accepted that international business contains a significant 'web of culture traps'. However, some evidence of shift in perspective began to emerge. One participant concluded, 'Let's agree to differ', which was the first time that a glimpse of collective intelligence could be sensed: differences and agreement met in a sentence, unity was expressed as diversity. This proposal touched a collective nerve and created spontaneous overall acceptance. The energy changed and participants switched from a mood of 'listening to respond' to an attitude of 'listening to inquire'. In other words they started to collectively suspend their immediate judgments, beliefs and disbeliefs, thus gaining new perspectives. They left the 'battle field' and entered a new collective sensitive field, called the 'Mental field' (see tool 'The field of fields') where respect started to prevail. Constructive confrontation became possible and collective interaction became a learning experience.

In order to deepen this creative process of connecting, participants were asked to identify their major cultural prejudgments as well as their consequences in terms of behavior, intention and collective atmosphere and to exchange in groups of three. They shared the perception, that when working with people of different cultures (and gender) everybody had hidden assumptions influencing individual reactions, relationship patterns and emotions. They recognized that under stress, or when feeling excluded, everyone had a tendency to become prisoners of their own stereotypes, thoughts and emotions. They accepted that there might be a genuine intelligence of each culture, that culture is about collective programming and that each individual represented a part of his or her culture soul.

Invited by the coach to experience more of appreciative cross-cultural communication, team members explored the option of speaking in their own language, expressing their intention without words and sharing different frames of efficiency. As they started to respect each other's opinion and make sense from the various points of view, the level of misunderstandings declined and they started to develop a common language. They were able to collapse the various misunderstandings into a shared field of knowledge and meaning. Words were no longer a hidden invitation for semantic discussions because collectively they now felt and sensed what they really meant in this group and this specific context. They perceived their diversity as a major ingredient for coming closer together and recognized that misunderstandings were the natural fuel for meaningful conversation more than its death. They realized that feeling they were at a 'dead-end' with nowhere to go had provoked a common will to create some new common understanding. One participant concluded that session by expressing the idea that 'to listen in depth we have to operate at the speed of sound rather than at the level of light'. The group was aware of their new emergent capacity of thinking and learning collectively.

Loops of creative conversations, the field of inquiry and emergence of collective intelligence

The second part of the coaching process was designed to re-create a positive collective field and to focus on developing collective intentionality. This part was introduced by a collective exercise, 'called breakthrough exercise' (so called by the French Coaching School, International Mozaik): the group was first asked to get a position on a tablecloth and then invited to invert it without anyone 'leaving' the tablecloth physically. The effective combination of imagination, improvisation and interactivity helped the group to access their collective intelligence on a different, more vicarious level. The debriefing process, organized in dynamic conversation rounds inspired by the World Café philosophy (Brown, Isaacs and the World Café Community 2005), helped participants focus on what was happening between them in terms of communication and dynamics. One person from each table, the host, was asked to observe the creative process of connecting and to share his or her insights with the next table, thus acting like a key pollinator for collective meaning through the whole session.

Entering the field of inquiry

For the next conversation round, participants answered the question: 'What is at stake for the future, which dilemmas do we face and what are the opportunities?' When sharing the outcome, the group noticed that they developed a common sense of what was at stake, such as 'creating our future', 'shaping our market', 'developing a culture of risk', 'turning permanent pressure on results into zones of freedom' and, 'stopping justification and initiating conversation'.

When sharing the answers to the next question: 'What is our added value as a management committee?' they pointed out that 'We have to break the old patterns of this business culture', 'We are pioneers and we challenge the traditional way of doing business' and, 'We are on the edge and we are in a leap of faith'. When expressing their added value as a feeling they mentioned 'Thrill', 'Endurance' and 'Aufbruch-Stimmung' (excitement of departure). The group was surprised to notice that they unconsciously developed a collective intentionality of 'pioneering, breaking the rules and doing things differently' and to share a common field of feelings oscillating between excitement and fear, between thrill and uncertainty.

In the next phase, tables were organized as business and cultural environments. Participants were asked to connect their collective intentionality to their business mission of creating significant business results in a short time and to stretch their collective awareness of organizational dynamics. One participant was to present the mission to another business line, one to Chinese clients, another to the top management committee and another to German partners. When facing the various reactions of resistance and/or alliance, the group became aware of the different fields of influence existing in their company and the need to adapt communication to cultural mindsets. 'From market share to mind share' became their shared slogan. They expressed their mission in pictures, symbols, poems and paintings. They played with the position of cultural exaggeration where the Italian responded as German and the French as American (which by the way cleared up some of the former interpersonal difficulties) so as to really feel their mission in all its facets.

The team experienced a web of relationships and had to juggle a variety of channels of communication. Influenced by the forces of this new collective sensitive field of inquiry, they practiced appreciative listening and inquiry. They explored 'meaningful confrontation' 'productive resignation' and 'choice creating' (Isaacs 1999). One participant summarized his experience this way: 'Our future emerges through our conversations.' Another added, 'Because we change the way to speak to each other we are able to co-create new meaning which then opened the window for new possibilities'. Another stated, 'New ideas emerged through the meeting of our differences'. To finalize, they experienced the field of inquiry and touched the field of emergence (see tool 'The field of fields') where trust and hope prevail, emergence of the new is the rule and energy is dense and focused.

From collective intelligence to collective leading: reframing the notion of leadership

During the next 'conversation day' two weeks later, the group discussed the concept of leadership, its various cultural 'translations' and the consequences of those on their role as a leadership group. They started to think that leadership could be something different from an individual attitude. One group proposed that leadership could be 'the process of leading'. Participants were then invited to experience what was happening when they spoke to the 'center of the table' rather than to each other. This shifted the nature of their conversation again. Through focus on the centre, participants were able to stay in a more impersonal mode, thereby helping them to suspend their personal issues and judgments. When inviting them to listen to what the centre of the table was trying to communicate, rather than arguing with individual proposals or positions, it became easier for this group to embrace the underlying and emergent idea of collective leadership.

One participant initiated the next question: 'What if collective leadership is a new possibility to cope with today's and future challenges?' The consensus was that the current leadership framework was outdated, and not capable of adapting to the dynamic of unforeseen challenges and disruptive changes faced by the group. They agreed that within that context, which included inherent and ongoing changing power balances, no leader alone would be capable to stand up, create a vision, download the vision to the organization and align its key processes. The idea of identifying one strong and/or inspiring individual leader in an environment where there were numerous potential leaders seemed inappropriate. Further, it risked jeopardizing the process of creative connecting and collective intelligence, thus slowing down any process of transformation and freezing their collective intentionality of creating a better future. They developed the idea of creating a different frame of attention by looking at leadership not as a thing, a task, or a capacity but to observe it as a process of leading, a kind of non-linear assembly line of various leadership tasks. They canvassed the idea that a group does always need an established leader to be effective but that at the same time a living system also needs a representative or 'speaker' who expresses the common unconsciousness of the group and launches initiatives. Subsequently, others may take on the role of speaker and follow and propose actions and take the initiative to the next level.

In order to nurture the team's reflection on collective leading, the coach invited people to imagine how they could lead their mission collectively, what they would have to let go, what they would like to do differently and what they would have to do more of. They agreed that for each 'conversation', one team member would take responsibility for carrying the shared decisions and the collective spirit through to the next meeting. Whoever wanted to take a specific initiative was free to act, provided that they shared the detail of the activities during the next conversations. They began to feel that collective leading was more powerful than investing an official 'team leader' with the burden of leadership, thus lessening collective responsibility and possibilities. They started to re-compose their collective patterns.

When the 'virus of collective intelligence' affects the whole system . . .

During the following conversation rounds, the team created their own questions and exchanged on who could help them to make a next step. They worked out small next steps, and decided to explore the 'strategy of creative organizational prototyping' when launching an initiative. They regularly eliminated disturbing 'cultural viruses' (fears, frustrations) and agreed to maintain their 'wisdom circles' and culture of 'meaningful conversations'. They invited 'resistant people' to their conversations and spread the conversation processes and content. They knew that they were pioneers, meaning that they were likely to face strong resistance. But instead of reverting to accepting collective failure, they agreed on leading collectively.

The group discovered that an effective change process starts from within. They experienced that, through the stream of conversations, they were able to integrate different initiatives of the whole business system. However, they also mentioned that the pressure on immediate and visible results was not easy to handle. They shared an impression that some official leaders seemed to feel a certain loss of control over the system and were taking initiatives to stop this new stream of ongoing conversations . . . without success. The collective initiative had developed resilience.

Later the team decided to create conversation circles with clients. They also organized co-development groups to create new solutions in real time through conversation. In this way they managed to create new networks of conversation and to spread their culture of conversation, collective action and effective support. They managed their conversation rounds on a regular basis, sometimes via phone conference. They learned to cultivate their diversity and to avoid its pitfalls. Too rapid consensus was challenged and too much comfort was interpreted as a sign of 'we are not discussing the important things here'. When different technical points of view met, they discussed them through, and agreed on, a collective set of options to maintain agility and the integrity of ideas. Small successes were shared, amplified and spread through the whole system. They consciously searched for opportunities to share learning from 'positive deviance', starkly contrasting with the old 'rule of silence' and conformity.

Witnessing the process of transformation

The coach's role was to hold the group far from equilibrium so that they stayed engaged in this collective process of silent transformation, which no individual was capable of controlling. It was their collective intention and interactions that explored and discovered new realities, behaviors and ideas. In the end, they achieved better-than-expected results, created fruitful relationships with their clients and proposed new organizational designs to the CEO. Without consciously so doing, they created a learning network and a business case for collective intelligence.

AND THE LEARNING IS . . .

The collective approach helped the team to leverage their cultural diversity, to overcome individual resistance from within, and manage individual anxiety and the tendency of 'group think'. One of the real dangers that a connected group can face is that of emphasizing consensus over consent and to exacerbate the human tendency to prefer the illusion of certainty to the reality of doubt, unpredictability and loss of control (Surowiecki 2004: 175; Zohar 1994: 254). The experience illustrated that a diversity of cultures, opinions and approaches is the single best guarantee that a group will avoid group think and instead leverage the sea of possibilities emerging through conversations. The active search for minority standpoints forces a majority group to interrogate its own positions more seriously if the conversation container is safe enough. Searching for cultural dilemmas enables a group to sense what is at stake and to look for new possibilities instead of fighting for a single superior outcome or approach.

All the conversations nurtured collective intelligence and the intention to create shared meaning. They allowed the team members to handle uncertainty, individual anxiety and a feeling of loss of control, and to embrace the possibility of 'no concrete action now'. There was something which allowed this team to continue this process of collective intelligence and to avoid the collapse of their creative potential of diversity into the former habitual pattern of technical discussions and endless argumentation. I suggest, consistent with José Fonseca (2002), that this something was a combination of curiosity, hope and trust: curiosity to experience the next step of the collective process, hope because it represents the necessary energy pioneers need and diffuse when they go forward and trust in the process, trust in the people and trust in their collective intelligence.

AND WHAT ARE THE TOOLS?

The Hidden Angel – exploring the effectiveness of invisible support

The 'Hidden Angel' exercise is a powerful tool to generate new perspectives and encourage collective intelligence. In this exercise, each participant randomly picks another participant to become his or her hidden angel for a certain period of time, i.e., a day. The job of the hidden angel consists in supporting and taking care of his or her protégée without revealing his or her 'hidden angel identity'.

This exercise introduces an interesting context of goodwill, protection and intention. People are inclined to pay more attention to what happens around them, they become more sensitive to synchronicities and are somehow 'forced' to participate in the field of collective protective intelligence. The key factor of success is that nobody knows their hidden angel but will be highly influenced by the fact that they know that there is someone looking out for them.

This exercise generates cross-contextual situations, facilitates debriefing and creates an exceptional taste of supportive and creative relationships. Since our clients are generally more accustomed to competition and survival than to protection and hidden support, this exercise is a great learning experience and can sometimes shift major individual and/or collective assumptions of the nature of support. And it is also interesting to notice that some hidden angels forget to do their job; they sometimes even do not remember at the end of the day who they were supposed to support . . . And the debriefing of this exercise under the cultural perspective often opens new insights since participants discover that each culture has its own myth of protection and support. A different and very interesting exercise that can be used by coaches is collective storytelling, described by Patricia Shaw (2002: 98).

False friends – go for the difference

Main business concepts such as leadership, management, strategy, concepts, efficiency, creativity, performance mean different things to different people in different contexts. Asking a group to identify these words, their various 'cultural translations' and the consequences for the business of different translations is a powerful exercise. In order to make this exercise a breakthrough approach, it is important to invite participants to 'go for the difference' more than for the common understanding, to 'force the gap' more than to close it, to 'hold the diversity' of perspectives instead of fixing it. In the end, people will experience a deeper level of connection where they experience a meeting through their differences. Additionally, participants can be invited to identify their major prejudgments and stereotypes and their respective consequences in terms of individual behavior and collective ambiance. Helping them to transform their prejudgments instead of denying them, to accept them instead of criticizing others turns out to be a powerful way of coaching groups and organizations navigating within an international environment.

The 'white whole' or the 'field of fields'

Creating transformational conversations and meaningful experiences are the starting point for collective emergence. Different conversations are influenced and created by different forms of underlying fields. Fields are spaces in which there is a particular quality of energy and exchange. Each of these fields has a different pattern of collective intelligence (thinking, learning and creating) and outcome. To guide a group from one field to the other requires the opening of gateways, the acceptance that people can be in different fields at the same time and that energy may flow without control and hence influence a group transformation. The invisible underlying field connecting these various fields and energies I term the 'White Whole' – the opposite of a 'Black Hole'. Whereas a Black Hole absorbs all energy and light in the universe, the White Whole represents possibility, contains the future, generates energy and makes emergence possible through creative connecting. The different collective fields are summarized in the following 'field of collective fields' (Figure 7.2).

In order to move through these different fields, participants need to develop at least three different skills, the capacity to:

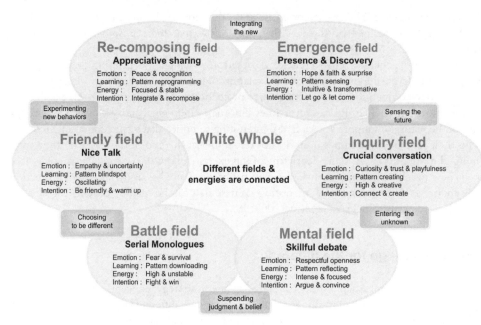

Figure 7.2 The 'White Whole' or the 'field of fields'

1   Suspend judgments, beliefs and disbeliefs;
2   Give up individual control and explore the unknown; and
3   Share at all levels (head, heart and hands).

As coaches, we can assist this skill development and in so doing nurture individual excellence and cultivate collective intelligence. The role of the coach consists of:

- creating the container for collective intelligence to emerge;
- facilitating the combination of vicarious experience and inspiring conversations;
- leveraging the architecture of the invisible (collective fields) and making collective 'un-discussables' (hidden rules and patterns) collectively discussable;
- providing structure and nurturing creative chaos;
- promoting the law or requisite variety and developing cultural sensitivity;
- inventing a different language to facilitate new perspectives; and
- inviting organizational prototyping of actions instead of rolling out detailed and aligned action plans.

CONCLUSION

Most of us are looking – individually and collectively – for meaningful breakthroughs in order to create the answers to the big questions we ask ourselves. Coaching collective intelligence may help us to create both individual and collective answers. However, when we want to promote creative transformational chaos, far from equilibrium states, silent collective transformation and 'suspicious' conversation streams, we have to make fundamental and simultaneous changes in our way of looking at, connecting with and managing our worlds. We have to change the way we look at organizations, our way of connecting and our way of leading. We need to focus on dynamics more than on 'things', we have to decode and leverage the invisible more than managing the visible. We have to give up our desire for control and we have to replace it with our capacity of facilitating emergence and connections. We have to invent a different language, such as the White Whole, Emotional Viruses, Future Fields, Mind Share, etc., to create new empowering perspectives. We have to give up our idea that there is 'me' and 'them' and leverage the creative tension of insiders and outsiders. We have to let go of our obsession for defining objectives and believing in the 'world of measurement' and replace them by communicating meaningful intention and creating space for people to share. Instead of silent individual thinking we have to provoke meaningful sharing; instead of formal synergy groups we have to invite transformational conversation circles; instead of individual leadership we have to inspire collective leading.

If we can help a group of international leaders to oscillate between a protective structure and creative chaos, to understand the dance between emotional fields and collective intelligence and to combine individual commitment and collective leading, they may be able to create a different future. If we succeed in helping a team and an organization to put their 'culture of relationships' and their 'matrix of connection' at their center of observation we may enable them to get access to a whole new world of possibilities, the world where collective intelligence is at work. In the quantum world, relationships are the key determiner of everything. Visible particles come into form and are observed only as they are in relationship to something else. And most importantly, relationships are not things, they are not predictable, they are not fixed in a specific form. Instead they are dynamic, they change their form regularly, and they are always in transition (Wheatley 1999: 11). If this is true for quantum physics and the atomic level, how much should this be true when human beings are involved in meaningful conversations and collective intelligence? It may be one way of creating the possibility of international leaders succeeding together.

Bibliography

Aburdene, P. (2005) *Megatrends 2010*, Charlottesville: Hapton Roads Publishing.

Ashby, W. R. (1956) *An Introduction to Cybernetics*, London: Chapman & Hall.

Bloch, S. and Whiteley, P. (2007) *How to Manage in a Flat World: Get Connected to Your Team – Wherever They Are*, Harlow: Financial Times/Prentice-Hall.

Bohm, D. (1996) *On Dialogue*, London: Routledge.

Brafman, O. and Beckström, R. A. (2007) *Der Seestern und die Spinne, Die beständige Stärke einer kopflosen Organisation*, Weinheim: Wiley-VCH Verlag.

Brown, J., Isaacs, D. and the World Café Community (2005) *The World Café, Shaping Our Future through Conversations that Matter*, San Francisco: Berret-Koehler Publishers Inc.

Bryan, L. L., Joyce, I., and Claudia, I. (2007) *Mobilizing Minds: Creating Wealth from Talent in the 21st Century*, New York: McGraw-Hill.

Capra, F. (2004) *Les connections invisibles*, Paris: Editions du Rocher.

Cholle, F. (2007) *L'intelligence collective*, Paris: Eyrolles.

Fonseca, J. (2002) *Complexity and Innovation in Organizations*, London/New York: Routledge.

Frenzel, K. (2004) *Storytelling*, München/Wien: Hanser.

Frenzel, K. (2006) *Storytelling*, München/Wien: Das Praxisbuch, Hanser.

Ganascia, J-G. (2007) *L'intelligence artificielle*, Paris: Le Cavalier Bleu.

Gardner, H. (1993/2006) *Frames of Mind: Theory of Multiple Intelligences*, New York: Basic Books.

Hammond, R. (2007) *The World in 2030*, Zarautz, Spain: Yago.

Isaacs, W. (1999) *Dialogue and the Art of Thinking Together*, New York: Currency.

Klein, E. (2004) *Petit voyage dans le monde des quanta*, Paris: Flammarion.

Lewis, R. D. (2007) *The Cultural Imperative: Global Trends in the 21st Century*, Boston, MA: Intercultural Press.

Lovelock, J.E. (1990) *La terre est un être vivant, l'hypothèse Gaïa*, Paris: Flammarion.

Naisbitt, J. (2007) *Mind Set! Wie wir die Zukunft Entschlüsseln*, München: Carl Hanser Verlag.

Noubel, F. (2004/2006) *La révolution invisible*, article published in 2004, revised in 2006, PDF File, see also: the transitioner.org *La révolution invisible*, <http://thetransitioner.org>.

French text: 'L'intelligence collective est la capacité d'un groupe de personnes à collaborer pour formuler son propre avenir et y parvenir en contexte complexe in Intelligence Collective'.

Parikh, J. (1999/2005) *Managing Relationships: Making a Life While Making a Living*, West Sussex: Capstone Publishing Ltd.

Prigogine, I. and Stengers, I. (1984) *Order out of Chaos*, New York: Bantam.

Ridderstrale, J. and Nordström, K. (2008), *Funky Business Forever: How to Enjoy Capitalism*, Stockholm: Book House Publishing.

Scharmer, C. O. (2007) *Theory U: Leading from the Future as it Emerges*, Cambridge: Society for Organizational Learning.

Sepheri, P. and Wagner, D. (2002) 'Diversity und managing diversity', in Sybille Peters and Norbert Besensel (eds), *Frauen und Männer im Management, Diversity in Diskurs und Praxis*, Wiesbaden: Gabler.

Shaw, P. (2002) *Changing Conversations in Organizations*, London: Routledge.

Stacey, R. (2005) *Experiencing Emergence in Organizations, Local Interaction and the Emergence of Global Pattern*, Okon: Routledge.

Surowiecki, J. (2004) *The Wisdom of Crowds*, New York: Anchor.

Théry, B. (2002) *Manager dans la diversité culturelle*, Paris: Editions d'organisation.

Thomas, R. R. Jr. (2006) *Management of Diversity*, Wiesbaden: Gabler Publisher.

Trompenaars, F. and Hampden-Turner, C. (2004) *L'entreprise Multiculturelle*, Paris: Editions Maxima.

Wheatley, M. J. (1999) *Leadership and New Science, Discovering Order in a Chaotic World*, San Francisco: Barret-Keoehler Publishers Inc.

Zara, O. (2005) *Le management de l'intelligence collective, vers une nouvelle gouvernance*, Paris: M2 Editions.

Zeldin, T. (1998) *De la conversation*, Paris: Fayard.

Zohar, D. (1990) *The Quantum Self*, New York: William Morrow & Co.

Zohar, D. and Marshall, I. (1994) *The Quantum Society: Mind, Physics and a New Social Vision*, New York: William Morrow & Co.

THE HEART OF CROSS-CULTURAL CREATION

Inclusion and presence that produce something greater

Danièle Darmouni and Margaret A. Krigbaum

In ancient Chinese, to write 'mind', you draw a heart.

In our current vernacular, the term 'cross-cultural' is used with great frequency. Often, it is assumed that a cross-cultural business will be more effective in a global world. In those instances, the term is used to define a desired business end. While much time is spent discussing how to be cross-cultural and why that is good for the business, little time is spent discussing what type of cross-cultural organizations will bring the expected efficiencies or what implications cross-culturalism has for the people in a corporation. As a result, an essential element is commonly missing from the foundational discussion that is necessary to create and implement a truly successful, truly sustained, cross-cultural environment.

Every profound, complete, and sustainable change process, whether in an organizational or social setting, is the result of a journey that includes both internal and intangible dimensions. This tacit portion, which involves the engagement of sustainable emotion, is infrequently given a place in the conversation commensurate with its importance to cross-cultural success. Genuine cross-cultural models, and the cross-cultural coaching that helps build and support them, build in another dimension – the heart. Gratton and Ghoshal (2002: 209) emphasize this concept in their international research, extending over five years. They found that the more successful and creative companies were invariably those which had fostered internal conversations in the mode of 'creative dialogue', i.e., high in both analytical rationality (the head) and emotional authenticity (the heart).

This chapter will focus on the human reason that cross-cultural principles are necessary: they create an understanding that enables leaders and managers to be fully present with their employees and allow them to feel fully included rather than being outsiders. These two human conditions, when attended to, allow the entire organization to create access to a larger field of possibility and to actually build self-sustaining forms. Without understanding these heart- and spirit-based human conditions, organizations achieve only the appearance of cross-culturalism and that illusionary appearance will fail in a short time. Consequently, any real cross-cultural initiative must start by understanding the science, art, and importance of human emotion.

WHY THE INTERNAL OR TACIT IS IMPORTANT

Mary O'Hara-Devereaux (2004: 104) proposed that 'Doing business across cultures is advancing with persistence through the uneven and surprising weather systems generated by multiculturalism' (O'Hara-Devereaux 2004: 104). We recognize and accept that storms and typhoons are rarely predictable and do not fit in with the 'rational forecast' – such recognition should be applied to our approach in doing team work across cultures.

We already understand that, with cultural differences, interpretations of the world vary from individual to individual and from group to group. In an organizational context, there are as many truths as there are people, though many of these realities may share common features. This understanding may persuade us that by sharing our interpretations of reality, we will reach the 'real' truth. However, no matter how factualist we try to be, it is still through the structure of the brain that we perceive the world. The brain is not just a place of rational perception, but also a place of emotional perception.

Research continues to deepen the established finding that our brains react very little to external factors and input – much of our brain's activities rely on what has already been acquired, what is settled or programmed (Maturana and Varela 1987; Senge, Sharmer, Jaworski and Flowers 2004). An individual's current rational and emotional construct in the brain will control that individual's perceptions of change. Thus, the mind will cling to known and predictable patterns and structures unless and until the heart, spirit, and mind are made comfortable with uncertainty and with newness. If we accept this theory, it is clear that the coach helping a team or organization develop a cross-cultural way of being must help that team or organization develop their capacity to adapt to new facts, meanings, and perceptions by challenging and shifting the emotional and rational constructions previously accepted as unshakeable truth.

The key lies in transforming the individual's and the group's capacity to see, and their capacity to create. Research from the Society of Learning (Senge et al. 2004) strongly suggests that these new and necessary constructions and the insights that will emerge from them rest in building three integrated new capacities:

1 Observing that no longer fragments the observer from what's observed; consistent with established participatory action research and action science models (Greenwood and Levin 1998; Argyris, Putnam and Smith 1985; Lewin 1946);
2 Stillness that no longer fragments who we really are from what's emerging; and
3 Creating alternative realities that no longer fragment the wisdom of the head, heart, and hand.

These three integrated capacities allow the individual and the team to be comfortable in the uncertainty and the disruption that always begins the cross-cultural evolution process. It allows the movement from domain expertise to the sharing of a wide variety of outlooks and perspectives. The inherent emotional and heart safety in the integration of observer and observed, stillness with authenticity, and the rational and spirit mechanisms of the mind and body allow dynamic interactions between diverse groups to begin. It is the coach's job to assist this integration in a powerful and yet strongly quiet way so that cross-culturalization can begin at a deep level.

CASE STUDY: AN EXAMPLE OF INTERNAL INTEGRATION LEADING THE WAY

A major European corporation decided to expand into the Asia-Pacific region. The first step was to conceive a strategy to create a headquarters in that region. The executive in charge was the Asia-Pacific general director and it was anticipated that the general director and executive team would create a two-year process for the definition and deployment of the expansion strategy. The general director brought in a coach to coach the team through this important process. The start was a three-day meeting in Jakarta with leaders from several divisions and countries who were potential team members and who would have ultimate responsibility for combining the various divisions and countries into a well-functioning, productive, and effective cross-cultural unit.

The beginning, however, was not auspicious. The coach arrived and was informed by the general director that the participants all had different obligations abroad, the time to be given to the work was fragmented, and that there would be constant comings and goings. In spite of this lack of commitment, the coach decided to proceed. The coach recognized that this lack of commitment represented the current rational and emotional construct of the participants. The participants were driven by what was known and predictable; i.e., their current commitments. They were avoiding the new unpredictability of the new entity that was to be developed and they reflected a greater commitment to current definable work than to future work that had yet to be defined. Therefore, the coach's work was to help the individuals and team do the internal integration that would produce a commitment to the new future.

The coach was helped by the weather. A major storm prevented everyone from leaving for their current, known commitments. Now, the work on integration could begin.

The first step of the coaching was to set up a discussion that created a new language so the brain could be open to the future. The coach wanted to connect the participants to each other as observers and observed and also to begin to plant the seed of new reality and capacity as a team. This was done using image and metaphor to begin to share perceptions of each participant's own culture as well as strengths they had observed in past cross-cultural experiences. This analogical representation was expressed as the making of a mosaic. In a mosaic, every piece is a different piece of art and the sum of these pieces creates a new, larger, richer and, maybe most importantly, a more meaningful work of art. In this instance, the team began to treat each share, each observation, and each observer as a contribution to the mosaic they were creating.

The coach then asked the team to silently think about what emerged from the conversation and to claim what was most emotionally meaningful for them. Once that place of silence and emergence was visited, the coach asked the team to share the emotional impact and meaning of the mosaic that had been created. With this foundation set, the coach invited the team to create the future out of the wisdom that the team had just developed. The coach tapped into the team's more integrated thinking, thinking that was mental, emotional, and physical, by asking the team:

1   Can you imagine the future together, cross-culturally?
2   Are you able to make the relevant change in time?
3   How do you create a larger, global 'We' without losing your differences?

The coach also asked each participant to open new possibilities for a more fully integrated individual role by asking:

- What is my 'Self'?
- What are some of the core questions which are central to my own work?
- How can I contribute to build a sustainable future?

These questions took the team into deeper, more extended, and more connective conversations where the new 'We' began to emerge that both used and celebrated their differences while creating a new 'All One' entity. This open 'melting pot' and deep creative dialogue about their future allowed them to co-create vibrant alternative realities that were challenging and sustainable, exciting, and achievable, and that were no longer fragmenting the wisdom of the head, heart, and hand.

At the end of an intensive three days' work, all participants had experienced a vivid feeling of the 'welcoming process' presented in the next section of this chapter. With a specific focus on welcoming the 'unpredictable flooding' as the first of the surprises that this new 'We' had to offer, they felt they could also welcome the new environmental opportunities and constraints with which they would have to deal through the following years. As a unit and a team, they were ready to lead the entire division toward a collective community that would be a model for the whole company.

Most importantly, they recognized the advantages that were inherent not only in their own cross-culturalism, but also how cross-culturalism could be used in a broader way to grow their own teams and the entire Asia-Pacific unit. As a result, they emerged from the meetings as a single productive group, with individuals feeling that they were accepted members of the group. Ensuing group meetings became a priority and a time for continued strengthening of the emotional relationships with one another. The subsequent successful and complete implementation of their strategy was simply a natural result of that emotional and rational integration.

'THE WELCOME' IS IMPORTANT

The internal integration discussed above is an absolute prerequisite to successful cross-cultural team building. There is, however, another prerequisite as well. That prerequisite is what we call 'The Welcome'. The Welcome requires that from the very first moment a cross-cultural initiative is started, each individual on a team must feel included, must feel important, must feel that they belong, and must feel loved. Mary O'Hara-Devereaux writes, 'Many potential global leaders ultimately fail because they are not able to learn enough about other cultures to be effective in situations where leadership is shared. In this increasingly global business world the goal must be maximum inclusion of all cultures within a global web of alliances' (O'Hara-Devereaux 2004: 104). The Welcome is a vital first step in ensuring a successful and inclusive cross-cultural journey.

Successful coaches of cross-cultural processes understand the emotional and heart aspects of cross-cultural work. Such coaches share Humberto Maturana's understanding of perception centers: individuals are not passive observers of an external world; rather, individuals know their world through interacting with it, and the individual's emotions can limit or enrich that interaction. The emotional framework for perception is so strong that, as Maturana says, 'love, allowing the other to be a legitimate other, is the only emotion that expands intelligence' (Maturana and Varela 1987: 178). In short, if the individual does not feel included and 'loved', the individual's rational knowledge supporting change will be limited.

The elements of The Welcome that a coach helps the leader of cross-cultural change develop are simple and powerful. The first is the development of welcoming language. The coach can play a part in this linguistic patterning and the language should occur in three forms:

1 The coach must help the leader develop the invitation to all individuals to bring the best of their cultures, the learning and wisdom from their cultures, and 'who they are

culturally' to the table, and assure participants that all aspects of their cultures will be welcomed and learned from;

2   The coach must help the leader develop language to invite the team, group, and others in the company, if applicable, to become learners and to welcome learning from each other; and

3   The coach must help the leader develop language to welcome the creation of a new entity, a new state of being, that is more complete and powerful than simply the sum of the individuals and cultures at the table. The leader, in fact, welcomes the birth of a new community. When such a welcome occurs authentically and sincerely, the encounter transforms itself into relationship.

Once the initial language of welcome is developed and begins to be used, a second welcome must be issued. The coach helps the leader and the team begins to welcome new possibilities of deeper relating at all levels and for all participants. The leader welcomes, encourages, and models not comfort, but the profound adventure that is inherent in playing joyfully with difference. This starts with the leader 'modeling' by intently listening to everyone: to mavericks, strangers to one another, atypical talents. The leader and team develop language that reflects meaningful listening to different views and voices. This ongoing welcome creates a fertile ground for a joined, sustained relationship, and continues on to create joined, joyful innovation.

Finally, the coach helps the leader create The Welcome for shared leadership. To start and then sustain cross-cultural paradigms, the leader must invite and welcome leadership from each culture within the paradigm. Anything less will be viewed as exclusionary and the rational knowledge of those who feel excluded will limit their ability to expand into both the vision and reality of a multicultural team or organization.

THE ART OF PRESENCE

Internal integration and The Welcome provide a sound foundation. It takes more, however, to sustain the cross-cultural journey to completion. It takes courage to learn in a fast and unstructured environment full of high stakes. In the short run, globalization is highly disrupting. Faced with the constant need and search for security, individuals tend to turn to habit and repetition. The dark side of this tendency is that these worn-out behaviors are difficult to turn off. This automatic repetition of old mind-sets, usually based in rational domain maintaining, no longer produces desired results and often damages the long-term worth of the person or the organization.

The coach's job, then, is to help a team or organization find a way to step and cross from the land of domain and fear of failure to the land of adventure – to build a calm place that allows the participants to engage on the critical highway of fast learning. To do that, the individual participants must be assisted to connect with the inner place from which each individual operates; that is, for each individual to become emotionally present to themselves. The coach must then help the clients to become emotionally present to environment and relationships and then to the possibility of a new definition of self and whole.

Research led by Otto Scharmer on the learning process provides both the coach and the leaders they coach with excellent guidance (Scharmer 2007). Scharmer's research holds that our courage in the unknown depends on how we connect to the inner place from which we operate. That connection occurs and the ensuing learning process and actions can occur at various levels. Each level will impact the individual's ability to both cope with and be a leader in the change process. Scharmer indicates that individuals can connect in four different ways to their inner being and each creates subsequently richer opportunities enabling the future to become reality:

1 Downloading: out of habit, action is the repetition of the past and thus results in no change;
2 Open the Mind: to access the source of creativity, one must suspend the VOJ, the Voice of Judgment;
3 Open the Heart: to allow oneself to be touched by the other's point of view, one must shut down the VOC, the Voice of Cynicism; and
4 Open the Will: to let go of an old identity and welcome a new sense of 'We', one must shut down the VOF, the Voice of Fear (fear of death, ridicule, the unknown).

'Downloading' is obviously the limited, 'current-knowledge-only' based method of presencing to one's self, relationships, and environment. As stated before, this limited rational construct will stifle the ability to engage in the adventure of cross-cultural change and will keep an individual married to the status quo. If downloading is the presencing mechanism for a leader or team, the coach must work toward the next three stages of presencing before any meaningful, sustainable cross-cultural results can be achieved.

'Opening the mind' is the act of becoming present to the sense of the individual's and team's potential for creativity. It requires a willingness to become present to the pleasure of experimentation and to suspend judgment for fear of failing in the experiment. Presencing to the act of creation and to potential change that is worth the emotional risk of failure is central to an individual's and team's ability to sustain themselves and others during the inevitable times of great challenge. It is the coach's great privilege to invite the participants to find the levels at which they are willing to be present to their own and their collective creativity and experimentation.

'Opening the heart' is also central to sustaining the journey. Coaches often encounter clients who are protective of their hearts. Cross-culturalization, however, requires the embracing of new relationships and new viewpoints. This requires a risk of the heart. The coach can help the participants become aware of where their presence to their heart and their protection of their heart are shrouded in fear and cynicism. The shut-down of cynicism, which is based on old beliefs about the self, about others, and about the world, is the powerful key to the opening of the heart. When these voices are silenced, participants can reach the inner space that is willing to be at risk in relationships.

The coach can assist the participants to meet the fears and shadows that protect, but also limit, access to the heart. The coach can then help the client define a new way of being vulnerable in the uncertainty of new relationships in a way that transforms the energy blocked by fear, into a new energy necessary to realize personal and organizational mutations and to become a main ally allowing entrance into a new dimension of relationships.

The final level of presencing is 'Opening the Will'. This is the presencing to a larger context beyond oneself. It is the emotional act of letting go of an old, small identity that is fully self-contained and welcoming a new larger identity that is a sense of 'We' which seeks the whole to emerge. In order to presence at this new and at times confusing level, the participants must be willing to shut out the voices that protect the current identity and environment. These 'voices of fear' will only be quelled by a larger vision and sense of self as part of a larger group and more complete reality. The strong cross-cultural coach challenges the participants to define and become present to the emotional whole they seek to create, and also allows each individual to find and define their part and contribution to the whole. This presence to the new identity of the whole and the individual and the two as joined entities creates a powerful and sustainable highway to a meaningful cross–cultural environment and organization.

In order to assist clients to 'Open the will', coaches must assist individuals who will be members of a cross–cultural team to define:

- Their old identity as an individual and what needs that identity met;
- The current comfort level of their environment and how that comfort level will shift, and where the individual might be emotionally uncomfortable in the new cross–cultural environment;
- A new identity, where the individual is part of a larger whole, and a more diverse environment;
- What meaningful and substantive potential gains and learning exist for the individual as part of this larger whole and why these potential gains are valuable to the individual;
- Each member's contribution to the whole and why that contribution is important; and
- Each member's merger into and contribution to the new cross–cultural environment in a way that will allow them to move with and then beyond the voice of fear.

This same process can and should be repeated with the team as a whole for the emotional connection that sustains cross–cultural evolution to be developed.

CASE STUDY: 'THE WELCOME' AND THE 'OPENING OF THE MIND, HEART, AND WILL' AT WORK IN BUILDING A CROSS-CULTURAL TEAM

The largest organization of coaches is the International Coach Federation (ICF). Early in 2008, ICF's membership surpassed 14,000, and the numbers continue to grow rapidly on a global scale. In 1999, ICF's credentialing program had been conducted only in English and only in English-speaking countries – the United States, the United Kingdom, and Canada. The credentialing criteria and program had been developed almost exclusively by North American coaches. At that time, the sole cross-cultural aspect to the program was that the developers of ICF's Definition of Coaching, Core Competencies, and the testing process itself came from approximately eight main coach-training backgrounds. As a result, coaches outside North America viewed the credentialing as 'exclusively American' or 'exclusively for English speakers'. Few members outside North America were inclined to participate in any meaningful way.

In 2000, ICF's Credentialing Committee began to contemplate the future of the credentialing program. The committee was the only ICF entity that contained a significant number of members from outside of North America. The committee concluded that it wanted the credentialing program to become a truly cross-cultural program with a cross-cultural team of assessors. The committee therefore recommended to ICF's board of directors that a plan be developed to move credentialing beyond English-speaking countries with a commitment to building a true global culture of credentialed coaches and a cross-cultural assessment team. ICF's board approved that recommendation. ICF was, however, faced with the same challenges of any organization trying to move toward cross-culturalizaton. How could it extend the welcome, and open the mind, heart, and will to build a team and a program that was a global culture, particularly when the credentialing program had been viewed with suspicion by non-English speakers?

The committee's first thinking focused on analytic strategy without adding the emotional authenticity advocated by Senge et al. (2004) and Gratton and Ghoshal (2002), to name a few. The committee attempted to develop a practical plan and step-by-step process that would yield a cross-cultural credentialing assessor team, which was a necessary precursor to taking the actual credentialing process global. The initial attempts to implement that plan stumbled.

The committee then asked a smaller group from ICF's assessor team to start considering what would be necessary to build a global assessment team. The task force consisted of members from both within and outside North America. Thus, the group of six contained one member from each of France, Germany and the United Kingdom, and three people from North America (all of whom worked internationally). All six had been part of the credentialing committee conversation and all had shared in the committee's frustration at its lack of progress in implementing a cross-cultural strategic plan.

The group decided that it had to leave the prior conversation behind. It was clear that it was not achieving the desired result and in fact, was causing division. The group concluded that there was no emotional motivation or call to those beyond the English-speaking coaches. They concluded, in terms of this chapter's language, that there had been no 'Welcome' or process to 'presence' international coaches to encourage people to engage with a cross-cultural assessment team.

When the group came to this conclusion, a significant and profound change occurred in their thinking. The group started to share almost melancholy feelings that had been unspoken and unrecognized. One member from the United States described it this way: 'While I am called a master coach, there is so much about coaching around the world I do not know. I wonder what I haven't learned that I need to?' Another said, 'I feel incomplete – as though my connection to the world is not complete. I think I am tired of living in the same conversations with my same colleagues, much as I love them'. A third common theme was: 'I thought as coaches we could connect with everyone in a way that made us whole and yet, we seem to fall into some of the same thinking that plagues the world. I had hoped we could move beyond that. This is an opportunity to prove that we can be whole.'

The members individually and collectively began, as Peter Senge and Otto Scharmer (Senge et al. 2004) said, to 'presence' themselves to the internal and intangible dimensions of the calling to build a global assessor team. They began to see the deepest source of their needs and to claim those sources as the reason, inspiration, and passion for the work. Those deepest sources were a need to be a whole community and a community of joined learners. Out of these sources, the group began to frame and extend The Welcome.

The group decided that they needed to call the most experienced, well-known coaches from each national or cultural area. They told these coaches that they needed their wisdom, their commitment, and their courage. They laid out the vision of having a credentialing program and an assessment team that connected coaches throughout the world. They invited the coaches to join them in creating a vision for their area of the world and the coaching profession as a whole. The coaches who were contacted responded to the energy and excitement of the potential vision. More importantly, they responded because they could see and palpably feel how much they were wanted, needed, and welcomed.

The next challenge was to open the heart, mind, and will. That resulted from joint work of the original group from ICF and the coaches who had indicated a willingness to explore going through the credentialing process and then become an assessor. The key to this phase was the idea that the credential would build a fully connected, fully global, fully cross-cultural profession. This vision was big enough to move those involved from the 'Me' orientation to the 'We' or whole orientation. In addition, a second vision of a community of continuous learners from one another, both culturally and professionally, propelled the opening of the heart, mind, and will by defining both the community of the whole and the role each assessor individually, and the assessor team, would play in building that community. With these two larger visions as a firm emotional context, the group, which had become a true cross-cultural team, began to implement the strategic and analytic portions of the plan with significant success.

Within nine months, the assessor team had assessors from 11 countries and had given exams in 15 countries in 5 different languages. It continued to build as a global team where people of different cultures worked easily and well together, who expanded one another's capacity as learners and coaches, where the conversations were forwarding, and evolution continued at a vigorous pace.

CONCLUSION

Every aspect of the cross-cultural journey requires a presencing to and an integration of the emotional, spiritual, and mental aspects of the participants. The research and the authors' experiences in coaching multinational teams reflect one certainty: the heart does not always follow the mind. Instead, the mind follows the heart. Coaches and leaders of cross-cultural initiatives need to clearly focus on the emotional integration and growth of the participants. We have drawn attention not only to the need to start strongly through The Welcome, but also to continue the forward movement of the emotional side during those times when it is challenging and turbulent. The authors encourage coaches and leaders to focus on building the necessary foundational presence and connection before attempting to build rational strategy. This will most ensure success, for in order to have the minds of participants, you must first have their hearts.

A tool: the heart of cross-cultural coaching; principles and practices for sustainable change

Below is a summary framework of principles and practices of being that the coach must help implement to create the heart of cross-culturalism with teams who are struggling to create a 'we' from a collection of internationally diverse individuals.

Principles

Through all stages, the coach is an engaged and active participant to:

1   Include and connect the observers with the observed – the 'Me' to the 'We';
2   Create stillness in an environment of great challenge;
3   Encourage the possibilities for and the creation of alternative realities; and
4   Encourage intensive listening for values in culturally diverse dialogue.

Process

The coach is a holder of and a partner in the process of harnessing diverse realities to facilitate group successes:

1   The Welcome: ensure that the group takes time and gives attention to beginning together:

   a   Invite cultures to the table;
   b   Cultivate a new language for shared learning; and
   c   Promote structures that reflect a shift from 'Me' to 'We'.

127

2 Presencing: model and bring forward a space for individual and collective presencing which includes emotional self-and-other connection:

    a Move past downloading – enable group members to let go of or unlearn habitual emotional, cognitive, and behavioral patterns that do not help build the collective 'We':

    b Open the mind – encourage individual and group challenges to Voices of Judgment and invite group members to open their minds to new ideas and feelings and ways of being:

    c Open the heart – encourage individual and group challenges to Voices of Cynicism and enable heart-led dialogue that is authentic; and

    d Open the will – encourage individual and group challenges to Voices of Fear and provide support for courageous choices.

3 Leadership: explicitly invite the group to leadership sharing from cross-cultural strengths and to create a new definition of leadership out of those cross-cultural strengths.

Bibliography

Argyris, C., Putnam, R. and Smith, D. (1985) *Action Science*, San Francisco: Jossey-Bass.

Gratton, L. and Ghoshal, S. (2002) 'Improving the quality of conversations', *Organizational Dynamics*, 31 (3), 209–23.

Greenwood, D. J. and Levin, M. (1998) *Introduction to Action Research: Social Research for Social Change*, London: Sage.

Lewin, K. (1946) 'Action research and minority problems', *Journal of Social Issues*, 2: 34–46.

Maturana, H. and Varela, F. (1987) *The Tree of Knowledge*, Boston, MA: Shambhala Press.

O'Hara-Devereaux, M. (2004) *Navigating the Badlands: Thriving in the Decade of Radical Transformation*, San Francisco: Jossey-Bass.

Scharmer, O. (2007) *Theory U: Leading from the Future as it Emerges*, Cambridge, MA: Society for Organizational Learning.

Senge, P., Sharmer, O., Jaworski, J. and Flowers, B.S. (2004) *Presence: Human Purpose and the Field of Future*, Cambridge: Society of Organizational Learning.

STIMULATING ADVERSARIAL GROWTH IN CULTURAL UNCERTAINTY

A survival guide for international executives and their coaches

Eddie Lievrouw

I've had many catastrophes in my life, some of which actually happened.

(Mark Twain)

Did you say survival? With my background as a military survival instructor for aircrew, I was surprised to be asked to write a chapter on international business coaching. I accepted the challenge and wisely engaged support from my friends and partners of the European Institute for Intervention and Research on Burn Out. Patrick, a neuropsychiatrist and international specialist in burn out provided some solid science. Fatima, multicultural coach, assured a female touch and some creative perspectives.

In international business, as in nature, survival and success require adaptation and attraction (Nordström and Ridderstrale 2005: 213). Increasingly, business life for those with a bent for global ventures, travel and excitement can be extremely dangerous, way too dangerous for survival instructors. Obvious dangers include volatile political situations, disease, crime, accidents, and so on. Less obviously, but sometimes even more destructive, are the insidious often-masked impacts of stress and pressure that are inherent in the high voltage life of the senior international executive. This latter threat can be just as great at home as in some exotic location far away. In their daily life, executives and their families, colleagues and reports can get trapped in a danger zone without even knowing it. As Daryl Paulson explained, 'At least in Vietnam, you knew when you were shot. In business, you can be half-dead before you ever know you're a target' (Paulson 2002: 11).

What is certain is that those who are genuinely engaged in international business will experience setbacks and difficulties that are intense and possibly life-threatening. In this chapter, an analogy will be drawn between the coping mechanisms required by businesspeople (and their coaches) to the survival mechanisms of humans facing crises and disasters. We suggest that there are 'critical success factors' (CSFs) that can assist those who want to engage with and benefit from playing in the fast-paced and stressful environments of cross-border acquisitions, overseas assignments, global ventures, virtual teams, and so on. That is where coaching comes in – to work with clients to promote awareness of what happens when people are put under high pressure with rapid response times and high stakes. Also coaching can help their clients and client-organizations to plan and execute actions consistent with what the research says are CFS.

The defense mechanisms in our brain do not differentiate between the rain forest of Amazonia and the business jungle of New York, Tokyo and Paris. The roaring of the CEO might freeze us to the spot, as might a quick inspection of the plane about to fly us to check a possible factory site in a regional outpost of a developing country. The reaction is the same one exhibited by our ancestors in reaction to the roaring of the saber-toothed tiger. Even if the objective consequences of the present danger are (hopefully) not quite the same as it was for our ancestors, the CEO's roaring and the plane's poor repair may lead to very intense emotions. Although caution is advised, the general structure of a survival situation can be applied to the situation of business executives operating in the global environment.

Perception determines whether we process the information in an adapted way, or whether our sensory perceptions and thoughts make us act dysfunctionally. The characteristics of the subjective experience of the event, rather than the event itself, influence our choices and determine whether or not we survive. Further, survival is not enough: in a capitalist world of economic Darwinism, companies and their managers have to grow; grow against all odds in spirals of adversarial growth to outperform the competitors.

There is an important distinction between (1) our survival situations where the threats are clear (tigers, angry CEOs, rusty planes, etc.) and (2) the daily business context where threats to our well-being and health are less visible. In business life, the environment is so complex, so busy and bullied by surface forces that in those surface difficulties we find a perfect busy excuse not to face the more essential difficulties of survival and meaningful existence (Whyte 2001).

In real disasters, people are only asked to survive. Two modeling approaches have been adopted. The most common one describes a disaster structurally in terms of its properties, usually along different dimensions such as natural or man-made, duration and geographical range. The second approach models disasters according to their impact on human behavior (Leach 1994: 2). Indeed, a closer study of the make-up of disasters reveals consistency across apparently unrelated events. Behavior tends to follow a structured pattern across different types of disasters (Leach 1994: 5). The resultant models are useful for the more extreme of situations faced by globally active executives, and even for the executive in a more habitual business environment. The broad sequence of the models (see Figure 9.1) follows from a pre-impact phase, through the physical disaster itself to the post-trauma and recovery phases. The following phases can be very distinct.

PRE-IMPACT

People come to perceive that there exists a risk to their lives. This period has been subdivided into two phases: threat and warning. During the threat phase there exists a possibility of a misfortune striking. It may come or not, but the potential is there. The warning phase, on the other hand, is that period before impact when the impending danger becomes all too real. A business example might be of people involved in oil exploration in areas of Africa where there has been a recent history of kidnapping.

IMPACT

The period of impact may not always be preceded by a period of pre-impact. A disaster may strike so suddenly that it catches people completely unaware (take for recent example the pilots of a regional New Zealand flight who were attacked by a woman attempting to hijack the plane). Whether expected or not, the immediate result is an overwhelming of the senses. So much information strikes the victim that he or she is often unable to process and comprehend it and consequently becomes bewildered and numb. No amount of training will entirely remove the psychological response. Behavior varies individually but across the spectrum there does appear to be an identifiable pattern of responses which is consistent throughout many independent studies and can be divided broadly into three bands (Leach 1994: 4):

1   In the first band, 10–20 per cent of people will remain relatively calm during impact. A few will become exceptionally calm and rational. They will be able to assess the situation, make a plan and act upon it;

2   The second and largest band comprises approximately 75 per cent of the population. These people will quite simply be stunned. They will find their reasoning significantly impaired and that thinking is difficult. They will behave in a reflexive, almost automatic manner. Their field of attention becomes restricted and visually they may suffer 'tunnel vision' or, more correctly, perceptual narrowing. The sense of the passage of time also alters. These people are unable to express any emotions and will later report that they completely lacked any such emotional sensations; and

3   The third band is made up of 10–15 per cent of the population. These people will tend to show a high degree of inappropriate behavior that is not only ineffective in coping with a life-threatening situation, but also adds to their danger.

Recoil begins once the initial dangers have been removed, either naturally or by the survivors having made their escape. Recoil typically begins with confusion. This followed by a gradual return of awareness and reasoning ability. The recovery of the survivors can be immediate and complete, or persist because the survivor cannot be rescued or is unable to regain friendly territory. Long-term survival Post-Trauma Stress Disorders may become entrenched long before a rescue occurs. During the period of post-trauma survivors will attempt to rebuild their lives. It is during this phase that acute psychological dysfunction may develop into a more chronic psychiatric disorder.

As a coach, when you hear the stories of executives who have worked extensively in developing countries and volatile environments they will invariably relate situations that are very much akin to disaster situations. Brushes with death are surprisingly common – serious illness,

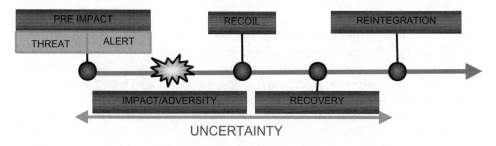

Figure 9.1 Three phases in responding to a disaster

transport accidents, hold-ups, earthquakes, civil wars, industrial accidents, etc. Beyond these extremes, their daily life invariably consists of small, never-ending and interfering waves of shallow disasters that can, in the figurative sense, devour them in the long run.

INDIVIDUAL REACTIONS

Let's examine the approximately 75 per cent of individuals that, during a disaster situation, do not react in a rational way. (You might reflect on the behavior of any clients, colleagues, managers or reports you deal with in the business context who are in this category.) There can be a variety of individual responses.

Despite popular belief, panic is not common. Leach (1994: 31) explains the elements characterizing panic. There is perceived time or space limit, such as in a building fire; people will become aggressive; behavior is irrational and this behavior is contagious and waves out quickly. You may observe this in executive teams where the equilibrium is disturbed by a dramatic change in events (e.g., a hostile takeover bid by a foreign competitor).

Paralyzing anxiety, often known as 'freezing to the spot', as distinct from 'fear'. The business equivalent might be the manager who, faced with an immediate crisis, simply does nothing – to the frustration of those around who are seeking immediate instruction on how to cope.

Denial is the most commonly reported behavior shown by people in a disaster. After the Hiroshima atomic bombing the Japanese called this phenomenon *burabura*, the 'do-nothing sickness'. Denial may take the form of a simple refusal to believe that the event is happening, stereotypical behavior, perceptual distortion or intellectualization. It is frequently reinforced by previous experience. Denial prevents people from planning to survive. Stereotypical behavior is a form of denial. Victims do not reflect on what is happening and fall back on previously well-learned or over-learned behavioral patterns no matter how inappropriate these are to the circumstances. The survivor is doing what he knows how to do, rather than applying the skill which would be helpful. The tendency to make this mistake seems to increase as fatigue and general stress levels increase (Rollins 2004). Take the example of a CEO who continually tells the good news story and encourages business-as-usual in the face of an obvious threat from an offshore competitor offering 30 per cent cheaper prices for an equivalent or better product. Even as debt mounts and the corporation bleeds, the news from the CEO is to 'have faith and keep going'.

Hypo-activity tends to be manifested as a depressed reaction and apathy. It is compounded by denial. People showing this behavior will not look after themselves and are at risk from secondary dangers such as dehydration. Perhaps the business equivalent is that of the under-pressure expatriate managers who in daytime retreat into their offices. At night, they share misery over too many gin and tonics at the local expat bar.

Hyperactivity is an intense but undirected liveliness. People who become hyperactive are dangerous because they give a misleading impression of purposefulness and leadership, which those who are stunned and bewildered will follow. Their actions are frequently inefficient and inappropriate and their ideas worthless. Most victims will show temporary hyperactivity during their recovery from a depressed reaction and apathy. An executive who has been demoted or sidelined may exhibit this kind of behavior.

Anger is a universal reaction among victims. It is characterized by being irrational and even rescue workers have come under verbal and physical attack. In very senior positions in highly competitive corporate environments, anger is not an unusual reaction to crisis – in more toxic corporate cultures it might even be encouraged!

Guilt is frequently reported in survivors during post-trauma but may also be encountered during the period of recoil. Where there has been a corporate takeover and heads rapidly roll, the executive 'survivors' may well exhibit this reaction.

Psychological breakdown is more a result of the above-mentioned reactions, than a specific behavior. It is the most desperate problem facing a victim. It is characterized initially by irritability, sleep disturbance, mild startled reaction, social withdrawal, loss of interest, apprehension, general psychomotor retardation and confusion. The ultimate consequence of psychological disintegration is death. Death may occur passively ('give up') or actively (suicide).

COPING BEHAVIOR

Amygdala hijack

The above reactions are mainly triggered by the amygdala. Drawing on findings from neuroscience using increasingly advanced technology, Goleman explains in his books *Emotional Intelligence* (1997) and *Social Intelligence* (2006) how a sensorial signal is first transmitted to the thalamus, where it is translated to brain language. Most of the information is then sent to the appropriate part of the cortex for analysis for an appropriate response. If the response is emotional, a signal is sent to the amygdala, the specialist in emotional matters and part of our limbic brain (a more ancient part of our brain). However, a small part of the initial signal passes right from the thalamus to the amygdala, provoking this way a quicker yet less-precise reaction. The amygdala is thus able to trigger an emotional reaction before the cortical centers have understood the meaning (Goleman 1997: 40). This lack of precision of our emotional brain is worsened by the fact that many heavily emotionally charged memories are stored from the very early years of childhood. That's why we are often very confused about our emotional reactions during a dangerous situation, because we cannot explain with words the memories that created them (Goleman 1997: 44).

In our changing social universe the neuronal alarms sent by the amygdala are often inappropriate. In other words, the new realities of our western civilization are evolving so rapidly that our biological evolution can't keep pace. Our neuronal circuits guiding our emotions have functioned relatively well during thousands of generations, but there is an increasing gap between technical and biological evolution. Trying to solve highly complex problems with a psychological panoply dating from Peistocenos (Goleman 1997: 20) can turn perceived disasters to real disasters.

For global executives, the situation is compounded because they are constantly confronting situations which are completely new. The emotional centers of the brain have to do the best with what they have got – i.e., not very much. The automatic emotional responses are likely to be at best ineffective. At worst the outcome may be highly destructive for the individual, the business and probably the unfortunate host nationals who have to cope with a pressured and ineffectual expatriate manager.

Accurate thinking

The response patterns above are not encouraging for the highly volatile and stressful international business environment. In crisis situations, inappropriate emotional responses are driving the decision-making processes of around 75 per cent of people. Extrapolate that into

133

board rooms and executive offices around the world and the picture is not pretty. For executives and the coaches charged with assisting them to survive and thrive in the global environment, there are lessons. Two steps seem mandatory:

- Impulse control – or our capability to counter the amygdala hijack, and not to give in to the first, very strong emotion. It is that control that can prevent jet pilots in severe difficultly from ejecting immediately, choosing instead to stay long enough for the crash to avoid a highly populated area. The prefrontal cortex acts as an inhibitor to these impulsive responses and allows a more considered reaction (Goleman 1997: 48). The more emotional information is available in the prefrontal lobes, the bigger the chance that an appropriate reaction occurs. The basis of cognitive behavioral therapy is that in between a stimulus (S) and the automatic response (R1) is a brief opportunity for the advanced cognitive processes (T) to step in and check the appropriateness of R1. Other responses (R2, R3 . . .) can be then considered and enacted; and
- Emotional regulation – even when the cognitive intervention signals to us that R1 might not be appropriate, we are still in-the-moment and the amygdala may still override saner voices that might be coming from our cognitive centers. After all, the situations we are talking about are dramatic events that elicit very strong emotions. Amygdala hijackers are well equipped, with a variety of emotional weapons, and are not easily dissuaded. Going with the amygdala-driven approach, however, will probably amplify emotions and result in inappropriate behavior. The amygdala hijackers are persuasive in making us believe that our immediate gut/emotional responses are valid and we even have a duty to play out our anger, frustration, fear, and so on. Even more confusingly, sometimes R1 is the right response.

Intuition/gut feeling

In a survival situation, by-and-large you should be highly suspicious of acting from your initial emotional reactions – your gut feelings. Exceptions might include people who are highly trained and experienced in survival/disaster situations. Intuition is the synthesis of the conclusions of all our systems condensed in one powerful gut feeling. The question for each person in a disaster situation is: 'To what degree can I trust my intuition in this situation?'

The executive on international assignment who is faced with a dramatic situation that requires a rapid response should be wary about trusting his or her gut. This is the case even for experts who, according to naturalistic research with military leaders, fire-fighters and nurses (Klein 1999; Klein 2003), in their home environment can be very confident that their intuition will produce a good result. The difficulty is that where the environment is unfamiliar, the automatic responses learned over time in one environment might be entirely inappropriate in a different environment. Novices need to take particular care since their gut responses are not going to be based on any experience that is akin to what they are facing. Armed with this knowledge, international business coaches can check with their clients as to the appropriateness of following their intuition in response to crisis situations as they arise.

Robert Cooper, who puts intuitive flow as one of the cornerstones for emotional intelligence, writes that there is one time, in particular, when it may be wise not to trust what you feel: when you are tense and tired from long hours at work (Cooper and Sawaf 1996: 18). This description of life might be familiar to those placed in overseas postings with demanding project objectives, or those operating around the clock to demanding deadlines as part of global virtual teams.

Conclusion

To give your advanced cognitive processes a chance of working for you, there are three challenges:

1 Learn to be aware of your emotions;
2 Know how to control them before you take action; and
3 Acquire the appropriate secondary emotions that are appropriate to the situation you are in.

Then, your intuition can be trained and trusted to fit the environment you are operating in and allow you to do things you'd never believe possible. It is a marriage of the head and the heart. Laurence Gonzales (2003: 33) synthesizes this beautifully in the following passage:

> The human organism then, is like a jockey on a thoroughbred in the gate. He's a small man and it's a big horse, and if it decides to get excited in that small metal cage, the jockey is going to get mangled, possibly killed. So he takes great care to be gentle. The jockey is reason and the horse is emotion. . . . The jockey can't win without the horse, and the horse can't race alone. In the gate, they are two and it's dangerous. But when they run, they are one, and it's positively godly.

CRITICAL SUCCESS FACTORS (CSFs)

Most studies are focusing only on the negative aspects of adversity, which can lead to a biased understanding of our reactions. Any understanding of reactions must take account of their potential for positive as well as negative changes if it is to be considered comprehensive. However, given the inconsistency of different studies few conclusions can be drawn (Linley and Joseph 2004). The research is more consistent on identifying factors that predict successful survival through disasters and crises. These CSFs contain important information for international executives and for their coaches.

Purpose

Finding a purpose to one's existence is an excellent aid to survival. Viktor Frankl's experiences in a Nazi concentration camp are testament to the power of inner purpose and meaning in sustaining survival (Frankl 1985/1946).

Attachment

Strongly linked to a purpose is the attachment to principal loved ones. The strong social bond between the survivor and his kin provides a powerful force for reunion and hence survival. John Peeters was a pilot in the first Gulf War. His jet was downed and he was captured by the Iraqis and imprisoned for 119 days. He reported that the main motor that kept him going was that he wanted to see his son Guy playing in a football team. Guy was two years old at the moment of the capture (Peeters 1996).

Action plan

Purpose must be coupled with an action plan. The act of planning can bring some relief, because making a plan automatically implies a future and thus hope. Hope feeds the struggle to keep going. Planning breaks down the aim into simple tasks so that life can be managed one step at a time.

Inner focus

Inner focus is both impossible to define and observe. Leach (1994) calls this 'personal spirituality'. It is equally found amongst atheists and those of a religious persuasion and works in a simple way: when a person who has lived for himself and his immediacy is thrown into a new and frightening environment, he becomes uprooted and disorientated and is unable to adapt to the change in circumstances. His world has sunk and him along with it. On the other hand, those people who possess a personal ideal will carry it with them, wherever they go, and wherever they happen to find themselves. They are able to put down roots and to anchor their own personalities. Inner focus enables one to command a quiet superiority over the enforced circumstances, refusing to allow one to succumb to circumstances. Again, Viktor Frankl's account of his time in a Nazi concentration camp is a perfect illustration of the power of inner focus to aid survival through times of intense pressure and deprivation (Frankl 1985/1946).

Prayer

A military maxim puts it, 'There are no atheists in foxholes'. Indeed, even those who do not profess a religious belief, catch themselves praying. Praying as a behavior has been reported too many times for it to be ignored. Many such prayers are straightforward pleas of fear. Praying is a form of adaptive behavior that helps a person's survival by reducing anxiety and keeping hope alive. In the same realm, many people will adopt tokens which they endow with the power to keep them safe and well. Often people are not consciously aware that a particular object has taken such significance for them. This process is well illustrated in the movie *Castaway*, where Tom Hanks starts a magical relationship with Wilson the ball. However, as magical thinking and prayer may give some relief, it should always be coupled with action. Many victims have perished while waiting for God, or other Forces, to help them out instead of recognizing that, whether or not you believe in a god, you must help yourself. Global executives are often isolated and experience times of dislocation and loneliness. Pragmatically, the challenge for each individual is to work out strategies that will not just get them through the day, but give them strength to motivate others and achieve success. Prayer is one such strategy.

Humor

At first sight it may seem incongruous that a person under threat should have any opportunity for the luxury of humor. Indeed it is the first behavior to be lost and the last to return. However, humor is not a luxury, but a vital organ to survival. Frankl described humor as 'another of the soul's weapons in the fight for self-preservation' (Frankl 1985/1946: 63). Deliberately ignoring the seriousness of a situation, even if it is for only a few seconds, often allows a reframing of a situation. This attitude of black humor is often found in subcultures dealing with high-risk activities such as fighter pilots, fire-fighters or alpine climbers. If humor is out of personal bounds, at least a positive approach is needed because anxiety undermines our intellect and uses mental resources made unavailable for the processing of other information. In this way our black prophecies might draw us towards the catastrophe they are predicting.

The literature on global executives and crossing cultures gives minimal attention to the use of humor as a mechanism for coping with stressful situations, which is a gap. In a study of British executives living in Singapore, humor has been shown to predict positive psychological adjustment (Ward and Kennedy 2001). The findings support the strategy of taking an active, positive approach:

> The avoidant coping style, which encompasses behavioral disengagement, denial, venting of emotions, the inability to see the potentially positive aspects of change, and mental disengagement, was inversely related to psychological adjustment. Using humor to cope with stress and employing an approach coping style, which included planning, active coping, and suppression of competing activities, predicted good psychological adjustment. (640)

One caution which is common is that executives working cross-culturally must be aware that humor is contextual and, if not used carefully, may make a difficult situation even worse. Jean-Louis Barsoux, a specialist on humor in international business at INSEAD, advises people to wait until they have achieved a certain familiarity with their local counterparts before employing humor (Marx 2001: 76).

Resilience

Another success factor is resilience, where the victim seeks to establish a new behavioral fit between himself and his new, hostile environment. By doing this he ceases to be a victim, and instead becomes an actor, responsible for his survival. The American Psychological Association Practice Directorate describes resilience as the process of adapting well in the face of adversity and bouncing back from difficult experiences. Leach found people who do succeed in adapting well to a new environment appear to do so within about three weeks (in Goleman 1997: 172). However, each individual executive is going to react differently to new and high-pressure situations. There are some patterns of adjustment, but these are based on large-scale studies which tend to wash out individual differences. The art of coaching in this area is to validate individual experiences, raise awareness with clients about their own levels of resilience, and help them find strategies that will help them – in their unique context – to utilize their resilience potentials.

REGRESS OR PROGRESS

When we regress to cope there is a return to an earlier stage, a simpler solution, or a previous perspective to respond to a specific problem. Once the danger is past or the problem solved, the system snaps back to home position (Beck and Cowan 2003). There is no permanent change as such, only a period of adjustment. However, the longer we stay in a perceived survival situation the bigger the risk that we regress to a level inappropriate to the social environment we are living in. Regression stops mental growth, retards interactions with our environment and finally creates risks of physical integrity through increased chance of illness. Executives who regress to earlier stages of coping may use such strategies as anger, stubbornness, avoidance, aggression, and so on that are not going to be very helpful in generating long-term positive outcomes in their situations.

However, we should not forget the 10–20 per cent of people who react appropriately to a high-stress environment. As these individuals try to deal with the problem, their base systems are temporarily stretched to a more complex expression, i.e., the envelope is pushed to achieve a specific temporary objective. Because this is not a natural position, a 'snap-back' will occur to the base belief structures and habitual ways of behaving. The question is, how long is temporarily? Everybody has a breaking point ('At the end everybody talks', to paraphrase a military interrogator). This breaking point is the beginning of burn out, of anger, hopelessness and revolution. One is trapped by barriers that seem insurmountable – a difficult time because part of the perception is a near-total lack of power to do anything about it (Beck and Cowan 2003: 89).

The coaching challenge is to engage the executive in dialogue that raises awareness about what is happening to them and around them in the situation. If there are serious issues that do not seem resolvable in the short term, the coaching strategy is to assist the client in a major change process. The costs of burn out for expatriate managers is particularly high, often resulting in the need for relocation of the individual and their families and the rapid engagement of a new manager – highly expensive and highly destructive all round.

TRIGGERING MICRO-DISASTERS

In most cases, we respond appropriately to the events of our daily life. However, some specific setbacks make us react differently. These events are our personal micro-disasters, our trigger adversities. A base-jumper colleague explained it this way: 'What is a terrifying abyss for some is paradise to others. When we're confronted with our trigger adversities, we are more likely to derail because our thinking tends to get blurred and problem solving becomes difficult.' He is describing a mini-amygdala hijack. A common outcome of a trigger event is embarrassment. Embarrassment is an acute loss of self-esteem, caused not by any behavior, but rather by our knowledge that the behavior has been observed and negatively evaluated by others (Reivich and Shatte 2002). However, an audience is not a necessary condition. Embarrassment may occur when we have acted in a way that is inconsistent with our personal values.

Coaching can help individuals to identify which adversities are triggering problems, and promote insight into how these adversities undermine self-control. The triggers are various and with complex patterns between them. In a new cultural and organizational environment, there is a bewildering array of new stimuli, some of which are likely to cause grief for new players. Some people are derailed by particular communications styles of others; others have problems chairing meetings with unfamiliar people, or maintaining balance between work and family (critical in overseas posting). Identifying patterns can help people create appropriate solutions.

MORPHING: TRAVELLING GUIDE IN THE DANGER ZONE

With a better understanding on how we can act within a survival setting, one can ask for a general applicable process for avoiding the danger or exiting. We call this process 'Morphing'.

Originally used to design 'digital imaging metamorphosis', a technique used to change one object smoothly into another in movies, the word spread quickly to other domains. Beck and Cowan (2003) used the term to define a gracefully altering course in a company's or culture's history without getting trapped. We prefer this term to 'resilience' which is related to 'bouncing back', to regain its original shape as quickly as possible. In survival this attitude is totally acceptable, as there is hope that this situation will once end and another life will start. In international business life, however, executives are often charged with coping with and implementing profound change. Assignments are often professionally, personally and organizationally transformational in positive ways. The aim is not to return to a former shape. The following paragraphs describe the elements of approaches conducive to effective morphing, many of which are familiar components of sound coaching programs.

Goal setting is a crucial element in morphing. Goal setting in a high-stress environment has to be rooted in the realm of our personal values and our significant relationships. This purpose can then be broken down in concrete sub-objectives and action plans.

A positive mental attitude is based upon a stable and enabling belief system that we possess the resources to achieve our goals, whatever they are. Survival instructors in different military survival schools add the adjective 'appropriate'. An exaggerated positive mental attitude can result in missing key elements of a situation, or can result in hostile reactions from other survivors, or enemies. Coaches can work with individuals to give them awareness about their temperament – noting any tendency towards overly negative or positive frames of mind. Strategies can then be devised to make appropriate changes that will promote improved performance and coping. An appropriate positive attitude is linked to self-efficacy, the belief that one masters the course of his own life and that one has the ability to accept the challenges that are presented (Goleman 1997).

Trivial events begin to shape an accident long before it happens so it is important for individuals to be able to perceive what is really happening. The coaching task is to assist people to notice things in their complex environments and to monitor how they are interacting with others. What clues might they be missing? What doesn't make sense? Are they accurately gauging their knowledge and skills?

We have noted above the need for impulse control and emotion regulation. This separation of facts from feelings enhances our ability to accurately identify the elements of the adversity and the tension between the present situation and the desired one, concretized by our expressed goal. Emotional regulation thus allows a better situational awareness.

Once we are aware of the situation – where we are and where we want to go – we can select the criteria for retrieving appropriate options, and not just jump on the first option that pops up. The task is to scan the situation to look for the option which is most likely to work, and to rapidly identify elements that can be used as resources. The task is to find an option that will work – not a perfect one! Life-threatening thirst need not be quenched by sophisticated sports drinks!

It is useful also to do a final check for possible obstacles through 'pessimistic' eyes. Once all options are identified we can decide to select the most appropriate one, based on a realistic risk assessment, available resources and time. If it appears that no option is going to work, it is necessary to start the process again, possibly with a changed goal or new approaches that will generate new options.

Once the option has been chosen, this intention must be translated into 'immediate action', remembering that the situation being faced is one of a current or impending crisis. In Figure 9.2 the process flow is synthesized in a flowchart.

While this chart may look complex, the aim is to move through each step at speed. Coaching

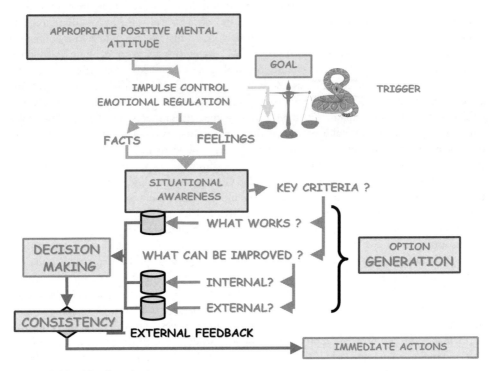

Figure 9.2 Morphing flow chart

can assist individuals to identify the process and develop their own strategies for coming up with in-the-moment solutions to crisis situations. Coaching strategies may include:

- Role playing likely scenarios;
- Debriefing past situations (both successful and unsuccessful); and
- Setting up meetings with others who have been in similar situations and thrived.

INSTALLING THE 'MIND-WARE'

Coaches can work directly with their clients on the 'mind-ware' – i.e., what mental processes are clients currently using and how can they best be shaped to equip them for future crisis situations? Is the executive missing any elements? If so, how can they be effectively integrated?

Morphing map

No model or map can accurately capture the complexity of the real world – particularly the real world of international business. Maps must be continuously (or at least regularly) updated to check position and counter contradictions and inconsistencies. Emotions affect our capacity to accurately and effectively keep our maps current. Anxiety, sadness, anger, guilt and embarrassment are linked to our mental maps via our belief system – our general rules on how the world ought to be and how we should operate within that world. We can distinguish deep-rooted, fundamental beliefs which apply to many different adversities (Reivich, in Reivich and Shatte 2002, calls these 'iceberg beliefs') and surface beliefs, floating on the surface of our awareness, linked directly to the ongoing event and driving our emotions and behaviors.

Enabling 'iceberg' beliefs

Sometimes the awareness of surface beliefs is not enough to identify the one that is driving our behavior. Iceberg beliefs are often fixed, frozen beliefs we don't often consciously think about. They lurk beneath the surface of awareness and can sink us: 'People must respect me at all times', 'A man doesn't show his emotions' are examples of such beliefs. Some underlying beliefs are adaptive, many others, because of their rigidity, minimize our effectiveness in responding to adversity. The make-or-break pillar enabling iceberg belief is that 'Life change is possible'.

Checking the presence of enabling beliefs is the very first step towards an adaptive information processing model. Coaches can check for underlying beliefs that may be blocking the morphing process. The root question is: 'What beliefs might the client be holding that are preventing him or her from coping with high pressured crisis situations?'

Values

Values are those things (or notions) that we are willing to expend resources for, or to obtain resources to have. For executives operating in different cultural environments, the values around them may be very different to their own. Coaching can help individuals clarify their own values, check how they fit in the environment, and position the executives so that values are drivers and motivators in times of crisis – and not potential derailers of the morphing process.

Mental programs

A mental program can be described as a structure, a sum of patterns installed within a person and which (1) determines his or her representation of the world, (2) conditions the processing of perceived data, and (3) leads to a reaction (Fevre et al., 1999). Morphing requires that the individual has a healthy and functioning mental programming capacity. There are numerous elements involved and coaching interventions can assist in building capacity – through awareness-raising and through experimentation.

An ability to dissociate is required in order to respond to a stressful situation. Associated, the person is part of the event – he or she views events through a subjective and often distorted lens. Dissociated, the individual sees the event from the outside without emotional connection – seeing him- or herself as an object. With this perspective, it is easier to manage feelings, observing the event with a certain distance. There is a choice whether to react with thinking or feeling, or a combination. This capacity has received considerable attention in developmental psychology and its application to coaching (Berger 2006).

One needs the ability to equally match and mismatch. To understand a situation it is important to have a full scope, to understand which pieces are working, and what does not work.

Strong mental programming includes the ability to chunk both specific and global. Chunk size relates to how people best receive and incorporate information. The ability to move from details to the big picture and back again allows shifting from concrete, specific details to a broader, yet more abstract level.

Internal and external frames of reference are necessary. The 'frame of reference' filter determines whether a person judges the responsibility for his or her actions through reference to internal or external data. A person with an internal frame will know if he has done a good job based upon his own internal reference system. This capacity, mandatory in a real survival situation where you cannot rely on objective data, is certainly useful in a stressful situation. However, it is useful to link this with an external check. In case of inconsistency of the external data with the internal knowing, a change in evaluation is possible.

CASE STUDY

Philippe, a senior HR manager, referred one of his direct reports to me for coaching. We had 10 sessions over approximately one year.

Diana had been the welfare officer at a French company with one thousand employees. The company had been taken over by Philippe's company, resulting in a cross-border entity of over 6,000 employees. After the merger, relations between Philippe and Diana deteriorated, even to the point that Diana made a formal complaint against Philippe for harassment following some very heated discussions. In his initial discussions, Philippe reported that he had indeed lost his cool with Diana, mainly because she stubbornly refused to understand just how tight the budget was and, consequently, refused to accept that major operational changes were necessary.

In the first session Diana said that she felt that she was receiving little or no support from her supervisor, the HR manager. He apparently saw no need for the luxury of a welfare officer and had told her that she might be fired.

It was clear from the first session that Diana was in a kind of survival situation. In working with her, I therefore drew on the models and approaches described in the preceding pages, giving attention to raising her awareness about what was happening in the situation and how she was approaching these new and fast-moving challenges.

After having defined a clear goal we started working on the beliefs and the mental programs. Empathic, ready to help, with a matching approach, she had excellent qualities for helping people, but few resources to defend their and her case in the business-frame thinking of her superior. So we worked on differentiating people from their belief systems. Over time, she realized that it was possible and desirable to effect a change in her belief system. Following this realization, bit-by-bit her belief system did indeed change. We started to work also on the practice of separating facts from feelings. This positioned Diana to better assess difficult situations. Finally, we worked on an inclusive match and mismatch option generation and a balanced internal/external outcome review.

The flowchart she constructed (Figure 9.3) shows how she finally schematized her new way of approach. It is similar to the earlier flowchart, yet different and personal, corresponding to her perception. In June 2004, at the beginning of the seventh session she asked if it was useful to continue. I asked her the same question and we decided that the goal was reached.

Six months later we met again for a follow-up session. Her working attitude and, in consequence, her relationship with her boss had changed dramatically. She was not fired and felt good with this new way of being. She stopped psychotherapeutic help and anti-depressant medication. She told me that she had also been able to make major and positive changes in her personal life, including separating from and divorcing her husband.

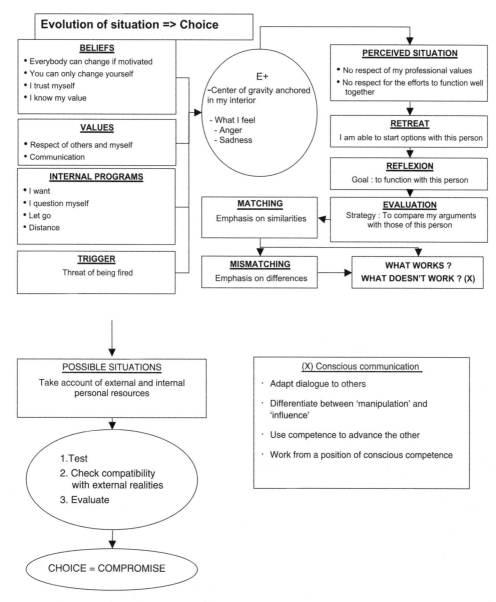

Figure 9.3 Case study – morphing flow chart

CONCLUSION

Every person comes to a place, at one time or another in their maturation, of complete loss and deadness, a stark and frightening absence of creativity and enthusiasm, where life seems to retreat from us like a tide (Whyte 2001). Every time we arrive at such a place, or even at less frightening and dramatic places, there are several pathways (whether we see them or not) leading us to new crossroads. Morphing is a simple model to help us confront the hugeness of our lives and our adversities.

I have drawn analogies between the situations of executives who choose to work in the pressure cooker of international business and those in survival situations in disasters and war zones. One difference is that executives have the opportunity and the resources to get support from professional coaches. Informed by the theories and models above, skilled coaching can allow international executives to survive and thrive by allowing them to see more paths, avoid traps and build value-driven futures that benefit them and those with whom they engage. In all of this, the aim is not to remove the hardship or challenges, because they are part of the attraction of the lifestyle. More, the aim is to ensure that individuals and their organizations receive appropriate support so that (1) they are not destroyed by the challenges, and (2) they play a part in constructing a healthy and sustainable business and social environment wherever they may go.

Bibliography

Beck, A., Emry, G. and Greenberg, R. (1985) *Anxiety Disorders and Phobias*, New York: Basic Books.

Beck, D.E. and Cowan, C. (2003) *Spiral Dynamics*, Malden: Blackwell Publishing.

Berger, J. G. (2006) 'Adult development theory and executive coaching practice', in D.R. Stober and A. M. Grant (eds), *Evidence Based Coaching Handbook: Putting Best Practices to Work for Your Clients*, New York: John Wiley and Sons.

Combs, A. (2002) *The Radiance of Being*, Saint Paul: Paragon House.

Cooper, R. and Sawaf, A. (1996) *Executive EQ: Emotional Intelligence in Leadership and Organizations*, New York: Berkeley Publishing Group.

Dilts, R. (1986) *Changing Belief Systems with NLP*, Cupertino: Meta Publications.

Fevre, L., Servais, C. and Soto, G. (1999) *Guide du maître Praticien en PNL*, Lyon: Chronique Sociale.

Frankl, V. E. (1985/1946) *Man's Search for Meaning*, New York: Simon & Schuster Inc.

Goleman, D. (1997) *L'intelligence emotionnelle*, Paris: Editions Robert Laffont.

Goleman, D. (2006) *Social Intelligence: The Revolutionary New Science of Human Relationships*, New York: Bantam.

Gonzales, L. (2003), *Deep Survival*, New York: W. W. Norton & Company.

Goudsmet, A. (2002) *L'athlète d'entreprise*, Bruxelles: Editions Kluwer.

Klein, G. (1999) *Sources of Power: How People Make Decisions*, Cambridge, MA: MIT Press.

Klein, G. (2003) *Intuition at Work: Why Developing Your Gut Instincts Will Make You Better at What You Do*, New York: Random House.

Laborde, G. (1987) *Influencer avec intégrité*, Paris: Inter Editions.

Leach, J. (1994) *Survival Psychology*, London: The Macmillan Press.

Linley, P. A. and Joseph, S. (2004) 'Positive change following trauma and adversity', *Journal of Traumatic Stress*, 17 (1): 11–21.

Marx, E. (2001). *Breaking through Culture Shock: What You Need to Succeed in International Business*, London: Nicholas Brealey Publishing.

Mesters, P. and Peeters, S. (2007) *Vaincre l'épuisement professionnel*, Paris: Robert Laffont.

Nordström, K., and Ridderstrale, J. (2005) *Karaoke Capitalism*, West Port, CN: Praeger.

Paulson, D. (2002) *Competitive Business, Caring Business*, New York: Para Press.

Peeters, J. (1996) personal communication.

Reivich, K. and Shatte, A. (2002) *The Resilience Factor*, New York: Broadway Books.

Rollins, Dr K., Colonel (2004) US Joint Personnel Recovery Agency, Personal communication, 30 Nov.

Shapiro, F. E. (2001) *EMDR: Basic Principles, Protocols and Procedures*, New York: The Guilford Press.

Ward, C. and Kennedy, A. (2001) 'Coping with cross-cultural transition', *Journal of Cross-Cultural Psychology*, 32 (5): 636–42.

Whyte, D. (2001) *Crossing the Unknown Sea*, New York: Riverhead Books.

Wilber, K. (2001) *A Theory of Everything*, Boston, MA: Shambhala.

FOSTERING INDIVIDUAL AND COLLECTIVE DEVELOPMENT USING THE CULTURAL ORIENTATIONS FRAMEWORK (COF™) ASSESSMENT

Philippe Rosinski

THEORETICAL FRAMEWORK: COACHING ACROSS CULTURES AND THE CULTURAL ORIENTATIONS FRAMEWORK

Business coaching, originating from the USA, has developed essentially from common sense (e.g., set priorities, manage time) and psychology (e.g., behavioral psychology, emotional intelligence). The cultural dimension was missing or at best given anecdotal and superficial attention. Coaching, defined in this chapter as 'the art of facilitating the unleashing of people's potential to reach meaningful, important objectives' (Rosinski 2003: 4), assumed a worldview that was not universally applicable. My book (Rosinski 2003) *Coaching across Cultures'* purpose was to help unleash more human potential by tapping into the richness of cultural diversity. This chapter gives attention to the use of the Cultural Orientations Framework (COF, see Figure 10.1), which is explained in detail in the book. The COF is an integrative framework designed to assess and compare cultures. It is a coaching-specific measurement tool that can be invaluable for introducing meaningful dialogue about culture into coaching and coach-training. The COF can be used to establish individual and collective COF profiles, while providing the scope for creating new cultural dimensions that reflect unique contexts.

Coaching across cultures (also referred to as 'intercultural coaching' or 'global coaching') enables more effective work across cultures (in an international sense and also generally when working with people from various organizations and backgrounds). More fundamentally, intercultural coaching is in essence a more creative form of coaching. The approach challenges cultural assumptions. It propels you, the coach, and your coachees beyond previous limitations. It offers new options in the form of alternative ways of thinking, communicating, managing time, and engaging in our various activities.

A group's culture can be defined as the set of unique characteristics that distinguishes its members from another group (Rosinski 2003: 20). These characteristics include external/ visible behaviors as well as internal/buried traits such as norms, values and basic assumptions. The poet David Whyte once said that 'difficulties can fall away when we make our inner territory larger, while simplifying our outer work' (Whyte 2000). Intercultural coaches help their coachees raise their awareness and expand their worldview (internal reality) to address

Categories	Dimensions	Description
Sense of Power and Responsibility	Control/ Harmony/ Humility	Control: People have a determinant power and responsibility to forge the life they want. Harmony: Strive for balance and harmony with nature. Humility: Accept inevitable natural limitations.
Time Management Approaches	Scarce/ Plentiful	Scarce: Time is a scarce resource. Manage time carefully! Plentiful: Time is abundant. Relax!
	Monochronic/ Polychronic	Monochronic: Concentrate on one activity and/or relationship at a time. Polychronic: Concentrate simultaneously on multiple tasks and/or people.
	Past/ Present/ Future	Past: Learn from the past. The present is essentially a continuation or a repetition of past occurrences. Present: Focus on the "here and now" and short-term benefits. Future: Have a bias towards long-term benefits. Promote a far-reaching vision.
Definitions of Identity and Purpose	Being/ Doing	Being: Stress living itself and the development of talents and relationships. Doing: Focus on accomplishments and visible achievements.
	Individualistic/ Collectivistic	Individualistic: Emphasize individual attributes and projects. Collectivistic: Emphasize affiliation with a group.
	Hierarchy/ Equality	Hierarchy: Society and organizations must be socially stratified to function properly. Equality: People are equals who often happen to play different roles.
	Universalist/ Particularist	Universalist: All cases should be treated in the same universal manner. Adopt common processes for consistency and economies of scale. Particularist: Emphasize particular circumstances. Favor decentralization and tailored solutions.
Organizational Arrangements	Stability/ Change	Stability: Value a static and orderly environment. Encourage efficiency through systematic and disciplined work. Minimize change and ambiguity, perceived as disruptive. Change: Value a dynamic and flexible environment. Promote effectiveness through adaptability and innovation. Avoid routine, perceived as boring.
	Competitive/ Collaborative	Competitive: Promote success and progress through competitive stimulation. Collaborative: Promote success and progress through mutual support, sharing of best practices and solidarity.
Notions of Territory and Boundaries	Protective/ Sharing	Protective: Protect oneself by keeping personal life and feelings private (mental boundaries), and by minimizing intrusions in one's physical space (physical boundaries). Sharing: Build closer relationships by sharing one's psychological and physical domains.
Communication Patterns	High-Context/ Low-Context	High-Context: Rely on implicit communication. Appreciate the meaning of gestures, postures, voice and context. Low-Context: Rely on explicit communication. Favor clear and detailed instructions.
	Direct/ Indirect	Direct: In a conflict or with a tough message to deliver, get your point across clearly at the risk of offending or hurting. Indirect: In a conflict or with a tough message to deliver, favor maintaining a cordial relationship at the risk of misunderstanding.
	Affective/ Neutral	Affective: Display emotions and warmth when communicating. Establishing and maintaining personal and social connections is key. Neutral: Stress conciseness, precision and detachment when communicating.
	Formal/ Informal	Formal: Observe strict protocols and rituals. Informal: Favor familiarity and spontaneity.
Modes of Thinking	Deductive/ Inductive	Deductive: Emphasize concepts, theories and general principles. Then, through logical reasoning, derive practical applications and solutions. Inductive: Start with experiences, concrete situations and cases. Then, using intuition, formulate general models and theories.

Figure 10.1 Cultural Orientations Framework (Rosinski 2003)

complex challenges and enable effective actions (external reality). In turn, these experiences enrich coachees' cultural repertoire, fostering an upward learning spiral.

To systematically integrate culture into coaching, we need a language to talk about culture, a vocabulary to describe cultural characteristics. The task may appear daunting: there are almost an infinite number of possible behaviors, norms, values and basic assumptions. The good news is that, pragmatically, we can choose to focus on the most relevant and salient aspects, building upon the work of eminent interculturalists. The Cultural Orientations Framework (Rosinski 2003, Part II) includes a range of cultural dimensions/orientations grouped in seven categories of practical importance to leaders, professional coaches and anyone striving to unleash human potential in organizations:

- Sense of power and responsibility;
- Time management approaches;
- Definitions of identity and purpose;
- Organizational arrangements;
- Notions of territory and boundaries; and
- Communication patterns; and Modes of thinking.

The COF builds upon the findings of anthropologists, communication experts, and cross-cultural consultants, including Florence Kluckhohn and Fred Strodtbeck (1961), Edward Hall (1976), Geert Hofstede (2001), and Fons Trompenaars (1997), among others. A 'cultural orientation' is an inclination to think, feel or act in a way that is culturally determined, or at least influenced by culture. For example, in the United States people tend to communicate in a direct fashion, saying what they mean, and meaning what they say. The message is clear, but it can also be perceived as offensive. Their cultural orientation, then, is 'direct communication', in contrast with Asians' typical indirectness. Asians don't necessarily spell out what they mean, at the risk of being misunderstood, because they wish to avoid hurting someone's feelings.

Cultural orientations are not black-and-white. In other words, no one is totally direct or indirect, but individuals and cultures lie somewhere on a continuum bounded by the extreme on both ends. For example, you may be inclined to be direct 75 per cent of the time and indirect in the remaining 25 per cent (see Figure 10.2).

The COF has a number of uses:

- *Assess cultures* – The COF provides a language to describe the salient traits of a culture and focuses your attention on key cultural variables and tendencies;
- *Discover new cultural choices* – You may recognize an orientation for, say hierarchical organization and compare it with a preference for a flat structure. Patterns that seemed so natural and universal suddenly appear relative and even biased when contrasted with their

Example: Direct–Indirect communication cultural dimension

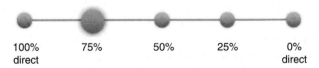

100%
direct

75%

50%

25%

0%
direct

Direct communication orientation   *Indirect communication orientation*

Figure 10.2 Sample of COF measurement scale – indirect communication

opposites. Orientations that had been overlooked or undiscovered offer new choices for dealing with challenging situations;

- *Assess cultural differences* – Stewart and Bennett's (1991) research found that the core difficulty in cross-cultural interaction is a failure to recognize relevant cultural differences. When several cultures are involved, the COF gives you a systematic approach to clarify the nature of cultural differences among them as well as similarities;
- *Bridge different cultures* – Having pinpointed specific cultural differences you can then focus your energy next on bridging the gaps;
- *Envision a desired culture* – The COF provides a vocabulary to describe an ideal culture. It then becomes a matter of bridging the current culture with the desired one. The challenge is still great, but it becomes manageable at least; and
- *Leverage cultural diversity* – With cultural alternatives clearly identified, you can strive to have the best of the two or three viewpoints for each dimension. Whenever possible, you will make the most of cultural differences and achieve synergy.

Several important nuances distinguish the COF from previous models. Among these nuances:

- *Merit* – The choice of words should convey the potential merit of each orientation. For example, I chose the term 'humility' instead of 'subjugation to nature' coined by Kluckhohn and Stodtbeck (1961: 4);
- *Essence* – I have clung closely to the essence of dimensions, which lie in the etymology. For example, I have defined 'monochronic' time simply as, 'concentrate on one activity and/or relationship at a time' in contrast with 'polychronic time' ('concentrate simultaneously on multiple tasks and/or relationships'). Hall's original concept (1976) includes other notions such as 'scheduling' and 'compartmentalization', which do not necessarily relate to the 'monochronic/polychronic' time duality time per se (Rosinski 2003: 96).
- *Dialectics* – Most importantly, I am less interested in describing static and binary traits of a culture (e.g., the French are like this, the Americans are like that) than in having a vocabulary to depict dynamic and complex cultural features. Aristotle declared that 'out of two contradictory propositions, if one is true, the other must be false'. Ironically, this is true and false at the same time! Binary thinking (or) tends to promote polarization and division. Dialectics (and) is called for to find new ways to reconcile alternatives, leverage differences and enable unity in diversity (Rosinski 2003: 57–8).

THE COF ASSESSMENT

The advantages of using the COF assessment to foster individual and collective development derive from the following hypotheses, which have been verified in my experience and from reports by other coaches who have used this tool in various ways:

- When habitual solutions don't work, as is typically the case with recurrent and complex challenges, it is necessary to review our cultural assumptions and examine our reality from alternative perspectives;
- Cultural orientations we are overusing might get us into trouble (e.g., direct communication, when overdone, might bruise people and disrupt communication); and
- Cultural orientations we are overlooking represent developmental opportunities (e.g., showing more sensitivity through appropriate indirect communication).

The COF assessment can facilitate a fruitful exploration around questions such as:

1   Referring back to your challenge, which cultural orientations may you be overdoing in this situation?
2   Describe how this gets you into trouble.
3   Which cultural orientations are you overlooking?
4   Describe how this would represent a growth opportunity for you.
5   What would be different if you mastered that?

This chapter draws in part from the use of a paper (PDF) version of the COF assessment used in November 2006 with an international group of 15 coaches during an advanced executive coaching seminar. Following the successful use of the instrument in the PDF format, a COF online assessment has been developed. The online version makes the COF easily accessible to individuals around the world and also provides flexibility for use of the tool with groups, including geographically dispersed teams. (Individuals can use the tool free-of-charge at <www.philrosinski.com/cof>. Further information can be obtained from the author.)

A project manager, specifically trained to use the COF, can administer it to an entire team, division, organization and even several corporations in the case of a merger. Aggregate results can be viewed globally and through sorting (e.g., per country, per division, per hierarchical level, and in fact per any combination of categories). Data concerning several projects in the same organization can be further aggregated to establish an organization profile. The tool allows users to:

• Aggregate individual results and establish group profiles on a project basis (e.g., team profile, organization overall profile as well as profiles per categories/fields the project manager has predefined such as division, nationality, management level, merging entities, etc.); and
• Add customized supplemental cultural dimensions beyond the COF's 17 standard dimensions.

In truth, the cultural profile concept is somewhat of a stretch. Cultural orientations depend indeed to a large extent on the cultural context (unlike psychological preferences). This means that orientations frequently change (at least to some degree) depending on the situation (e.g., low context at work, high context with family and with close, long-time friends). Therefore, how can we establish a reliable cultural profile? One solution is to devise a cultural profile in each situation. The cultural profile would be accurate, but only in that situation. Another solution is to accept that an individual cultural profile is only meant to represent a default, an overall tendency.

A cultural profile does not always determine actions. For example, you might have an orientation toward competition, yet choose collaboration in a particular situation. Consequently, your cultural profile does not limit your potential. The opposite is true. Aware of your profile, you can discover new options outside your profile and tap into this unexpected potential. Coaches can help their coachees though similar processes.

Methodological considerations: usefulness versus validity

Intercultural coaching assumes a 'multiple realities' view of the world. Culture from this perspective is highly contextual, dynamic, and fluid. Capturing data through the COF in a moment of time is useful for generating conversations and making sense of change processes, but not so helpful in seeking definitive truths about individuals, groups or societies.

The questionnaire gives preference to simplicity and straightforwardness. The items are directly derived from the definition of each cultural orientation (see Figure 10.2). The aim is for participants to establish cultural profiles that constitute a useful basis for further discussion, rather than a truly valid measure. Paradoxically, this may sometimes yield more valid results than properly validated psychometric instruments. Indeed, the validation process often produces an illusion of absolute accuracy, which does not hold true in practice. Even the best researched and most popular assessments include inevitable assumptions and biases that might prove incorrect. For example, the Bar-On Emotional Quotient Inventory is considered by many as the best instrument to evaluate someone's emotional intelligence and is certainly a useful coaching assessment tool (Bar-On 2002). Still, I recently had the chance to review a report that showed a low score for 'problem solving'. As it turns out, one item that drove the score down had to do with a 'step-by-step' approach. The assumption built into the instrument implies that this method is a panacea whereas, in my view, it reveals a 'Sensing' (using the Myers-Briggs Type Instrument terminology) psychological bias or/and a linear cultural bias. Intuition may prove more appropriate to solve certain problems. Rather than solely relying on step-by-step, creativity is essential, defined as the 'faculty to find original ideas, different approaches, when confronted with a problem or a challenge that resists habitual solutions' (Rosinski 2003: 187).

Another example has to do with the apparent contradictions between separate conceptualization and research, both derived from Carl Jung's seminal work around psychological types (Jung 1971/1923): the popular Myers-Briggs Type Instrument (MBTI, Myers et al. 1998) and Dr Katherine Benzinger's Cerebral Cortex's Four Modes of Thinking (Benzinger 2006). Dr Benzinger's model distinguishes four modes of thinking through a physical representation in the brain:

- Frontal right;
- Frontal left;
- Basal right;
- Basal left.

The MBTI model includes four dichotomies of:

- Extraversion (E) – Introversion (I);
- Sensing (S) – Intuition (I);
- Thinking (T) – Feeling (F); and
- Judging (J) – Perceiving (P).

Without going into the detail, the Judging–Perceiving (J–P) dichotomy is absent in Dr Benzinger's model. What is confusing for someone familiar with the MBTI is that her description of the four modes de facto seems to assume either J or P in addition to the functions. For example, Frontal Right equates to Intuition Feeling (NF) and P. Having an ENFP preference, this works for me but what about someone with an NF and J preference? Dr Benzinger explains that she uses only parts of Jung's core model that have a solid physiological base, and that her work represents the synthesis of more than thirty years of neuroscience with psychology (Benzinger 2007). In sum, both schools can boast solid research to support their findings, which in fact are mostly consistent. Yet the existing contradictions suggest that these findings are still merely hypotheses that should not be confused with an absolute truth.

The best scientific research implies paying close attention to what does not fit with current conceptualization. Openness and curiosity are called for. Einstein once said, 'I have no special talent. I am only passionately curious'. He also noted, 'The important thing is not to stop questioning. Curiosity has its own reason for existing. One cannot help but be in awe when one contemplates the mysteries of eternity, of life, of the marvelous structure of reality' (Singh 2004: 98–9). All these qualities are also essential in global coaching and should hopefully inspire us to exert caution when using theories, models and psychometric instruments. We should avoid two extremes when analyzing results: dismissing or accepting results too quickly. An open mind together with healthy skepticism is required to learn from any assessment. The feedback giver needs the combination of rigor and curiosity to move beyond the illusion of absolute accuracy, to understand the instrument's biases and limitations and to treat findings as working hypotheses.

Building a valid cultural psychometric instrument would be even trickier for several reasons including:

- The notion that culture can be assessed with a questionnaire is already culturally biased;
- Language is an issue: English is fortunately widely known in international business but is certainly still far from being mastered by everyone. Translations, on the other hand, raise various difficulties. For example, some concepts may not have an equivalent in a foreign language; and
- Even within a given culture, built-in assumptions can distort results. When you add the cultural variable, risks that assumptions linking observable manifestations to concepts will not hold true multiply.

This is not to suggest that the COF is immune from difficulties. For example, participants in certain cultures might be reluctant to express disagreement and are therefore likely to skew measures of abilities. However, and paradoxically, the COF assessment may prove advantageous by striving to merely enable useful conversations without claiming to be valid. In intercultural business coaching, it is important to give prime importance to conversations that flow from data rather than to the data themselves or to the tools from which they are derived. With any instrument – the COF included – it is critical to carefully launch the assessment process, by giving clear instructions, warning against possible issues that might distort the results, and mostly by creating a safe and constructive environment, which encourages candidness and growth from the onset.

In my experience, the COF assessment is well accepted by coaching clients. However, other options exist to address the cultural dimension topic. For example, inductive approaches (Rosinski 2003: 618) can be used on their own or in combination with the COF assessment. To be able to help clients in this area, it is essential that coaches give attention to their own cultural orientations and how they might be impacting on the coaching assignment. Coaches need also to understand the cultural assumptions associated with the tools and approaches they are using. The COF in coach training can assist coaches to gain insights about the way culture influences their own work, as well as skill them in raising awareness of how culture might be impacting the lives of their clients.

CASE STUDIES

Individual executive coaching

The COF assessment is typically of greatest value when used systematically in the initial assessment phase of executive coaching and when referred to subsequently in connection with the client's concrete situations. The COF assessment can effectively complement other commonly used instruments such as the Myers–Briggs Type Indicator and the Fundamental Interpersonal Relations Orientation–Behavior (FIRO-B), with the underlying common philosophy of making a constructive use of differences. The FIRO-B (Waterman and Rogers, 1996) explores three critical areas related to interpersonal relationships:

- Inclusion (social interactions);
- Control (taking the lead, making decisions, empowering); and
- Affection (personal relationships, openness).

It distinguishes behaviours we initiate (Expressed) from behaviours we expect from others (Wanted).

In this case study, I use the example of a Belgian senior executive, country manager for Belgium in a large international corporation. Some details have been changed (including name) to protect confidentiality.

Tom's FIRO-B scores in the Affection category were unusually high (8 for 'Expressed Affection', 7 for 'Wanted Affection', on a scale from 0 to 9). The COF assessment showed a clear orientation for sharing (versus protective) coupled with only a fair self-perceived ability to use the protective orientation when necessary. These combined results facilitated a constructive discussion around what was preventing Tom from spending sufficient time in Belgium (both at his home office and with his family) and cut down on his tiring international travel. They also allowed him to decipher patterns of delaying confrontation when handling difficult interpersonal situations. High Affection scores enabled Tom to naturally show empathy and promote bonding in his team. This was highly appreciated. However, this tendency worked as a double-edged sword. An unconscious tendency to 'please' implied that he was sometimes too patient with sub-par performance and this prevented him from confronting certain team members.

The COF assessment clearly revealed the necessity to erect boundaries, and to firmly set limits (protective orientation). As a result of the coaching dialogue, Tom started to confront one of his direct reports, whose results had been below par for over a year, giving him three months to show significant improvement and reach mutually agreed targets, as a condition to continue the collaboration. Incidentally, learning from the MBTI as well, Tom consciously moved outside his Intuition Perceiving (NP) comfort zone by devising and adhering to a detailed developmental plan in a Sensing Judging (SJ) fashion. The COF gave him a chance to realize that he was not really at ease with very direct communication, that is, in a conflict or with a tough message to deliver, getting his point across clearly at the risk of offending or hurting. Tom explained that, although his behavior was appropriate in a Belgian context, his straightforwardness was insufficient in the Netherlands and in Denmark where more directness is expected. Moreover, his orientation toward affective communication coupled with a higher ability made him realize that he sometimes overlooked the importance of precise and concise communication.

His FIRO-B scores in the Control area were relatively high (7 for Expressed Control, 6 for Wanted Control). The COF results for control–harmony–humility shed light into these results:

humility being both less preferred and less mastered than harmony and control. Tom could not conceive that his direct report was simply not taking his responsibilities. A sense of ownership coupled with Tom's sensitivity further explained why he had not confronted poor performance more quickly: Tom had over-sympathized with the hardship his direct report had indeed gone through. Tom realized his 'rescuer' role was only maintaining his direct report in a 'victim' position, in which he continued to use personal problems as an excuse. Temporarily difficult life circumstances alone could not explain the poor performance. Tom had to make sure his direct report would accept and tackle his issues.

Other COF dimensions contributed insights for Tom's future career choice. He interpreted his orientation for polychronic time and change as confirmations about the importance of having variety in his work. Continuing on the path of general management would allow him to best honor his preference. The combined psychological and cultural awareness have allowed Tom to identify personal tendencies that had proved counterproductive (as well as highlight many assets he had), and most importantly to discover new choices that helped him become more effective as a leader than he already was. In this case, the following guidelines were applied in assisting Tom to make sense of the data from the instruments:

- Interpretations are primarily the responsibility of the client;
- The coach mostly invites the executive to articulate what struck him or her in the results, as confirmations, new insights, or questions;
- The coach may tentatively propose interpretations, carefully framing remarks as hypotheses;
- The observations of the coach are linked where possible to the concrete challenges the executive is facing; and
- The coach facilitates a discovery process in which the executive him- or herself uses the assessment to see his or her reality from new perspectives, to identify strengths as well as pitfalls, and to conclude with specific new choices and actions to address challenges.

An advantage of both personality and cultural profiles is that they help reframe difficulties in terms of underused preferences rather than personal deficiencies. Awareness and conscious attention can go a long way to address difficulties. It would not be the same if issues were attributed to personal deficiencies that might decrease self-esteem and self-confidence, thereby undermining the resolution process.

TEAM EXECUTIVE COACHING

This section presents some of the COF aggregate results of an international group of 15 coaches who took part in an advanced cross-cultural coach training. Although this seminar was not a team coaching session per se, the results should nevertheless give a sense of how the COF can be used with a group and of the type of insights that can be gained through this process. The professional coaches (12 women and 3 men, aged between 40 and 60) were all experienced, from countries including the United Kingdom, Belgium, France, Turkey, Israel and the United States.

Orientations that are underrepresented might be overlooked by the group and may well include the wisdom, perspectives and skills necessary to address challenges that resist habitual solutions. This is helpful for identifying new growth opportunities and new choices for dealing with complex challenges. In other cases, the group could systematically recognize and

153

build upon its assets. Its cultural inclinations might already be particularly suited for addressing certain challenges. Insights can be gained both at the individual and group level. Examining the COF results can help facilitate growth for both a team as a whole and individuals within the team.

Examining in detail all the results is beyond the scope of this chapter. I have focused on select dimensions and given some examples of questions a coach might use with a group to raise awareness about each of the COF dimensions. The aim, as noted earlier, is always to encourage clients to generate their own interpretations rather than for the 'expert' coach/facilitator to impose interpretations. The assumption is that the clients are experts in their own professional and cultural contexts. This does not exclude sharing, when appropriate, other examples and insights, notably on how to leverage differences, and referring to the book *Coaching across Cultures* for more information.

Control–harmony–humility

The orientation is primarily toward 'control' with 92 per cent declaring to be good or excellent at taking responsibility. This is an invaluable asset for setting targets and achieving them, sometimes against all odds. On the other hand, the orientation toward the 'humility' perspective is almost absent. Furthermore, only 43 per cent of the group self-scores favorably on ability to use 'humility'. (Generally speaking our assumption is that responding with 'slightly agree'/fair suggests a hesitation and is therefore not considered favorable. In this case, 43 per cent is the addition of 29 per cent 'agree'/good and 14 percent 'strongly agree'/ excellent.)

Possible questions for a coach/facilitator to assist clients to explore the data might be:

- What are the advantages of a control orientation?
- In what situations might a control orientation be less helpful?
- What alternatives might there be?
- Looking at individual results, did anyone see a marked variation in their own orientations on this item in relation to the group?
- What might this mean in practice?

The current results would suggest that learning to accept natural limitations is a developmental opportunity. Embracing 'humility' (leveraging it with 'control') should help the group aim for realistic and sustainable success, resisting the possible temptation to do whatever it takes to succeed, at the risk of going to excesses, breaking down, etc. – and help their coachees do the same.

Scarce–plentiful time

The orientation is clearly toward 'scarce' versus 'plentiful', reflecting the bias that 'time is money' and that we should strive to use time efficiently. Furthermore, only 28 per cent of the group scores favorably on the ability to use the 'plentiful' time orientation. The possibility that time could be viewed as 'plentiful' seems to be overlooked by the group and represents a developmental opportunity (the value of slowing down, of 'giving time time'). However, despite the scarce time orientation and the fact that coaches are often called upon to help coachees

Table 10.1 Control/harmony/humility – orientations

Orientations

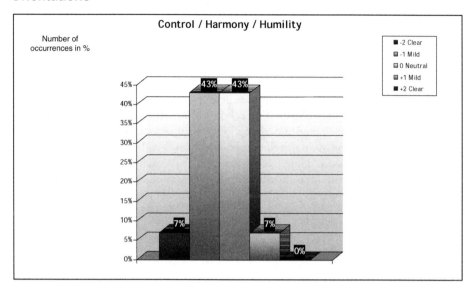

manage their time more productively, 35 per cent of the group members still admit difficulties in using time efficiently.

The coach/facilitator might observe that the group orientation reflects a mainstream Western bias and invite discussion about alternative approaches and possible advantages. He or she could highlight the paradox that by taking the time (as if time was plentiful) one might better

Table 10.2 Control/harmony/humility – abilities

Abilities

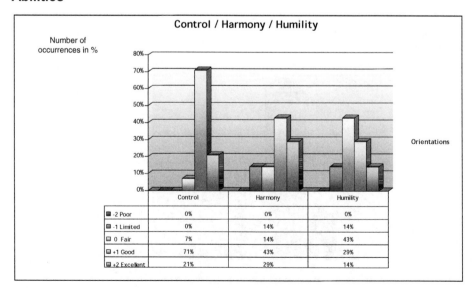

	Control	Harmony	Humility
■ -2 Poor	0%	0%	0%
■ -1 Limited	0%	14%	14%
▣ 0 Fair	7%	14%	43%
▣ +1 Good	71%	43%	29%
▣ +2 Excellent	21%	29%	14%

appreciate its scarcity, the eternity in one moment. It is easier to see what is really important when stepping back and slowing down. The coach might ask the group how specifically they would go about treating time in a plentiful fashion for more effectiveness, how they could improve on their efficiency and how they could leverage both perspectives.

Being–doing

The orientation distribution is close to a normal curve (even bell shape) and abilities scores are high both for 'being' and 'doing'. These results echo the thesis that executive coaches contribute significantly by leveraging 'being' and 'doing'. They bring precious help into corporations where the emphasis is often on 'doing' at the expense of 'being'. As I have argued, more 'being' can paradoxically help increased 'doing' (achievements). The coach/facilitator might explore the views of the group on the ideal distribution for a group of coaches. A question might include the invitation for people to provide examples of where being and doing worked well together.

Stability–change

The dominant orientation is 'change' with an impressive 100 per cent of favorable scores on the ability to work well in a dynamic environment where adaptability and innovation are promoted. Coaches are indeed often referred to as change agents but change is not the only, nor always the best choice we have. With a limited inclination and self-evaluated ability for stability, the questions might be:

Table 10.3 Scarce/plentiful time – orientations

Orientations

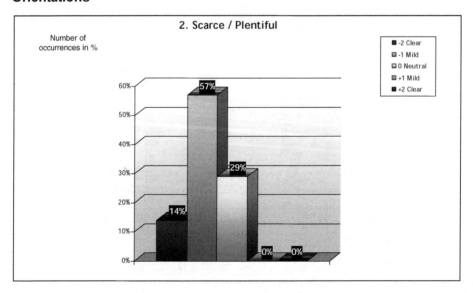

Table 10.4 Scarce/plentiful time – abilities

Abilities

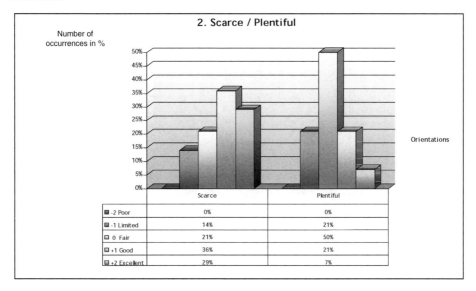

	Scarce	Plentiful
■ -2 Poor	0%	0%
■ -1 Limited	14%	21%
▢ 0 Fair	21%	50%
▢ +1 Good	36%	21%
▣ +2 Excellent	29%	7%

Table 10.5 Being/doing – orientations

Orientations

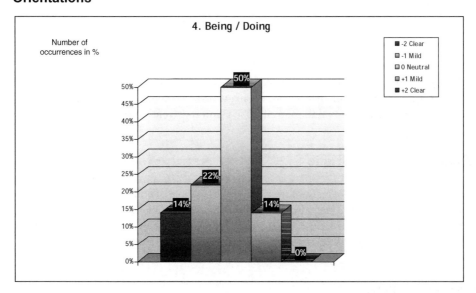

Table 10.6 Being/doing – abilities

Abilities

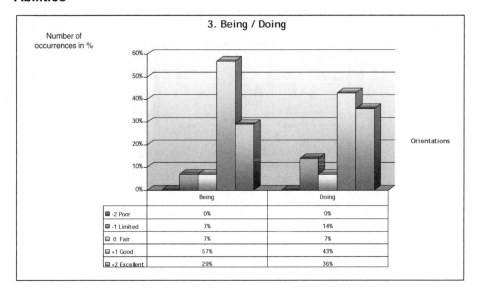

	Being	Doing
■ -2 Poor	0%	0%
■ -1 Limited	7%	14%
■ 0 Fair	7%	7%
■ +1 Good	57%	43%
■ +2 Excellent	29%	36%

- What are the merits of stability that you might overlook?
- In your coaching, do you remember that the ideal combination often includes periods of changes alternating with periods of stability (notably for recuperation and consolidation)?
- Moreover, how can you paradoxically promote change by reframing 'resistance to change' into a positive 'preference for stability'?

For the group, the danger would be to strive for new and radical changes at times when consolidation, disciplined maintenance and systematic improvement of existing processes would be necessary. How then can you find motivation in rigorous execution and disciplined practice?

Individualistic–collectivistic

The distribution is close to normal and the group looks capable of emphasizing both individual projects/attributes and affiliation with the team. This seemed apparent during the seminar, when participants showed the richness of their individuality and cultures, while constructively contributing to the group's harmonious functioning and its shared ideals.

Hierarchy–equality

The dominant orientation is 'equality', as can be expected with the equality bias inherent in coaching. I have argued in *Coaching across Cultures* that coaching assumes equality but that it can nevertheless also benefit from a 'hierarchy' orientation. Moreover, 93 per cent of the group scores favorably on the ability to use equality. However, 43 per cent seems to have difficulties working well in an hierarchical environment.

Table 10.7 Stability/change – orientations

Orientations

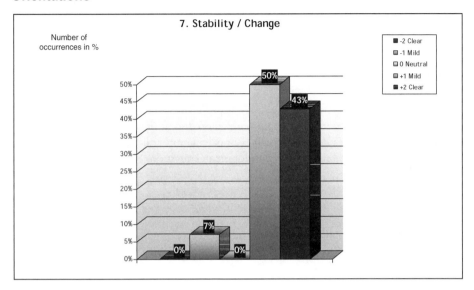

Table 10.8 Stability/change – abilities

Abilities

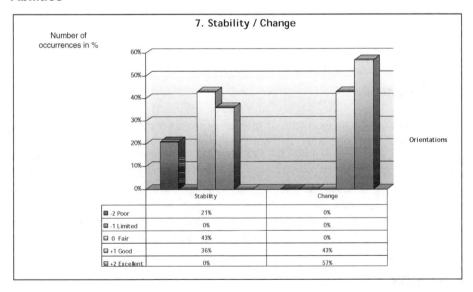

Questions for discussion might include:

- How prepared are you to help your coachees deal effectively with hierarchies?
- Are you able to help them engage in 'constructive politics'?
- Do you run the risk of overlooking that possibility and ignore politics?

Universalist–particularist

The dominant orientation is 'particularist' and 79 per cent of the group scores favorably on adapting to particular circumstances by promoting tailored solutions. The group is likely to be flexible. With 'universalism' underrepresented as an orientation, and only 35 per cent favorable scores on the corresponding ability, useful developmental questions for the group could be:

- How can you take better advantage of economies of scale?
- How can you achieve better coherence when working collectively?

The challenge is to strive for both consistency and flexibility.

Direct–indirect

Over 42 per cent of the group prefers 'direct' communication (although only 7 per cent clearly prefers directness). Half the group, however, is either neutral or inclined toward indirect communication. This is significantly different from traditional coaching, which has assumed direct communication and disregarded indirect communication. The abilities scores suggest that group members can learn from one another, to be both clear and sensitive when communicating in difficult situations.

Analytical–systemic

The majority in this group prefers systemic thinking (with 86 per cent of members considering themselves good or very good at it). This profile is probably unusual in Western society. This group of global coaches is culturally inclined to help others explore connections between elements, establish links and focus on the whole system. This cultural orientation is becoming increasingly necessary in today's global and interconnected world (e.g., we notably have to work in concert and across disciplines to address new global threats such as global warming and to preserve our planet). Analytical thinking is still needed, however, and 35 per cent of the group declares to have only a fair or limited ability to dissect a problem into smaller chunks.

CONCLUSION

Beyond the data and interpretations we can offer, it is important that we, as global coaches (1) ensure deep awareness is built, which goes beyond a superficial intellectual understanding of these concepts, and (2) foster actual development building upon the new awareness. Experimentation is critical. My experience in training coaches in advanced techniques of cross-cultural coaching has shown that role plays can facilitate learning. This is particularly the case when participants have the chance to role play challenging situations both one-to-one and in team interactions and these are videotaped and then debriefed. Role plays used in creative ways can be valuable when coaching executive teams across cultural boundaries, where there is considerable diversity. Concrete situations help participants appreciate how their cultural orientations (both individual and collective) play out and the debrief conversations help them identify new choices that might prove more effective. The questions asked by the intercultural coaches must be tailored to each particular group. One of their tasks is to inform their questions by knowledge of their clients and the international context in which they are operating. Some groups in some cultures may be more receptive to more hierarchical interventions from the 'teacher as role model/expert perspective'. At the same time, the facilitator may use the COF to challenge the group's perception of his or her cultural orientations and to invite new ways of interacting.

The following questions, when tailored to the particular group, have proven useful:

- What are your cultural orientations?
- How do these orientations possibly vary depending on the context?
- How do your cultural orientations impact the way you coach/lead?

Referring to their particular challenges dealing with a different culture:

- What are their orientations and the key differences with yours?
- How do you reconcile the differences?
- How are you learning/growing from this (enriching your own cultures, expanding your options when coaching/leading and living)?

There are countless questions a coach could ask to generate discussion and awareness around issues of culture. Additional questions might include:

- What are the dominant orientations in the team?
- How do you – as an individual – seem to be similar and different? What implications does this have on the ground?
- What cultural orientations are not represented in your team?
- How can you compensate for this absence?
- Who are the key people in the organization that you deal with the most? What are their orientations – or what do they seem to be? Are there implications for the way your relationship has developed? How might you use this knowledge?
- To what degree are your colleagues aware of their and your orientations?
- What different orientations are operating in different parts of your organization?
- Are there dominant orientations? If so, how does your profile fit with these?
- How might you leverage differences?
- How is national culture relevant in the situation?
- Where are the potential synergies and conflicts? And so on.

The orientations in the COF are derived from very sound research across cultures. However, as I have explained through this chapter, culture is not so easy to capture. My experience is that individuals and groups will sometimes find a unique orientation that is contextual. Unlike other instruments, the COF provides for additional orientations to emerge through dialogue. In fact, this is almost a preferred outcome since it shows that participants are engaging with culture. The COF online assessment includes the option of adding supplemental cultural dimensions that can be tailored to a specific client context. I used this feature for example at a conference about Service with a large group of international executives. Preliminary interviews, apart from uncovering several connections with the COF dimensions, also revealed two interesting dichotomies that I captured in the form of two supplemental dimensions including 'nobility–servitude' (service viewed as a noble activity versus as servitude). Not surprisingly, a large majority of 90 per cent expressed a preference for 'nobility' (60 per cent even expressed a clear preference). However, the 'servitude' orientation was defined in a way that was not without merits: those who view service as servitude tend to recognize the importance of setting the necessary boundaries to avoid being exploited. Remarkably, 70 per cent had unfavorable responses in their abilities to set appropriate limits when serving clients. When reviewing these results, the group's conclusion was twofold:

1 Taking better of care of oneself and of one's employees should be emphasized (conversely, abusing their goodwill for meeting clients' demands at all costs should be avoided); and

2 Service is fortunately not a zero-sum game: serving others with generosity and care is often a source of personal satisfaction, pride and meaning. In other words, you serve yourself by serving others.

In sum, the COF assessment offers various possibilities for helping executives deal constructively with cultural diversity in general and particularly in an international context. Above all, it offers a language for coaches that is easy to introduce into organizational contexts and to help coachees make sense of what is going on. The COF assessment assumes a dynamic and inclusive concept of culture, which contrasts with traditional intercultural approaches. Cultural diversity, when leveraged, becomes an opportunity for personal and collective growth. However, the COF cannot be applied mechanically if we want to avoid detrimental polarization and stereotyping. By developing unity in diversity internally, we executive coaches will become more credible and better equipped to promote it externally.

Bibliography

Bar-On, R. (2002) *Bar-On Emotional Quotient Inventory*, Toronto: Multi-Health Systems Inc.

Benzinger, K. (2006) *Thriving in Mind: The Art and Science of Using Your Whole Brain*, Carbondale: KBA, LLC.

Benzinger, K. (2007) E-mail correspondence with Philippe Rosinski.

Hall, E. (1976) *Beyond Culture*, New York: Doubleday Books.

Hofstede, G. (2001) *Culture's Consequences Comparing Values, Behaviors, Institutions and Organizations across Nations* (2nd edn), Thousand Oaks, CA: Sage.

Jung, C. (1971/1923) *Psychological Types*, Princeton: Princeton University Press.

Kluckhohn, F. and Strodtbeck, F. (1961) *Variations in Value Orientations*, New York: Row Peterson.

Myers, I. B., McCaulley, M.H., Quenk, N.L. and Hammer, A.L. (1998) *MBTI Manual* (3rd edn), Palo Alto: Consulting Psychologists Press.

Rosinski, P. (2003) *Coaching across Cultures*, London: Nicholas Brealey Publishing.

Singh, S. (2004) *Big Bang*, New York: Fourth Estate.

Stewart, E. and Bennett, M. (1991) *American Cultural Patterns: A Cross-Cultural Perspective*, Yarmouth, ME: Intercultural Press.

Trompenaars, F. (1997) *Riding the Waves of Culture* (2nd edn), London: Nicholas Brealey Publishing.

Waterman, J. and Rogers, J. (1996) *Introduction to the FIRO-B*. Palo Alto: Consulting Psychologists Press, Inc.

Whyte, D. (2000) Workshop, ICF Conference, Vancouver.

INTERCULTURAL COACHING TOOLS

A constructivist approach

Monika Verhulst and Rebecca Sprengel

Do not ask someone who knows about your way. You are at risk of not getting lost.

(Jewish proverb)

EPISTEMOLOGY AND THEORETICAL FRAMEWORK BUILT UPON CONSTRUCTIVISM, ETHNOMETHODOLOGY, COGNITIVE AND SOCIAL PSYCHOLOGY

Effective executive coaching is part of a process where cognition, attitudes and emotions come together in order to bring about change. Change in executive clients is achieved through concrete actions which bring new results. The coaching tools in this chapter represent a support intended to foster and sustain this change. They are selected and analyzed to take particular account of the international business environment where the executives' integration of diverging viewpoints is of outstanding importance to the success of a global enterprise.

Intercultural business coaching is different from other coaching settings as it is intended to increase the client's awareness of other cultures and systems where fundamentally different processes are at work. 'Awareness' not only means 'knowledge of' but also a deep understanding and acceptance that even what seems to be most evident for the client is also part of a certain personal, social, organizational and cultural understanding. Hence, consistent with the constructivist paradigm put forward by those such as Glasersfeld and von Foerster (Watzlawick 1984; Von Foerster et al. 2006), our basic understanding of 'reality' is a construct of our mind.

Ethno-methodologist Harold Garfinkel (1967) has shown how we all, including scientists, proceed to elaborate reasoning in order to make sense of our daily social interactions: we automatically assume that the people we interact with share our fundamental understanding of reality. It is this assumption which makes social interaction possible and plausible to all the participants. In an international business context executives will no longer be able to rely on their own basic understanding because there are so many individual realities at play, emanating from diverse and connected national, organizational and social environments.

As a complement to this constructivist outlook, cognitive and social psychology explain the individual's reasoning with complementary theories:

- Which are the actions that an individual generates in order to make sense of the world? (Heider 1958)
- How consistent is an individual in the implemented actions according to similar or different situations? (Kelley 1967)

> How does an individual reach an explanation of what happened once actions (be they inconsistent) have been carried out?
>
> (Festinger 1957)

These are fundamental processes of 'making sense' with particular expressions in different cultures. They are part of a systemic framework where all elements of the system interact and retroact on the outcomes that are relevant in a given environment.

Being aware of, accepting and even understanding the ways in which individuals from foreign cultures make sense of their social interactions is insufficient, however, for giving evidence of different human mental programs. It is precisely when we learn by doing, particularly in critical situations, that these understandings can be integrated by the individual in order to bring about new action schemes. Therefore, action and interaction within the coaching setting are essential to sustain client change (Hofstede 2001). Coaching in intercultural business contexts requires an understanding of the complexity of each situation, and the need to challenge clients to work with and from different perspectives to (1) implement effective actions, and (2) learn from actions in ways that will creatively inform new actions. The constructivist paradigm underlying this action learning process requires all of the players to accept that a solution created in one context will not necessarily work in another which appears – on the surface – to be similar or the same.

The coaching tools presented in this chapter address all these areas of potential learning and provide coaches and clients with means by which they can raise awareness, and engage with new and emerging realities in tough and fast-moving business environments. Their presentation follows the assumption that, starting with a sharpened self-awareness, the client can then question his or her understanding of reality and a culture's 'universal values'. It is the aim of the

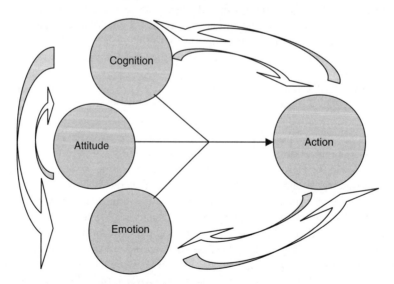

Figure 11.1 Interactive components of change

constructivist paradigm to outline the relativity of all these values and the cultures within which they reside. With new insights, the client can then make more sense of the process which operates in commercial and social interactions between individuals from different teams, departments, regions, and nations.

Nevertheless, starting a coaching process with such a focus on the understanding of the individual represents in itself an essentially Western approach. More collectivistic cultures primarily concentrate on the needs and goals that concern a whole organization before (if ever) addressing the question of individuality. A constructivist coaching approach should take into account such different perspectives: whichever the chosen outlook, the presented tools can be implemented in an altogether different order. What matters are not so much the executives' insights into new contents but their ability to learn from different kinds of process building. The understanding of processes is not simply relevant to national culture, but is equally applicable to team, organizational and community cultures, all of which come into play at different times in the ongoing messiness of intercultural business.

Self-awareness of the client's basic, taken for granted assumptions

The systemic approach in coaching maintains that, in order to influence a system, a client can act upon only his or her own person, even in intercultural settings. The first implementation of coaching tools therefore aims at giving evidence of the ways in which the client selects pertinent information according to initial attitudes, and how this selection leads to thoughts, emotions and further actions. A coaching process can therefore start with the client performing his or her self-assessment. In other words, clients first need to be aware of their own identities and cultural influences and how they affect others, before becoming familiar with other individual and cultural influences. Questionnaires are a practical and efficient way of beginning an exploration of these themes.

Questionnaires

There are various questionnaires which take into account a multi-variable approach. They are based on parameters which, throughout different cultures, underpin an individual's understanding of societal reality. The Schwartz Value Survey (SVS) (Schwartz 1992, 1994) forms a spectrum which articulates values as:

- Openness to change: stimulation, self-direction and hedonism;
- Conservation: security, tradition and conformity;
- Self-enhancement: achievement, power and hedonism; and
- Self-transcendence: universalism and benevolence.

Related research (Schwartz and Bardi 2001) suggests underlying preferences across this universal hierarchy of values. Across nations, benevolence, self-direction, and universalism values are consistently found most important; power, tradition, and stimulation values are least important; and security, conformity, achievement, and hedonism are in between. Coaching dialogue that encourages awareness around values preferences and connections may assist executives in making sense of their reactions and actions in key moments and in gaining greater clarity in decision making.

Philippe Rosinski's Cultural Orientations Framework (COF) (Rosinski 2003) focuses on values in an organizational environment, distinguishing at the same time between personal preferences (attitudes), abilities and behaviors. The theory and application of this coaching-specific tool is given attention by Rosinski in Chapter 10 of this *Companion*. The worksheet outlines dimensions like Sense of Power and Responsibility, Management Approaches, Definitions of Identity and Purpose, Organizational Arrangements, Notions of Territory and Boundaries, Communication Patterns, Modes of Thinking.

Questionnaires tend to imply that a given business culture is a static element. Any culture can be considered, however, as the product of an ongoing process (Garfinkel 1967; Seel 2000) where boundaries change according to permanent negotiation between the different components of that culture. This is particularly valid for business organizations where actions and decisions have in many cases measurable outcomes in terms of success or failure. Even though a culture description (implemented through questionnaires) is in itself a beginning which makes change possible, it is important that the implementation of concrete action as well as the reflection on processes is also part of executive coaching.

Activities

Beyond awareness rising, through dialogue related to questionnaire responses, coaches can stimulate learning through activities. The following tools are examples of effective activities. They are intended to lead the client beyond knowledge towards first practical actions. Activities can be implemented in a pair relationship with the coach or, with enhanced effectiveness, in team coaching sessions. Michel Moral's chapter gives further attention to team coaching activities. Their aim is to show how individuals construct their basic and self-evident understanding of the world, and to equip them to take effective action in evolving and complex business situations.

Garfinkel (1967) has shown in a number of examples how individuals make sense in the course of their interactions with others. Through questioning and analysis of daily routine actions in the conduct of business, the client can be encouraged to experience how deeply our common sense is based on a shared agreement and shared meanings. When these are questioned, there is discomfort. The coaching sessions can be a safe opportunity to explore and challenge assumptions around shared meanings in day-to-day interactions. Later, executive clients can experiment with new actions and challenge assumptions in 'real time' in the workplace, thereby generating opportunities for new shared meanings.

In practice, the coach may, for example, insist that the client provides specifics around commonplace remarks such as: 'How are you today?', 'It is a nice day', 'I am tired.' Garfinkel (1967: 44) cites an experiment where he tests unconformity to such banal interaction settings. In this experiment, a subject (S) waved his hand cheerily, asking: 'How are you?' The experimenter replied, 'How am I in regard to what? My health, my finances, my work, my peace of mind, my . . .?' The subject was very agitated and replied (red in the face), 'Look! I was just trying to be polite! Frankly, I don't give a ** how you are.' This short example is an illustration of how an individual expects his or her counterpart to react in the most basic daily interactions. Clearly, the assumption in a Western culture is that the question: 'How are you?' requires a simple, 'Fine, thank you!' and not any other more elaborate enquiry. Even an answer like, 'Oh, not very well' might be a source of discomfort and embarrassment. In most cases, an ordinary interaction, particularly in a business context, does not allow the participants to go into lengthy personal details. In any culture, such a basic shared understanding is so much taken for granted that it is beyond the consciousness of individuals.

Executive clients who deal with complex challenges may find it particularly difficult to focus on such banal interactions. Nevertheless, they consistently represent a potential source of conflict. Such exchanges, if not approached with the knowledge that even the most evident 'normality' relies on shared understandings, are often a barrier to business – particularly in trust-building. There may therefore be scope to put forward an activity which questions shared assumptions, meanings and reactions related to day-to-day 'mundane' business exchanges. It is a first step to valuing differences and a basis for the next activity which enlarges the focus on business culture.

'The Visitors from Mars' activity is designed to help clients become aware of their own business cultures and how they affect others. The activity can be carried out in an individual coaching situation or with monocultural groups. The coach provides the client(s) with the following briefing:

1   Imagine a delegation from Red Earth, a Martian company, is visiting your company for the first time to discuss a possible joint venture.
2   You are aware that they might also be visiting your competitors.
3   A successful joint venture would mean huge profits for your company and the opportunity for better relations for your two planets.
4   They have never visited your country or your company before.
5   They have asked you to send them a list of cross-cultural dos and don'ts to read during the flight.
6   You want to help your visitors as much as you can, including positioning your company as distinctive and significant.
7   Decide what you are going to tell them and also how you are going to manage the visit.

If clients run out of ideas, the coach can use the prompts below and encourage them to come up with more:

•   Body language, gestures
•   Business cards
•   Business entertaining
•   Communication patterns
•   Decision making
•   Dress codes
•   Drinking, toasting, tipping
•   Etiquette
•   Feedback (giving and receiving)
•   Gender and minority issues
•   Gifts: giving and receiving
•   Greetings
•   Humor and small talk
•   Negotiating (prices, concessions)
•   Personal space
•   Presentations
•   Problem solving
•   Punctuality
•   Religion
•   Taboo topics.

The coach could also use the items from the Rosinski COF or Schwartz Values Survey to generate discussions. As with all activities, the debriefing is as vital as the activity itself. The following are suggestions for the debriefing:

- Find out why participants chose the different issues and get them to think of the underlying values;
- Ask them which culture clashes might occur and how they would deal with them best;
- Explore the company *v* country levels of culture; and
- Ask questions about how the executive might find out about the Martian culture – and any particular features of the Red Earth culture.

Techniques for self-management

Clients often mention the difficulties they experience when receiving feedback. In a systemic paradigm, any statement is, in fact, a feedback to a statement made by the person with whom we are interacting (Mucchielli 2003). There are significant cultural factors at play in feedback. Communication styles in different cultures vary from High Context to Low Context, from Direct to Indirect, from Affective to Neutral and from Informal to Formal (Rosinski 2003) and are therefore a source of major misunderstandings. In addition, different corporations also have very diverse feedback cultures, ranging from regularly solicited feedback to 'name, blame and shame cultures'. This naturally adds to the confusion, especially within cross-border projects and mergers. Individual executives, particularly new recruits, are often at sea when presented with feedback patterns that are completely foreign to them. Their capacity to make sense of new situations is severely limited – as is their performance. For example, an executive from Asia who might be used to very indirect critical feedback (and never in public) might be completely derailed if thrown into a situation where it was acceptable to deliver critical feedback immediately and directly. Therefore, the coach may explore:

1 What is the client's level of awareness about how feedback is delivered in this business environment?
2 If awareness is low, how can the client find out more about it?
3 If it is a cross-border/multinational team that is being established, how can the client ensure that a mutually acceptable feedback system is established?
4 How can the client ensure, regardless of (1), (2) and (3), that he or she can access and deliver feedback in ways that will be satisfying and effective (understanding that the client might not be in a position to engineer a suitable feedback system)?

With the following tool for self-awareness, clients can learn how to cope with and develop, particularly through negative feedback (Kumbier and Schulz von Thun 2006). It invites particular attention to loaded words and phrases that may have damaged the feedback process.

1 Ask clients to pair-up and describe to each other a real situation regarding feedback in their business context which is or has been confusing or difficult.
2 Encourage clients to recall – and even role play – the actual words and phrases that were used in the interaction.
3 Invite clients to 'replay' the situation using more neutral language that would bring about a more effective outcome.

4 Encourage dialogue about what the language seemed to reflect about the cultural values of the people involved. (Also, on reflection, how accurate was the initial assessment?)

5 Explore to what extent did different understandings of terms affect the feedback interaction?

6 Ask clients to also look for the exact counterparts of the loaded terms: one representing the 'zone of aversion', the more neutral one describing the 'area of possible development'. Together, the terms define the whole spectrum of the clients' values in the given communicative situations.

As an example, one French client was told by her German colleagues that she was 'totally unstructured' in her presentations. During the coaching process, she admitted that she was in fact quite proud of her capacity to be 'spontaneous and flexible', and the feedback of being unstructured offended her the more so as it had touched upon her area of vulnerability. On the other hand, she said she would have hated to make 'rigidly planned' presentations like those delivered by her former German colleagues. Their feedback showed her, however, that her presentations could be 'better structured and planned beforehand'.

Subsequently, the coach can use a 2 × 2 (Figure 11.2) to explore with the client the relationships between the terms being used.

In this context, feedback can be seen not as devastating criticism, but as a possibility for personal development which is particularly useful in an intercultural environment. When debriefing this activity (clients present their findings to the group) the coach then has the opportunity to show how more feedback can be given in a more positive manner. This will also lead to the next level where clients have to be sensitive about other cultures when giving feedback.

Knowledge of different cultures: becoming aware of others

At this second level, there are various coaching tools that can assist in generating a better understanding of other cultures by the client. In line with the cognitive framework of concept and representation generation, clients will be able to interact with foreign colleagues or customers in a more constructive manner if they are able to build positive associations of foreign values, cultural achievements and philosophy.

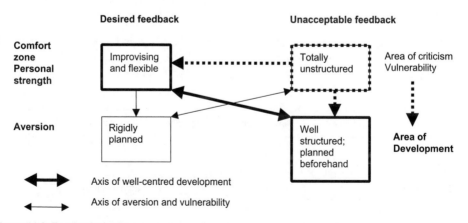

Figure 11.2 Feedback matrix

Introductory activity: building intercultural sensitivity

If faced with an intercultural situation for the first time, clients usually focus on either the differences or the similarities to other cultures. Bennett (1986, 1993) has shown that these are the first steps in a process where an individual starts to experience intercultural differences. The Developmental Model of Intercultural Sensitivity (DMIS) shows six stages where the individual evolves from an ethnocentric to an ethnorelative understanding. After a first stage where denial of cultural differences is observed, a second stage leads to defense against other cultures and one's own culture is experienced as the only valid one. A later stage of minimization of cultural differences leads then to the ethnorelative understanding with acceptance, followed by adaptation and a final stage of progressive integration.

The Intercultural Development Inventory (IDI) is a questionnaire designed to follow these different stages (Hammer 1998) of each individual's intercultural sensitivity. Clients are invited to think about the way in which they perceive other cultures as well as their own. They might find that their representations vary from one culture to another, and it might occur that even within their own culture there are areas of defense and minimization.[1] Once these points of relativity are outlined, clients may see the following aids for intercultural understanding in a different light. Coaches should be prepared to deal with clients' resistance to change, especially if the clients are in the 'denial' or 'defense' stage. Rosinski (2003) takes this one step further, suggesting a seventh stage of 'Leveraging Differences' where coaches facilitate creative synergies between different approaches.

Consultants' reports on foreign countries

Reports on foreign countries can be a convenient tool for firms who provide intercultural coaching. Recent consultant reports, information held by, for example, the US State Department, books, toolkits, and so on can be used with clients, as well as with their families, who often appreciate this kind of ready-made, easily accessible information. If such collections of 'dos' and 'don'ts' are sometimes quite operative and useful, it should be borne in mind that the information they transmit is, in too many cases, bristling with unnoticed commonplaces of cultural stereotyping. It might also be outdated, and/or just plain wrong. In a constructivist perspective, such an approach is at best insufficient and more often misleading, if the relativity of the underlying analytical framework fails to be explored.

Media, literature, movies, etc.

Newspapers, magazines, radio and television, as well as literature and movies from other cultures, are more valuable material for first impressions, as each medium does not pretend to represent anything else than the specific purpose it was designed for (daily news, art, etc.).

Figure 11.3 Developmental Model of Intercultural Sensitivity (Bennett 1986, 1993)

Journals and essays by other sojourners are useful sources of insight for people new to a culture (noting that these are, by nature, subjective accounts with their own biases and perspectives). Essays and novels written by multicultural authors often give particular insight in the under-lying assumptions of two given cultures. With exposure to a range of material from various sources, the client can develop his or her own interpretations of cultural specificities. From a constructivist outlook, coaching conversations can help in this sense-making process.

> As an example, a French-speaking expatriate manager from Switzerland had a very difficult start in India. Six months of complete disorientation made him quite inoperative and frus-trated in his interactions with his team of local colleagues. In particular, he was unable to understand the Indian way of 'decision making'. He reported real difficulties in communicat-ing, due to his colleagues' 'equivocal way of agreeing and disagreeing'. In a coaching ses-sion, he discussed an essay he had come across written by a French author (Kalda 1996) who had lived in India for years. According to the client's words, he had, 'on each single page, a true insight on the ways Indians make sense of their daily environment'. With the increasing numbers of transcultural migration, this kind of literature is flourishing. It is therefore an important source of information for coaches and their clients equally.

Questionnaires

The use of questionnaires can be valuable, particularly in a foreign organizational culture. They can shed light on the different processes in the fields of communication – within the team and with contacts outside the organization – the styles of team work, decision making and hierarchy, conflict management as well as negotiation. However, these are often protected trademarks and accessible via payment only.[2] They may also carry inbuilt cultural biases. The above-mentioned issues can also be approached by means of other techniques, particularly with a constructivist approach which examines the different steps that lead to a particular process (e.g. the detailed steps for decision making, expression of disagreement, negotiations, and so on). The coach can help individuals and teams to work through the different themes by asking questions such as the following:

- How do you proceed in order to reach a compromise – assuming a compromise is the desired outcome? (conflict and agreement management);
- How does a manager gain the authority in order to be able to implement an unpopular decision? How does a manager then show this authority to employees? (hierarchy); and
- How do you negotiate with trade unions, difficult partners and colleagues? (negotiation culture, communication styles).

In line with the overarching constructivist approach, particular emphasis is made on the ques-tion of 'How?', which examines the progressive construction of a process. As a systemic approach suited to a complex business environment, it is opposed to the question of 'Why', which implies a linear thinking.

ACTIVITY: THE INNER TEAM

The last tool in this section is designed to help clients become aware of their own intercultura-lity. Each client identifies an inner diversity of characters which tend to give different answers in a single situation. This concept of the 'inner team' (Schulz von Thun 1998) reflects the fact that individuals are not monolithic beings but personalities with sometimes antagonistic views, tendencies and stances. The individual perception of a coherent identity is therefore not so much a condition with metaphysical origins, but appears to be a rather circumstantiated outcome of a permanent negotiation among the inner team. When clients evoke, in a second step, culturally different behaviors which seem to be inexplicable in their perspective, the coach can help them to find one character, within their inner team, which would have reacted in a similar way, given certain circumstances (Trompenaars 1997). It becomes plausible that reactions which may initially be perceived as 'strange' are finally understandable in a set framework of values. By being aware of the relativity of different cultures, a skilled coach can guide clients through experiencing and becoming competent in the systemic dynamics of intercultural interactions. This issue is addressed in the following section.

Intercultural processes: becoming competent in intercultural interactions

The previous activities will generate in clients a degree of understanding of intercultural processes and a better sense of what is going on in the cultural and organizational context. However, the particular nature of intercultural dynamics can only be experienced through direct interactions and relations which simulate specific situations.

Activity: the 'Diplomatic Suitcase'[3]

The Diplomatic Suitcase is a setting which aims to demonstrate that various difficult situations are constructed by the involved parties tending to externalize their internal tensions and transfer them to intercultural relations.

Participants are divided into groups of five. In each group there are two pairs and one intercultural 'diplomat'. Beforehand, the coach has constructed realistic but paradoxical situational tasks which are adapted to the organizational environment of the participants. The two negotiating pairs have antagonistic sub-goals for a given common goal. It is now up to the diplomat to bring the two parties together in a win–win solution, taking upon him or her, the ambitions, achievements as well as the tensions of the two pairs without betraying either one of them.

> The following case study illustrates this activity. A British Corporation has decided to introduce European standards across its subsidiaries in the booming service industry. In line with this policy, head office in London has developed a concrete proposal for the implementation of the new standards in the French subsidiary. The local goals of the subsidiary, however, are quite different from the plans of the head office. In addition, both parties are experiencing a number of internal tensions (leadership, dysfunctional teams, and competing projects) which they have to first overcome before they are able to turn themselves to the international project. An intercultural specialist is delegated to implement the standards project within the group.
>
> At first, both entities seem very cooperative and ready to make concessions. However, as the specialist progresses towards concrete implementation of the project, she experiences that everyone involved simply shifts to her the different paradoxes with which they are confronted. That is, all involved parties entrust their expectations of and frustrations about the business partners to her. In addition, the British in head office become suspicious of the French subsidiary about their involvement in the project. At the same time, the relationship between the two organizations becomes more and more critical up to the point that it risks

breaking up. The intercultural specialist mediates between the concerned parties: she becomes the unofficial 'diplomat' who has to carry out the delicate goal of resolving all the antagonistic aims and goals among the different teams and companies. By now the diplomat is carrying a heavy suitcase filled with frustrations, individual ambitions and contradictions that come from both national organizations. Aware of her delicate position, she cautiously starts to 'unpack' her suitcase and diplomatically confronts the two organizations with their internal contradictions, which she has experienced in a systemic process. Unveiling the process rather than discussing the content, she helps the two national entities to step out of the usual framework of conflict. Deconstructing the difficulties by focusing on the question of 'how' rather than 'why' the situation became so inextricable, was the key to the solution.

The Diplomatic Suitcase can be adapted to real situations of the participants and be illustrated with small suitcases, goal cards, and the like. The role of the diplomat is a critical one as this person collects the contradiction of the two involved pairs. Even when there is a positive outcome to the negotiation with a win–win solution, but particularly when a compromise cannot be found, a debrief must follow. A coach can facilitate meta–communication about the processes that have progressively led to the success or the failure of the overall objective. Particular emphasis should be made on how the diplomat unpacks the suitcase, how she delivers the bad news, to whom, how it is received, lessons learnt, etc. With this activity, participants show their ability to take upon themselves internal and intercultural contradictions, in order to promote an overarching goal.

Game I: the Prisoner's Dilemma

The Prisoner's Dilemma (Rapoport and Chammah 1965; Watzlawick 1977; Poundstone 1992) sheds light on the ability of two individuals to trust each other while both are in a critical situation. It is adapted from game theory in mathematics. The game is played in threes – two 'prisoners' and an 'interrogator'. The prisoners have a choice:

1   To betray the other, and decrease their own jail time from two years to, say, six months. This choice increases the jail time for the other by, say, eight years; or
2   To stay silent.

The aim of the prisoners is to get the shortest possible sentence for themselves. The prisoners make their choices (to betray or to stay silent) simultaneously. This way, they know that their

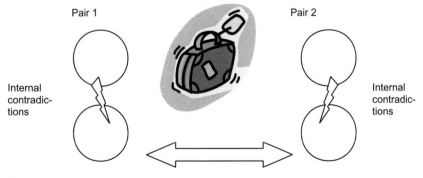

Figure 11.4 Intercultural contradictions

173

choice cannot affect the choice of the other. The situation provides a dilemma because if each of the prisoners makes the obvious choice (to betray), both will end up serving ten years of jail time, while they both could have received just the two years if they had stayed silent. This paradoxical situation has been widely adapted to different situations. It is particularly pertinent in a context of intercultural relations where trust and the common search for win–win solutions are of importance.

Game II: Barnga

Barnga (Thiagarajan 1990) is a popular simulation game of intercultural conflict where clients learn how one set of rules and codes can be interpreted in profoundly different ways in different cultural settings. The game demonstrates that even though interactions may be based on good-will, this alone will not guarantee clash-free interactions. In addition, the game also highlights the fact that 'winners' and 'losers' cannot be defined by linear thinking. Rather, the winning and losing positions progressively emerge within a systemic process to which all participants contribute from the start of the game.

Game III: The Invasion

The Invasion (DeLozier 2008) is another activity intended to show how different perceptions and attitudes may be an obstacle for implementing win–win solutions. Participants are divided into two groups. Group 2 has knowledge of an imminent catastrophe but Group 1 doesn't. This group can survive only if it is able to get support from Group 1 within a five-minute time span. However, the absence of a common language between the two groups makes communication and persuasion very difficult: only non-verbal interactions are allowed. As Group 1 has been living without contact with the outside world, it is resistant to any change, and worried if approached by foreigners.

Different instructions are given to each group according to the indications set out in Table 11.1. The debrief should take into account the emotions and thoughts of both parties.

Case studies and critical incidents

Case studies and critical incidents, such as the example below, are another classical tool and can be adapted to many different learning situations.

> The following critical incident involves German and UK managers. Dr Dieter Kunze (not his real name), 42, worked as a senior manager for a large automobile manufacturer in Germany. His company set up a joint venture with a small-parts manufacturer in the UK, and Dr Kunze

Table 11.1 Intergroup communication

	Group 1	Group 2
Objective	Defend themselves Resistance	Save the other group at all costs
Communication	Non-verbal, try to avoid physical contact with members from Group 2	Non-verbal, but may try to gently 'force' members of Group 1
Attitude	Defensive, anxious, shy, introverted	Well intentioned, positive, extroverted

was sent over to England for six months to help with the project. His English was a little rusty but as he had studied English for nine years at school, he was confident he would be able to communicate with his British counterparts.

After a couple of weeks in the UK, he realized that things were not going very smoothly and that the development of the parts was way behind schedule. After having prepared himself in great detail he called a meeting with the various heads of departments for nine o'clock the next morning. He was the first to walk into the meeting room just before 9am. He sat down and unpacked his folders and equipment. At 9.20am when the last people had arrived, a rather irritated Dr Kunze got straight down to business as he saw that time was running short. He set out exactly what mistakes they had made. They listened, smiled and commented politely. He felt satisfied and relieved that they all agreed with him, although he was a little unsettled by the humorous remarks some of them had made.

Finally, he suggested another meeting in a week's time as he thought that most issues would be dealt with by then. However, the meeting never eventuated as most of his British colleagues had other appointments or were travelling. By this point, Dr Kunze was very angry and wrote a detailed report to his vice president in Germany, who in turn wrote a four-page letter to the managing director in the UK, complaining about the delay and the lack of professionalism of his staff.

Dr Kunze was working with an executive coach. The coach in this instance suggested that he view the issue with a 'Babel Fish' in his ear (Adams 1979). A Babel Fish can understand all languages in the universe and can also whisper in the ear of its owner the underlying thoughts of the speaker(s) in front of him or her. The aims of this outlook are for clients to:

1   Achieve a degree of dissociation from their own mental frameworks; and (at the same time)
2   Try to understand and integrate into their reasoning the cultural and individual backgrounds of their negotiating partners.

The coach role played various people in the scenario; Dr Kunze went to work with his new fish. In the discussions that followed, Dr Kunze gained new insights and explored various ideas about what had gone wrong and how he could have approached the situation. In the coaching sessions, he explored the interactions of national and company culture and came to a number of conclusions, including:

- He realized he had been too direct with his criticisms;
- He needed to formulate his thoughts in a less direct manner, in line with the English communication style;
- He should have checked the company processes and culture and found out that meetings did not start exactly on time (common among UK companies);
- The normal approach was for meetings to begin with a few minutes' light conversation and a cup of tea or coffee before getting down to business;
- He had made no effort to motivate his colleagues to new action;
- He should have spoken to them individually rather than just focusing on the task. In general Germans are more task-oriented, whereas the British tend to be more person-oriented;
- He had mistaken their politeness for agreement. He realized through discussion and investigation that in the UK office people had a subtle and indirect way of signaling disagreement;
- He realized that his British colleagues probably didn't go to the second meeting as he had offended them; but did not want to say so directly so as not to 'rock the boat';
- He discovered that oral communication was given high value in the British office;

- He and his boss had escalated the situation dramatically and unnecessarily by communicating in writing.
- It became obvious to him that interpretations of the rigidity of a deadline in his new situations were very different from those in his previous situation in Germany; and
- As a simple measure, before taking on the assignment, he should have done more to improve his English.

Depending on the level of cultural knowledge of the client, this kind of discussion could be assisted with use of the Cultural Orientations Framework (COF) (Rosinski, 2003).

CONCLUSION

Act always so as to increase the number of choices.

The world, as we perceive it, is our own invention.

(Heinz von Foerster)

The global business environment is no longer merely complicated; on the contrary: it has become truly complex (Angel, Amar, Gava and Vaudolon 2005). Mainly promoted by trans-national companies, a coaching culture is progressively emerging in the countries such as the BRINCs (Brazil, Russia, India, Nigeria and China) Central Africa, and East Asia. Shell provides coaching to its Nigerian managers, hence introducing a coaching culture also in Africa. However, the trend is no longer a simple transfer of Western management cultures to non-Western business organizations. On the contrary; in a context where companies merge with what Westerners consider to be jewels of their national industry – like the Indian Tata group who now control Jaguar and Land Rover – an increasing understanding and acceptance will be needed for different non-Western management cultures. When the former French minister of Education, Ségolène Royal, maintained during a visit in New Delhi that Indian managers would benefit from training in French elite schools,[4] she did not consider that the exchange could also take place the other way round. Japanese companies like Toyota have long been at the forefront of this trend. Considering that in the coming years, the BRINCs will definitely be the source of global growth and knowledge, they send their executives to be trained within these non-Western management cultures. Recently, the few Indian schools located in Tokyo have been confronted with a soaring number of applications from Japanese children looking for entry into this highly selective school system as a way of securing admission into Indian elite universities.

As globalization is moving forward rapidly, coaching itself has to follow this overall evolution. Coaches can no longer consider that their monocultural coaching tools based on underlying national/ethnocentric values can continue to be efficient and relevant to the international business realities faced by their clients (Moral 2004). It therefore seems important that tools are consciously chosen for their neutrality in respect to national cultures. The alternative is for coaches to use their and others' knowledge to change tools so that they are more culturally transportable.

However, while clients' thinking will have to be adaptive, they also need to constantly rely on their own solid values and identities. Knowing precisely who they are and how they react, particularly in situations of stress, are important abilities for internationally active executives. Coaching can assist clients to gain higher levels of self-awareness and to build on their capacities to deal with the unexpected and the stressful. Paradoxically, such knowledge will then position clients for future transformational change that comes from rich experiences in the ongoing action learning cycle of exploration, awareness, action and reflection.

Coaching tools which are conceived within a constructivist paradigm will take into account this double perspective of thorough self-knowledge and openness to others. In such a context, a framework of linear thinking that attributes causes and origins of success and defeat to individual actors, organizations or even nations is no longer always valid. The emphasis has shifted towards the progressive co-construction of an interactive process, where each individual has to understand how he or she contributes to and interacts within a broader, systemic process. We then can envisage a paradigm where more integrative thinking can create the conditions for true win-win solutions. These represent the only option that can guarantee constructive intercultural relations in the long term.

Notes

1 This part of the activity prepares for the activity in the last paragraph of section 2 where clients reflect on their own inner multiplicity.
2 The 'Culture in the Workplace QuestionnaireTM' is based on Geert Hofstede's research (Hofstede 2001). Another questionnaire is the 'Cultural Perspectives Questionnaire' of IMD in Lausanne (CH). Participants can get their individual profile for no fee, if they agree to have their data stored in the IMD database. It is possible to download the questionnaire in 21 languages. Cf. <https://applications.imd.ch/external/surveytool/printMain.jsp?target_id=1>.
3 Tool based upon a systemic and constructivist approach, created by M. Verhulst, 2007.
4 During a brief visit in 1999, missioned by the former French President, Jacques Chirac.

Bibliography

Adams, D. (1979) *The Hitchhiker's Guide to the Galaxy*, London: Pan Macmillan.
Angel, P., Amar, P., Gava, M.-J. and Vaudolon, B. (2005) *Développer le bien-être au travail, stress, épuisement professionnel, harcèlement, une réponse innovante: Les programmes d'aide aux salariés*, Paris: Dunod.
Bennett, M.J. (1986) 'A developmental approach to training for intercultural sensitivity', *International Journal of Intercultural Relations*, 10(2): 179–96.
Bennett, M. J. (1993) 'Towards ethnorelativism: A developmental model of intercultural sensitivity', in Michael R. Paige (ed.), *Education for the Intercultural Experience*, Yarmouth, ME: Intercultural Press.
DeLozier, J. (2008) Personal communication. <http://www.nlpu.com/judybio.htm> for contact details, accessed 20 April 2008.
Festinger, L. (1957) *A Theory of Cognitive Dissonance*, Stanford: Stanford University Press.
Garfinkel, H. (1967) *Studies in Ethnomethodology*, Englewood Cliffs, NJ: Prentice-Hall.
Hammer, M. R. (1998) 'A measure of intercultural sensitivity: the Intercultural Development Inventory', in Fowler, S. and Fowler, M. (eds), *The Intercultural Sourcebook* (Vol. 2), Yarmouth, ME: Intercultural Press.
Heider, F. (1958) *The Psychology of Interpersonal Relations*, Wiley: New York.
Hofstede, G. (2001) *Culture's Consequences, Comparing Values, Behaviors, Institutions and Organizations across Nations*, London: Sage.
Kalda, A. (1996) *Promenade en Inde*, Paris: Grasset.
Kelley, H. H. (1967) 'Attribution in social psychology', *Nebraska Symposium on Motivation*, 15: 192–238.
Kumbier, D. and Schulz von Thun, F. (2006) *Interkulturelle Kommunikation: Methoden, Modelle, Beispiele*, Hamburg: Rowolt Taschenbuch Verlag.
Moral, M. (2004) *Le Manager Global: Comment piloter une équipe multiculturelle*, Paris: Dunod.
Mucchielli, A. (2003) *Théorie systémique des communications, Principes & applications*, Paris: Armand Colin.
Poundstone, W. (1992) *Prisoner's Dilemma*, New York: Doubleday.
Rapoport, A. and Chammah, A. (1965) *Prisoner's Dilemma*, Ann Arbor: University of Michigan Press.

Rosinski, P. (2003) *Coaching across Cultures: New Tools for Leveraging National, Corporate & Professional Differences*, London: Nicholas Brealey Publishing.

Schulz von Thun, F. (1998) *Miteinander Reden, Das 'Innere Team' und Situationsgerechte Kommunikation*, Hamburg: Rohwolt Verlag.

Schwartz, S. H. (1992) 'Universals in the content and structure of values: Theoretical advances and empirical tests in 20 countries', in M. Zanna (ed.), *Advances in Experimental Social Psychology*, San Diego: Academic Press.

Schwartz, S. H. (1994) 'Beyond individualism/collectivism: new dimensions of values', in U. Kim, H.C. Triandis, C. Kagitcibasi, S.C. Choi and G. Yoon (eds), *Individualism and Collectivism: Theory Application and Methods*, Newbury Park: Sage.

Schwartz, S. H. and Bardi, A. (2001) 'Value hierarchies across cultures: Taking a similarities perspective', *Journal of Cross-Cultural Psychology* 32 (3): 268–90.

Seel, R. (2000) 'Complexity and Culture: New Perspectives on Organisational Change', *Organisations & People*, 7 (2): 2–9.

Thiagarajan, S. (1990) *Barnga: A Simulation Game on Cultural Clashes*, Boston, MA: Intercultural Press.

Trompenaars, F. (1997) *Riding the Waves of Culture: Understanding Cultural Diversity in Business*, London: Nicholas Brealey Publishing.

Von Foerster, Heinz, et al. (2006) *Einführung in den Konstruktivismus*, München: Piper Verlag.

Watzlawick, Paul (1977) *How Real is Real? Confusion, Disinformation, Communication*, New York: Random House.

Watzlawick, Paul (ed.) (1984) *The Invented Reality*, New York: W. W. Norton & Co.

Section 2

Organizational challenges and opportunities – individual

COACHING EXPATRIATE EXECUTIVES

Working in context across the affective, behavioral and cognitive domains

Geoffrey Abbott and Bruce W. Stening

Over the past half century, there has been steady growth in the number of executives assigned to manage operations in foreign countries. While increasingly (for reasons of cost and local expertise) many firms are seeking to employ host national managers, the fact remains that expatriate managers are in considerable demand. Expatriate executives face many challenges. Among the expectations held of them are: to rapidly acculturate to the new environment; to become highly productive in often difficult circumstances; to thrive professionally and personally in unfamiliar and often highly complex environments; to cope with cultural and linguistic differences; as well as to operate as quasi-ambassadors for the home office and sometimes the home country.

This chapter provides theory and evidence as to why executive coaching, working from a multidisciplinary evidence base – particularly informed by psychology and intercultural research – can provide invaluable support for expatriate executives through what is usually a time of high pressure and rapid change. The case for coaching expatriate executives has been made before (Abbott et al. 2006). The argument is that professional coaching will be effective with expatriate managers because it can operate interactively in-the-moment across the individual's affective, behavioral and cognitive domains, facilitating contextually appropriate and creative change processes through all points of the expatriate experience.

Executive coaching can be cost-effective preventive medicine to guard against two potentially debilitating 'ills' of expatriate assignments:

1   Premature departure – with the associated high personal and company costs of relocation, disruption and replacement; and
2   Staying on, yet failing to cope with the complexity and challenges of the sojourn – with associated costs of inefficiency, stress, and increasingly negative reactions from host nationals.

In addition to providing a theoretical basis for expatriate coaching, the chapter draws on specific evidence – including the first author's intensive study of expatriate managers in Central America (Abbott 2006) – to give an overview of the types of coaching approaches that may be particularly effective in the expatriate manager context.

As noted above, coaching can be particularly powerful because it has the capacity to work interactively in situ across the cognitive, behavioral and affective domains, thereby engaging with the complexity of the expatriate context. Support for this coaching framework in a cross-cultural context is provided by recent work on 'cultural intelligence'. Cultural intelligence describes the ability to adapt to and flourish in a new cultural environment (Earley and Ang 2003; Thomas and Inkson 2004). Earley and Ang stress that successful acculturation requires that individuals:

1   *Know about* how to work across cultures (cognitive);
2   *Have the skill* to put that knowledge into practice (behavioral); and
3   *Want to* change their behavior to acculturate (affective).

The coaching framework also fits with our understanding of 'culture shock', that is, the high impact effects of entering a new cultural environment. Ward et al. (2001) give considerable emphasis to interactivity across the three domains in their discussion of the nature of culture shock and strategies for successful acculturation. Further, the theoretical framework is consistent with (and to some extent based on) cognitive behavioral therapy and its coaching derivatives (Grant and Greene 2001; Greene and Grant 2003).

Coaching conversations invariably and deliberately raise awareness about, and make sense of, the relationships between feelings, thoughts and behavior. They can also anchor coaching clients in core values – an essential element of sustainable individual change processes. The action focus of coaching, with its strong goal-setting emphasis can encourage expatriates to work through complex issues in real time. The theory and the evidence suggest that each expatriate situation will be unique because the variables at play are numerous and complex. A major study of global executives found that, 'By far the greatest number of derailments could be understood only by examining the context in which they occurred' (McCall and Hollenbeck 2002: 164). There is, then, no one approach or model that will always work. Solutions are situational – as is coaching.

The interactive coaching model is essentially an experiential action learning process, consistent with the learning theories of Kurt Lewin (1946), John Dewey (1938) and, more recently, David Kolb (1984). Kolb's experiential learning cycle (see Figure 12.1) includes four stages of 'concrete experience' (doing or having the experience), 'reflective observation' (reviewing or reflecting on the experience), 'abstract conceptualization' (drawing conclusions and learning from the experience) and 'active experimentation' (planning and trying out new actions based

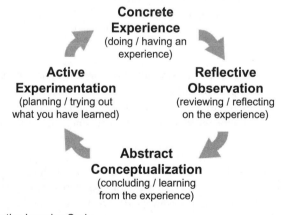

Figure 12.1 Kolb's Action Learning Cycle

on the new learning). These stages are generally viewed as sequential, with people moving in cycles of action learning.

Most sound coaching approaches propose some kind of similar action learning process. However, this is even more important when expatriates are operating in environments where their acquired expertise may need fine tuning. The gut-feeling or intuition which drives expert decision making is based on templates built up through experience (Klein 1999, 2003). Radically different environments may render those templates irrelevant or inoperative. Coaching can assist experienced expatriates in the fine-tuning process.

Coaching expatriates requires an approach that is grounded in experiential learning but is broader in scope than some of the individualistic executive coaching models favored in Western cultures. That is, coaches need to encourage expatriate managers to identify and engage with the cultural complexity (family, team, organizational, community, national, and so forth) that inevitably influences their contexts. To be of assistance in this broader role, coaches must be knowledgeable about culture, as well as being experienced and successful in navigating cultural difference in their own careers and personal lives. Coaches' cultural antennae need be tuned at all points during the coaching process to ensure that their clients have opportunities to take advantage of subtle but often powerful cultural influences.

Coaching expatriates requires that a cultural perspective supplements whatever other coaching approaches might be favored. This includes raising client awareness of the potential value of viewing cultural difference as an opportunity rather than an obstacle or threat. Research on cultural dimensions and orientations by Hofstede (2001), Schwartz (1999), Smith et al. (2002), Trompenaars and Hampden-Turner (1998) and others can inform the coaching intervention and increase impact. At the same time, there is a need for coaches and clients to be cautious when using cultural dimensions to explain or predict individual behavior, and in particular to avoid cultural stereotyping.

At the end of this chapter there is a 'Ten Phase Expatriate Coaching Framework' that provides some guidance to issues that face expatriates at various stages of their sojourns and the kinds of questions coaches may pose to their expatriate clients to generate situationally appropriate action strategies. The questions are designed to draw attention to cultural issues within the emotional, cognitive and behavioral dimensions, and also to ground the coaching process in the fundamental values of the client.

An expatriate executive's experience is complex and has many paradoxes and contradictions, as Osland (1995), Thomas (1998), McCall and Hollenbeck (2002) and others have noted and the following examples illustrate:

1   A direct positive relationship exists between expatriate adjustment and effectiveness – but the same characteristics that make an expatriate effective can also make it more difficult for them to adjust;
2   Married executives adjust better – but the main reason for expatriate failure is the failure of the spouse to adjust;
3   Cultural differences between home and host cultures result in adjustment difficulties – but cultural novelty may facilitate certain types of adjustment;
4   Support from the expatriate's homeland can assist adjustment – but too much contact with home can hinder adjustment;
5   The strengths displayed in the homeland environment which helped gain an expatriate role can become fatal flaws abroad;
6   Host-country language skills are positively related to adjustment – but over-proficiency can lead to suspicion; and

7   Prior expatriate experience assists adjustment – but not always. It has to be positive and of a similar kind.

These paradoxes add to the difficulty of making sound selection decisions and designing inter-ventions to address issues facing expatriate managers.

There is a further issue which has added to the challenge of supporting expatriates. The typical profile is often of an executive from a North American or European background, male, mid-forties, married, with children. However, there is now greater diversity in the backgrounds of expatriate executives, partly as a result of a larger number of countries becoming more active in the global economy and partly because of equal employment legislation creating greater numbers of women executives taking up overseas assignments. Many, if not most, of the models and theories that have been constructed in this field have been based on samples reflecting a 'typical' expatriate executive that is increasingly atypical. The advantage of coaching is that it is by nature contextual – that is, issues are dealt with on a case-by-case basis in situ. No assump-tions are made about what is going on. Of course, theory and experience inform the coach and the client, but they do not dictate outcomes, as the participants in the coaching program design solutions appropriate to the here and now.

It is remarkable that despite the vast knowledge base from research and experience on the factors that make for a successful sojourn, very often individuals are selected primarily on the basis of professional expertise. Even worse, when there is pressure to get someone on the ground quickly, selections are frequently made with little consideration of the cultural context of the assignment or the real suitability of the candidate (Harris and Brewster 1999).

Once a selection is made – good, bad, or indifferent – the practical challenges of providing effective training are immense. A growing body of research has shown that training, particularly cross-cultural skills training, can be effective in facilitating adjustment to a foreign culture and in improving work performance abroad (Bhaskar-Shrinivas et al. 2005; Hechanova et al. 2003; Mendenhall et al. 2002; Mol et al. 2005; Morris and Robie 2001). However, there are serious practical difficulties in getting results from training. It is costly and difficult to: (1) locate or develop sophisticated and comprehensive cross-cultural training programs; (2) ensure that the programs are appropriate to the backgrounds and circumstances of attendees; and (3) deliver the programs to the right people at the right time. Training methods have frequently concen-trated on the cognitive and behavioral aspects of the expatriate experience, but have given very little attention to the crucial affective aspects of acculturation. Cross-cultural training has gener-ally been regarded as something that is usually conducted at the beginning of an assignment, whereas acculturation is something that is not confined to the early months of interaction but, rather, is an ongoing process of adjustment. Too often, operational priorities put training on the back burner, or individual's judge pre-packaged training programs to be irrelevant to their particular circumstances. The net result is that the rigor of training varies. It has been argued (Ward et al. 2001) that most training programs are not sufficiently comprehensive in content and implementation, and simply do not hit the mark. Not surprisingly, the results of studies of the impact of training have been mixed, and complicated by the fact that outcome variables differ (Mendenhall et al. 2002).

Earley and Peterson (2004) have proposed that training programs should aim to increase the cultural intelligence of managers, focusing on broad meta-cognitive skills, motivation and behavioral skills. However, the approaches they have suggested for increasing managers' cultural intelligence carry some of the limitations of the current cross-cultural training approaches noted above.

Many expatriate managers have mentors within their organization, either through their own initiative or formal mentoring programs. By definition, mentors pass on their personal and professional skills, life experience and knowledge to their protégées and protégés (Clutterbuck 2003; Stead 2005). There are clear strengths in being guided by someone who has their own personal experience to share, and senior company executives have an important role to play as mentors in acculturation (Harvey et al. 1999). However, what worked well for the mentor might not always be appropriate for the protégée. A mentor may have been a successful sojourner but have gained the experiences in a cultural context completely different from that of the protégée. Moreover, the mentor's personal qualities and leadership style might be quite different from those of the protégée, so that what was effective for the mentor might fall flat. In most cases, the mentor is not on-the-ground with the sojourner and can provide support only at a distance. Furthermore, formal mentoring programs may lead to inappropriate matches between mentor and protégée. In short, the mentoring role has a high degree of 'hit and miss'.

For obvious reasons, then, organizations seek ways of supporting expatriates, yet the traditional approaches of training and mentoring are unlikely – alone, at least – to have a high impact. Professional 'evidence-based' executive coaching, therefore, warrants serious consideration by both theoreticians and practitioners as a form of preventive medicine for the ills we know afflict expatriates in acculturating. Evidence-based coaching refers to, 'the intelligent and conscientious use of *best current knowledge* integrated with *practitioner expertise* in making decisions about how to deliver coaching to *individual coaching clients* and in designing and teaching coach training programs' (Grant and Stober 2006: 6).

Coaching is already being used in cross-cultural contexts. Philippe Rosinski (2003) has developed a coaching process that places the emphasis on leveraging cultural differences at the national, corporate and individual level. However, coaching has not yet been widely used as a systematic intervention to support expatriate managers. Rosinski (2003) outlined a global coaching model that is holistic and draws on multiple sources of evidence to ensure contextual nimbleness for the coaching relationship. Geoffrey Abbott and Philippe Rosinski (2007) examined how global coaching and the cultural perspective interconnect with the following coaching perspectives: (1) cognitive-behavioral; (2) psychoanalytic; (3) adult development; (4) action learning; (5) systemic; and (6) positive psychology.

Rosinski (2003) has given attention to the cultural perspective in coaching. The Cultural Orientations Framework he has developed from the cross-cultural research of Hofstede and others provides a tool and a language for coaches by which they can both raise awareness about cultural differences that are relevant in the client situation and leverage those differences to advantage.

Put simply, an executive coach with a high degree of knowledge and expertise in acculturation can provide considerable support to an expatriate by engaging in creative dialogue relevant to the emotional, cognitive and behavioral aspects of issues that are of great importance in complex overseas assignments. The support can traverse personal and professional boundaries with global, 'whole-of-person' strategies developed and played out in action learning cycles of planning, action and reflection.

CENTRAL AMERICAN CASE STUDY

An increasing amount of evidence has become available that points towards exciting opportunities to use coaching in innovative ways in cross-cultural business situations, and specifically to support expatriate managers. Geoffrey Abbott (2006) described and analyzed 15 individual case studies of executive coaching, working with expatriate managers from diverse backgrounds in

Central America. There were significant findings from this study that supported the conceptual case made earlier.

First and overall, the study established that evidence-based executive coaching can be of value as an adjunct intervention to assist those who work in cross-cultural business environments. Specifically, executive coaching was shown to offer significant benefits for expatriate managers in the form of improved work performance and enhanced personal satisfaction. Second, the 15 richly descriptive case studies were written of what actually happens in executive coaching, providing a rare view of coaching (and acculturation) from the 'inside'. Third, the study laid out a solid methodological and philosophical basis (grounded in pragmatism and critical realism) for executive coaching from a cultural perspective, and potentially for the emerging profession of evidence-based executive coaching. Fourth, the study provided an example of how evidence-based executive coaching can be used as a form of action research, with the capacity to get inside decision-making processes in organizational settings, illustrated by the specific context of expatriate managers. Fifth, an analysis was undertaken of how executive coaching worked in this specific context; why it seemed to contribute to successful acculturation by the participants; and how it might be applied as an intervention in other contexts. Regarding 'how and why', the conclusion is that executive coaching facilitated expatriate acculturation because it:

1   Was tailored to the individual needs of diverse individuals in diverse cultural contexts;
2   Applied sound models from coaching and acculturation interactively across the affective, cognitive and behavioral domains, giving particular attention to the often-ignored affective domain;
3   Encouraged expatriate managers to operate from a basis of trust in professional cross-cultural relationships;
4   Clarified and worked from the personal values of the individual expatriate managers;
5   Facilitated reflective thinking, allowing the expatriate managers to step back from their complex and pressured situations to better-understand themselves and their contexts and to plan effective actions;
6   Provided a medium to transfer and apply knowledge (theory, research, and experience) from other contexts into local situations; and
7   From a cultural perspective, promoted the leveraging of individual and group differences.

The research methodology involved the researcher/coach delivering individual executive coaching programs to participant-clients and then analyzing the impact of the coaching, giving particular attention to the criteria of performance and personal satisfaction. The research was established within an action research framework with the implicit intention of facilitating action learning. Abbott and Grant (2005) conceptualize executive coaching as a form of action research. In cross-cultural environments action inquiry and learning are absolutely essential if clients are to make sense of their often complex and changing environments.

All coaching sessions were taped, transcribed, coded and analyzed with NVivo qualitative research software. An extensive post-coaching questionnaire was administered and a post-coaching interview conducted with each client. The strength of the design was the retention of the narrative with text of actual dialogue, illustrating the nature of the coaching conversations and the complexity and richness of the expatriate experiences. Other features of the design were the depth of engagement with participants, the longitudinal element (coaching programs over three months to two years), and the rigor of data collection and analysis. A limitation was the use of one coach in one location and the study recommended further research on a larger scale.

In the remainder of this chapter, we will examine one case study from this action research project to illustrate these findings, particularly the capacity of coaching to cope with contextual issues that are unique to individual clients. Personal and company details have been changed.

The case is of Jack Trimboli, a US-born senior manager in an American multinational company, based in Nicaragua. He worked with a coach/researcher (Geoffrey Abbott) for 21 sessions over 18 months. (If readers are interested in exploring other case studies from the original research, they can contact the first author.) He had been in the country for five years and was fluent in Spanish. Previously, he had held an expatriate position in Guatemala. Jack was in his late thirties, white American and was married with two sons. At the commencement of the coaching Jack was country manager for Nicaragua. He was soon promoted to regional manager for Latin America. This promotion was the presenting issue for the coaching. After a year of coaching, he left Central America to successfully launch his own beverage company in the United States. The coaching continued by phone (and face-to-face when Jack visited Central America).

The coaching with Jack covered many issues and events:

- Promotion to regional manager;
- Consolidation at the new level;
- Development of a new company as an entrepreneur;
- Succession planning for a new country manager;
- Repatriation from Central America to the USA;
- Change in employment from a salaried manager to owner-founder-president of a new company; and
- Evolution of his company from an uncertain start-up to a functioning business.

Jack was interested in self-help and saw coaching as an opportunity to learn more about himself and to increase his effectiveness as a manager. He had been coached before – with mixed results. The coaching became more focused and important for him as he took on new challenges. The initial coaching sessions were directed to assisting him in working at the new regional manager level. Over time, Jack developed a goal with a higher priority – to leave the multinational and to set up his own business in the United States.

Jack provided positive feedback about his coaching experience and gave a maximum rating on all items in a post-coaching questionnaire. Jack said that the coaching encouraged him to reflect and to take practical steps to change. He emphasized the value of learning to trust his instinct (something we noted earlier as a matter of great importance provided it is done with an eye to the cultural nuances). Jack described the coaching as, 'business psychotherapy'. He said that he found the questioning to be of immense value in enabling him to gain new perspectives. He used his coach as, 'a reasonable, insightful and informed person who could give an independent perspective of his situation and encourage him to look at things differently'.

Culture was prominent at times, for example through generating strategies for Jack to approach situations in his role as regional manager and later with investor issues. However, Jack's comfort with cross-cultural situations was a strength that provided insights which proved valuable for the coach in working with other clients. The remainder of this section provides examples of outcomes from coaching that contributed to Jack's work performance and personal satisfaction and development.

Anxiety

Jack's level of anxiety about the major changes that he was generating was high, particularly early in the engagement. As Jack stepped up to each new level he became anxious about his capacity to handle the challenges. Coaching sessions assisted him to manage his anxiety and allow him to move forward. A positive psychology approach (Seligman 1994; Seligman and Csikszentmihayli 2000) was used to move him away from anxiety through enhanced self-efficacy and confidence. The tension between his ongoing career with the multinational and his desire to become an entrepreneur caused Jack some additional anxiety. It was a major element of most of the coaching sessions for almost a year. In Session 2 we talked about this tension:

Geoffrey Abbott (Geoff): The better the job you do here the more difficult it is do decide not to be here. This is a paradox.
Jack Trimboli (Jack): It is an absolute paradox. It is not my nature to do the job poorly to make the decision easier.

In the post-coaching interview and questionnaire, Jack reported that the coaching seemed to have the greatest impact in increasing his general confidence and positive mood when he was faced with situations that previously would have been anxiety-provoking.

Self-reflection

One of Jack's major strengths was his capacity for self-reflection – though he did not always use it. He was able to step away from situations and look at himself objectively, and he was relatively comfortable with paradox (i.e., when he did see internal consistencies he did not feel obliged to rush towards a resolution). He used coaching as a way of enhancing and harnessing this self-reflective capacity. Once trust was established, I freely explored Jack's perception of himself without being too concerned about triggering resistance.

Jack said that one of his limitations was that he was essentially lazy, though in terms of efficiency and pace of his activities this was hard to accept. Nevertheless, one of the outcomes of his purported laziness was Jack's unwillingness to deeply self-question and sort through paradoxes and contradictions. Coaching did two things. First, the coaching sessions provided spaces where laziness was not an option – I had permission to call him out of it. Secondly, it provided a realization that by making a conscious decision to get out of a 'lazy zone', he could make better use of his self-reflective capacities.

Procrastination

I encouraged Jack to examine underlying issues that might be guiding his behavior. In the following passage he talks about his procrastination, a recurring theme which he related to his inherent laziness:

Jack: I want to organize a training course and I don't know what to do with it. I want to get all our managers together here at the beginning of the year and to train people on deal-making. I cannot for the life of me decide what this meeting needs to be. It is simple. I do this all the time. All I have to do is sit down and write it. I have been sitting on it for two months. I don't know why at times I make great decisions and other times let things sit forever. I don't trust myself that I am so good subconsciously that I know this is one of those times not to make a decision.

Geoff: It might be.

Jack: Maybe, but shouldn't I know that? Shouldn't I know if it's instinct?

Through dialogue and reflection, Jack realized that in fact he was working subconsciously on not making a decision, an insight he valued immensely. Jack observed after the coaching had finished:

> This was critical. You helped me to realize and trust that I needed more information to make the right decision. Previously I was self critical if doubtful about a decision. I realized that maybe that is a sign that I don't have information.

Jack realized he had been unwilling to trust his instinct, even while knowing that often it had proved correct in the past. Through the course of the coaching he began to better trust his instinct, and himself.

Regional managers' conference

The training session developed into a regional managers' workshop that Jack ran in Miami. We devoted a session to preparation. Jack was anxious about the event and was still looking for clarity around its purpose:

Jack: I'm sort of over my fear of whether or not I can do this. I am now looking to take the steps that are necessary. I haven't completely answered the question about my goals and my approach to the region. The question is, in my interaction with these managers, whether they are autonomous and we interact occasionally as autonomous professionals, or whether there is a formal hierarchy and decisions are made through me. Do they interact as independent professionals or as linked peers? This meeting is going to help because we will draw out from the individual businesses what are the common needs.

He was comfortable with a degree of uncertainty and successfully ran the conference. This was an example where coaching allowed him to work through his anxiety. The post-conference coaching debriefing was useful in cementing Jack's planning of individual approaches with his managers on common issues such as closing customer deals.

Coach confidence – an investors' meeting

Early in his negotiations with investors for his new company Jack hit an issue of investor confidence. He had received some unexpected resistance to important changes in the rates of return for investors. I asked him questions and made simple reflective observations about what he was saying. The use of this technique was deliberate because:

1   It was not a content area where I had expertise and could make suggestions: and
2   Jack had been quite explicit in wanting me to examine and explore the issues around his relationships with investors:

Geoff: It makes me slightly uncomfortable going through this conversation. I am not from that mindset, the entrepreneurial mindset.

189

Jack: I am not coming to you for that. I thought of you specifically for these types of questions, 'How are they seeing it?'. You are adding value in those particular areas. Don't worry. I am not going to hold you liable. From my personal perspective on my thought processes on the way I am evaluating this, you give good feedback.

When reflecting on coaching, the occasions where Jack reported that he had found the coaching less helpful were when he sensed that I doubted my own role and impact. He commented:

There were times when I sensed that you questioned the applicability of some of the things you were suggesting to my new situation. You had self-doubt on how to do that when you proved you don't need to do that.

My learning was that no matter how experienced or capable a coach may be, it is impossible that he or she could be knowledgeable or experienced in the myriad of challenges being faced by expatriate managers. Value can still be added, providing the coach remains confident in his or her skills, knowledge, insights, capacities, and so on.

Directness/indirectness

Jack reported that he was experiencing problems with his own indirectness in interactions with his local employees, contrasting with the generally accepted American cultural preference for direct communication. There was one person in particular with whom he was struggling on some issues of performance. He said that he would get tired or feel sick and get bogged down and less inclined to address the issue because it was confronting – instead of just dealing with it. Through discussion, he worked out that partly what was going on here was that Jack was aware of Latin sensitivity to directness, and was therefore reluctant to follow his instinct to deal with the problems. Over several sessions we worked on his taking a more direct approach to make the progress he wanted. He was able to resolve the situation.

Discussions of the appropriate degree of directness and indirectness help him to extend his cultural and interpersonal repertoire. He was aware of the importance of establishing high trust in a relationship before using a more direct style. Post the Miami conference, Jack felt confident that a direct approach would be appropriate with his Bolivian country manager:

Jack: In Bolivia we have some major issues where we have an audit that came back very poorly. I sent the manager some information and when I was on the phone to him I was very matter of fact and very direct, 'You have a problem and it is something you need to work on'. It wasn't taken as a personal affront. I think he took it as exactly that – something constructive rather than just bitching him out.

The Miami workshop and other initiatives had provided a foundation of trust, allowing him to deal with issues in a direct but culturally appropriate way. Coaching gave him clarity about what was happening and encouraged him to make behavior changes.

Succession management

Jack's sales manager in Nicaragua (Rodrigo) was a natural successor to Jack but there were problems with his 'polish' and communication skills. We discussed this issue:

Jack: I need a different approach to Rodrigo because I have addressed this with him again and again. I am getting through to him to a certain extent because I have seen him make an effort to take this job. I see him making some effort with English. But the style thing has been difficult. Part of the problem is that I am not sure I have the right words for it and I am uncomfortable with it – with the fact that you know this is something I really think shouldn't matter. I feel frankly a little bit guilty about.

Geoff: Is it a cultural thing in the company?

Jack: No, it's like, you know. I guess I have come to accept the fact that, um, how do I say this? [pause] I generally get the benefit of the doubt. I feel like I have had, um, a lot of lucky breaks. I feel that the reason I am in this role is certainly I have proven I do good work. But it certainly doesn't hurt that you know that I am white, American, not ugly, in reasonably good shape and I can charm a lot of people. I recognize in a certain way that those are assets, those are skills and abilities that serve me well. They would serve anyone well in a business environment. Yet at times I think I feel a bit of guilt. When I sit across from somebody like Rodrigo that doesn't quite get that – doesn't quite see it.

Geoff: But he can't be white American.

Jack: He can't. My boss's response was, 'Jack, is Rodrigo part of "the class"?' He meant the class in all Latin America – including Nicaragua – that runs things. I agreed he was not. My boss was worried that customers and partners would not accept him at the high level. The discussion really bothered me because I believe in a certain level of meritocracy and our company should be that way. The world should be that way but it's just not. Yet, I look around and I see people that aren't from that class who have achieved positions of power and authority. I said, 'I know I am still an outsider despite my 13 years experience in Latin America, but I think you need to get to know Rodrigo a little bit better.' And he did, and he changed his perspective and he was willing to give him a chance. We went through a very fair process and another candidate won out. I have had discussions with Rodrigo about that – formally and casually over beers. It is a very tough one. I have tried to be direct. I have tried to be casual about it.

Geoff: When you were discussing it, what was the point you were trying to make?

Jack: He has got to recognize that the way he dresses, the way he presents himself, the way he writes a report, makes a presentation, his language – all those things do not have the level of polish that give other people the confidence that he knows what he is talking about. This guy knows the business inside and out but when he makes a presentation and when he drinks a little too much – he gets a little bit sloppy.

Geoff: Do you say it in those words?

Jack: Yes.

Geoff: This is about – as you say – this is about skills you can acquire and still deal with people from that class.

Jack: Exactly. That is where I may have missed an opportunity and that is calling it skills. If he could [learn the new skills] he could score professionally. When we discussed the issue of presentation, Rodrigo started to get a little teary, 'I thought this company was different. I thought it was more of a meritocracy'. And I sense that this is deep for him and I can only imagine in this society that it is always there.

Geoff: He may perceive a block that isn't there or may not be as big a block as he perceives?

Jack: There are a lot of little things he could do that could make a difference. The sense I get is that this is deep for him. I am cautious to really go deep with him on these issues but I think that is what it would really take.

The dialogue above provides a good illustration of the complexity of the expatriate coaching situation. In the one segment, the following observations were possible:

1   The issues of an expatriate manager from the United States attempting to bring in a local manager as country director – creating potential tension with head office culture;
2   The need for careful succession management;
3   Highly emotionally charged issues regarding cross-cultural management;
4   Evidence of the coaching process exploring beneath the surface to assist the client gain clarity on a difficult issue which touched on some of his underlying issues and assumptions;
5   Behavioral issues around a manager struggling to operate effectively at a new organizational level with cultural complexities; and
6   Cultural influences across national, organizational and social class boundaries.

Rodrigo was subsequently coached and was appointed into the country manager role behind Jack.

Spouse re-acculturation

In the expatriate context, the prominence of family issues as matters which impact on the success or failure of the sojourn virtually requires coaches to discuss emotionally sensitive family and personal issues. This was the case with Jack. For example, on re-entry to the USA, Jack's wife experienced some adjustment problems. The coaching discussions helped to inform Jack about the nature and risks of re-entry. He was able to use this information in ongoing discussions with his wife to assist her with the adjustment process. Generally, the coaching sessions were an opportunity for Jack to talk through various issues relating to family.

Values

The mission and values of Jack's business reflected his personal values. As an entrepreneur, Jack was interested in making profit. However, he was also passionate about environmental sustainability. The company mission included to 'Create a market for an alternative agricultural product that stimulates development in certain tropical countries in an environmentally and economically sustainable way'. The values of the company reflected the way Jack aimed to live his own life, including achievement, integrity, risk-taking, self-awareness, passion, and fun. The knowledge that these values underpinned Jack's work gave me confidence to return Jack to basics when he doubted his direction with the company and his career. Values were prominent in our discussions. For example, Jack set a level of 5 per cent of company profits to be put into a foundation once his new business became profitable. The coaching conversation reinforced his conviction that this needed to be embedded in shareholder agreements early in the process.

CONCLUSION

The narrative and dialogue in the previous section of the chapter are designed to illustrate the huge range of issues facing expatriates. Coaches must be prepared to be challenged and be equipped with a variety of approaches that can help expatriates to make sense of personal and professional complexity. Jack's case demonstrated how a coach can assist an expatriate manager by working through various stages of the sojourn. Some of the issues faced by Jack and other expatriates sound like 'normal' coaching issues. To some extent this is true, but they are made more intense by embedded cultural issues which render void an expatriate's tried and true approaches; the effect is that they add considerably to the pressure and complexity. This is where a coach working in this field needs to have some expert process knowledge – specifically, around how to raise awareness of cultural issues.

We have also stressed the interplay of affective, behavioral and cognitive factors. The model below, adapted from Greene and Grant (2003), illustrates the coaching process as a community of houses, each house representing an individual coaching process, with connected situational, behavioral, cognitive and emotional 'rooms', underpinned by values. Coaches work with different individuals, looking at connections that are culturally based and raising awareness about broader organizational, societal and community influences. This model can assist coaches (and their expatriate clients) in analyzing and progressing interventions.

Following is a 'Ten Phase Expatriate Coaching Framework' designed to provide a very broad, practical framework for coaches as they work with expatriates, highlighting issues that may be relevant across the emotional, cognitive and behavioral domains. However, coaches need to expect the unexpected and to understand that there will be times when both client and coach will be rather overwhelmed by the sheer scope of the issues and events that emerge on expatriate assignments, many of which are undertaken in volatile and dangerous environments. At the same time, the client has a parallel life at home with its own complexities – increasing the stress and the challenges.

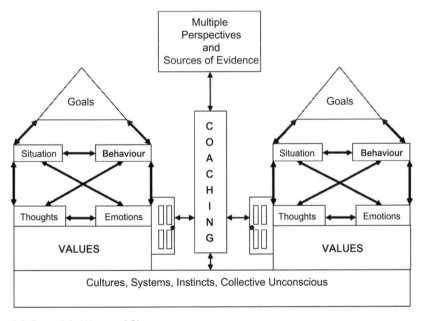

Figure 12.2 Remodeled House of Change

Source: adapted from Grant and Greene (2001)

COACHING TOOL: A TEN-PHASE EXPATRIATE COACHING FRAMEWORK

Phase 1: contemplation

(The executive is not in an expatriate role but is considering this as a possible career direction.)

Issues

Cognitive

- What is the client's level of understanding of the nature of the expatriate existence/lifestyle?
- What are the consequences for family and career of pursuing an overseas sojourn?
- What particular criteria is the client looking for in an overseas assignment?

Behavioral

- What is the client's current skill base in relation to the skills required for an overseas assignment?
- What was the nature of prior experiences (home and overseas) that could be relevant to taking on an overseas assignment?
- What is the spouse/partner going to do?

Affective

- What is the client's emotional preparedness for culture change?
- What impact is the change going to have on the client's primary relationship(s)?
- What are the core values of the client that are likely to provide motivation and grounding during the pressures of an overseas assignment?

Possible coaching strategies/tools

- Cultural Orientations Framework (Rosinski, 2003)
- Aptitude tests (e.g. Intercultural Adjustment Potential Scale (ICAPS); Multicultural Personality Questionnaire)
- Tolerance of Ambiguity Scale
- Values exercises

Additional/alternative interventions

- Mentoring by someone with experience overseas
- Networking with former expatriates
- Cross-cultural training
- Specific skills training to develop strengths (or overcome major deficiencies)
- Travel

Phase 2: offer of appointment

(The client has been offered a position. The lag time may be very short (even overnight)).

Issues

Cognitive

- What is the client's level of awareness of the logistics of the position including location, role and duties, salary, accommodation, timing, length of assignment?
- How can the client increase knowledge and clarity around the offer and decision?
- What are the cultural issues that might be relevant – of the country, the company etc.

Behavioural

- Does the client have the requisite skill set in relation to the position?
- How is the client handling the negotiation process with the company?
- Are there any behavioral norms in the new country that the client may be challenged by? If so, what can the client do to prepare for this?
- What conversations can the client set up to increase knowledge of the area and role?

Affective

- What is the client's deeper emotional reaction to the offer (e.g. fears, anxieties)?
- Are there any values-clashes in the nature of the assignment (e.g. company policies, political situation in the country, religious issues, etc.)?

Possible coaching strategies/tools

- Revisiting of Cultural Orientations Framework in relation to the new country

Additional/alternative interventions

- Discussions with mentor, spouse, colleagues and others
- Travel for a pre-decision inspection of the proposed overseas location

Phase 3: acceptance/predeparture

(The client has accepted the position. This phase covers the time until departure.)

Issues

Cognitive

- How aware is the client of the complexity of the task of personal and professional transition into the new country/position?
- Is the client aware of the possible impact of culture shock and strategies to cope (making reference to theory/research as appropriate)?

195

- How clear is the client about the expectations of the organization regarding the new position and the client's role in it?

Behavioral

- What planning has the client done for departure including all aspects of logistics?
- Is there a need for specific skills development (such as strategies for language learning and exploring the client's individual learning style)?
- Is the client aware of the 'dos' and don'ts' in the new environment (both in terms of the local culture and differences between the home office and the country office)?

Affective

- Working with the emotional state of the client and family in relation to the disconnection from home

Possible coaching strategies/tools

- Cross-Cultural Adaptability Inventory
- Intercultural sensitizers (culture assimilators)

Additional/alternative interventions

- Language training
- Specific–country research
- Networking with people with role and task knowledge, and country knowledge
- Diversity training

Phase 4: arrival

(The client has just arrived in the new country.)

Issues

Cognitive

- Does the client have sufficient knowledge of the country and support to cope with the practical challenges of housing, schooling, transport, safety, communication, etc?

Behavioral

- What does the client need to do to ensure a smooth entry?
- What support does the client need to give or arrange for family?

Affective

- How is the client coping in this early phase?
- How is the family coping?

- What are the levels of stress apparent in the client and significant others?
- How do host nationals appear to be reacting to the client?

Possible coaching strategies/tools

- Identification of knowledgeable expatriates

Additional/alternative interventions

- Language tuition

Phase 5: establishment

(The client is in the new role and has organized basic living needs.)

Issues

Cognitive

- What appear to be the main challenges?
- Are there changes that need to be made that appear 'obvious' to the client that have not been made by others? What might be going on?
- What are the strengths of the client that seem to be most valuable? How can these be effectively applied?

Behavioral

- Are there things that the client is doing that are particularly effective or ineffective? What needs to be done differently?
- What are others doing that seem unusual or different?
- Does this suggest some need for change on the part of the client?
- What does the client need to do to maximize opportunities for integration with the local culture/community?
- Are there risks involved?

Affective

- How is the client coping with the initial phases? What are the levels of anxiety? How consistent is the mood of the client? How is the family (in the country and at home)?
- How is what the client doing fitting with his or her core values?

Possible coaching strategies/tools

- Assessment of psychological health and socio-cultural adaptation

Additional/alternative interventions

- Identification of an in-country or in-region mentor
- Contact with existing mentor

Phase 6: maintenance

(The client is well established in the new position and seems – on the face of it – to be set for the period of the sojourn.)

Issues

Cognitive

- Is the situation as the client expected it?
- What new things have emerged that might not have been apparent at the start?

Behavioral

- What is working? What is not working?
- Are there new skills that need to be acquired?

Affective

- How is the situation with the client's emotional well-being?
- What has been the pattern since arrival?
- How is the family?
- What relationships are key and what factors are at play that are aiding or restricting relationship-building with host nationals and others?

Possible coaching strategies/tools

- 360-degree Performance Appraisal (with attention to cultural implications and appropriateness)

Additional/alternative interventions

- Development of a reflective journal

Phase 7: transition

(The period before the sojourn ends when the client and others are beginning to think seriously about the situation when the client has moved on.)

Issues

Cognitive

- How clear is the client on 'what next?' professionally and personally?
- Is there a succession plan in-country?

Behavioral

- What skills are required for the next assignment?
- What skill training is needed by the new person (particularly if the replacement is in-country)?

Affective

- How is the client feeling about the impending move?
- What are the other significant people feeling about the departure?
- Where are the areas of discomfort and do these have links with values of the client?

Possible coaching strategies/tools

- Life transition conversations
- Social readjustment rating scales

Additional/alternative interventions

- Skill assessment measures

Phase 8: immediate pre-departure

(The period immediately before the expatriate and family leave the sojourn to return home or move on to another expatriate location.)

Issues

Cognitive

- Has the client worked through the various issues involved in the move?

Behavioral

- What still needs to be done?

Affective

- Are there any major emotional issues that have emerged that require special attention?
- Has there been transformational change in the client?
- Have there been changes in core values or identity?
- What implications might there be?

Possible coaching strategies/tools

- Mental mapping of the home culture and organization

Additional/alternative interventions

- Pre-return training and orientation
- Disengagement discussions with local and expatriate colleagues and friends
- Significant re-engagement with a home–country mentor
- Establishing home–country information sources

Phase 9: re-entry/reassignment

(The client arrives home or in a new position in a different country.)
   Note: Revisit Phase 4.

Issues

Cognitive

- What is different from when the client left?
- What is the same?
- How is the client different (transformational issues)?

Behavioral

- How should the expatriate best manage discussions of the sojourn with friends, colleagues and family?

Affective

- How is the client feeling about 'being back' and 'being away' (from the previous country?)
- How are significant others coping?

Possible coaching strategies/tools

- Revisiting the Cultural Orientations Framework *vis-à-vis* the home culture

Additional/alternative interventions

- Discussions with home-country mentor
- Networking with home-country colleagues
- Support for spouse and family

Phase 10: re-acculturation

(The client is established back home or in the new position. Logistics are sorted out.)

Issues

Cognitive

- How is the client finding the new role in terms of challenges and opportunities?
- Is there a sense of *déjà vu*?
- Looking ahead, what might happen next?
- What seems different?

Behavioral

- What does the client need to do differently in the new role?
- How are behaviors learnt on the sojourn being applied in the new role?
- What needs to change?

Affective

- How is the client coping emotionally with settling back home (or in the new country)?
- How are others coping?
- How is the new situation fitting with deeper considerations of meaning and purpose?
- How are relationships (former, new, family)?

Possible coaching strategies/tools

- Assessments of psychological health and socio-cultural adjustment

Additional/alternative interventions

- Values exercises

Bibliography

Abbott, G. N. (2006) 'Exploring evidence-based executive coaching as an intervention to facilitate expatriate acculturation: fifteen case studies', unpublished PhD thesis, Australian National University.

Abbott, G. N. and Grant, A.M. (2005) 'Evidence-based executive coaching and action research: A natural fit', in I. F. Stein, F. Campone and L. J. Page (eds), *Proceedings of the Second ICF Coaching Research Symposium: November 3, 2004, Quebec City, Canada*, Washington, DC: International Coach Federation.

Abbott, G. N. and Rosinski, P. (2007) 'Global coaching and evidence based coaching: Multiple perspectives operating in a process of pragmatic humanism', *International Journal of Evidence Based Coaching and Mentoring*, 5: 58–77.

Abbott, G. N., Stening, B.W., Atkins, P.W.B. and Grant, A.M. (2006) 'Coaching expatriate managers for success: Adding value beyond training and mentoring', *Asia Pacific Journal of Human Resources*, 44 (3): 295–317.

Bhaskar-Shrinivas, P., Harrison, D.A., Shaffer, M.A. and Luk, D.M. (2005) 'Input-based and time-based models of international adjustment: Meta-analytic evidence and theoretical extensions', *Academy of Management Journal*, 48 (2): 257–81.

Clutterbuck, D. (2003) 'Diversity issues in the mentoring relationship', in M. J. Davidson and S. L. Fielden (eds), *Individual Diversity and Psychology in Organizations*, Hoboken: John Wiley & Sons.

Dewey, J. (1938) *Experience and Education*, New York: Simon and Schuster.

Earley, P. C. and Ang, S. (2003), *Cultural Intelligence: Individual Interactions across Cultures*, Stanford: Stanford University Press.

Earley, P. C. and Peterson, R.S. (2004) 'The elusive cultural chameleon: Cultural intelligence as a new approach to intercultural training for the global manager', *Academy of Management Learning and Education*, 3 (1): 100–15.

Grant, A. M. and Greene, J. (2001) *Coach Yourself: Make Real Change in Your Life*, London: Pearson Education Ltd.

Grant, A. M. and Stober, D. R. (2006) 'Introduction', in D. R. Stober and A. M. Grant (eds), *Evidence Based Coaching Handbook: Putting Best Practices to Work for Your Clients*, Hoboken: John Wiley & Sons.

Greene, J. and Grant, A.M. (2003) *Solution-Focused Coaching: A Manager's Guide to Getting the Best from People*, London: Pearson Education Ltd.

Harris, H. and Brewster, C. (1999) 'The coffee-machine system: How international selection really works', *International Journal of Human Resource Management*, 10 (3): 488–500.

Harvey, M., Buckley, M.R., Novicevic, M.M. and Weise, D. (1999) 'Mentoring dual-career expatriates: A sense-making and sense-giving social support process', *International Journal of Human Resource Management*, 10 (5): 808–27.

Hechanova, R., Beehr, T.A. and Christiansen, N.D. (2003) 'Antecedents and consequences of employees' adjustment to overseas assignment: A meta-analytic review', *Applied Psychology: An International Review*, 52 (2): 213–36.

Hofstede, G. (2001) *Culture's Consequences: Comparing Values, Behaviors, Institutions and Organizations across Nations* (2nd edn), Thousand Oaks, CA: Sage.

Klein, G. (1999) *Sources of Power: How People Make Decisions*, Cambridge: MIT Press.

Klein, G. (2003). *Intuition at Work: Why Developing Your Gut Instincts Will Make You Better at What You Do*, New York: Random House.

Kolb, D. A. (1984) *Experiential Learning: Experience as the Source of Learning and Development*, Englewood Cliffs, NJ: Prentice-Hall.

Lewin, K. (1946) 'Action research and minority problems', *Journal of Social Issues*, 2 (4): 34–46.

McCall Jr., M. W. and Hollenbeck, G.P. (2002) *Developing Global Executives: The Lessons of International Experience*, Boston, MA: Harvard Business School Press.

Mendenhall, M. E., Kuhlmann, T.M., Stahl, G.K. and Osland, J.S. (2002) 'Employee development and expatriate assignments', in M. J. Gannon and K. L. Newman (eds), *The Blackwell Handbook of Cross-Cultural Management*, Oxford: Blackwell.

Mol, S., Born, M.P., Willemsen, M.E. and Van Der Molen, H.T. (2005) 'Predicting expatriate performance for selection purposes: A quantitative review', *Journal of Cross-Cultural Psychology*, 36 (5): 590–620.

Morris, M.A. and Robie, C. (2001) 'A meta-analysis of the effects of cross–cultural training on expatriate performance and adjustment', *International Journal of Training and Development*, 5 (2): 112–25.

Osland, J. S. (1995) *The Adventure of Working Abroad: Hero Tales from the Global Frontier*, San Francisco: Jossey-Bass.

Rosinski, P. (2003) *Coaching across Cultures: New Tools for Leveraging National, Corporate and Professional Differences*, London: Nicholas Brealey Publishing.

Schwartz, S.H. (1999) 'A theory of cultural values and some implications for work', *Applied Psychology*, 48 (1): 23–47.

Seligman, M. E. P. (1994) *What You Can Change and What You Can't: The Complete Guide to Successful Self-Improvement*, Sydney: Random House.

Seligman, M. E. P. and Csikszentmihayli, M. (2000) 'Positive psychology: An introduction', *American Psychologist*, 55: 5–14.

Smith, P.B., Peterson, M.F. and Schwartz, S.H. (2002) 'Cultural values, sources of guidance, and their relevance to managerial behavior: A 47-nation study', *Journal of Cross-Cultural Psychology*, 33 (2): 188–208.

Stead, V. (2005) 'Mentoring: Model for leadership development?', *International Journal of Training and Development*, 9 (3): 170–84.

Thomas, D. C. (1998) 'The expatriate experience: A critical review and synthesis', *Advances in International Comparative Management*, 12: 237–73.

Thomas, D. C. and Inkson, K. (2004) *Cultural Intelligence: People Skills for Global Business*, San Francisco: Berrett-Koehler Publishers.

Trompenaars, F. and Hampden-Turner, C. (1998) *Riding the Waves of Culture: Understanding Cultural Diversity in Global Business*, New York: McGraw-Hill.

Ward, C., Bochner, S. and Furnham, A. (2001) *The Psychology of Culture Shock*, Hove: Routledge.

13

COUPLES COACHING FOR EXPATRIATE COUPLES

A sound investment for international businesses

Andrew L. Miser and Martha F. Miser

Successful expatriate programs are increasingly vital to fulfilling corporations' global business strategies. Expatriate assignments are developed to expand business in new international markets, to strengthen leadership capabilities cross-culturally and to transfer both technical knowledge and corporate culture. As a result, there is much at stake in the success of expatriate assignments and the costs associated with failed expatriate assignments can be enormous. The high costs associated with failed expatriate assignments and the role of spousal and family adjustment in such failures are well documented. In addition to the services already offered to expatriates and their families, international companies could greatly benefit from offering couples coaching as an available service throughout the life cycle of an expatriate assignment. A couple's coaching relationship, if made available and requested by the expatriate employee, can assist an expatriate couple in promoting the healthy and satisfactory adjustment of their whole family in a foreign country. Such a service, coaching for expatriate couples, represents a sound investment in the success of expatriate assignments and, ultimately, in the corporation's business enterprises internationally.

THE EXPANDED USE OF EXPATRIATE ASSIGNMENTS IN INTERNATIONAL BUSINESS

In today's trend toward globalization, multinational companies are relying more on expatriate assignments to fulfill their global business strategies, to expand business in foreign markets, to transfer technical knowledge and to build leadership expertise internationally (Corporate Leadership Council 2002a). Each year for the past 12 years, GMAC Global Relocation Services has provided data on trends in global mobility from international companies around the world. The *2006 Global Relocation Trends Survey Report* (GMAC 2007), found that 69 per cent of the 180 responding companies reported an increase in expatriate employees in 2006 and that a similar percentage of companies expected an increase in the use of expatriate assignments in the year 2007. International corporations are increasingly hiring talented expatriate executives in order to be competitive in the international marketplace (Tye and Chen 2005).

The financial investment in the success of expatriate assignments for multinational companies can be substantial. The cost of a single three-year overseas assignment has been estimated to be $1 million (Corporate Leadership Council 2002b). The significant investment in training, relocating and compensating expatriate employees and their families requires companies to provide comprehensive expatriate services to ensure the success of every phase of expatriate assignments from the families' transition to their host country, to their successful adaptation in the new culture and to their relocation and/or repatriation at the end of their expatriate assignment. Even though companies, in recent years, are utilizing shorter-term expatriate contracts and using local talent to minimize financial costs, most international companies still have a lot riding on the success of their expatriate assignments.

THE COSTS OF A FAILED EXPATRIATE ASSIGNMENT

The costs, both direct and indirect, associated with failed expatriate assignments can be significant:

- Swaak (1995) and McCaughey and Bruning (2005) reference research studies that estimate the failure rates of expatriate assignments from 10 to 45 per cent;
- In the mid-1980s, the estimated cost of failed expatriate assignments to United States companies was as much as $2 billion per year and that figure has increased significantly in the last twenty years (Punnett 1997);
- The total cost of a single failed expatriate assignment can range from $200,000 to $1.2 million and be three to four times that of the employee's annual salary (Swaak 1995; McNulty 2001); and
- Studies cited by McCaughey and Bruning (2005) estimate the cost of relocation of an executive and their family to range from $60,000 to $250,000.

The consequences of failed expatriate assignments impact more than just the financial bottom-line. Substantial indirect costs include a failure to achieve organizational strategic objectives, lost productivity, the physical and mental well-being of the expatriate employees, an inability to attract other employees willing to relocate, and the lost investment in recruitment, training, and compensation of new expatriate employees (McNulty 2001).

In the US, businesses have typically underestimated the impact and the role that the well-being of marriage and families have in the financial outcomes of for-profit corporations (Turvey & Olson 2007). Turvey and Olson (2007) provide a case for how healthy marriages of employees can increase the long-term profitability of domestic US companies and how failing marriages contribute to decreased profitability. Forthofer et al. (1996) found that, in the United States, companies lost upwards of $6 million as a result of decreased productivity related to the marital difficulties of their employees. Only recently have more US companies been willing to invest in the marital health of their employees as a strategy to impact the financial bottom-line. Turvey and Olson (2007) conclude that it is financially, socially and ethically responsible for companies to focus directly on how marriage affects a company's financial future. Today, many more multinational companies are recognizing the connection between the health of expatriate family relationships, the success of their international assignments and the realization of their international business strategies.

THE ROLE OF THE EXPATRIATE'S SPOUSE AND FAMILY IN EXPATRIATE ASSIGNMENT FAILURES

Among the companies included in the 2006 GMAC *Global Relocation Trends* report, 60 per cent of expatriates were married and 85 per cent of the spouse or partners accompanied the expatriate employee on their foreign assignment, representing almost 50 per cent of all expatriate assignments. There is growing research and experience within companies that the successful adjustment of expatriates' spouses and families goes hand in glove with the success of international assignments (Corporate Leadership Council, June 2002b). The expatriate's spouse and family's inability to adapt to the new culture, cope with the challenges associated with the expatriate assignment and deal with limited spousal employment opportunities have been cited as contributing to a significant number of failed expatriate assignments (Ely & McCormick 1993). Of the many factors that are implicated in the failure of expatriate assignments (e.g., work adjustment, staff selection, performance issues, etc.), the adjustment of the expatriate spouse and family, often seen as outside an international company's control, has been repeatedly implicated in expatriate failures (McCaughey & Bruning 2005).

Expatriation can put a significant strain on a marital relationship, even if a couple has been together for a long time. It can take many months for expatriate family members to begin to feel at home in a foreign country; however, mechanisms for expatriate couples to talk about continuing family difficulties in adjusting to life in their host country are often not readily available. Common dilemmas for expatriate couples include a loss of connectedness and belonging, a lack of understanding of the host culture, and a sense of family instability as family members learn to live in a new country. Nevertheless, expatriate executives often do not talk about these or other potential issues involved in moving their family overseas (Pascoe 2003). Almost half of the 200 expatriate executives interviewed in the GMAC survey had not even thought about how the move might impact their family (GMAC 2004)! In developing and providing expatriate services, multinational companies cannot afford to ignore the expatriate executive's marital relationship and family.

THE IMPACT OF MARITAL RELATIONSHIPS ON BUSINESS PROFITABILITY

Paying attention to the marital and family health of employees has been found to improve the profitability in US companies (Turvey & Olson 2006). Employees who have healthy marital relationships also contribute other positive benefits for domestic American companies. Happily married couples are more loyal and stable employees (Turvey and Olson 2007), are healthier (Waite & Gallagher 2000), have a positive impact on productivity and a lower turnover ratio (Gallagher 2002)

What is more, relationship skills, such as communication, problem-solving, and negotiation can all be improved through increased marriage education and couples coaching, and can be found to transfer from home to the office (Turvey & Olson 2007). American businesses are recognizing the interdependence of business and marital relationships and that it makes good business sense to invest in the marital health of its employees (Turvey and Olson 2007).

This recognition of the relationship between healthy employee marriages on the long-term profitability of businesses has extended beyond the borders of the United States into the expatriate communities of multinational companies. Information collected from international corporations as part of *The Global Relocation Trends Survey* by GMAC Global Relocation

Services over the ten-year period from 1993 to 2004 revealed that the percentage of those companies offering expatriate support had risen from 52 per cent in 1995 to 86 per cent in 2003 (GMAC 2004). Although, in the last decade, there has been greater emphasis on improving support services to expatriates and their spouses and families, still more can be done.

THE CHALLENGES OF AN EXPATRIATE ASSIGNMENT FOR EXPATRIATE COUPLES

The challenge of taking an expatriate assignment can be daunting for couples and their families. In addition to the magnitude of the logistical tasks of moving to a foreign country, expatriate couples experience a number of challenges, including being disconnected from family and friends, negotiating everyday life in the new culture, dealing with an uncertain future, and experiencing disruption in their family life. Given such realities, what does an expatriate assignment require of a couple to be happy, successful and fulfilled?

First, taking on an expatriate assignment requires an aligned commitment on the part of both partners to have their life be fulfilling in the new country. There is plenty of research and anecdotal evidence to suggest that, if the trailing spouse feels that she (or he) had little choice in making such a significant life decision to move overseas, adjustment difficulties at home can start almost immediately (Pascoe 2003). In contrast, the couple can expand their prospects for expatriate success if each partner has the opportunity to consider all the pros and cons of moving internationally and experiences having choice in the matter.

Accepting an expatriate assignment requires a couple to be in partnership in handling the myriad of operational details. Prior to their move, couples must have conversations to envision living abroad and to begin creating a future together in their host country. They must have conversations to work out new roles and responsibilities, to take care of important logistical tasks with their move, and adjust to the unique cultural expectations and norms in their new country. These are times when it is important for couples to establish an anchor for when the winds of change become overwhelming and turbulent.

Life for expatriate couples requires new levels of communication, problem-solving, negotiating roles and responsibilities, resolving conflict, planning, and taking action together. It requires continuous attention to the health, well-being and happiness of each partner, their relationship and their entire family. Expatriate life requires couples to see the world from new perspectives, to be cognizant of the life they want, to be in alignment about their goals, to plan successfully together, and to learn from their experience.

It is safe to assume that most expatriate couples want to succeed in their assignment and in their life in their new country. The problem is that, no matter how much preparation or training the couple receives prior to the move, they will not know what life as expatriates will be like until they have taken the step and moved abroad. It is only after couples leap into their new life, with everything at stake, that they find out what is really required and that they are on their own, in a foreign land, wondering what they have just signed on to. As Dorothy said to her dog, Toto, when they dropped into the Land of Oz, 'We are not in Kansas, anymore'.

A GAP IN EXPATRIATE SERVICES

Some of the initial services included in a company's program of expatriate services include participation in the selection and planning processes for the expatriate couple to understand the scope of the international assignment, visiting the host country to have an experience of its culture and daily life, meeting with an international relocation manager to review the terms of the expatriate assignment (relocation services, housing, education, tax services and family support) and participation in cross-cultural training to learn about their new country's norms, customs and etiquette (Corporate Leadership Council 2002a; Corporate Leadership Council 2002c).

As the transition process gets underway, multinational companies will provide relocation services – often contracted out to a relocation company that will work with the expatriate to arrange for the moving of household belongings, to purchase or rent housing, to contact school officials, and to engage governmental agencies around such issues as work permits, residency permits, driver's licenses, bank accounts, etc. Follow-up and evaluation services foster regular contact with the expatriate and their family at various intervals in the expatriation process in order to assess their cross-cultural adjustment, to troubleshoot persistent difficulties and to discuss overall family acculturation and career development. Some companies will offer coaching services for the spouse, the children or the family as a whole to assist the family to adjust to the demands of their new culture.

Finally, at the end of an expatriate assignment, multinational companies will provide repatriation services designed to ensure the expatriate's successful assimilation back to their home country and to take advantage of the expatriate's newly learned cross-cultural expertise in the company. The goal of such programs is to maximize the company's return on investment and to ensure a smooth repatriation transition for the whole family.

Progress is being made in developing services to expatriates and their families who take on both the adventure and the potential risks of an international assignment to fulfill personal, family and organizational goals. There is also growing awareness among leaders in international expatriate services, such as NetExpat and Grovewell LLC, that coaching specifically for expatriate couples is a vitally important service to be included in expatriate service offerings. Yet, this important service, one that could address the very heart of an expatriate family's adjustment, is often found missing in most programs of expatriate services. Given the scope of the investment and the fact that the success of an expatriate assignment seems to be so heavily dependent on the expatriate's spousal or partner relationship, one further service should be available during *every* phase of the expatriate assignment and in *every* international program of expatriate services: couples coaching for expatriate couples.

COUPLES COACHING: MEETING THE CHALLENGES FACING AN EXPATRIATE COUPLE

The field of professional coaching is ideally suited to helping couples meet the challenge of expatriate living. Diane Stober (2006) outlines four guiding principles that are underpinnings for coaching from a person-centered, humanistic perspective. These include the importance of designing a trusting and collaborative relationship between the coach and the couple, the recognition that the expatriate couple is responsible for their experiences and for the change they desire, the stance that the couple is whole and unique, and a perspective that the professional coach is a facilitator of the couple's growth and development.

The foundations of couples coaching include a framework in which both individuals and their relationship are held as creative, resourceful and whole, and in which there is nothing inherently wrong and nothing to be fixed (Whitworth, Kimsey-House, and Sandahl 1998). Distinct from therapeutic approaches focused on pathology, coaching is a paradigm of possibility in which the coach is a collaborator with the couple in designing and creating the life the couple wants to achieve. The coach is responsible for the process of coaching and committed to the coaching outcomes the couple has articulated. The coach asks powerful questions which open up inquiry and exploration for the couple to discover and set their life path and course of action.

A coaching relationship provides a forum in which expatriate couples are able to focus on what is going on in their lives, what they see for their future and how they are going to achieve their goals and objectives. A coach can assist the couple in creating and choosing empowering perspectives in areas of their lives that are troublesome for them. In a coaching relationship, couples can also focus on effective problem-solving, redesigning roles and responsibilities, creating personal or family projects and taking action toward their goals. Fundamentally, a coaching relationship is a forum in which an expatriate couple can create a life that they love and are living fully.

There are a number of key aspects and specific advantages that a couples coaching relationship can provide expatriate couples:

1   In the context of a coaching relationship, the expatriate couple always has choice over their contact with and utilization of a professional coach. The expatriate couple can request such a coaching relationship on their terms. The coach and the expatriate couple design a professional alliance so that it works for both the couple and the coach in building a relationship of trust and confidence (Whitworth et al. 1998).

2   Where possible, coaching can be done in the couple's home, at an agreed-upon location or over the telephone. This kind of relationship is ideally suited for expatriates who may be separated from key support personnel by long distances. A couple and their coach can speak to each other at times that work for all of them and from wherever they are in the world.

3   Expatriate couples can also contract with a professional coach who is from their home country and who speaks their own language. In some cases, this kind of arrangement is vital to adjustment in the host country where a significant language barrier may be a critical obstacle for success.

4   The paradigm of professional coaching very often allows a couple to achieve desired outcomes in relatively short periods of time. Coaching engagements may be from six weeks to four to six months and will focus on the couple's agenda and concerns at specific points in the life cycle of their assignment.

5   Coaching can also be less stigmatizing and more 'user friendly' for an expatriate couple than traditional mental health services, with which the couple may not be as familiar in their host country. In short- or long-term expatriate assignments, expatriate couples, by investing in a coaching relationship, have greater control over when and under what circumstance they might engage their coach.

6   The coaching relationship can be viewed as an ongoing flexible and responsive resource that would be available for an expatriate couple to utilize as they need over the course of a two to three-year expatriate assignment. The couple and their coach can make a short-term agreement to focus on an area of their lives at one point (e.g. during the initial transition) and, then later, can renegotiate another kind of agreement to focus on another aspect of their lives (e.g. repatriation). A couple's coach can provide needed support both in a timely fashion and consistently across the life cycle of the entire assignment.

7   A trained certified coach can also spot situations in which a couple may be experiencing

more intense problems that are outside the professional capabilities of the coach, and can assist the couple in seeking therapeutic help within the local community. In this regard, Williams and Davis (2002), draw key general distinctions between traditional therapy and professional coaching. While therapy often focuses on the client's past, coaching focuses on what the client desires for the future. Clients often initiate therapy to eliminate some source of suffering, while clients who request coaching see themselves as wanting support in creating future possibilities in their lives. Finally, coaches tend to develop a collaborative relationship with their clients to promote personal growth and the attainment of life goals whereas therapists tend to be regarded as experts who have the knowledge and skills to help their clients solve or heal personal problems. With this as a context, professional coaching would never be considered as taking the place of mental health services, counseling, psychotherapy or marriage and family therapy, if such services were needed by an expatriate couple.

8   There are several additional important professional requirements of any coach who is contracted to participate in an expatriate program of services for the purpose of working with expatriate couples. These include the following:

a   The coach should be professionally trained and certified in an independent coaching training program, such as The Coaches Training Institute or Coach University, or in a university coaching training program, such as those at The University of Texas at Dallas, Georgetown University or The University of Sydney. These programs typically earn accreditation through an international accreditation association, such as the International Coaches Federation or the European Mentoring and Coaching Council.

b   A professionally trained coach should be someone who understands the importance of confidentiality, adheres to the coaches' professional code of ethics and has met a basic set of agreed-upon professional competencies in the industry.

c   The professional coach should be a person who has the professional credentials and background to work with couples and families, including training in general systems theory or marital and family systems.

d   Strongly recommended is a professional coach who has had an expatriate experience with their partner and who can appreciate some of the family dilemmas inherent in living in a foreign country. In order to facilitate understanding, it may also be necessary to match an expatriate couple with a coach who is from the same home country.

THE OPPORTUNITY OF COUPLES COACHING FOR EXPATRIATE COUPLES

During the course of an expatriate assignment, there are critical points where coaching could be invaluable for couples who are faced with having to consider choices, make plans, and/or deal with change. Making available coaching for expatriate couples throughout the life cycle of their expatriate assignment has many benefits to the couple and to the viability of the expatriate assignment. Here are a few specific areas where a couples coach could bring valuable coaching tools and methods to assisting expatriate couples in having their expatriate assignment be rewarding and successful:

Clarifying motivation for accepting an expatriate assignment

During the pre-assignment assessment, couples could use a coaching relationship to help them clarify their reasons for exploring an expatriate assignment, the questions they have about the nature of the assignment, and the life they wish to create for themselves in the process. Couples coaching can be viewed as a forum for intentional conversation and partnership. There are tools that a coach brings to assist the couple in determining whether an expatriate assignment is right for them.

Connecting with values

When exploring an expatriate assignment, couples can find it very helpful to engage in conversations about what is important to them in their lives. Coaching provides an intentional structure for conversation where a couple can clarify what they value and find compelling about an expatriate assignment.

Exploring from a meta-view

A coach can also encourage the couple to pull back from their immediate circumstances and examine an expatriate assignment from a larger life perspective. What is calling to them at this stage in their life together? What possibility does an expatriate opportunity present for themselves and their family?

Creating a vision for the future

A vision for the future allows a couple to be aligned on the kind of life they want together. By holding clients to what is important to them, a couples coach can assist a couple to create a vision for their future and to assess whether an expatriate assignment is part of that future.

> Cheryl and Joe sought the services of a couple's coach as they were considering an international move from the US to Germany. Cheryl had the opportunity to take a position as the head of the global marketing department for an international clothing firm. While Cheryl was in mid-career, Joe, who was significantly older than Cheryl, was considering closing his private practice as a chiropractor, a practice he had built over 25 years. This was a significant choice for both of them and they wanted to make sure they were each considering their own needs as well as the needs of their three grown children, one of whom was newly married. This job was career advancement for Cheryl at a time when Joe would be stepping into the role of househusband at home. Before making the choice to accept the position (or not), this couple wanted to clarify their motivations and concerns for making what appeared to them an exciting but risky choice to uproot their family and head to Europe for three to four years.
>
> Their coach, who was contracted through the company's human resources department, assisted the couple in identifying their concerns and goals for coaching, in bringing to light what was important to them in their stage of life and in considering how such an expatriate assignment could meet their individual as well as couple needs. In this case, the coaching engagement was time-limited, four sessions at most, but helped both of them to consider the expatriate assignment in earnest. They gathered the additional vital information they needed for them to be able to respond meaningfully to Cheryl's offer of an international assignment.

Facilitating the choice

The choice to accept or to decline an offer of an expatriate assignment is one of the most important discussions a couple might have with a couple's coach. Being aligned in shared values and in the kind of life they want for themselves provides a couple a sense of intentional partnership in dealing with all the risks and challenges they may face during an expatriate assignment.

Making the choice

Making the choice powerfully together requires a couple to fully consider all the 'pros' and 'cons' for both accepting a potential expatriate assignment as well as declining the assignment. A coach can help to facilitate a couple to have this discussion completely and over a period of time. When considering all the plusses and minuses of the potential impact of an expatriate assignment, the couple can be fully responsible for the myriad of logistical, financial, and emotional aspects of the assignment once they have made their choice. Making their choice in partnership may be the most important single accomplishment a couple shares to ensure a successful expatriate assignment.

Creating a project supporting their family's transition

Once the couple chooses to accept an offer for an expatriate assignment, their worldview shifts dramatically. A whole host of logistical issues and decisions will flow from their fateful choice. A coach can work with the couple in creating a project that involves, not only the logistics of the relocation, but also the transition issues for each member of the family.

> Jim and Mary had been considering a move overseas for some time. Jim was an executive in an international financial services corporation and had been offered a similar position in The Hague, The Netherlands. Mary was a psychologist in private practice in Atlanta where they had lived for 20 years. They had two children, ages 12 and 15 years. Mary was quite resistant at first about giving up her private practice. Jim and Mary had sat down together with the company's talent manager to gather information on Jim's potential job opportunity, its role and responsibilities, and its salary and benefits package. This couple also sat down with the firm's relocation manager to talk about what was involved in setting up the move, finding a place to live and getting acclimatized to the foreign country. They also made arrangements for Mary to accompany Jim on an international trip to meet and speak to staff at the international headquarters in The Hague.
>
> Over a two-month period, Jim and Mary gathered a lot of information, bought books about The Netherlands and spoke to their families and friends. At the point when they needed to make a decision, they independently hired a coach to help them to facilitate their choice. On the one hand, the move presented opportunities to experience life in another culture, to travel in Europe and to redesign their family life that had become quite hectic in the Atlanta area. On the other hand, their children had expressed unhappiness about leaving their friends, Mary was reluctant to give up her private practice and find new work in a new country and the couple each had concerns about living abroad in the turbulent times following the attack on the World Trade Center in September, 2001. By asking powerful questions and keeping this couple anchored in their values, the coach was able to support Jim and Mary in making the choice that was right for them. They each chose to proceed with accepting the international assignment. By engaging in such a choice process together, they were better able to support their children together in the actual move and relocation process.

211

Facilitating problem-solving

After the choice is made, the three months before relocation and the three months after moving represent a period of intense problem-solving and activity for the expatriate couple. The following coaching conversations and tools are invaluable for a couple at this juncture of an expatriate assignment.

Creating a partnership

A coach can assist the couple in developing a partnership that can sustain them through this time of intense change. Accepting an expatriate assignment requires fact-finding, brainstorming, planning, communicating with other family members, and making important life decisions.

Forwarding the action and problem-solving

A coach can assist a new expatriate couple to articulate what is happening and to gain insight into their family's adjustment during the months after their move. A coach can work with the couple in adjusting roles and responsibilities, keeping focused on short-term goals, identifying roadblocks and obstacles, and working together to solve problems in the process. Couples can benefit from having a coach with whom they can reframe disempowering perspectives as the 'rubber' begins to really meet the 'road'. A coaching relationship can assist the couple in maintaining their focus on their larger life goals as they face the uncertainty before them.

Understanding national cultures

One of the major opportunities of an expatriate assignment for a couple and their family is their understanding of different cultural expectations, customs and social values. A couple in a coaching relationship can gain insight into differences between their native culture and the culture of their host country and the impact these differences have in their daily life.

> Kees, a Dutchman, and Veronique, a Flemish Belgian, met just after graduating from college when they were both working at a Dutch logistics firm.[1] They married a few years later. Kees had been identified as a high potential employee on the fast track within the company. The company sponsored him to get an MBA at the London Business School and Veronique went along for the adventure. They really enjoyed their time in London and his career really started to take off upon their return to The Netherlands. Kees was then offered his first foreign expatriate assignment as country manager for the firm in Switzerland. As they were preparing to move, Veronique discovered that she was pregnant with their first child.
>
> The adjustment to Switzerland was a difficult one. Kees and Veronique were living in a small village just outside of Zurich and she was not working outside the home for the first time in her life. This move and all the subsequent adjustments put a severe strain on the marriage. His adjustment seemed to be easier because he was working in a familiar company culture. For her, everything was new and different, but she gradually adjusted to all of these life changes. She found an expatriate women's group in Zurich and she started a business from her home doing cross-cultural training and consulting. Then, two years later, they had a second child.

Three years into their posting in Switzerland, Kees was offered a global position back in the head office in The Netherlands. He was very excited about the offer, but Veronique was not. She felt she had gone through a great deal in order to adjust culturally to living in Switzerland. After having established a support system with the international women's group, Veronique was not ready to make another international move to support his career. At that point, with their marriage at some risk, they found a coach who helped them clarify and work through the issues around the decision to move back to The Netherlands.

The couple's coach assisted Kees and Veronique in listening to each other's needs, problem-solving, putting their partnership ahead of Kees' short-term career goals and choosing together to stay in Switzerland, with their two children, both of whom were under four years of age.

Assessing local opportunities

Within three to six months of arriving in their host country, a couple can begin to look further into the future. As a couple and their family begin to get settled in their new country, a coach can bring additional tools for assessing the local opportunities for the couple and for fulfilling the vision they created before they moved.

Creating a longer-term view for their expatriate experience

Many expatriate assignments are two to three years in duration and the future beyond the current assignment is often cloudy at best. At this point, an expatriate couple can benefit from taking a step back and taking a longer-term view of their future. What do they see for themselves five years down the road? Where do they see themselves living? What kind of work are they each engaged in? What are the children doing? A coaching relationship can be a forum in which an expatriate couple can create the kind of expatriate life they want to have that inspires them.

Planning and fulfilling family projects

In a coaching relationship a couple is able to assess opportunities, make plans and take committed action. Traveling, going on sightseeing excursions, volunteering, building a new social network, finding a job, or building a business are all projects that require planning and taking action. A coach can assist the couple in troubleshooting problems, taking effective action and achieving results.

Reflecting on the expatriate experience

A rewarding aspect of an expatriate experience is the understanding of one's cultural adaptation through reflection and shared learning. In a coaching relationship, a couple can gain insight and awareness of themselves through self-reflection and inquiry. The coach is trained to ask powerful questions to assist the couple in integrating their observations and the lessons they are learning.

Jim and Mary, six months after they settled into their new home in Den Hague, The Netherlands, had begun to build a social network with other expatriates, most of them

213

American and from Jim's company. Jim was working long hours and Mary was getting restless to design a family life that worked for everyone, to find a way to contribute, and to create opportunities to travel. Jim and Mary worked briefly with a coach to sort out what kind of life they wanted to create for themselves in The Netherlands.

The couple first shared about the kind of family life style they wanted. In Atlanta, they had both worked long hours and had wanted to get off the 'treadmill'. They knew they didn't want to recreate that life in the foreign country. Jim agreed to be home by six and to start to leave his work at the office. Mary, who had been a full-time professional psychologist, happily took on the bulk of the household responsibilities to be able to promote a healthier family life style. They got into the habit of eating dinner together as a family many nights, something they rarely did in Atlanta. Jim and Mary created a project they called, 'Seeing the Sights', in which Mary would take the lead in planning family day excursions on the weekends and trips to other European countries during their children's vacations. Mary also got involved volunteering at her kids' school. At the first year mark, Jim and Mary began to feel at home in the new country.

Repatriating

Toward the end of an expatriate assignment and the beginning of repatriation, a couple can use a coach to help integrate their expatriate experience into their lives and to facilitate their transition home.

Re-examining their lives and looking to the future

A couple's coach can further work with a couple to help them re-create a vision for their new future as their expatriate assignment comes to a close. At the end of an expatriate assignment, the couple comes full circle and is again examining what is important to them. Coaching can help a couple stay anchored in what they value as they plan for their journey home or to their next expatriate destination.

Completing the expatriate experience

Toward the end of an expatriate assignment, a couple is dealing with closure and assessing life lessons that they and their family have learned. They are saying goodbye to friends and integrating their expatriate experience into their lives. A coaching relationship can be helpful for an expatriate couple in coming to terms with the benefits and the drawbacks of their experience as expatriates. Focusing on repatriation to their home country can be even more difficult for a couple than the original move overseas. Fully acknowledging the lessons learned, the international friendships gained, and the memories captured can facilitate a smoother transition for the couple.

Six months after their choice to remain in Switzerland, Kees and Veronique faced a new challenge. The company had come back to him with yet another offer for a position in their Asian-Pacific regional headquarters in Kuala Lumpur. The couple called their coach to help them with this new dilemma.

In their follow-up coaching engagement, the couple began to deal with some issues, avoided previously, in a forthright way. This couple was confronting fundamental value differences in what was important to them. They recognized that their conflict revolved around a sense of inequality that resulted from a disproportionate focus on Kees' career.

Veronique was more assertive in what she wanted, which was equality in the relationship. She was no longer willing to be second fiddle to her husband's climb to the top of the corporate ladder. Veronique had developed a cross-cultural business and was part of a network of international women leaders. Veronique wanted her husband to negotiate a more comprehensive expatriate package including quality international schooling for the children and an upscale suburban residential placement for the family. In the coaching relationship, Veronique was able to negotiate with her husband from a position of being equal partner and, as a result, this couple was able to establish a more powerful negotiating stance with Kees' company. They moved within six months to the company's Asian-Pacific regional headquarters in Kuala Lumpur, Malaysia.

The coach supported this couple in listening to each other's concerns, in dealing powerfully with a long-standing conflict and in negotiating with each other from an equal footing. This coaching engagement was critical to this couple's ability to choose what was right for each other, their relationship, and their family.

For the expatriate couple, the benefits of having a coaching relationship available to them throughout the expatriate assignment are many. At every step of the way, an expatriate couple can get the support they need in creating their lives, in cooperating together, and in being responsible for their shared expatriate experience. With the expatriate employee and their spouse as full partners in the life cycle of an expatriate assignment, their marital relationship can stay strong and the expatriate assignment can be rewarding.

CONCLUSION: THE PROMISE OF EXPATRIATE COUPLES COACHING

Companies make a large investment in moving top talent internationally. Expatriate couples take big risks moving themselves and their families around the globe. Supporting expatriate couples and their families directly through the use of couples coaching as part of an expatriate services program can have a positive impact on the well-being of expatriate couples and on a company's bottom-line. An expatriate executive or manager is better able to 'hit the boards running' in his or her new international position, being confident that the marriage partnership is strong and supported. The corporation also sends a very loud and positive message to the executive and his or her partner that communicates that their relationship is important. This is a 'win-win' family-centered corporate focus.

Happy and satisfied expatriate relationships and their families provide a strong foundation for the executive to be fully engaged on the job. The executive is able to make a substantial investment in the company over the long term and participate more actively in the company's growth internationally. Satisfied executives, supported by their spouses at home, translate into retention of top talent for the company. As the retention of talent improves, the company's investment in expatriate services pays off greatly. There is a reduction of lost talent and large financial costs associated with failed expatriate assignments. With a more stable expatriate workforce, companies are able to sustain their investment and their growth internationally.

This chapter has made a case for the central inclusion of couples coaching in a company's program of services to expatriates and their families. The extraordinary cost of failed expatriate assignments is well documented. It is also clear that a large percentage of those failures are due to expatriate spousal and family adjustment problems. While many companies provide extensive services to expatriates and are increasingly including the spouse (and the family) in pre-assignment planning, cultural training, relocation services, and repatriation planning, companies could well afford to include couples coaching as a service offered throughout the duration of an expatriate assignment.

A coaching relationship, if made available and requested by the expatriate employee, can focus on the adjustment and satisfaction of the expatriate couple and their family, areas that traditionally have been outside the control of multinational companies and have been implicated in the success or failure of expatriate assignments. A professional coach assists couples in exploring what is important to them, in making choices that are consistent with what they value, in problem-solving, in creating a vision for their lives, and in fulfilling their aspirations. In short, a professional couples coaching relationship can focus directly on what is important to the couple in fulfilling their life together in a new country. By supporting expatriates and their spouses more directly by making couples coaching available to them, companies make a vital and sound investment in the success of expatriate assignments and, ultimately, in the future of their business enterprises internationally.

Note

1   The authors wish to thank Ann Houston Kelley of Nomadic Life in Voorschoten, The Netherlands, for contributing this case study.

Bibliography

Corporate Leadership Council (2002a) *Successful Expatriate Assignments and Repatriation Processes*, Arlington, VA: Corporate Executive Board.

Corporate Leadership Council (2002b) *Expatriate Programs: Staff Selection Process*, Arlington, VA: Corporate Executive Board.

Corporate Leadership Council (2002c) *Expatriate Programs: Staff Development*, Arlington, VA: Corporate Executive Board.

Ely, R. and McCormick, J. (1993) *The New International Executive: Business Leadership for the 21st Century*, A Global Research Report Published by AMROP International/Harvard University.

Forthofer, M., Markman, H., Cox, M., Stanley, S., and Kessler, R. (1996) 'Associations between marital distress and work loss in a national sample', *Journal of Marriage and Family*, 58: 597–605.

Gallagher, M. (2002) *Why Supporting Marriage Makes Business Sense*. Corporate Resource Council. Available online at <www.corporateresourcecouncil.org/white_papers/Supporting_Marriage.pdf.> (accessed 7 April 2008).

GMAC (2004) *Ten Years of Global Relocation Trends: 1993–2004*, Woodbridge, Ont.: GMAC Global Relocation Services.

GMAC (2007) *Global Relocation Trends: 2006 Survey Report*, Woodbridge, Ont.: GMAC Global Relocation Services in association with the National Foreign Trade Council.

McCaughey, D., and Bruning, N.S. (2005) 'Enhancing opportunities for expatriate job satisfaction: Human resource strategies for foreign assignment success', *Human Resource Planning*, 28: 21–9.

McNulty, Y. (2001) *International Mobility and the Bottom Line*. Amsterdam: Expatica Communications BV.

Pascoe, R. (2003) *A Moveable Marriage: Relocate Your Relationship without Breaking It*, North Vancouver: Expatriate Press Ltd.

Punnett, B.J. (1997) 'Towards effective management of expatriate spouses', *Journal of World Business*, 32 (3): 243–57.

Stober, D.R. (2006) 'Coaching from the humanistic perspective', in D.R. Stober and A.M. Grant, *Evidence Based Coaching Handbook*, Hoboken: John Wiley & Sons.

Swaak, R. (1995) 'Expatriate failures: Too many, too much cost, too little planning', *Compensation and Benefits Review*, 27 (6): 47–55.

Turvey, M.D. and Olson, D.H. (2007) *Marriage and Family Wellness: Corporate America's Business*, Available online at <www.marriagecomission.com/files/May31ReportCopy[1](1).pdf.> (accessed 7 April 2008).

Tye, M.G. and Chen, P.Y. (2005) 'Selection of expatriates: decision-making models used by HR professionals', *Human Resource Planning*, 28 (4): 15–20.

Waite, L.J. and Gallagher, M. (2000) *The Case for Marriage*, New York: Broadway Books.

Whitworth, L., Kimsey-House, H., and Sandahl, P. (1998) *Co-Active Coaching: New Skills for Coaching People towards Success in Work and in Life*. Palo Alto: Davies-Black Publishing.

Williams, P. and Davis, D. (2002) *Therapist as Life Coach: Transforming Your Practice*. New York: W. W. Norton and Company.

14

COACHING WOMEN MANAGERS IN MULTINATIONAL COMPANIES

Katrina Burrus

WOMEN IN MULTINATIONALS: MISUNDERSTOOD AND UNDERUTILIZED

The way to the top in multinationals is clearly built abroad; overseas assignments provide rich learning and a definitive proving ground in both operational and intercultural experience (Bennis 1989; Caligiuri and DiSanto 2001; Schein 2003; Weber 1996). Yet, women comprise only 14 per cent of the expatriate population (Koretz 1999). Why? Peter Brabeck-Letmathe, chief executive officer of Nestlé SA, one of the 50 largest companies in the world (see Forbes 2006), told me:

> This is the reason why it is more difficult to find women in top-management positions. Women are as competent as men. However, if you want to have a career at Nestlé, you must be open to relocate frequently. You cannot judge from here what is really happening there. It is necessary to be exposed to and have lived in those countries. This means that during your career you have to live in one or several of those areas. Up to now, it has been easier to find men willing to move frequently. Whether this will continue to be the case in the future, who knows? This is perhaps the one aspect which makes an international career more difficult for women.
>
> (Quoted in Burrus-Barbey 2000: 498)

Every woman in business has experience with the glass ceiling, the illusive barrier to C-suite success (Acker 2006; Bible and Hill 2007; Eagly and Carli 2007; Noble and Moore 2006; Valian 1998). But how does the gender barrier play out in international business? What is the experience of women in multinationals, particularly those in or vying for the coveted expatriate spots? How do leadership perspectives and styles, family roles and responsiblities, and cultural and gender prejudices impact the woman working abroad, and her opportunities to even get or succeed in such a job? This chapter identifies the myths, paradoxes, and facts about international businesswomen; the issues of women in international posts; and strategies for coaching these women on navigating the complex multicultural environment of global organizational life.

Understanding and appreciating the experience of international women executives is critical to the global organizations who deploy them, their human resources (HR) teams and the women and their families and, of course, their coaches. The evidence of bottom-line business advantage for businesses that embrace diversity is overwhelming (Catalyst n.d.; Ghoshal and Bartlett 1997; Kanter 1995; Kouzes and Posner 1995; Pfeffer 1998). Thus, coaching these women is crucial to facilitating and ensuring their success, and promoting greater diversity, intercultural competency, and business competitiveness.

CEILINGS, WALLS, AND MAZES: BARRIERS BY ANY OTHER NAME

Various metaphors have been used to describe the poor representation of women executives in business. The glass ceiling connotes the invisible barrier on the way to the top of the organization, beyond which one can see, but not go (Hymowitz and Schellhardt 1986). A new, more accurate, and more powerful metaphor has recently emerged: a labyrinth – 'walls all around' (Eagly and Carli 2007: 63–4) – to contradict and supplant the simplistic, breakable notion of the glass ceiling with a much more complex maze of obstacles on the path to C-suite success.

> Metaphors matter because they are part of the storytelling that can compel change. Believing in the existence of a glass ceiling, people emphasize certain kinds of interventions: top-to-top networking, mentoring to increase board memberships, requirements for diverse candidates in high-profile succession horse races, litigation aimed at punishing discrimination in the C-suite. None of these is counterproductive; all have a role to play. The danger arises when they draw attention and resources away from other kinds of interventions that might attack the problem more potently. If we want to make better progress, it's time to rename the challenge.
>
> (Eagly and Carli 2007: 64)

So what are the facts that confirm women's poor representation in international business and expatriate roles? Women make up half of the population, and over 40 per cent of the ranks of managerial positions in US business, for instance (Eagly and Carli 2007). So far, so good. But that's where the equity breaks down. Women do not have equal access to entry – or mid-level positions, much less strategic roles leading to the top (Eagly and Carli 2007; Valian 1998). Women hold only 15 per cent of corporate officer positions in US-based companies, and a mere 7 per cent of the top earner positions. Within their 15 per cent of the officer positions, 73 per cent of those women are in staff roles, and only 27 per cent are in line roles, the gateway positions to top leadership (Catalyst n.d.). In other industrialized nations, women's status is similar. In the 50 largest publicly traded companies in each of the EU countries, women hold an average of 11 per cent of the top executive positions (Eagly and Carli 2007). And the trend is static to declining (Catalyst n.d.).

The cause of this dismal situation is embedded in patriarchal culture, a status quo maintained by various myths and paradoxes (Bourdieu and Paseron 1977; Eagly and Carli 2007; Valian 1998). Changing the cultural status quo is extremely difficult, as resistance to change is systemic (Kotter 1995; Schein 1992). Yet the myths that help sustain the status quo signal how and where change might get a foothold.

THE MYTHS: SHE WOULDN'T GO, AND IT WOULDN'T WORK ANYWAY

Even the most progressive organizations promulgate myths which support and maintain the existing culture and undermine efforts toward change (Kotter 1995; Schein 1992). Fallacious and discrimatory assumptions about women's fitness for and performance in expatriate roles engender unfounded bias in expatriate selection, HR policy and practice, leadership and management decision-making, expat supervision and interaction, and in-country expat support (Mayrhofer and Scullion 2002; Tzeng 2006; Vance, Paik and White 2006).

Various reasons cited by business leadership for not giving overseas assignments to women who work for multinational corporations include:

- Lack of motivation to pursue such positions;
- Lack of qualifications;
- Inability to manage work and family responsibilities in an expat environment;
- Physical safety concerns for women in underdeveloped countries;
- Concern for women's ability to cope with isolation and loneliness in a foreign country;
- Spousal career concerns; and
- Severe gender prejudices, especially in developing countries (Adler 1994; Antal and Izraeli 1993; Izraeli, Banai and Zeira 1980; Tzeng 2006; Tye and Chen 2005; Vance et al. 2006; Wah 1998).

Thus, even as the ranks of women in the executive pipeline have increased toward formidable parity, these fallacious assumptions about women's readiness and capabilities to serve in expat posts persist.

Private sector organizations' expat selection, 'is carried out largely on the basis of technical competence, with minimal attention being paid to the interpersonal skills and domestic situations of potential expatriates' (Anderson 2005: 567) and HR often has a limited role. When HR *is* involved, selection decision-making consistently places 'greater emphasis on stress tolerance and less emphasis on such characteristics as gender and home country (domestic) job performance' (Tye and Chen 2005: 15). In contrast, NGO selection practices differ markedly in that psychological testing is widely used and the family is treated as a unit and included in the selection process (Anderson 2005: 567).

Thus the facts begin to emerge. But these disparities, false assumptions, and unfair practices are compounded by ironic paradoxes relative to the woman expatriate and her male competitors.

THE PARADOXES: DAMNED IF SHE DOES, DAMNED IF SHE DOESN'T

The gender barrier often manifests in a double bind in which women in business find themselves (Jamieson 1995). Simply put, what works for men doesn't work for women, or actually works against women when they emulate the same behavior and performance as men (Eagly and Carli 2007; Shames 1997; Wah 1998). These contradictory expectations of women were identified early in the glass ceiling research:

- Take risks but be consistently outstanding;
- Be tough without sacrificing feminity or being 'macho';
- Be ambitious without expecting equal treatment to men; and
- Take responsibility but strategically follow the advice of others (Morrison, White, Van Velsor and Center for Creative Leadership 1987: 57).

Some of these dichotomies are systemic in business itself. Organizations talk teamwork, yet laud, value, and promote individual achievement (Lipman-Blumen 1996). The double bind plays out for women in multinational business particularly in terms of leadership style and marriage and family issues.

WOMEN'S LEADERSHIP STYLE

Male leadership connotes assertiveness, control, ambition, and self-confidence. Yet a woman with these more aggressive characteristics may be perceived as less effective and not engaging the more democratic (Goleman 2001) and communal style expected of women (Eagly and Carli 2007; Shames 1997; Wah 1998). In certain cultural environments this paradox can be even more detrimental to women in international business, as exemplified by the following quote of an Asian employee talking about her expat boss (personal correspondence):

> Her style is confrontational and aggressive and it does not work in an Asian market. If we feel that aggression, we will simply not carry out her orders. Some people do not want to work with her and only agree to deal with her through emails. This situation makes her even more aggressive.

Usually women use more participative and collaborative styles than men (Eagly and Carli 2007; Helgesen 1990, 1995; Lipman–Blumen 1996). When a man emulates these qualities, he is lauded and rewarded (Eagly and Carli 2007). But when a woman emulates the male leadership style, it is perceived as detrimental and may backfire.

MARRIAGE AND FAMILY ISSUES FOR WOMEN IN MULTINATIONAL COMPANIES

Another common barrier, particularly for expatriates, is marriage, family, and relocation to other countries. The paradox here is simple: 'Marriage and parenthood are associated with higher wages for men but not for women' (Eagly and Carli 2007: 65). Yet the fact that women are the childbearers and continue to take on more of the family responsibilities than men makes solutions less obvious, both emotionally and pragmatically. Clearly, a woman may decide to terminate or delay a mobile career because of marital and maternal responsibilities (Tzeng 2006).

But, beyond childbearing itself, the facts of family life abroad for the executive, trailing spouse and children are complex and poorly understood (Tzeng 2006), and may surprise decisionmakers who 'often assume that mothers have domestic responsibilities that make it inappropriate to promote them to demanding positions' (Eagly and Carli 2007: 68). This perception may apply even when a woman executive has forgone a family life for a career.

These are not just women's issues (Pomeroy 2007). Companies would benefit by providing generous support to expat employees and their families to contribute to their in-country well-being, performance, and successful repatriation and retention (Andreason 2003; Kraimer, Wayne and Jaworski 2001; Lazarova and Caligiuri 2001; Richey 1996; Rosinski 2003; Shaffer and Harrison 1998; Stahl, Chei Hwee Chua, Caligiuri, Cerdin and Taniguchi 2007; van der Zee, Ali and Salomé 2005).

Thus, though men and women both face family obligations and inherent challenges in balancing work and family life abroad, the challenge is perceived as culturally different for men and women. As such, the coach's support can be tailored to the executive woman's adjustment needs in developing culturally specific behavioral strategies to adapt to her new environment. Coaches can also gather 360° feedback data, which, when debriefed with cultural sensitivity, may explain the paradoxes and the fine line between being damned or praised in cross-cultural environments.

THE FACTS: IT'S NOT A GENDER ISSUE – ALL EXPATS NEED SUPPORT

The stereotypes, false assumptions, and biases don't stand up when multinationals research the facts about men and women in international assignments. Research demonstrates that gender is unrelated to:

- Interest in and qualification for expatriate assignments (Adler 1994; Selmer and Leung 2003; Tharenou 2003; Tzeng 2006);
- Expatriate performance (Caligiuri and Tung 1999; Sinangil and Ones 2003; Tye and Chen 2005);
- Expatriate turnover intentions (Caligiuri and Tung 1999; Tye and Chen 2005);
- Expatriate adjustment abroad (Selmer and Leung 2003; Tucker, Bonial and Lahti 2004; Tye and Chen 2005), although women may experience higher interaction and work adjustment (Selmer and Leung 2003) particularly in countries with masculine values (Caligiuri and Tung 1999), while men may experience greater psychological adjustment (Selmer and Leung 2003); and
- Work/life balance (Brett and Stroh 1994; Pomeroy 2007); female expats actually find work/life balance easier than in home-country roles because domestic help is often provided (Adler 1994).

Thus objective criteria of expatriate success are gender neutral. In a gender-neutral environment, in fact, it's conceivable that women's success rate might be even be higher than men's due to their leadership styles and intercultural sensitivity. Yet substantive gender biases remain in other cultures around the world, and thus may continue to promulgate bias and impact local perceptions of women expats abroad (Keillor, Thomas and Hauser 2006). Coaches, therefore, are well served to understand and address the issues that their women clients in international roles face, and work to facilitate their selection for, and adjustment and success in, these strategic roles. The next section illustrates some of women expats' experiences in the field.

THE EXPERIENCE OF WOMEN IN MULTINATIONALS

Women expats experience day-to-day gender- and culture-driven challenges, particularly in less developed countries (Adler 1994; Antal and Izraeli 1993; Izraeli et al. 1980) and/or countries with masculine-based values (Caligiuri and Tung 1999; Shames 1997; Wah 1998). Women expats' success, particularly relative to gender, can be viewed in four categories: women's individual characteristics, their organizations, their families, and the local host nationals with whom they work (Caligiuri and Cascio, 1998). The issues of women expats in each are illustrated with actual vignettes from published research and my own practice.

Challenges expatriate women managers may face

Gertrude was a business turnaround wizard, and had succeeded brillantly in emerging markets. Her straightforward, all-business style had served her well. But in Asia, this same leadership style created resistance, avoidance and, finally, isolation from her employees.

Angela had argued with her local Vice President. She insisted on being included in the negotiation dinner with their bankers. Her VP insisted that such a plan would result in them losing the funding for their next expansion (Wah 1998).

Like most women expats, Patrizia was single, and threw herself into her work abroad. In the US, Hong Kong, and London, she worked long hours and her social life was completely business-related. In Latin America, however, her hours and dedication were frowned upon by local colleagues, and her lack of personal life became a concern for her global management as well. Having no one to talk to about this increased her despondency. Having no one to talk to increased her sense of isolation.

A coach can create the space in which the woman expat can step back, reflect, and view the situation from her colleagues' perspectives. With this insight, she can overcome these gender-specific cultural barriers by devising appropriate behavioral strategies, and learn on-site even greater intercultural sensitivity. This being said, women expats' leadership skills, cultural savvy, and local adaptation remain key to the success of women in multinationals. Like men, women chosen for expat assignments should fulfill the qualities and characteristics required of such roles upfront (Caligiuri and DiSanto 2001; Rosinski 2003).

Women expats and their organizations

Stefanie's functional expertise landed her the overseas role. But in their haste to get her on site, the company skipped over intercultural training in favor of immersion language classes. Once overseas, Stefanie's key asset, her expertise, was ignored when her behavior was viewed as inappropriate for her gender. She was then treated as a low-level employee by local management and clientele.

Lydia had traveled the globe for years, providing counsel for the firm's operations world-wide. But when she relocated to open up the new region, she found herself alone, with no one to fill the off hours or share her new experiences. Being single, she was invited once to each of her local colleagues' homes, but as the months passed, she felt increasingly isolated and shunned socially by her male colleagues, who were hesitant to share meals or make trips with her because she was a single woman:

I was anxiously fidgeting with the papers I was going to distribute when suddenly the general director appeared in front of me. He very kindly told me that they were looking forward to my intervention. They were resolving important issues and would appreciate the relaxation during my 10-minutes speech. He said he would call me in a few minutes. He then disappeared behind those large, heavy doors.

(Burrus 1997: 212)

Organizational support and mutual intercultural competence are key for expats and their host-country colleagues. Importantly, research confirms that helping the expat establish a full life experience in the host-country environment is pivotal to expatriate success. The adjustment is, of course, a family issue as well.

223

Women expats' families

Alexandra was notified while traveling that her son had broken his leg at the football tournament. Her husband was presenting at a conference abroad too, so their in-country au pair was the only one to hold their son's hand at the hospital for the first few days. The parents' guilt and their son's loneliness, fear, and resentment frequently came up in subsequent family squabbles.

Nina and her husband were grateful to have been home when their daughter was injured by a pedicab. But they did not trust the local medical care, staff, or facilities, and had a long and stressful ordeal trying to locate and move her to adequate care abroad while maintaining their work responsibilities.

The demands of family life for women in multinationals can be extremely stressful, particularly if a woman perceives herself as both caregiver and executive, struggling to strike a balance. This double bind is exaggerated in crisis situations such as those described above, and underscores the need for corporate support – funding, systems, and social networks – to fill the gaps and provide real-time resources for expat families: medical, legal, social, domestic, psychological, and community. Support networks will ease the pressure, but the prioritization process might be best facilitated by a coach.

Women expats working with local host nationals

Selena was astounded that her local director had set up the client briefing on the new line at a night club where the only women were scantily dressed on stage (Wah 1998).

Even though she outranked him, the local manager insisted on having the final say in decision-making that was clearly within Inger's authority and beyond his (Wah 1998).

When Rianna's local general manager introduced her to their key supplier, he thought Rianna was his secretary, and was confused when she joined them at the conference table (Tzeng 2006; Wah 1998).

Nicola laughed when reflecting on how the local director had arranged for her to join the local management's wives on the city tour during the conference (Adler 1994).

Nurit was refused a rental car in Indonesia because the locals were unaccustomed to a woman driving her own car; when she complained to her in-country supervisor, he suggested that her husband drive the car (Wah 1998).

Only months later did Lourdes understand why business associates had canceled their scheduled meeting; they questioned her credentials and would not attend if the only company representative was to be a woman (Wah 1998).

Many of the challenges for international businesswomen result from gendered cultural differences perpetuated by local organizations and their business contacts in-country. The executive coach can assist the woman expat to develop strategies to address such discrimination. Also, the coach, in consultation with the client, may be well positioned to appropriately intervene with each of these stakeholder groups – the expat's organization, her family, and her local host colleagues – to facilitate a successful expatriate experience for all.

Coaching women and their multinationals: tips and tools

The coaching relationship of course relies on managing expectations and delivering results responsive to the client's needs (Dagley 2006). Particularly in expat contexts, the organization and the individual assigned for coaching have a sense of urgency. Yet the coaching involves individual development, intercultural adjustment, and often organizational culture change, all of which, of course, take time and patience. Thus highlighting the process for the client company and individual can help to align expectations and facilitate the in-depth work that may be needed.

THE COACHING PROCESS

Whether coaching the individual woman expatriate or the organization's CEO, expectations can be better aligned if the client understands that coaching follows a path of increasing individuation of the executive, progressively exploring

- The executive's environment – the strategies, structures, and systems through which the expat operates, and particularly status defense mechanisms;
- The executive's behavior – the expat's communication methods and styles, particularly when under stress;
- The executive's attitudes – the expat's beliefs and values, and how she sees the world;
- The deep structure of the executive – her character, defenses, and unconscious beliefs; and ultimately
- The deepest structure of the executive – the expat's core identity and spirit (Webb 2006: 70–1).

As in all coaching relationships, focus on the right problems, a relationship of trust, and the coaching process delineated above are central. Yet, beyond these basics, little research exists on this specialized intercultural coaching (Lowman 2007) or successful expatriate coping strategies (Stahl and Caligiuri 2005). And even as the metaphors evolve, many aspects of gender in management remain absent in research and thus not well understood (Broadbridge and Hearn 2008). So caution and care – without assuming transferability of home-country coaching practices – are of utmost importance (Lowman 2007).

As Doug Riddle, the Center for Creative Leadership's global director of coaching and feedback services, notes, 'A skilled coach allows leaders to *own* their own feelings, needs, and goals', which Riddle calls 'the modified Socratic technique' (Jenkins 2006: 24). While it may be tempting to focus on culture-specific education, and even on offending executives in the organization, expert coaching of course goes beyond supplying solutions, to examine underlying values and beliefs that drive behavior and culture (Jenkins 2006; Schein 1992).

COACHING INDIVIDUAL WOMEN EXPATRIATES

First, women need to make clear their interest in international assignments. Women interested in such roles should prepare and educate themselves, not only on the expat track, but also in terms of language, intercultural competence, flexibility, and superior interpersonal skills.

Once chosen, women expats are foremost expected to do a job. Women's particular

225

leadership styles can be an advantage, including collaboration, a gentler approach, listening, relationship-building, willingness to share the credit, team play, becoming confidantes of male colleagues, patience, empathy, and sensitivity to cultural nuances (Eagly and Carli 2007; Helgesen 1990, 1995; Lipman-Blumen 1996; Wah 1998). Conversely, adopting men's leadership styles can backfire against women executives (Eagly and Carli 2007; Shames 1997; Wah 1998). Yet management and leadership remain culture-specific (Bennis 1989; Caligiuri and DiSanto 2001; Schein 2003; Trompenaars and Hampden-Turner 1998).

Prospective expats need training in not only language and customs, but also intercultural competence, a combination of specific, learned customs, and much more subtle, nuanced behaviors and sensitivities (Bennett 2004; Bennett and Bennett 2004; Caligiuri and DiSanto 2001; Rosinski 2003; Trompenaars and Hampden-Turner 1998; Zakaria 2000). Expats often report that their learning further increases sensitivity and introduces humility, 'compared to those who have not been on a global assignment, these individuals "know what they do not know" ' (Caligiuri and DiSanto 2001: 33).

Coaching can also help expatriate leaders leverage their cultural intelligence, leadership styles, and knowledge of the importance of relationships, short-term profits, hierarchies, ethics, risk aversion, and other factors which vary from culture to culture, for example, the ability to establish relationships in China: *guanxi*.

Finally, whether single or married, with partner and/or children in-country or abroad, expats need to take care of themselves and their families. The issues are the same if a woman has no family; but if a woman has family, more responsibility falls on her, her trailing spouse is a more awkward issue than for men expats, and her networking needs are greater. The woman expat should push for and take advantage of all available support systems, and recognize that her professional success and adjustment depend on her personal adjustment and that of her family (Andreason 2003; Caligiuri, Hyland, Joshi and Bross 1998; Caligiuri, Joshi and Lazarova 1999).

INTERCULTURAL COACHING ON A GLOBAL SCALE

'Globally competent managers are critical for the success of all multinational organizations' (Caligiuri and DiSanto 2001: 27). Receptive expats, organizational leaders, and well-trained cross-cultural coaches can team up to help achieve this goal (Jenkins 2006; Rosinski 2003). These specialized coaches, like their clients, need to understand the nuances of the cultures involved, and score high on intercultural competence themselves (Bennett 2004; Bennett and Bennett 2004; Caligiuri and DiSanto 2001; Trompenaars and Hampden-Turner 1998).

My experience coaching women executives in multinational organizations has been most rewarding. Although men and women executives have many of the same issues, I have been surprised by how much more the coaching conversation with women executives revolves around relationships and the balancing act of personal and professional demands. Is my perception coming from a preconceived mindset that views women as equals, or does it stem from the fact that I, too, am an outcome of a cultural upbringing which perceives women as more relational?

Bibliography

Acker, J. (2006) 'Inequality regimes: Gender, class, and race in organizations', *Gender and Society*, 20 (4): 441–64.

Adler, N.J. (1994) 'Competitive frontiers: Women managing across borders', in N.J. Adler and D.N. Izraeli (eds), *Competitive Frontiers: Women Managers in a Global Economy*, Cambridge: Blackwell.

Anderson, B.A. (2005) 'Expatriate selection: Good management or good luck?', *International Journal of Human Resources Management*, 16 (4): 567–83.

Andreason, A.W. (2003) 'Direct and indirect forms of in-country support for expatriates and their families as a means of reducing premature returns and improving job performance', *International Journal of Management*, 20 (4): 548–55.

Antal, A.B. and Izraeli, D.N. (1993) 'A global comparison of women in management: Women managers in their homelands and as expatriates', in E.A. Fagenson (ed.), *Women in Management: Trends, Issues, and Challenges in Managerial Diversity*, Newbury Park: Sage.

Bennett, M.J. (2004) 'Becoming interculturally competent', in J. Wurzel (ed.), *Toward Multiculturalism: A Reader in Multicultural Education* (2nd edn), Newton, MA: Intercultural Resource Corporation.

Bennett, J.M. and Bennett, M.J. (2004) 'Developing intercultural sensitivity: An integrative approach to global and domestic diversity', in D. Landis, J. M. Bennett and M. J. Bennett (eds), *Handbook of Intercultural Training* (3rd edn), Thousand Oaks, CA: Sage.

Bennis, W. (1989) *On Becoming a Leader*, Reading, MA: Addison-Wesley.

Bible, D. and Hill, K.L. (2007) 'Discrimination: Women in business', *Journal of Organizational Culture*, 11 (1): 65–76.

Bourdieu, P. and Paseron, J.C. (1977) *Society, Culture, and Education*, Beverly Hills, CA: Sage.

Brett, J.M. and Stroh, L.K. (1994) 'Turnover of female managers', in M.J. Davidson and R.J. Burke (eds), *Women in Management: Current Research Issues*, London: Paul Chapman.

Broadbridge, A. and Hearn, J. (2008) 'Gender and management: New directions in research and continuing patterns in practice', *British Journal of Management*, 19: S38–S49.

Burrus-Barbey, K. (2000) 'Interview: leadership, global management, and future challenges: an interview with Peter Brabeck-Letmathe, Chief Executive Officer of Nestlé SA', *Thunderbird International Business Review*, 43 (5): 495–506.

Burrus, K. (1997) 'National culture and gender diversity within one of the universal Swiss banks: An experiential description of a professional woman officer and president of the Women Managers' Association', in S.A. Sackmann (ed.), *Cultural Complexity in Organizations: Inherent Contrasts and Contradictions*, Thousand Oaks, CA: Sage.

Caligiuri, P. and DiSanto, V. (2001) 'Global competence: What is it, and can it be developed through global assignments?', *Human Resource Planning*, 24 (3): 27–35.

Caligiuri, P.M. and Cascio, W.F. (1988) 'Can we send her there?: Maximizing the success of Western women on global assignments', *Journal of World Business*, 33 (4): 394–416.

Caligiuri, P.M., Hyland, M.M., Joshi, A. and Bross, A.S. (1998) 'Testing a theoretical model for examining the relationship between family adjustment and expatriates' work adjustment', *Journal of Applied Psychology*, 83 (4): 598–614.

Caligiuri, P.M., Joshi, A. and Lazarova, M. (1999) 'Factors influencing the adjustment of women on global assignments', *International Journal of Human Resource Management*, 10 (2): 163–79.

Caligiuri, P.M. and Tung, R. (1999) 'Comparing the success of male and female expatriates from a U.S. based company', *International Journal of Human Resource Management*, 10 (5): 763–82.

Catalyst. (n.d.) *2007 Catalyst Census of Women Corporate Officers and Top Earners of the Fortune 500*. Available online at <www.catalyst.org/knowledge/2007cote.shtml> (accessed 28 April 2008).

Dagley, G. (2006) 'Human resources professionals' perceptions of executive coaching: Efficacy, benefits and return on investment', *International Coaching Psychology Review*, 1 (2): 34–45.

Eagly, L.L. and Carli, A.H. (2007) 'Women and the labyrinth of leadership', *Harvard Business Review*, 85 (9): 62–71.

Forbes (2006) 'Largest companies in the world', *Forbes*, 177 (8): 111–14.

Ghoshal, S. and Bartlett, C.A. (1997) *The Individualized Corporation: A Fundamentally New Approach to Management*, New York: Harper Collins.

Goleman, D. (2001) 'An EI-based theory of performance', in C. Cherniss and D. Goleman (eds), *The Emotionally Intelligent Workplace: How to Select for, Measure, and Improve Emotional Intelligence in Individuals, Groups, and Organizations*, San Francisco: Jossey-Bass.

Helgesen, S. (1990) *The Female Advantage: Women's Ways of Leadership*, New York: Currency/Doubleday.

Helgesen, S. (1995) *The Web of Inclusion: A New Architecture for Building Great Organizations*, New York: Currency/Doubleday.

Hymowitz, C. and Schellhardt, T. D. (1986) 'The corporate woman (a special report): The glass ceiling – why women can't seem to break the invisible barrier that blocks them from the top jobs', *The Wall Street Journal*, March 24: 1.

Izraeli, D.N., Banai, M. and Zeira, Y. (1980) 'Women executives in MNC subsidiaries', *California Management Review*, 23 (1): 53–63.

Jamieson, K.H. (1995) *Beyond the Double Bind: Women and Leadership*, New York: Oxford University Press.

Jenkins, J. (2006) 'Coaching meets the cross-cultural challenge', *Leadership in Action*, 26 (5): 23–4.

Kanter, R.M. (1995) *World Class: Thriving Locally in the Global Economy*, New York: Simon and Schuster.

Keillor, B.D., Thomas, A. and Hauser, W. (2006) 'A gender comparison of national identity: Implications for sales managers', *Marketing Management Journal*, 16 (2): 38–49.

Koretz, G. (1999) ' "A woman's place is . . .": men frown on female execs abroad', *Business Week*, 3630–960: 12.

Kotter, J.P. (1995) 'Leading change: Why transformation efforts fail', *Harvard Business Review*, 73 (2): 59–67.

Kouzes, J.M. and Posner, B.Z. (1995) *The Leadership Challenge* (2nd edn), San Francisco: Jossey-Bass.

Kraimer, M., Wayne, S. and Jaworski, R. (2001) 'Sources of support and expatriate performance: the mediating role of expatriate adjustment', *Personnel Psychology*, 54 (1): 71–99.

Lazarova, M. and Caligiuri, P. (2001) 'Retaining repatriates: The role of organizational support practices', *Journal of World Business*, 36 (4): 389–401.

Lipman-Blumen, J. (1996) *The Connective Edge: Leading in an Interdependent World*, San Francisco: Jossey-Bass.

Lowman, R.L. (2007) 'Coaching and consulting in multicultural contests: Integrating themes and issues', *Consulting Psychology Journal: Practice and Research*, 59 (4): 296–303.

Mayrhofer, W. and Scullion, H. (2002) 'Female expatriates in international business: empirical evidence from the German clothing industry', *International Journal of Human Resource Management*, 13 (5): 815–36.

Morrison, A.M., White, R.P., Van Velsor, E. and Center for Creative Leadership. (1987) *Breaking the Glass Ceiling: Can Women Reach the Top of America's Largest Corporations?*, Reading: Addison-Wesley.

Noble, C. and Moore, S. (2006) 'Advancing women and leadership in this post feminist, post EEO era: A discussion of the issues', *Women in Management Review*, 21 (7): 598–603.

Pfeffer, J. (1998) *The Human Equation: Building Profits by Putting People First*, Boston, MA: Harvard Business School Press.

Pomeroy, A. (2007) 'Work/life balance not a gender issue', *HRMagazine*, 52 (4): 16.

Richey, M. (1996) 'Global families: Surviving an overseas move', *Management Review*, 85 (6): 57–61.

Rosinski, P. (2003) *Coaching across Cultures*, London: Nicholas Brealey.

Schein, E.H. (1992) *Organizational Culture and Leadership* (2nd edn), San Francisco: Jossey-Bass.

Schein, E.H. (2003) 'The learning leader as culture manager', in R. Brandt and T. Kastl (eds), *Business Leadership*, San Francisco: Jossey-Bass.

Selmer, J. and Leung, A.S.M. (2003) 'International adjustment of female vs male business expatriates', *International Journal of Human Resource Management*, 14 (7): 1117–31.

Shaffer, M. and Harrison, D. (1998) 'Expatriates' psychological withdrawal from international assignments: Work, nonwork, and family influences', *Personnel Psychology*, 51 (1): 87–118.

Shames, G. (1997) *Transcultural Odysseys: The Emerging Global Consciousness*, Boston, MA: Intercultural Press/Nicholas Brealey.

Sinangil, H.K. and Ones, D.S. (2003) 'Gender differences in expatriate job performance', *Applied Psychology: An International Review*, 52 (3): 461–75.

Stahl, G.K. and Caligiuri, P. (2005) 'The effectiveness of expatriate coping strategies: The moderating role of cultural distance, position level, and time on the international assignment', *Journal of Applied Psychology*, 90 (4): 603–15.

Stahl, G.K., Chei Hwee Chua, Caligiuri, P., Cerdin, J-L. and Taniguchi, M. (2007) 'International assignments as a career development tool: factors affecting turnover intentions among executive talent', *INSEAD Working Papers Collection*, 2007 (24): 1–43.

Tharenou, P. (2003) 'The initial development of receptivity to working abroad: Self-initiated international work opportunities in young graduate employees', *Journal of World Business*, 35 (3): 241–55.

Trompenaars, F. and Hampden-Turner, C. (1998) *Riding the Waves of Culture: Understanding Diversity in Global Business* (2nd edn), New York: McGraw-Hill.

Tucker, M.F., Bonial, R. and Lahti, K. (2004) 'The definition, measurement and prediction of intercultural adjustment and job performance among corporate expatriates', *International Journal of Intercultural Relations*, 28: 221–51.

Tye, M.G. and Chen, P.Y. (2005) 'Selection of expatriates: Decision-making models used by HR professionals', *Human Resources Planning*, 28 (4): 15–20.

Tzeng, R. (2006) 'Gender issues and family concerns for women with international careers: Female expatriates in Western multinational corporations in Taiwan', *Women in Management Review*, 21 (5): 376–92.

Valian, V. (1998) *Why So Slow? The Advancement of Women*, Cambridge, MA: MIT Press.

Van der Zee, K.I., Ali, A.J. and Salomé, E. (2005) 'Role interference and subjective well-being among expatriate families', *European Journal of Work and Organizational Psychology*, 14 (3): 239–62.

Vance, C.M., Paik, Y. and White, J.A. (2006) 'Tracking bias against the selection of female expatriates: Implications and opportunities for business education', *Thunderbird International Business Review*, 48 (6): 823–42.

Wah, L. (1998) 'Surfing the rough sea', *Management Review*, 87 (8): 25–9.

Webb, P.J. (2006) 'Back on track: The coaching journey in executive career derailment', *International Coaching Psychology Review*, 1 (2): 66–74.

Weber, G.B. (1996) 'Growing tomorrow's leaders', in F. Hesselbein, M. Goldsmith and R. Beckhard (eds), *The Leader of the Future: New Visions, Strategies, and Practices for the Next Era*, San Francisco: Jossey-Bass.

Zakaria, N. (2000) 'The effects of cross-cultural training on the acculturation process of the global workforce', *International Journal of Manpower*, 21 (6): 492–510.

15

COACHING MANAGERS IN MULTINATIONAL COMPANIES

Myths and realities of the Global Nomadic Leader

Katrina Burrus

Peter, based in Hong Kong, is an executive working for a multinational headquartered in Switzerland. His company's executive team keeps him on the radar as he is being groomed to be a future C-suite executive. He is leading the company's teams in India, Singapore, and China to develop the new Asian markets. He has lived in Hong Kong for the last two years. His wife and children like the place, as life there is easier than in Bogota, his previous post. He spent the first years of his life in Italy. His parents have now returned to the US, after retiring from a transient diplomatic career. For the next New Year holidays, he and his family will visit his sister in Bangalore, a trip he likes, as it reminds him of the years he spent there. Where to spend occidental New Year came after a long debate; his sister had wanted him to share the holidays with her in Germany, where she is pursuing an advertising career. His brother insisted on meeting in Beijing, where he now resides. Peter mulled over where home might be. Should it be governed by his Swiss passport, even though he has never lived in Switzerland? Should it be determined by where his parents live? Or should he call Hong Kong home, having resided there for the last two years? Peter was hard pressed to decide upon the culture with which he identified. Finally, he decided that it did not matter where he met his family for the New Year, as he belonged everywhere and nowhere. Working for the same company, albeit around the world, was the constant in his life.

Do you recognize the coaching client in this description? Then surely you have coached an executive nomad: a multinational manager who has not one innate cultural reference, but several. Growing up, the executive nomad lived in numerous countries and today travels and lives all over the world for his or her company.

Executive nomads have unique personal characteristics with professional implications that benefit multinational organizations. These unique characteristics, developed to adapt and thrive while moving to different countries, are the same attributes that prove beneficial to high potentials in multinationals; a high potential being, among other things, a strong performer in changing environments. Although the global nomad's attributes are precious for organizations, their unique upbringing has both personal and professional consequences at different times during their careers. An understanding of this particular profile's strengths and challenges will enhance the executive coach's contribution both for the executive nomad and the organization.

230

WHY THE NEED FOR GLOBAL NOMADS?

Inherently, the executive nomad has what many multinational companies seek: innate intercultural instincts, mobility, and adaptability. Increasing globalization of markets and companies has compounded this need, making these profiles even more highly regarded and sought after by companies:

> The past CEO of General Electric has asserted to his managers on many occasions that his example of leadership cannot last in a global company and that a new breed of leader is needed. [Quoting Jack Welch] 'The Jack Welch of the future cannot be like me. I spent my entire career in the United States. The next head of General Electric will be somebody who spent time in Bombay, in Hong Kong, in Buenos Aires. We have to send our best and brightest overseas and make sure they have the training that will allow them to be the global leaders who will make GE flourish in the future.'
>
> (Black, Morrison and Gregersen 1999: 20)

Jack Welch realized that future leaders will work in a globalized environment, and underscored the need for leaders with experience on different continents. Yet, his ethnocentric mindset is still evident when he suggests that the company's 'best' need to go overseas and be trained – instead of recruiting and immersing lifelong multicultural leaders from around the globe who are capable of holding a perspective outside the restrictive cultural lens through which the monocultural 'best and brightest' peer.

The chairman and CEO of Nestlé, Peter Brabeck-Letmathe, also emphasizes the need for cultural understanding combined with first-hand international experience:

> You cannot limit yourself to knowing just one culture, for you need to have an understanding of and respect for different national cultures. . . . When you are selling food, . . . you are participating in the consumers' cultural relationship with food, and this requires a much stronger understanding of the country's culture. The consumers' relationship to food is highly emotional and culturally specific. Therefore, you need a manager who understands and respects different cultures . . . Frankly speaking, I cannot imagine a top manager at Nestlé who has not lived in several countries and who does not speak at least two or three languages. This is a basic requirement.
>
> (Burrus-Barbey 2000: 498)

While the mandate from multinationals is clear, a survey of *Fortune 500* firms completed in 1997 indicated that 85 per cent of firms responding did not have an adequate number of global leaders (Black et al. 1999: 7). And the demand for global leaders continues to accelerate with the pace of globalization.

WHAT IS THE DIFFERENCE BETWEEN THE GLOBAL NOMAD AND THE EXPATRIATE?

How does the executive nomad differ from the immigrant or expatriate? The immigrant leaves his or her country of origin for political or economic reasons and does not intend to return to live there again; the immigrant moves once and identifies with one or the other culture. The expatriate may have a similar lifestyle to the executive nomad as an adult but still identifies with his or her home country and intends to return. The executive nomad was exposed to multiple cultures while growing up and has a multicultural reference which can be referred to as 'third culture' or 'global nomad'. The global nomad identifies with several cultures and, if his or her partner does not decide otherwise, tends to maintain or recreate a mélange of homes in the different places they travel to at different times, and in the spaces in-between (Pollock and Van Reken: 1999).

A useful analogy rests in the global nomad's way of learning languages. A global nomad learns several languages when young, integrating the different cultural references of several languages concurrently, and discovers an understanding that could be expressed as in-between: beyond any particular culture or single language. If the typical executive learns a new language as an adult, he or she learns through the mother tongue's cultural perspective and language construction to understand the new language. The typical executive or expatriate thus takes an ethnocentric viewpoint to understand the new and different, even if he or she is open to a new perspective. Moreover, the expatriate traveling the world tends to retain an emotional cultural attachment to his or her home country, as demonstrated by this quote from a Swiss ambassador:

> There is not one day that I do not think of coming back home. The place I belong to is here. Everything I learn I want to contribute to developing my home town. The advantage of my travels is [that] I am more flexible. I have more perspective and a better understanding of the qualities and defects of my culture even though, at times, I feel like a stranger in my home town.
>
> (Personal correspondence)

A coach needs to assess whether a new client identifies with a specific culture, or whether he or she is in the in-between. In the above case, even if this Swiss ambassador feels estranged from it, he still identifies with his home culture, as is the characteristic of the expat. This contrasts with the executive nomad, who is at home everywhere, and nowhere. The personal paradox, discussed below, notwithstanding, this kind of mobility is highly valued by multinationals.

After defining how to differentiate the itinerant leader's orientation, from expat to immigrant to global nomad, further questions remain: what are the unique attributes of executive nomads that position them so well for these globalized, multinational leadership positions? What issues might a coach face with a global nomad? Sorting out the facts and dispelling the myths require a closer look at the executive nomad's background and skills, illustrated here through the stories and experiences of such individuals, gleaned from my years of interviewing and coaching these unique executives on their nomadic lifestyles, as well as being one.

THE CHARACTERISTICS OF EXECUTIVE NOMADS

Executive nomads represent a new and different type of corporate leader who is more adaptable, interculturally successful, and willing to work in a constantly changing environment. Executive nomads tend to have a certain humility when immersed in a new culture. Typical characteristics are flexibility, tolerance, and openness to integrating new experience. They are usually keen observers, acutely aware of cultural contexts and nuances. This combination of instinctive skills makes them particularly adept at navigating rapid change while balancing complexity and nuance. Each of these characteristics, instinctive to the executive nomad, is highly desirable for the multinational seeking success-prone managers for intercultural assignments.

HUMBLED BY AND EAGER TO IMMERSE IN NEW CULTURES

Many executive nomads grew up being physically different from those around them, an experience integrated into their self-perceptions. Some may have memories of being bullied by other children if they did not blend in. Blending in socially with the locals becomes the quickest way to camouflage differences or build a new network of friends in the host country. Contrary to the ethnocentric individual who looks at the world from his or her own perspective, a monocultural outlook of the world without diversity or dissension, the global nomad generally searches for the differences to assimilate and adapt. This humility in the face of difference provides stark contrast to the xenophobic behavior of those less experienced in diverse environments.

Executive nomads usually integrate into the local culture by speaking the language and socializing with local friends. In contrast, many expatriates recreate the cultural ghetto and live and socialize almost exclusively with other expatriates to recreate a community similar to that of their home country. Some can stay 20 years in a country without ever speaking the local language. Thus the expat tends to remain a visitor, while the executive nomad moves toward integration into the local experience. Multinationals benefit from having an executive who can adapt seamlessly to the local culture like a chameleon and leverage local attributes while understanding the multinational's agenda.

CURIOUS ABOUT AND AWARE OF CULTURAL NUANCES AND CONTEXTS

Executive nomads are curious, and this curiosity not only helps them adapt to the local environment but is also valuable for understanding the nuances of clients' and customers' subtle, specific, and tacit needs. Growing up as children constantly on the move, executive nomads have had to develop a keen sense of observation and a heightened awareness of context, enabling them to adapt and thrive in their ever-changing environments (Pollock and Van Reken 1999).

Early on, the executive nomad learns that there are many ways of perceiving and interpreting the same event. This intimate understanding of local perspectives may, in turn, provoke the executive nomad to ambivalence about following local requests or those of headquarters, particularly if the latter are not culture-informed. Viewed another way, many diplomats stay a limited period in the host country, for fear that, if they identify with and invest too much in the local country, they will no longer represent their home countries as fervently.

The global nomad does not identify with either the local or the headquarter culture completely, and can serve as a translator who negotiates, interprets, and explains the perspectives of the locals to headquarters, and vice versa, so that learnings can be leveraged from both perspectives. The locals will feel understood by the global nomad, and the organization will have a good representative of the company's objectives. Although this intercultural perspective may come with feelings of solitude and not belonging anywhere, the coach can be instrumental in highlighting the positive contributions of the leader's unique perspective.

ADEPT AT RAPID CHANGE IN COMPLEX SITUATIONS

'Nomads tend to think quickly on our feet and can take the initiative to troubleshoot – but we often do so in a context of understanding the currents and observing the situation first' (Carlson 1997: 2). Growing up in the multiplicity of countries and cultures, executive nomads observe (a) different and sometimes conflicting philosophical and political perspectives first-hand (e.g., Osama Bin Laden is a hero for some and a terrorist for others), and (b) cultures that are on two parallel paths (e.g., Western culture is time- and task-oriented, while, in Eastern cultures, interpersonal relationships are of great importance) (Burrus 2006; Rosinski 2003; Schneider and Barsoux 2002). The executive nomad's ability to negotiate and collaborate across cultural differences is a rare and highly valued talent.

Although cross-cultural experience affects adults as well as children, cultural experience during childhood develops as one's sense of identity, relationships with others, and view of the world are being formed. Growing up in a highly mobile world, where everything in their lives is constantly changing, may be so integrated into who nomads are that they thrive on this lifestyle as adults, or recreate the nomadism, especially if the work environment offers exciting new challenges.

I have found that some nomads, who have consistently moved every two to four years with their parents, become adults who have integrated this cycle of change into their lives and tend to reproduce a similar cycle in their professional careers. In other words, around the second to fourth years, the executive experiences a certain restlessness and might start looking for change. If a professional opportunity emerges in the marketplace at that specific time of restlessness, the global nomad might seize it without much thought.

The coach's role, in this case, is to help the executive explore this restlessness and whether there is any pattern in the timing of these changes. For other nomadic leaders, the itinerant lifestyle becomes a need, and a sedentary lifestyle causes a certain amount of anxiety, as the quote below reveals:

> I have to keep moving. It is scary to stay in the same place for a long time. I think it would have a dramatic effect on me. I would feel something is missing, like an engine that is no longer working. My career would be at a halt. It would be a nightmare for me to live in a little village with a small-town mentality where everyone knows each other.
>
> (Member of the executive team of a multinational consumer goods company)

The moving into new, challenging situations becomes a motor upon which global nomads thrive. Some companies leverage their mobility, especially if they are high potentials or functional specialists who are sent around the world to resolve issues requiring their expertise. One of the coach's contributions is to help the global nomad identify something constant in constant change, and help reevaluate what has meaning for the global nomad when the thrill of novelty and new challenges that drives the global nomad forward wears off. This brings us to some of the particular challenges of the global nomad.

WHAT ARE SOME OF THE EXECUTIVE NOMADS' ISSUES AND GAPS?

For all of their intercultural skills and instincts, executive nomads often have a few gaps in their experience. Their mobile lives and lifestyles often result in a lack of rootedness, or a sense of a place from which they came. Similarly, they do not enjoy the traditional sense of community, in terms of place and support. And because they are so adept at multiple perspectives, executive nomads often clash with the traditional status quo, questioning its underlying assumptions

If China can build the infrastruture for a magnetic train in Shanghai to cover 40 km from the airport to downtown in eight minutes, why not question the Swiss incessant need to debate, for the last 25 years, whether they should or should not build a 2 km tunnel under the lake? The itinerant leaders have multiple perspectives, which aids them to question underlying assumptions. Organizations may leverage these attributes to promote change.

ROOTLESSNESS: NO SENSE OF HOME

At one point upon their professional paths, or after an emotional event, the global nomad feels a sense of rootlessness, of not belonging, or of solitude. As in the prototype described above, family members may be dispersed around the globe, the job may come to a transition point, or there may be a career lull, when the nomad's sense of rootlessness drives a search to find a place to drop the suitcases and feel grounded. The following examples illustrate how global nomads deal with this rootlessness:

> For the younger executive nomad, buying a house simply allows the executive to continue the mobile lifestyle, while providing a better sense of roots and balance for the global nomad and his family. The real focus of the young nomad is often the curiosity and enthusiasm that go with a new job and a new place.

In another example:

> The Swiss Hungarian executive of a consumer goods company decided to buy a chalet in the Swiss Alps. He spends only two weeks a year in his chalet, but he calls it home. It provides him and his family with some sense of belonging, a place to which they could always fly back while relocating in different countries.
>
> Buying the home was his attempt to feel more grounded and keep something that epitomizes part of his cultural identity.

In this next example, the itinerant leader is an ex–McKinsey consultant, newly married for the second time; his wife, an expatriate, wanted to build a home:

> I get anchored in myself, my wife gets anchored in her surroundings. . . . She wants a home. I look forward to building and designing a house and calling it mine. I want to own land and watch the house grow old. To know I have a place that I will call home is appealing. I can come back to the same place. It will be a whole new experience and another level of anchoring.

The global nomad looks at the house from an outsider, reflective stance, 'I want to watch the house grow old'. The house is an object that he is observing. He does not see himself in it yet. It is a place he can 'call' home. He did not say it will *be* a home. The coach's discussion with the global nomad is identifying what 'home' and 'anchoring' represent for the global nomad, how these concepts might be different for his partner, and how each one's needs can be met with understanding.

This sense of rootlessness can be heightened after the death of parents, when the sense of loss is compounded with the sense of not belonging anywhere. In this fourth example, parents represent the anchor:

A diplomat said that, as soon as both parents passed away, he felt compelled to buy a flat where his parents had lived most of their lives; preferably, he wanted their flat.

The coach begins by exploring what the flat represents to the executive, what he needs to be constant, what can be mobile, and which culture has more meaning to him than others? This sense of uneasiness can also be instigated by a career hitting its glass ceiling, or an executive near retirement who needs to decide where he or she is going to retire.

Many companies send their global executives abroad as change agents to restructure affiliates or transfer critical functional knowledge. Although executive nomads thrive on being mobile, at some point, they tire of being challenged or changing everything year after year, especially if it creates havoc in their personal lives. When the mobile life loses some of its luster, or personal and family relations show serious strains from moving constantly, the global executive often enters a critical moment of reevaluating the nomadic lifestyle. Often there is an active and conscious search for a sense of being grounded. This desire for a home may be compounded by a desire to form a family, provide adequate childcare, or take care of aging parents. Whether accurate or not, such pressures may be perceived by companies as more intense on women executive nomads. A coach can highlight the developmental changes the executive is going through combined with the work/family reconciliation.

NO COMMUNITY OR SUPPORT STRUCTURES

Family challenges, particularly, highlight the nomadic issues of not belonging, being an outsider, and having no extended family or local community on which to rely for support. Yet executive nomads often work through the discomfort of being new. To counter the initial feelings of not belonging, nomads draw upon their curiosity and enthusiasm for new locales and cultures to bridge the gap. How does this differ from the expatriate? The expatriate carries this sense of community in and from the home country. The executive nomad's allegiance, by contrast, is to the here and now, to multiple peoples and institutions, without living long enough in any one area to develop a lasting allegiance to any particular community.

As respects the executive nomad's family, the multinational should provide or outsource logistical support to help in finding new schools, housing, and the various administrative matters that come with a family move to a new home and country. These key infrastructure issues aid and speed the transition, and provide local contacts and context beyond the company itself. Otherwise, all of this stress is added to the executive's and family's workload and pressures while trying to adapt to a new environment, home, job, lifestyle, and country. Even if the executive nomad thrives on the novelty of the situation and the new work challenges, the trailing spouse may not. Clearly, whatever support coaches and companies can provide to improve executive nomads' and their families' resiliency to serial adaptations is pivotal to their success and start-up time in such roles.

CLASH WITH THE STATUS QUO

As executive nomads grew up with many geographical changes, they seldom rely on normal moorings and support systems. This sense of confusion may make the executive nomad more self-assured than average, with a worldview more knowledgeable and circumspect than most. Moreover, having less of a sense of community, the executive nomad is more readily willing to challenge the status quo. As inveterate change agents, executive nomads can transpose their acute perceptions and adaptability to the work environment, insightfully seeing what needs to get done, and clearly articulating how to get there. 'Those that have never lived and worked outside of their home country don't question the pertinence of their decisions in the local culture. They make many assumptions and do not question them' (member of the executive committee of a multinational consumer good company).

Each of these aspects of the executive nomad has its strengths and inherent drawbacks. Yet the companies assigning executives to these posts want change, and know that executive nomads are most likely to be able to deliver it, despite or because of their rootlessness, illusive community support, and questioning of the status quo. As executive nomads are increasingly in demand for their rare skills, coaches will need to understand their unique characteristics and their implications on their personal and professional lives.

HOW THE GLOBAL NOMAD'S COACH CAN HELP

How can a coach leverage the executive nomad's competencies? When coaching expatriates or executive nomads – such as the prototypical executive at the top of this chapter – the coach's task is to:

- Help to identify and sort out the cultural contexts upon which the executive draws in normal and unusual situations;
- Identify the cultural and leadership needs and expectations of the local situation, and work toward finding a good fit between the local culture, the executive's many choices, and the skills and behaviors needed in a given situation (Burrus 2006); and
- Raise spouse/partner and family issues, work/family reconciliation, and organizational support for these key infrastructure issues for all executives abroad.

The executive nomads' key talents – flexibility, tolerance, observation, curiosity, appreciation of cultural detail and context – make them particularly adaptable to integrating new experience and adept at navigating rapid change while balancing complexity and nuance. Their unique upbringings, though, also render them vulnerable in the areas of rootlessness, community support, and challenges to the status quo.

The executive nomad lifestyle, while envied and in demand, remains little understood, and thus fraught with misconceptions and paradox. Multinationals and their coaches will be well served to work through coaching on an individual basis. Many of the specific issues facing executive nomads, men and women alike, and their companies, will continue to evolve rapidly. Coaching can be instrumental in accelerating the process and ensuring a good fit of executive nomads and multinational leadership needs.

Bibliography

Black, J.S., Morrison, A.J. and Gregersen, H.B. (1999) *Global Explorers: The Next Generation of Leaders*, New York: Routledge.

Burrus, K. (2006) 'Coaching the global nomad', *International Journal of Coaching in Organizations*, 4 (4): 6–15.

Burrus-Barbey, K. (2000) 'Interview: Leadership, global management, and future challenges: An interview with Peter Brabeck-Letmathe, chief executive officer of Nestlé SA', *Thunderbird International Business Review*, 43 (5): 495–506.

Carlson, D. (1997) *Being a Global Nomad: The Pros and Cons*, WorldWeave Publications. Available online at <www.worldweave.com/procon.htm> (accessed 18 November 2007).

Pollock, D.C. and Van Reken, R.E. (1999) *The Third Culture Kid Experience*, London: Intercultural Press.

Rosinski, P. (2003) *Coaching across Cultures*, London: Nicholas Brealey.

Schneider, S.C. and Barsoux, J-L. (2002) *Managing Across Cultures*, Harlow, UK: FT Prentice-Hall Pearson Education.

Section 3

Organizational challenges and opportunities – collective

WHEN FAR EAST MEETS WEST

Seeking cultural synthesis through coaching

Ho Law, Leon Laulusa and Grace Cheng

Many models of coaching come from Western cultural frameworks. For Westerners applying coaching models in the Eastern cultures, it is crucial for them to understand their cultures and be sensitive about their values and how these values manifest in their behaviours and interactions. For example, the value 'respect' is translated in Chinese language as 'save face'. In behavioural terms, this may mean one does not openly criticize others in public. The cultural learning or synthesis is a two-way process with many opportunities for cultural differences to be combined to make a superior third way.

INTRODUCTION

This chapter offers a two-way cross-cultural approach. It is hoped that a 'new paradigm' or a superior third way will emerge as a result of the exploration (as exemplified by three case studies). We aim to provide a strong theoretical framework that links to the themes of cross-cultural coaching and also relates to a review of relevant literature. We have also provided some practical guidance for coaches, consultants, leaders and managers who need to do business within the Chinese culture, through various opportunities that are emerging in the international scene.

CHINESE BUSINESS – NEW CHALLENGES

The way that people communicate has cultural implications. The cultural differences between East and West introduce an additional level of complexity in the arena of management in the global marketplace. As Chinese enterprises enter fully into the global marketplace, forming world alliances and competing domestically with multinational corporations, they will encounter diverse business cultures and dynamics. A recent study on comparative leadership styles between Chinese and Western executives shows that Chinese leaders tend to use more task oriented and intellectual styles than their Western counterparts (Cheng et al. 2006). The communications from Chinese leaders tend to be brief, to the point that they might be perceived by Westerners as blunt, inflexible or impatient. Western business executives might therefore erroneously conclude that Chinese leaders do not respond well to different views and may not be politically savvy. On the other hand, the Chinese would construe a stereotype of European/Western executives as people who tend to rely on logic and analysis in their decision-making, and create excessively formal relationships. Westerners might come across as being serious, opinionated, controlling, dominant and overly concerned with details.

The hypothesis of Chinese culture being the root of this disparity has been tested further by a comparison between the Chinese leaders and their counterparts in the Four Dragon countries, i.e. Hong Kong, Taiwan, Singapore and South Korea. The study showed that despite the fact that mainland Chinese and Four Dragon leaders were closer in leadership styles, the latter were more similar to their Western counterparts (reference). For instance, Four Dragon leaders tend to use more participative leadership styles in team dynamics. This was to say that both Four Dragon countries and international executives were more open to consensus decision-making and tended to deal with more issues at the same time. They might appear slower in decision-making, more ambiguous in communication and even more disorganized, but they were more ready to listen to alternative ideas, and placed more emphasis on participation and team building.

The reasons why Chinese business executives are different from their international peers may be due to the stage of international/cross-cultural development. For instance, Chinese enterprises are still young and are led by entrepreneurs who are hands-on in running their own business – they are so-called 'micro managers'. While this style is suited to running start-ups or when organizations are small, it may not be sustainable for organizations that grow larger in size and more complex in structure, hence the growth of Chinese companies themselves calling for changes in leadership styles. On the other hand, Western business executives who wish to do business with China face difficulties in understanding Chinese values and practice. In both cases, executive coaching may help managers to develop their cultural competence and provide solutions for business transformation internationally. We shall explore these complex coaching interactions further with three case studies followed by a description of a possible cross-cultural coaching framework. From the Western perspectives, very little is known about Chinese culture and values. The emergence of the growing socio-economic status of China poses many new challenges as well as opportunities for international businesses. Thus we argue a case for placing China as a focal point of our studies.

CHINA IN THE INTERNAL WORLD SCENE

China has enjoyed nearly thirty years of fast economic growth with an average annual GDP growth of between 9 per cent and 11 per cent. The huge market potential has made China the most favoured destination of international direct investment. In a single year (2006), FDI exceeded 60 billion. Today, for Western multinationals, China is already a major revenue generator, a manufacturing centre, a key part of the global supply chain and centres for Research and Development. In addition to this, we have seen the rise of Chinese companies and globalization of some of the national champions. Lenovo (previously called Legend) has recently acquired the personal computer business of IBM and has become the third largest computer manufacturer and marketer in the world. Lenovo has moved its global headquarters to the US and with that move the company has transferred many of its Chinese managers to the US. As of today, 5,000 Chinese companies have already established 10,000 companies overseas. Thus the probability of business executives and coaches coming across Chinese clients or colleagues is very high. To maximize the benefit of coaching, one must better understand the cultural dynamics in the coaching arena.

Framework for international coaching with reference to Chinese culture

From the above there is a clearly a requirement for coaches in the Western culture to learn about coaching clients within Chinese culture and vice versa. It would help if there was a body of knowledge to guide coaches to establish their own meta-framework. Moral and Angel (2006 noted the importance of adapting Western coaching models for the Asian environment due to the markedly different cultural perceptions between West and East. While there is a lot of literature on coaching models (e.g. Megginson and Clutterbuck 1995) and more recently in coaching psychology (e.g. Palmer and Whybrow 2006), we have found very little work done in cross-cultural coaching, especially about Chinese culture. Where there are studies that include Chinese culture, Chang (2000: 125) pointed out that the existing bodies of research are usually based on the Western cultural standard as a measurement and tend to include Chinese people, 'in all the wrong places'. The term 'wrong places' in a sense implies that 'the Chinese' are not an easily identifiable group. Historically, the majority of Chinese are descended from the Han dynasty. The so-called 'Han' people in China are very diverse with more than fifty different ethnicities; each group has different dialects. Apart from Mainland China, Chinese people live all over the world including in Africa, America, Asia, Australia, and Europe (Zhaung 1998). In order to understand Chinese people and culture, the studies should not classify the Chinese in terms of race or demographics (Chang 2000; Zukerman 1990) but learn about the cultural context of the local people within their own proximity.

The lineage of coaching in China could probably date back as early as the Confucian and Taoist ways of teaching. However, the actual term 'coaching' is very new in China. When translated into the Chinese language, its meaning is virtually the same as 'teaching' and 'training'. Most Chinese people do not know what it does and see it as something close to teaching, training, learning and development. At present, Chinese people still see training as classroom lectures; development as being conducted on the job; and coaching as something that is passed down from the older and wiser to the younger generation (while some European coaches would regard this as mentoring). In China, coaching is not yet seen as a management tool that can raise people's awareness of their potentials to be better managers and leaders. Thus the styles and expectations of the Chinese coaches/coachees may be very different from the West.

One of the challenges for Westerners doing business in China is that there has not been a critical mass of Western coaches with adequate familiarity with the Chinese culture. As Rosinski (2003: 20) observes, 'coaching with a national and corporate cross-cultural focus does not yet prevail . . . acknowledgement of this cultural reality has been missing in coaching'. Law et al. (2007) argue that the psychological coaching approaches should be grounded in a model of multi-cultures called the Universal Integrated Framework (UIF), which is described in more detail later in the chapter. The approach is based on cultural anthropology in addition to the basic principle of psychology such as learning theories. The model embeds a multicultural perspective and emotional intelligence that are grounded in the psychology of learning (Vygotsky 1962; Kolb 1984) and socio-cultural anthropology (Hall 1976; Turner and Brunner, 1986). The framework looks like an onion with multi-layers, which is consistent with those proposed by Geertz (1986), Hofstede (1991), and Trompenaars and Hampden-Turner (1997).

We shall first provide some definitions on cross-cultural and intercultural coaching and describe two case studies to demonstrate the dynamics of cross-cultural coaching. We shall then

243

draw from the experience of the case studies and relate it to the UIF. Tips and guidance are provided at the end of this chapter.

First, some definitions

For coaches working in the international scene, it implies that they would be coaching someone from different cultures. We define intercultural coaching psychology as 'for enhancing well-being and performance of individuals from different cultural backgrounds or with dual cultural heritage in their personal life and work domains'. For example, Law (2007) applied such a principle in narrative coaching in a community setting. Readers should note that cross-cultural coaching has a subtle difference from intercultural coaching. Cross-cultural coaching is for coaching individuals who come from different countries and hence with different cultures. While our definition is very similar to that adopted by the Special Group in Coaching Psychology (Palmer and Whybrow 2006, adapted from Grant and Palmer 2002), it is also in line with Philippe Rosinski's (2003) proposal that by integrating a cultural dimension into coaching, we can help our coachees unleash more of their potential to achieve meaningful objectives. In this chapter we focus on Chinese–European interaction within the coaching arena.

CASE STUDIES

Three case studies are described in this chapter as supporting evidence to illustrate the challenges and complexity in international coaching. Case study 1 illustrates how a Chinese entrepreneur attempts to establish international business in France with the support of cross-cultural coaching. In case study 2, a European chief executive working in a large company in China finds herself lacking in knowledge of Chinese culture, and seeks coaching to transform the working relationship to improve the corporate performance. Case study 3 shows increased complexity when a Chinese highflier who was educated in the West returned to lead an international company in China.

Case study 1 in France: French coach – Chinese coachee

Mr Chen[1] was a 45-year-old Chinese entrepreneur who originated from the province of Zhejiang. After having made several trips throughout Europe, he decided that he would like to work with European entrepreneurs, especially with French ones. He then got in contact with some French entrepreneurs through one of his Chinese friends living in France. Following the Chinese custom, Mr Chen brought over Chinese gifts each time he met the French entrepreneurs. He also invited them to visit his firms and house, welcoming them with hospitality by introducing them to important officials and the key leaders in the organization, and by organizing receptions in order to make them feel important. However, despite this excellent welcoming, the French entrepreneurs were somewhat disappointed because, first, they could not talk about business projects in detail with Mr Chen and second, they found this business protocol too showy and superficial. The entrepreneurs asked him to make a presentation of his group's activity and financial structure based in particular, on its financial statements. As an answer, Mr Chen just verbally threw some accounting figures in an allusive manner and described some of his firms like a tour guide would as if they were VIP visitors.

Besides, Mr Chen was used to communicating in an indirect way. When he disagreed, he never said, 'no' but rather, 'We cannot say that'. Alternatively, he would say, 'yes' with a smile. He also liked to make appointments with the French entrepreneurs without fixing a date a long time before but rather just two days before his arrival in France. He did not show obvious interest each time the projects were proposed. As a consequence, the French entrepreneurs did not feel confident about working with Mr Chen and abandoned their intention to build a partnership with him.

For Mr Chen, before doing business, he liked to get acquainted with and understand his business partners more and to appreciate potential social interactions. That was why he took his time and preferred to first look for a friendly relationship. If the relationship became friendly, Mr Chen would treat them like *zijiren* (insiders, in-group members[2]) and give *renqing* rule (Chinese reciprocity). After that, business projects would be taken seriously and fairly.

Due to this first experience, Mr Chen did not succeed in making use of some business opportunities. As he wanted to do business with French multinational groups, his Chinese friend asked one of the authors to advise Mr Chen. In fact, through this, his Chinese friend wanted us to change his behaviour and his way of making contact with French entrepreneurs. His friend had tried to make him change but did not succeed.

During our first meeting with Mr Chen, he gave us an account of his objectives and background during a friendly discussion. We took care to 'give face' to him in terms of respect, hierarchy, and politeness (*limao*)[3] by speaking to him in an indirect and non-direct manner, i.e., by following Chinese social norms. We discovered that Mr Chen was very keen on doing business with French entrepreneurs but for face reasons (prestige and ego), he did not want to give this impression. We knew that it would be difficult to make him change his point of view. We first adopted the following methodology: an informal discussion in order to discover his personality and a mutual learning approach. Mr Chen showed us his way of doing business in China and we shared our knowledge on doing business in France. During the mutual learning process, we anticipated that Mr Chen would assimilate another point of view. We gained the trust (*xinyong*) of Mr Chen through observing Chinese social rules (such as respect, courtesy, 'giving face', renqing, speaking in a non-directive manner) and indeed observed that he was keen on learning our point of view. Then, we proceeded with coaching through providing examples. We told stories about Chinese top executives who failed in managing businesses in France and encouraged him to speculate on why they had not succeeded. Afterwards, we described what had really happened. Through this process, we were encouraging Mr Chen to understand by himself, to assimilate, to study (*xue*),[4] in other words to 'acculturate' himself to the Western way of doing business. After a few months, Mr Chen started to change his behaviour. He brought his business executive summary including financial figures and fixed appointments at least one month in advance. He was willing to give some extra information when the French top executives required it. Of course, his Chinese behaviour continued, especially when the negotiation phase arrived, but now he had begun to integrate some French business behaviours.

Case study 2 in Southern China: a Chinese coach with a European coachee

The above case study demonstrates how Chinese business executives working in the West have to learn the Western style of interaction. What if Westerners were working in China? What problems would they encounter and how could a coach help them to work within the Chinese culture? Case study 2 illustrates the dynamics of this reversed power relationship.

Catherine, a businesswoman with an MBA and seven years' experience in an international company recently acquired a chief executive position in a division in China. She and her senior management team (SMT) were all white Europeans educated in the West with Western management styles and thinking. All other workers in the company were Chinese. She and the SMT found increasing difficulties in working with their Chinese colleagues. She thought the industrial relations would improve over time but feared that this would take too long for her to achieve the business objectives within the time frame. She consulted an international coach of Chinese origin who was educated in the West and understood both Chinese and Western cultures. From the first session, the coach established the situation and identified the problem areas, which mostly arose from a cultural misunderstanding of different expectations and values between the SMT and the workers. Catherine felt extremely frustrated about this.

She said, 'I cannot not give as much as I could because I am unable to see if other people are happy' (implying that the Chinese workers were inscrutable – a typical Chinese stereotype perceived by the Westerners).

'The SMT and I have a lot of problems in managing Chinese workers in the organization. Being a woman working in the West, I have learnt how to be business-like . . .' By that, she meant behaving like a male executive in management style. She had a very classic Western management style: a functional approach, with formal communication at meetings and ensuring that projects ran within budget.

'However, in China, I feel that that they do not expect a woman to speak up. In fact they do not speak up at all with me . . .' She felt that she had received very little feedback from their communication (both verbal and non-verbal). There is a significant gender difference within the Chinese culture that would not be expected by the Westerner. As a sign of respect, Chinese people do not confront/speak up to their superiors. This is perceived by Westerners as being submissive, lacking confidence or being inscrutable.

'What do you understand about Chinese values?' asked the coach.

'Nothing', said Catherine.

The coach provided Catherine with some clarification on Chinese values and communication styles with emphasis on the differences between the Chinese and European styles. These were then related back to Catherine's personal values at work, these included:

- equality;
- communication (direct/indirect) including feedback;
- knowledge management;
- responsibility;
- relationship;
- self-determination; and
- understanding cultures.

Catherine liked the Chinese 'can do' attitude; if only they could show-and-tell the SMT about their ideas. She saw her leadership role as being to inspire the workers. She hoped that if individual workers could see for themselves their responsibility, they would increase confidence in speaking to her about their issues and concerns.

At the end of the coaching session, the coach set Catherine some homework.

Give at least two examples from work to support the Chinese values as you understand them within the organization.

From the homework, the coach and coachee met again to come up with a plan of action on how to overcome the cross-cultural barriers that were identified.

After three sessions over a four-week period, Catherine perceived a noticeable change in attitude and behaviour of the workers towards her. She recommended a group coaching session for the SMT to see if the knowledge and skills could be transferred to the team. The coach suggested that learning should be two-way, and recommended that the workers should also be provided with training to understand Western-style MBA management. A cultural training programme was rolled out within three months. The training workshops were conducted in English for the senior and middle management team, while the training for the junior managers/supervisors and other workers was conducted in the local Chinese language. Today Catherine is leading a happy team, and the company has achieved all the performance targets set with an annual profit increase of 25 per cent.

Case study 3 in Northern China: developing international leadership styles? Chinese coach–Chinese coachee who were educated in the West

Susan was from Northern China and was in her late 30s. She had graduated from a top university in China and subsequently obtained an international MBA in the West. When she returned, as a young and fast-tracked business executive in a top global professional service firm in China, she was given every opportunity to grow from an associate to a managing director within a short time. From her MBA studies, she had learned that to be successful, she needed to be an individual performer. She was ranked one of the top executives in the Asia Pacific team and was a successful market-maker from the business generation perspective. Because of this, she was rapidly promoted to a regional role to lead a specialized business practice for the firm in the region, with 15 consultants reporting to her. She was the first PRC national to be elevated to such a regional role within her firm. For a while she walked around with the feeling of glory all around her. She was going to sweep her competitors off their feet. Initially, she had success and made her team the most successful in her business practice.

However, after 12 months at the year-end appraisal, Susan was not rated very highly by her boss. Revenue fell behind annual targets and three key consultants left the firm. Some new consultants were hired in their places but hardly had time to demonstrate their work. Team morale was low and new staff turnover happened following the year-end bonus payment. Susan was frustrated and consulted Jonathan, an executive coach, about this. Jonathan also originated from Northern China and was educated in the West for his postgraduate studies, but had recently returned to China.

In talking with Jonathan, Susan revealed that since becoming a regional practice leader she had worked twice as hard as usual and had spent almost 80 per cent of the period away from home. Her flight mileage had tripled and, together with that, her individual business generation had also nearly doubled. Wherever a country was running short of the revenue for a quarter or so she would fly in, meet the clients and walk away with some more business to make up the numbers for the country. In her own mind she had become a saviour and privately she wondered why everybody else on her team was so incapable. She was even calculating in her mind who she wanted to get rid of from her team in the coming year. However, when she spoke with the country managers, she met barriers from place-to-place. Susan was frustrated and wondered why her harder work had not brought the expected business results and appreciation from others. Susan, who was used to being praised for almost everything she did, for the first time in her life felt inadequate.

Jonathan's focus as an executive coach was to raise awareness and solicit changes in behaviours from the client. He therefore made a conscious effort to transform a difficult organizational situation into a realistic learning challenge matching the immediate needs of Susan. He shared some of his own cross-cultural learning with Susan and gently reminded her that the ego/euro-centric approaches about performance that were taught in the Western MBA schools might not work internationally across cultures. He also shared with Susan his own re-evaluation of Chinese culture and some of the virtue that Chinese values could bring into organizations and teamwork. At first, Susan was very defensive about Jonathan's view, as she believed that the Western management styles were far superior. However, after several coaching sessions, she gradually came to realize that different behaviours and skills were required from 'individual performers' than from 'team leaders'. When Susan was an individual performer, she became very efficient in getting things done and managing tasks. When she became a team leader she brought her 'task master' mentality into the new job and the result was far from satisfactory. What she had failed to see was that as a leader she had to become a people manager, and her job as a leader was to make the team successful. The secret lay in how to succeed through other people. Subsequently she made an analysis of all her team members, their strengths and weaknesses, their drivers and how to best motivate them. With respect to the Chinese culture, instead of conducting a formal team meeting and away-days, as she had learned from the West, she held informal face-to-face meetings with individual team members to understand their needs, and agreed on plans where she could best support them to be successful. Some of her team members even came up with some very good suggestions for improvement.

Susan was delighted with the changes happening to the team. She was grateful to Jonathan who had helped her 'see the light'. Staff turnover dropped and Susan was no longer flying out of her base 80 per cent of the time. The team was more motivated and Susan was no longer lonely and frustrated. 'Superstars' were emerging from her team and the goal of becoming the strongest practice became attainable!

TRANSACTIONAL ANALYSIS OF THE CASE STUDIES FROM CULTURAL PERSPECTIVES

In the introductory chapter, the editors cited the incident that happened in the 2006 football World Cup to demonstrate that players in the game might suffer from an 'emotional hijack', using Goleman's (1998) apt phase. That was the French captain Zinedine Zidane's violent *response* to the insults from an Italian player (the *cause*) which led to the undesirable *consequence* (*direct* result: the referee applied the penalty and *indirect* consequence: France lost the game). The editors further described the intercultural dynamics in terms of the needs of 'I' 'team us' and the 'family and cultural roots us'. How does this translate into the cross-cultural interaction in business coaching within international organizations as demonstrated in the three case studies above? We could explain how these intercultural dynamics work by using a psychological approach known as transactional analysis. Eric Berne (1970) translated Freud's psycho-dynamic self-concepts into everyday language as follows:

1 Id – Child
2 Ego – Adult
3 Super-ego – parent

Berne argues that person-to-person interaction could be understood by analysing the interaction among these three factors between two persons. Conflicts emerge if one person treats another person as a child while he or she expects to be treated as an adult. We could map the above concept coach–coachee interaction:

1 Child – I – coach/coachee
2 Adult – us/team/organization
3 Parent – cultural us

The three elements above mapped upon the coach–coachee interaction, which provides a complex interaction is shown in Figure 16.1.

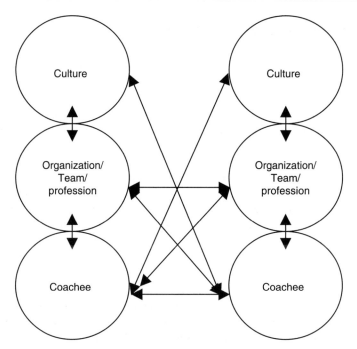

Figure 16.1 Transactional analysis of a double triad relationship between the coach and coachee of different cultures

With reference to Zinedine Zidane's situation, the conflicts occurred when both players acted like children while the expectations from the others (the audience) were operating at the team/cultural level. The two case studies show that individual expectations from another's culture may be perceived as 'peculiar' or 'inappropriate'. For example, in Case study 1, Chen wanted to *indirectly* show the French entrepreneurs his business power, his *guanxi* (social relationship, network) in China, to make them feel comfortable, create *gongqing* (friendly feeling and relations) and provide them with *respect* and *social status*, literally 'give them face' (*mianzi*). All these are important Chinese cultural values. However, these were evaluated by the French entrepreneurs as a lack of awareness of the French business culture. In other words, one tends to perceive and judge another person's behaviour according to one's own culture. Different cultural behaviours might be misconstrued as immature (not an adult–adult interaction). By the same token Catherine (in Case study 2) was frustrated as she felt there was a lack of communication between herself/SMT and the workers within the organization. Communication is two-way. Each participant/player should be coached with knowledge to decode each other's behaviour on three levels:

1 Basic human emotion;
2 Team/organizational sub-culture; and
3 Root cultural value.

The outcome would be a successful third way, as exemplified by Case study 3, in which Susan found a new approach that combined the Western business approach (such as a SWOT analysis) with Chinese values, and implemented it in a way that was respectful to the local culture (such as confidentiality to 'save face', and informed consensus).

DISCUSSION, CONCLUSION AND SUMMARY

International assessment work shows that as managers move up through an organization, their leadership styles change to adapt to new requirements. At the entry level, managers generally demonstrate task and intellectual styles and become more social and participative as they grow into more demanding leadership roles. One of the drivers for such development patterns may be the growing need for information at higher levels of management. Strategic business and people decisions require massive volumes of accurate information, which usually lie deep within an organization. In theory, a more sociable and open leadership style makes it easier to surface the information, share the knowledge and encourage cooperation across the organization. However, this may not be easily realized in practice internationally. Through the above case studies, we see that in both sides, i.e. Western and Chinese, the business social norms and coaching perceptions are not the same. For Chinese, coaching is seen more as a method of thinking, a philosophy; whereas in the West, it is considered more as a tool. The different cultural perceptions between East and West are shown in Table 16.1 with some differences.

It should be noted that the above table is for the purpose of providing readers an easy reference/summary. With increased mobility, and cross-cultural exchanges in business and education, the increased complexity and sophistications invariably make stereotypes – and even generalizations – unhelpful. As Case study 3 and the study of the Chinese leaders in China and the Four Dragon countries show, Chinese executives at the senior level (very often Western-educated), tend to have a similar leadership style to Western managers.

TOOLS AND MODELS

From the above case studies, we have found the following model and tools that would be of practical assistance to coaches/managers in the field. If coaches find that there are no general rules and/or no universal management system, then perhaps a generic framework may be useful. Law et al.'s (2007) Universal Integrated Framework (UIF) consists of the following four dimensions (Figure 16.2):

Table 16.1 Eastern v Western orientation

	Eastern orientation	*Western orientation*
Communication	Indirect Verbal Informal	Direct Written Formal
Hierarchy	Natural authority of the superior	Authority comes from the hierarchy line (function)
Logic	Affective/intuitive	Rational
Assumptions	Be in harmony with nature Emphasis on community and inter-dependence	Master the nature Emphasis on self-efficacy and independence
Time	Time-space continuum Money is not time	Chronological (time) Time is money

1 (Self) Personal competence
2 Social competence
3 Cultural competence
4 Professional competence

Dimension I: personal competence

These competences reflect how we manage ourselves. They consist of two parts:

1 Awareness of oneself (Self-awareness)
2 Management of oneself (Self-regulation/Self-management)

Self-awareness

This measures whether you accept and value yourself – an awareness of one's own internal states, feelings, emotions, cognition, preferences, resources and intuitions. It is regarded as a starting point to be aware of another culture. For example, Mr Chen in Case study 1 was not aware of the negative evaluation he might have received during the social interaction. Catherine in Case study 2 became aware of her own discomfort when interacting with Chinese workers.

Self-management

This is the ability to manage one's emotion and motivation, and control them productively. It measures whether you invite the trust of others by being principled, reliable and consistent (trustworthiness). Once aware of one's own feelings, one should be able to manage one's own emotions to achieve the optimal objective (emotional intelligence).

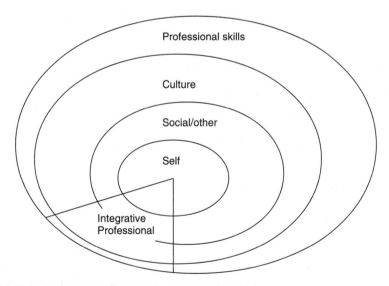

Figure 16.2 Universal Integrated Framework – a pragmatic model

Source: Law et al. (2007)

Dimension II: social competence

These competences reflect how we manage relationships. Social competence is a didactic process as individuals gain insight through social interaction and awareness of others. It consists of *empathy* (awareness of others as in Dimension 1) and *social skills* (management of others) that could be acquired through coaching and training.

Dimension III: cultural competence

These competences reflect how we manage organizational change. They consist of *awareness of other cultures* (enlightenment) and *management of organizational cultures* (champion).

Cultural competence measures (1) the extent to which individuals inquire into or respond openly to others' cultures, ideas and values, and (2) the willingness to challenge and question one's own assumption as well as others' (Law et al. 2007). International coaches should have the ability to mediate boundaries between cultures.

Dimension IV: professional competence

To be professionally competent, coaches within the international arena require a professional approach. However, the so-called 'professional' standard might vary from culture to culture. In coaching, what is important is a professional attitude. This is to give and seek authentic feedback to and from others that is appropriate to their cultural situation locally.

The above four dimensions with their eight elements are summarized in Table 16.2.

THE BASIC ASSUMPTION

The basic assumption of UIF is that a meta-model for intercultural coaching should consist of the following elements:

- Learning cycle (for example, see Kolb, 1984) with supervision and continuous professional development;
- Appreciation of the cultural environment;
- Coach/coachee fluidity – coachees have skills and knowledge; coaches learn as much as coachees;
- Integrative continuum – dimensions of competences are in a continuum and may be correlated;

Table 16.2 Dimensions of UIF pragmatic model

Competence	I. Personal (Self)	II. Social (Other)	III. Cultural (Culture)	IV. Professional (Competence)
Awareness	Self-Awareness	Empathy	Enlightenment	Reflective Practice
Management	Self-Regulation	Social skills	Champion	Continued Professional Development

Source: Law et al. (2007)

- Cross-cultural emotional intelligence (e.g. Goleman 1998) framework plus a cultural dimension;
- A pragmatic implementation model that embeds all of the above elements; and
- Communication methods and feedback mechanism – 360-degree feedback that is embedded in an on-line tool (Law et al. 2005; 2007).

VALIDITY

The UIF model was validated using the data from the on-line tool (Law et al. 2007). The data set was statistically analysed using the participant competency scores against overall rating scores (49 participants). The results show that personal competence and its link with authenticity was the best predictor of all-round competence ($p < 0.04$) and increased with age/life experience, as expected ($p < 0.00015$). The research showed that there were no gender differences ($p = 0.5$) and that there was a significant co-relationship between the personal competence, social competence and cultural competence ($r = 0.7$). More importantly the UIF users indicated that the highest-rated coaches were people with cross-cultural experience or dual cultural inheritance ($p = 0.06$).

UNDERSTANDING CHINESE VALUES (OR CULTURAL EXPECTATIONS)

Cultural Intelligence is as important as IQ and EQ for globally competent managers – and coaches. It consists of three components. These include: (1) knowledge of culture and the fundamental principles of cross-cultural communication; (2) the ability to pay attention in a reflective and creative way to cues in the cross-cultural situation; and (3) choosing the behaviour from a well-developed repertoire of behaviours that are correct for different intercultural situations (Thomas and Inkson 2004).

For Westerners operating in the Chinese culture, they may find that the Chinese culture shares similar characteristics with other cultures but these characteristics may be differently communicated. For example, the information may be implicitly conveyed rather than explicitly expressed (Victor 1992).

For Westerners working within the Chinese culture, they may find it helpful to understand the three values that Chinese people celebrate:

1   Luck (external dependent/blame);
2   Wealth (money); and
3   Long life (health).

Knowing that these values are treasured will provide international coaches in China with the following guiding light:

- Build a relationship (trust);
- Give due regard to respect ('save face'; local practice – their way of doing things);
- Be flexible; and
- Give substantive (tangible) advice and be technical and to the point.

International coaches could use the above model as scaffolding for their own cultural contexts.

TIPS/IMPLICATIONS

Some tips for coaches/business executives in China and their implications for coaching:

- Quick cognitive behavioural techniques and solution-focused coaching may not be applicable.
- Building trust/a relationship should be the initial focus.
- Be in accord with the culture of the client's condition.
- Be educational (but not lecturing).
- Be holistic (socio-economical as well as psychological and physical).

Notes

1 For confidentiality reasons, the main character's name has been changed.
2 Instead of outsiders, out-group members (*wairen*).
3 Gu (1990, quoted in Bond 1996: 315) suggested four qualities taken from the Confucian concept: 'respectfulness (concern for the other's face, status, and so forth), modesty (self-denigration), attitudinal warmth (demonstrations of kindness, consideration, and hospitality), and refinement'.
4 Also means to assimilate, to imitate.

Bibliography

Berne, E. (1970) *Games People Play*, London: Penguin.
Bond, M.H. (ed.) (1996) *The Handbook of Chinese Psychology*, New York: Oxford University Press.
Chang, W. C. (2000) 'In search of the Chinese in all the wrong places!' *Journal of Psychology in Chinese Societies*, 1 (1): 125–42.
Cheng, Y., Zhang, Z., Zhang, W. and Zheng, J. (2006) 'What leadership styles are missing from the Chinese executives?', *Harvard Business Review* (Chinese Version): April, 2006.
Goleman, D. (1998) *Working with Emotional Intelligence*, London: Bloomsbury.
Geertz, C. (1986) 'Anti-anti-Relativism', *American Anthropologist*, 86: 263–78.
Grant, A. M. and Palmer, S. (2002) 'Coaching psychology', workshop and meeting held at the annual conference of the Division of Counselling Psychology, British Psychological Society, Torquay, 18 May.
Hall, E. T. (1976) *Beyond Culture*, Garden City: Anchor Press.
Hofstede, G. H. (1991) *Cultures and Organizations: Software of the Mind*, London: McGraw-Hill.
Kolb, D. A. (1984) *Experiential Learning: Experience as the Source of Learning and Development*, Englewood Cliffs, NJ: Prentice-Hall.
Law, H.C. (2007) 'Narrative coaching and psychology of learning from multicultural perspectives', in S. Palmer and A. Whybrow (eds), *Handbook of Coaching Psychology*, London: Brunner-Routledge.
Law, H. C., Ireland, S. and Hussain, Z. (2005) 'Evaluation of Coaching Competence Self Review on-line tool within an NHS leadership development programme', Special Group in Coaching Psychology Annual National Conference. December. City University, London: The British Psychological Society.
Law, H. C., Ireland, S. and Hussain, Z. (2007) *Psychology of Coaching, Mentoring & Learning*, Chichester: John Wiley & Sons.
Megginson, D. and Clutterbuck, D. (1995) *Techniques for Coaching and Mentoring*, Oxford: Elsevier Butterworth-Heinemann.
Moral, M. and Angel, P. (2006) *Coaching, Outils et pratiques*, Paris: Armand Colin.
Palmer, S. and Whybrow, A. (2006) 'The coaching psychology movement and its development within the British Psychological Society', *International Coaching Psychology Review*, 1 (1): 141–56.
Rosinski, P. (2003), *Coaching across Cultures*, London: Nicholas Brealey.

Trompenaars, F. and Hampden-Turner, C. (1997) *Riding the Waves of Culture* (2nd edn), London: Nicholas Brealey.

Turner, V. and Brunner, E. (eds) (1986) *The Anthology of Experience*, Chicago: University of Illinois Press.

Vygotsky, L. S. (1926/1962) *Thought and Language*, Cambridge, MA: MIT Press.

Zhaung, G. T. (1998) *Overseas Chinese at the Turn of the Century*, Xiamen: Nanyang Institute of Overseas Chinese Studies.

Zukerman, M. (1990) 'Some dubious premises in research and theory on racial differences: Scientific, social and ethical issues', *American Psychologist*, 45: 1297–303.

17

EXECUTIVE TEAM COACHING IN MULTINATIONAL COMPANIES

Michel C. Moral

Twenty years ago, most multinational companies were organized by geography. Times have changed and today, most global enterprises are organized within a matrix structure where the control, role and influence of the individual countries tend to be balanced by other forces. Now, the driving forces are usually either the distribution channels or the business product units; selling being the prime corporate value in the first case, and innovating being the top cultural belief in the second. Furthermore, large companies are optimizing their costs by locating their activities where they will find the best financial and technical conditions. It is not unusual to find some product parts produced and assembled in China, software design implemented in India, basic administrative work carried out in Africa, call centers organized in Belarus, and so on. Consequently, executive teams with a dominant nationality are seen less and less frequently, and most are now likely to have three or more cultures represented.

Modern executive teams are confronted with a vast array of issues in their functioning. Cultural diversity and remoteness are two factors that characterize modern executive teams. The fact that they are multicultural might raise some specific problems but it can also be an advantage, depending on circumstances and the attitudes of participants. According to Leight and Maynard (1995) it is more difficult to reach a high level of team spirit with a multinational group of people if the decision-making and production centers are dispersed, the executive teams are themselves dispersed, and the day-to-day coordination of operations is rapidly adapting (requiring, for example, conference call techniques instead of regular trust-building face-to-face meetings).

On the positive side, many highly educated and well-travelled senior executives in multinationals are drawn to their roles by the international nature of the assignments. They are intrinsically motivated by interacting with their executive colleagues who – though from diverse backgrounds – often hold similar global world-views. Also, due to a better understanding of team dynamics and to the integration of appropriate tools, upper management teams within most enterprises tend to achieve quite high levels of cohesiveness and motivation. Team members' shared goals are usually well articulated, ambitious and well rewarded if achieved. Most high performance companies are familiar with, and have implemented techniques to improve team spirit and to maintain consistency in setting goals. Also, over time, more and more attention is being given to the high potential managers. Companies often spare little expense in ensuring resources are available for executive team training, communication and travel. This level of support can offset the negative effects of geographic dispersion and differences in cultural backgrounds. However, the current challenge is to go one step further, i.e. to reach the highest possible level of effectiveness.

In this chapter, we will take two examples to illustrate our point. Names and some details have been changed. In both cases we begin by addressing the same issue: an executive team unable to take care of a minor organizational or business problem without first seeking the approval and drive of the team leader. Consequently, the team leader is overloaded with a multitude of small decisions. We will then consider how to develop the team once this issue is resolved.

EXAMPLE 1: AUTOGLOBE

AutoGlobe is a small organization of approximately 100 people, highly specialized in the hiring and placement of international managers, specifically in the automotive industry. It has offices in France, Germany, Poland, Romania, the Czech Republic, India and China. The owner of the company, Lucien, of both French and German descent, is a very active, pushy and demanding person. He decided to initiate an executive team-coaching program within his company, not only to improve the efficiency, but also to acquire experience in the subject with the idea of setting up an international practice. He, in fact, intends to provide an additional service to respond to his clients' demand for coaching. His clients are large corporations which are in the process of relocating their back office, plants, or business units (like telesales or call centers), in countries where the salaries and infrastructure costs are low. Most often, an entire division of perhaps thousands of people is implanted in a relatively small town like Brno in the Czech Republic. AutoGlobe usually takes control of all of the human resource aspects of the operation, which consists of mass-hiring the workers (sub-contracted to a local service provider), hiring the middle management, and identifying local high potential people to be members of the organization's executive committee. An expatriate usually takes on the role of general manager for the first couple of years, arriving with one or two of his or her key people. In addition to attracting and selecting the local workforce, Lucien is also often asked to coach the general manager, the executive team and/ or the high potential managers.

TEAM COACHING METHODOLOGY

My own way of coaching an executive team invariably starts with observing the team in action. I insist on attending one of the regular executive committee meetings or an operational meeting. The theoretical frameworks and the different options on how to conduct team coaching have been reviewed by Giffard and Moral (2007). Team coaching is informed by the practice of action research. From this perspective, Greenwood and Levin (1998) describe the role of the action researcher as a 'friendly outsider' which is akin to that of a coach in the team coaching scenario. The friendly outsider can observe and describe things that the individual members of the team either cannot see or do not choose to see:

> He or she must be able to reflect back to the local group things about them, including criticism of their own perspectives or habits, in a way that is experienced as supportive rather than negatively critical or domineering.

> (1998: 104)

257

> Strictly speaking, the trope of irony centers on affirming in words that the facts or situations are precisely the opposite of what the listener understands them to be. Irony is a kind of displacement, a viewing of the world in reverse that often provokes humor but is also capable of openings up patterns of thought to new possibilities.
>
> (1998: 107)

In my own practice, I am particularly attentive in identifying behaviors that are slowing down the team momentum. The feedback I give is strictly related to observation and formulated as a question like, 'Why did it take so long to make a decision about this issue?', 'Are you going too fast into discussing details?', and 'Is there a reason for this?' Repetition of the same behavior is questioned: 'I notice that this is the third time that you have delayed the discussion about this item? Why?' Of course, the fewer questions the coach asks, the more powerful these questions are.

All teams have different processes but highly effective multicultural teams share certain characteristics, particularly mutual respect. For example, members of purely Italian or French teams usually talk simultaneously, which has been observed by social scientists in Latin cultures. Within a mono-cultural framework, there is no lack of respect. However, in a multicultural team, experienced executives from whatever background will generally follow the unwritten meta-rules in use in international groups: let the previous speaker finish his sentence and say something only if it contributes to the discussion. If the coach observes a perceived lack of respect among members emerging due to conflicting conversational styles, this issue can be explored and a workable approach agreed that is considered respectful by all.

During the observation phase, it is quite important to assess the following:

1   The maturity of the team;
2   The level of demand;
3   What and how.

The maturity of the team

Many different team maturity scales have been created over the years (for instance Lewin 1946; Schutz 1966; Tuckman 1965; Whitmore 1992; Katzenbach and Smith 1993; Devillard 2003, etc.) but they all say roughly the same thing: a team starts as an unorganized group trying to work together, then establishes some kind of structure in order to gain efficiency and, finally, reaches an ultimate state of smooth functioning, providing both success and pleasure. Distilling the literature, I have found it useful to identify the six levels of team maturity described in Figure 17.1 below.

It is useful to assess team maturity because it defines the framework for team coaching: if the team maturity level is low (Level 1 or 2) then, of course, coaching must start by creating cohesiveness, using one of the existing team building methodologies.[1] If the maturity level is already high (say Level 4 or 5), it is wise not to spend time on exercises which might be perceived as 'amusement', as the coach's capabilities could be questioned. Instead, the coach should immediately address the real question: performance and, ultimately, success. Figure 17.2 lists several criteria to determine maturity.

Compared to the adult developmental models (for instance Robert Kegan (1994) argues that there are five levels of adult development and managers must be at least at level four before they can survive in the current economic context). The team maturity model is similar but different.

TEAM MATURITY

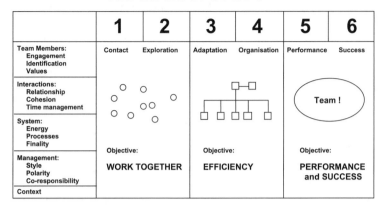

Figure 17.1 Team maturity levels

In the case of an individual, moving from a development level to the next is usually forever. Maturity levels of a team are much more fragile (1) because members may leave or enter and (2) because the 'collective spirit' is not something engraved in a unique coherent neuronal system like a brain. The circulation of information and emotions between the members of a team is not completely known. Nevertheless, there are some analogies between adult and team developmental models and similarities in how coaching can assist people and teams to move to higher levels of development through action learning exercises.

The level of demand

We call 'level of demand' the category of outcome that the team is explicitly requesting. Based on my research and experiences with customers, it appears that outcomes typically fall into three categories or levels, each one needing the previous one(s) to be reached before being addressed:

TEAM MATURITY

	1	2	3	4	5	6
Team Member Engagement Identification Values	None Role Work or "Me"	Motivation Group Friendship	Recognition Goal Rules	Unrestricted Project Performance	Unrestricted Performance Human	Unrestricted Success Work/"Me"
Interactions Relationship Cohesion Time management	Limited None Poor	Confident Limited Poor	Formal Ruled Discussed	Intense Passioned Ruled	Connivance Quiet Prioritised	Loyalty Productive Optimised
Action Energy Processes Finality	Dispersed None Inexistant	Coordinated Some Some	Managed Accepted Defined	Managed Efficient Endorsed	Collective Efficient Performance	Creative Optimised Inexistant
Management Style Polarity Co-responsibility	One to one None None	Paternalistic Needs Conflicts	Directive Needs Operational	Cooperative Wants Ops+Human	Delegative Methods Human+Ops	"Meta" Finality Human
Context	Ignored	Hostile	Existant	Cooperation	Synergy	Holistic view

Figure 17.2 Team maturity components

259

A Understand: the team is seeking help to either explore a domain, or share knowledge, or even to figure out who are the different members in terms of personality, culture or wishes;

B Create: the team has to imagine new solutions, a new product, design a new structure or invent innovative offerings; and

C Execute: the team has difficulties in deploying an action plan or transforming decisions into realities.

Let's take the case of a large banking institution that is creating a new division to open branch offices in China. In terms of team maturity, the members of this new executive team first need to work at getting to know each other, especially if they come from different countries. Given that they have probably been selected due to their relevant experience and leadership potential, it is likely the team will progress rapidly from maturity Level 1 to Level 4. Thus, the real objective of the team coaching is to help them attain Level 5 or even Level 6.

In terms of level of demand, this team has to understand the business environment (demand level A). Once the executives have shared enough knowledge (level A), they must then design a new organization (level B) and maybe even create new offerings for the Chinese market (level B). Eventually, they will execute by opening the network of branch offices (level C).

In real life, an executive team has simultaneously different levels of demand depending on the questions that arise. During an operational meeting, various disparate issues are considered: for instance, hiring a new director in Germany, opening a plant in Romania, restructuring a division, fixing the price of a product, deciding to bid in a highly competitive tender, and so on. Each one of these questions probably has a different level of demand: the Romanian plant is now built and production is about to start (demand level C), while restructuring a division requires creativity (level B).

What and how?

When observing an executive team, carefully recording the 'how' is much more important than analyzing the 'what' and all possible attention must be given to the circumvolutions of the decision-making process. Mapping the different issues and their levels of demand usually highlights patterns indicating what the team needs to significantly improve if it wants to maximize the performance and the well-being of its members.

Coaching the AutoGlobe executive team

How does this apply to the AutoGlobe executive team?

During the monthly face-to-face executive committee meetings, the following points (and others) were discussed:

- Engaging a large bid in Germany;
- Assessing the progress of the new information system;
- Considering a merger with a small company in the same business in India; and
- Improving external communication.

The coach observed that the AutoGlobe team was at around maturity Level 3. The executives were rarely operating at Level 4, despite the fact that a third of the team members were German (with the reputation of liking organizations where roles and processes are crystal clear). Here, mapping the level of demand revealed a common execution problem: many minor concerns were percolating up to the executive team meetings, making it difficult to focus on the really important matters.

The members of the AutoGlobe executive team were clearly divided into two groups: those who thoroughly enjoyed exploring and creating (the 'explorers') and those were eager to execute and make money (the 'executors'). The first group tended to spend a lot of time arguing on details while the second group displayed a preference to earn a dollar now rather than a million dollars next century. They were impatient to act.

During the first workshop, the team was asked to participate in a rope exercise designed to reveal execution dysfunctions. Team members were asked to configure a square with a 25 meter-long rope – blindfolded and silent. Before the execution phase, the team was given a ten-minute preparation phase during which time they could see and speak. In order to address the issue that was identified during the observation of the team in real action, the following regulation was introduced: the general manager may act as a resource but not as the leader of the team. The team must find its own way towards the solution.

The first attempt, at the end of the first day of the workshop, was a disaster: the group of 'explorers' took the lead and spent most of the preparation time arguing on how to check that the square was a square, excluding from their discussion the rest of the team. No execution plan was defined and once the team was blindfolded and forced to silence it became chaotic. The outcome was that the figure resembled a potato more than a square.

The dinner and evening sessions were tough, especially for the coach who had to cope with the hostility of both parties: from the 'explorers', who realized that their way of thinking was breaking the momentum, and from the 'executors' who were frustrated because of the failure. The following morning, the team members were presented with a new exercise. This time they had to use the rope to write the name of the company, in silence and blindfolded. The preparation phase was reduced to seven minutes and the general manager was still not allowed to lead the team. Things progressed much better, as leadership was taken by one of the 'executors' who made good use of the time, not excluding anyone during the preparation phase and making sure that a process was in place prior to the execution.

The debriefing provided an opportunity to increase the team members' awareness of their collective ability to find solutions without their boss. Several people in the group were rather shocked to learn that charisma does not mean efficiency.

EXAMPLE 2: ET-INDEPENDENT

ET-Independent is an independent division within a large European high technology company (EuroTech). The head of this relatively small entity is English and a member of the EuroTech corporate executive team. His ET-Independent management team counts 12 members, one third German, one third American and one third Italian. ET-Independent has a total staff of around 400 people located in Germany, USA and Italy. Its mission is to design, sell and administrate high technology products that are manufactured in Asia by the EuroTech group.

Here again, the same issue related to execution that emerged with the AutoGlobe team (minor concerns percolating up to the executive meeting), appeared during the observation of a real executive meeting. But, fixing this was not the coaching objective, which was clearly defined as: progress from maturity Level 3/4 to Level 5 or 6. As the team was already quite advanced in terms of execution, the exercise session with the ropes was not appropriate.

Instead, the coach decided to stimulate the creativity of the team with another exercise, called Breakthrough.[2]

The whole team was asked to stand on a tablecloth. The objective was to turn the cloth upside down without any body part protruding onto the floor. As with the previous group, the same new regulation was introduced: the general manager could not act as a leader and must let the team find its own solution.

On average, a group of 15 persons on a 2.5 × 1.5 meter tablecloth can take up to ten minutes to figure out how to flip the sheet. In the case of this executive team, it took only six minutes, and the team members were rather disappointed because they found the exercise far too simple.

This exercise is designed to create an analogy with real-life situations: usually obstacles exist because ideas receive limited support from the group, or even opposition from those who are looking for leadership or recognition. In order to implement the solution, only a couple of people need to drive the process, all others tend to act in strict compliance. This exercise can be valuable in raising awareness that in a successful organization, an idea:

- can originate from anywhere;
- needs to receive some support (by at least 7–10 per cent of the population); and
- can be implemented by change agents with limited or no opposition.

In the case of this group, after considering and rejecting several highly impractical ideas, the secretary was the one who suggested the approach that was successful. She received immediate support from two directors who started to implement the process. The rest of the group was extremely disciplined and the execution went smoothly to completion. Compared to other groups, the execution design phase took approximately the same time but the implementation process was much faster. During the debriefing session many analogies were made to real-life situations and a number of decisions were taken to improve team processes. For instance, it was decided to assign roles (such as, time keeper, decision pusher, facilitator, and meta-communicator) during the executive committee meetings (Cardon, 2003).

In these exercises, the team leader and his or her team are explicitly involved in the assessment and debriefing. As in the action research approach, the coach's role is to share observations and help the team to develop meanings that make sense in the context. That is, exercises that flow from the initial observations and assessments are presented – and understood – as contextually appropriate. Otherwise, the risk is that the coach is perceived – and acts – as outside 'expert' whose sole role is to administer externally sourced solutions. The 'friendly outsider' role allows expertise but injects participatory and more democratic foundations to interventions where team members are central in designing solutions.

A second risk is that the coach generates interesting and 'fun' activities that in the end do not have an impact on the team's functioning in 'real' life outside of the individual and team coaching sessions. Therefore, the coach must work with the leader and the team to ensure relevance. A fundamental element of briefing before and the debriefing after any team action learning exercise is to stress the connection between the activity and what happens in real business life for the team. Exercises can therefore be positioned with the team as a kind of laboratory where the team members can individually and collectively explore their functioning and growth.

THEORY

A team can be considered from different viewpoints; as a:

1 set of people;
2 set of interactions; and/or
3 a system (see Figure 17.3).

In any case, a team is pursuing some kind of objective and usually has a leader who provides business directives or precise targets.

In Figure 17.3, the system is similar to an 'us', in which members say 'we' or 'our'. Members are portrayed as circles, partially situated inside the 'us': this is what they contribute to the team. They also have a part situated on the outside, the part of their life where they say 'I' or 'me' or 'my' (e.g., commencing sentences with 'I believe that' or 'in my opinion'). In Figure 17.3, straight lines between members represent mutual interactions. However, this is an oversimplification that does not give the full picture. The interactions are more like twisted ropes, combining several strands, such as love, hate, indifference, complicity, respect, etc. But, let's keep it simple for a while!

In modern matrix organizations, employees report to several management lines. This is depicted in Figure 17.3, with short line segments emanating from each member's circle. It is possible that some team members are only moderately involved in the 'us' because they have responsibilities and loyalties to another group. A sales representative who belongs to a product division and also to a distribution channel might consider that his or her 'real' management line is the first one, where the salary increase is set. As shown in Figure 17.4, modern team members have to be part of several 'us' and still protect and grow 'me'. When the team is multinational, some members, due to their country culture, are more or less inclined to engage in the 'us' of a team. Interculturalists, according to Geert Hofstede's (2001) scheme, make a distinction between individualistic cultures, such as occidental culture, and collectivistic cultures, the Orient and Asia, where the group is more important than the individual. Within collectivist

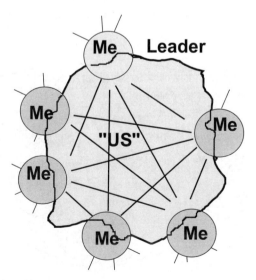

Figure 17.3 Representation of a team

cultures, some are loyal only to their group, like the Chinese, while others are ready to adopt the values of any group. Commitment patterns are therefore quite complex, with a residual 'me' surrounded by several 'us' (family, national culture, corporate culture, professional culture, etc.). Usually, all these loyalties are prioritized according to the current activity: I am fully loyal to my football team when I am playing football. Back at work, I am loyal to the team, or to the group of my peers, accountants or sales representatives. Back home, my family comes first.

Sometimes, the loyalty patterns are broken, as demonstrated by Zinedine Zidane at the very end of the football World Cup in 2006. Despite his loyalty to the French team, he made a mistake, which probably caused his team's defeat.

The team as a group of people

The idea of the team as a 'group of people' has been at the source of a large number of tools, such as Brain Thinking Styles (Hermann 1978), Social Styles (Marston 1928), Management Styles (Fiedler 1958; Hersey and Blanchard 1977; House 1971; Vroom and Yetton 1973) and Role Analysis (MBTI: Myers-Brigg 1962; TMS: Mergerison and McCahn 1985; Belbin 1981). Collective mechanisms, such as corporate or country culture and related tools (Schein 1985), also view the team as a group of people.

The team as a set of interactions

The idea of the team as a 'set of interactions' has instigated various approaches, depending on the kind of interaction that is being considered: power, information, emotions, conflict, love, hate, etc. Notions like cohesiveness or maturity are a function of the density and of the quality of interactions. Paul Watzlawick (Watzlawick et al. 1967) sees interactions as a series of messages. For many authors, there is no difference between interaction and communication: both are viewed as an exchange of information. Gregory and Marie-Catherine Bateson (1987: 172) define information as, 'a difference which creates a difference', thus including non-verbal attitudes and even implicit elements which need contextual rules to be understood.

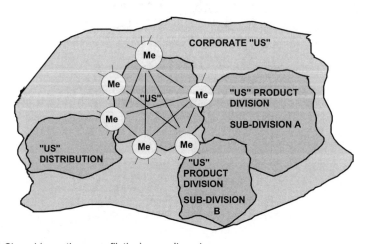

Figure 17.4 Shared (sometimes conflicting) commitments

The team as a system

Lastly, if the team is considered as a 'system', not only the 'whole theory' developed by Palo Alto, known as 'first systems theory' (von Bertalanffy 1947) applies, but also its derivatives, called 'second systems theory' (Von Foerster 1975) and 'third systems theory' (Varela 1991). Within the second, which includes concepts such as Nonlinear Dynamics (Kaufman 1995), Chaos-Theory (Lorenz 1996), and Sciences of Complexity (Langton 1992), the Catastrophe Theory (Thom 1972) is a specific branch of the 'bifurcation theory'. It studies sudden shifts in behavior caused by small changes in the environment, and considers only the cases where the long-term stable state has a minimum degree of chaos, thus a minimum of the so-called 'Lyapunov exponent', a number which determines the system's predictability over time.

All these different approaches are well known but it is quite interesting to note that, at a given period of time, most of the methodologies used by consultants were focusing on only one perspective: in the 1960s and 70s, the manager was seen as the driver of performance, and many management style models were designed on this basis (by Fred Fiedler, Robert Blake, Jane Mouton, Robert House, Victor Vroom, Philip Yetton, James Burns, etc.). All these models originated in Anglo-American culture. Ten years later, with the emergence of the commitment paradigms (Kiesler 1971) motivation models appeared and were better adapted to European culture. Systems Theory helped to produce interesting new methodologies more fitted to holistic Eastern cultures. Currently, consultants are enthusiastically exploring the analogy between organizations and living systems, based upon the Second Systems Theory. These apply to organizations (see Chapter 1 of this *Companion*) as well as to teams.

It is time now to discover ways of combining these three different perspectives of teams, not only to bring team performance to its maximum but also to go beyond performance towards success. The different approaches need to be interfaced with internationalization and interculturalization.

CREATIVE TEAM COACHING: THE COMMITMENT AWARENESS EXERCISE

In order to create maximum awareness of what is going on in the team and the context, the idea of the commitment awareness exercise is to combine all three perspectives of the team into a single exercise. This powerful approach should be used only if the team's maturity is at Level 4 and if the management layers below are empowered. It is very useful in matrix organizations with less rigid management lines. Also, the model is best handled by a facilitator or a coach who is experienced in team environments, including as an executive manager.

Members of a high performing team need to recognize the positive and negative aspects of communication and emotions within the group, which may be deeply embedded at the level of group subconscious. They must also be aware of the varying degrees of commitment that are likely to be present in the team, sometimes ranging from obsessive devotion to work to indifference and apathy. The objective of the following exercise is to surface all the various aspects of the team's existence and operations and to encourage the members to share their views and agree on how to behave collectively. It requires disclosing personal beliefs related to work, it is likely to surface strong emotions. But, it has nothing to do with some sort of 'new age' approach and it is derived from theory and sound practice. As noted, it requires a seasoned professional for successful implementation.

The exercise is executed in several steps. During the first step, team members stand around a rope that is lying in a loose circle on the ground. The inner circle represents the 'us'. The area outside is where the individual 'me' resides. Each person is given a cardboard disk, about one foot in diameter. They are asked to place their cards under the rope, so that the part inside the loop represents their commitment to the team (see Figure 17.5).

Then each team member is asked to comment on the positioning of his or her disk. Some might disclose that they favor their family over the team, or that they have strong commitments to another business unit in the matrix. Possibly, some may feel fully engaged and they will place their disks completely inside the rope. The discussion can then be expanded towards reaching an agreement concerning which type of behavior demonstrates commitment, and what limits must be established to protect each person's 'me' or identity. Furthermore, each team member's contribution needs to be described as it relates to the person's uniqueness. The coach's role is essential in preventing judgments and encouraging members to avoid sentences that may provoke unnecessary or destructive conflict (e.g., such as accusatory sentences beginning with 'you'). Where there is team dysfunction, it is likely that the coach will encounter group tension and even resistance to the exercise. The skilled coach will roll with the resistance, and manage the tension by insisting on the legitimacy of the 'me'.

The second step is a bit more complex in terms of facilitation. Each member is asked to describe how they see their communication with each of the other members. For this purpose, they use ropes of different colors (blue: good relationship, red: conflict, white: limited contact) and different rope diameters to symbolize the pattern of relationships within the group (see Figure 17.6).

The process continues until everyone has had the opportunity to demonstrate how they see their network and when everyone has proposed possible options to overcome the pitfalls that could hinder overall team performance. This element of the exercise requires a high level of group maturity.

This exercise was done with the ET-Independent client. It brought to light a high level of communication within and among the three cultural groups (German, American and Italian) but a low exchange of information among these groups. For example, an Italian team member disclosed that when looking for help, she was more inclined to go to her Italian peer rather than

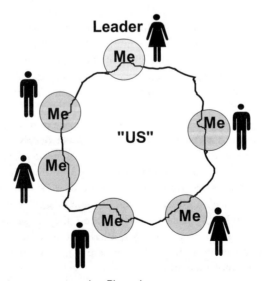

Figure 17.5 Commitment awareness exercise, Phase 1

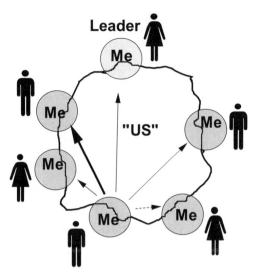

Figure 17.6 Commitment awareness exercise, Phase 2

to the German in charge of the problem. It also brought to light the fact that 'small' functions, such as those in Legal or Procurement Departments, were not involved in the strategic decisions and had poor long-term visibility.

CONCLUSION

We consultants and coaches need to refresh our toolboxes. It is true that modern management still shares some concepts as used by Roman, Huns or Mongolian armies. But, it is also true that concepts and technologies have made major strides during the last twenty years. The environment has also significantly evolved. Therefore, we need to exploit the opportunities that the information and communications systems currently provide as they will allow modern organizations to cope with the challenge. The role of the coach is to raise awareness about the issues going on in teams. The theory and tools above may provide some guidance and assistance to coaches in the challenging role of working with international teams.

Notes

1 Many team building approaches have been developed: 'goal setting', 'role model' developed by Belbin, 1981, 'problem solving', 'motivational', etc. All are detailed in Driskell et al. (2003).
2 Breakthrough has been invented by a French coach, Marc Guionnet, who holds an MCC accreditation from ICF.

Bibliography

Bateson, G. and Bateson, M. (1987) *Angels Fear: Towards an Epistemology of the Sacred*, New York: Macmillan.
Belbin, M. (1981) *Management Teams*, New York: John Wiley & Sons.

Cardon, A. (2003) *Coaching D'équipe*, Paris: Interéditions.

Devillard, O. (2003) *La dynamique des equipes*, Paris: Editions d'Organisation.

Driskell, J., Radtke, S. and Salas, E. (2003) 'Virtual teams: Effect of technological mediation on team performance', *Group Dynamics*, 7 (4): 297–323.

Fiedler, F. (1958) *Leader Attitudes and Group Effectiveness*, Urbana: University of Illinois Press,

Giffard, M. and Moral, M. (2007) *Coaching D'équipe, Outils et Techniques*, Paris: Armand Colin.

Greenwood, D.J. and Levin, M. (1998) *Introduction to Action Research: Social Action for Social Change*, London: Sage.

Hermann, N. (1978) *Les Dominances cérébrales et la créativité*, Paris: Retz.

Hersey, P. and Blanchard, K. (1977) *Management of Organizational Behavior*, Englewood Cliffs, NJ: Prentice-Hall,

Hofstede, G. (2001) *Culture's Consequences: Comparing Values, Behaviors, Institutions and Organizations across Nations* (2nd edn), Thousand Oaks, CA: Sage.

House, R. (1971) 'A path-goal theory of leader effectiveness', *Administrative Science Quarterly*, 16: 321–39.

Katzenbach, J. and Smith, D. (1993) *The Wisdom of Teams*, New York: Harper & Collins.

Kaufman, S. (1995) *At Home in the Universe*, Oxford: Oxford University Press.

Kegan, R. (1994) *In Over Our Heads: The Mental Demands of Modern Life*, Cambridge, MA: Harvard University Press.

Kiesler, C. (1971) *The Psychology of Commitment: Experiments Linking Behaviour to Belief*, New York: Academic Press.

Langton, C. (1992) 'Life on the edge of chaos', in C.G. Langton, C.Taylor, J.D. Farmer, J.D. and S. Rasmussen (eds), *Artificial Life II, Santa Fé Institute Studies in the Sciences of Complexity (Proceedings Vol. X)*, Redwood City: Addison-Wesley.

Leight, A. and Maynard, M. (1995) *Leading your Team: How to Involve and Inspire Teams*, London: Nicholas Brealey.

Lewin, K. (1946) 'Action research and minority problems', in G.W. Lewin (ed.), *Resolving Social Conflict*, London: Harper & Row.

Lorenz, E. (1996) *The Essence of Chaos*, Washington, DC: University of Washington.

Marston, W. (1928) *Emotions of Normal People*, New York: International Library of Psychology.

Mergerison, C. and McCahn, D. (1985) *Team Management: Practical New Approaches*, London: Management Books.

Myers, K. and Brigg, I. (1962) *The Myers-Briggs Type Indicator*, Palo Alto, CA: Consulting Psychologists Press.

Schein, E. (1985) *Organizational Culture and Leadership*, New York: Jossey-Bass.

Schutz, W. (1966) *The Interpersonal Underworld*, Palo Alto: Science and Behavior Books.

Thom, R. (1972) *Structural Stability and Morphogenesis*, trans. D. H. Fowler, Reading: Benjamin.

Tuckman, B. (1965) 'Development sequence in small groups', *Psychological Bulletin*, 63 (6): 384–99.

Varela, F. (1991) 'Structure and cognition in living systems', in A. Shibatani, N. Hokkyo and Y. Sato (eds), *Structuralism and Biology*, Kyoto: Yosioka Shoton.

Von Bertalanffy, L. (1946/1972) 'The history and status of general systems theory', *Academy of Management Journal*, 15 (4): 407–26.

Von Foerster, H. (1975/1995) *Cybernetics of Cybernetics* (2nd edn), Minneapolis: Future Systems.

Vroom, V. and Yetton, P. (1973) *Leadership and Decision-Making*, Pittsburgh: University of Pittsburgh Press.

Watzlawick, P., Beavin, J. and Jackson, D. (1967) *Pragmatics of Human Communication: A Study of Interactional Patterns*, New York: Norton.

Whitmore, J. (1992) *Coaching for Performance*, London: Nicholas Brealey.

COACHING WITH GLOBAL VIRTUAL TEAMS

An action learning perspective

Geoffrey Abbott

Virtual business is a hot topic in management literature. In particular, global virtual teams (GVTs) are getting attention. The recent attention on GVTs is not because experts and futurists are predicting the advent of this kind of management and collaborative approach; it is because it is already here. Virtual work and virtual teaming have not received the same attention in the burgeoning coaching literature. The focus of this chapter is the intersection between the advent of management by technology across borders and international business coaching practice. The analysis is informed by action research and action learning methodologies, based originally on the work of Kurt Lewin (1946) and more recently by Greenwood and Levin (1998) and others.

I suggest that a coach's role is best fulfilled as a 'friendly outsider' (Greenwood and Levin 1998) who can assist participants in exploring their challenges and context and in building satisfying, productive and sustainable ways of operating in the virtual world. The coach shines a light into areas that may need attention, challenges, supports, and also helps to apply theory and knowledge from other contexts in the unique situation of an individual GVT.

The chapter examines not only the difficulties and obstacles of virtual team work, but also potential and possibilities, drawing perspectives from solution-focused coaching (Greene and Grant 2003), positive psychology (Seligman and Csikszentmihayli 2000) and appreciative inquiry (Cooperrider and Whitney 2005). The chapter suggests how leaders and team members can make use of external coaches and coaching approaches. It may encourage coaches to increase their engagement with virtual coaching – noting the potential advantages that can flow in terms of:

1   Assisting clients with current issues; and
2   Getting meaningful engagements with internationally active organizations.

There are many books on virtual teaming and countless articles in the popular press and in academic journals. Appropriately, a very sound publication (Lipnack and Stamps 2000) is available free and online (www.virtualteams.com). Distilling the literature, a GVT is defined in this chapter as, 'A group of two or more people with a common purpose working together across different international locations that primarily relies on technology for communication and collaboration'. Note that a 'group' can be just two people, meaning that a GVT can comprise, at its leanest, a coach and coachee. There is no upper limit.

There are various ways that coaching and GVT activity connect. Consider the situation of each of the following:

1   At its simplest, a coach who is coaching a client via technology;
2   The leader of a GVT who is being coached (individually and/or with the team);
3   The leader of a GVT using coaching techniques;
4   A member of a GVT receiving group or individual external coaching;
5   An external coach who is coaching a GVT leader and/or team member;
6   A coach who is a member of a coaching group that works out of different locations and connects virtually (i.e. a GVT);
7   A leader of a team of coaches who are in different locations (a GVT);
8   A member of a study group in online learning (a GVT) who is using coaching techniques with his or her virtual classmates; and so on.

These variations may serve to highlight just how much virtuality there is in the current international workplace. These different roles also show that coaching can be applied in GVTs in ways other than through the engagement of an external coach. In business generally there is an increasing tendency for organizations to utilize the power of coaching through internal processes such as:

• manager-as-coach training programs;
• leadership development;
• self and peer coaching in self-managed teams; and
• internal coaching.

These applications are equally valid in the virtual team world. However, the model of the external coach working with GVTs in various ways at this stage is likely to be the primary way that coaching is going to add value. I suggest external coaches can play a very significant role in GVTs, particularly in supporting the sound leadership of GVTs and in helping to embed coaching practice into the virtual team environment.

I draw a strong link between the successful operation of GVTs and the application of action learning and action research principles. Coaching is conceptualized as adult learning which works through cycles of planning, action and reflection to explore the world of the client (Abbott and Grant 2005). This exploration includes setting meaningful goals and seeking to fulfill client potential (Rosinski, 2003). I borrow the concept of the 'friendly outsider' from the field of participatory action research to position the role of the coach. Greenwood and Levin explain this role: 'He or she must be able to reflect back to the local group things about them, including criticism of their own perspectives or habits, in a way that is experienced as supportive rather than negatively critical or domineering' (Greenwood and Levin 1998: 105). In the GVT world, 'local group' can be taken to mean 'virtual group' (though a local geographical perspective still exists). The friendly outsider role is very similar to the role of the consultant described by Peter Block (2000), who gives attention to the relational and reflective powers of the outsider. One thing is for sure, no outsider is going to be an authority on the unique context of each GVT. That authority resides only in the group.

Coaching in the role of the friendly outsider is mainly around asking insightful questions rather than giving instructions – teasing out cultural, technical, professional and other knowledge that is in the group and being created by the group. Powerful questioning gives attention to raising awareness and finding clarity, something that is crucial in very complex and uncertain international environments which GVTs traverse. The GVT environment is often task and goal driven. Working from an action learning frame, the coach calls people to action based on awareness, and then assists them to make sense of what happened, explore further, take new actions, and so on. Goal setting and attainment can be assisted by a supportive and action-results oriented coach. One defining feature of action research is that the researcher-explorer is positioned within the group as participant. The implications of employing this methodology in the GVT environment is that the coach will do more than have one-to-one interactions with a leader. He or she will be involved in many different and creative ways and work pragmatically to facilitate solutions to group challenges.

Early coaching approaches were often based on what worked for individual coaches on the dubious principle of, 'it worked for me so it *must* work for you'. More recent and rigorous interventions are 'evidence based' (Grant and Stober 2006), meaning that they draw on the best of contemporary knowledge and practice from a range of disciplines. The approach is to work in partnership with individual and organizational clients; evidence-based coaches practice in the mode of the participatory action researcher. Stober and Grant (2006: 361) argue for a contextual model of coaching and propose seven principles of effective coaching, all of which are central to the successful function of GVTs:

1   Collaboration;
2   Accountability;
3   Awareness;
4   Responsibility;
5   Commitment;
6   Action; and
7   Results.

Evidence-based coaching connects research, theory and good-practice into new contexts. Well-informed and experienced coaches can validly offer suggestions – but the application has to be owned, localized, contextualized and adapted by the group. At times an external coach working in the GVT environment may have to play more of a consultancy role than some of the 'purer' forms of coaching taught in coaching schools where a coach may not often be forthcoming with 'advice'. In a mix of coach/consultant, the external GVT coach can be armed with knowledge of what has worked elsewhere with GVTs and be forthcoming about making suggestions to leaders and teams. The art is to put forward the hypothesis, 'This strategy has worked elsewhere in a similar GVT and may be useful in this situation', then, paradoxically, work hard to disprove the hypothesis even if the group accepts it with open arms. That way, a safeguard is provided to protect contextual appropriateness.

In the following paragraphs, I aim to bring to the attention of coaches and GVT operatives some of the theory and practice relating to GVTs and how coaching might assist in implementing these in different contexts. There are five related themes:

1   Leadership;
2   Culture;
3   Communication;
4   Common Purpose; and
5   Trust.

LEADERSHIP

A vital issue for GVTs is leadership. GVTs face the challenges of all teams as they move through from establishment to task performance and completion (or ongoing working practices). The virtual environment adds to the pressure and complexity of leadership – a point made many times in the literature (Nemiro et al. 2008a). It is absolutely essential for people involved with GVTs in any capacity to understand that no one approach to leadership works. As with all teams, there are various leadership options for virtual teaming. Context will determine the best fit. Options include:

- permanent (i.e. one assigned leader);
- rotating;
- Managing partners (someone in the company but outside the GVT overseeing the team);
- Facilitator/coordinator (almost in the role of a coach and without leadership authority); and
- Leaderless (self-managed) (Nemiro 2004).

Each has its advantages and disadvantages. Virtual teams are often fluid in their make-up, have uncertain timeframes and often carry very high-powered memberships with specialized skills. Alternatively, a GVT may be a hastily thrown together group of people with undefined skills, have vaguely defined parameters and objectives, and be highly diverse (culturally, technically, personally, and so on). Assumptions about how any group should be led should be tested and decisions made carefully and with group input. One of the great advantages of GVTs is that there is scope for imagination, fluidity and creativity in leadership processes. The virtual world opens up – rather than closes – possibilities in this regard. Coaches can help participants to explore these possibilities and arrive at workable leadership approaches.

The essence of GVT leadership is distilled by Brake (2006: 116) to challenges of building community and clarity, 'We can only beat isolation through building community, and we can only beat confusion by promoting clarity'. The following sections expand these areas. Building community means establishing a team culture that is embracing of cultural differences. The team community needs strong communications systems internally and with external stake-holders; a common purpose; and the glue of trusting relationships. Clarity is required regarding the elements and linkages across these themes. Coaching conversations are powerful in assisting individuals and teams to gain clarity. The role of the coach as the friendly outsider is in supporting the leader(s) to foster community and clarity in the face of often daunting complexity in the multiple, shifting and overlapping challenges.

Increasingly, coaching practice has been connected to leadership. Goleman (2000) cites coaching as one of six leadership styles, and the one that is least utilized and with great potential. He stresses situational leadership with great leaders being able to utilize all six styles. This is even more crucial in the GVT environment where nothing is fixed or predictable. The GVT environment is not necessarily conducive to traditional leadership and management approaches and the creative dialogue generated by coaching may assist teams and their leaders to find approaches that are uniquely effective in the situation. A leader of a GVT could use the services of an external coach to sharpen and challenge his or her leadership approach and decision making. Bethanis (2004) observes that a global leader has to know when to be virtual and when not. A coaching conversation is the perfect medium for determining these kinds of judgments. It may be that the external coach takes on a temporary leadership role in leading with expertise in systems or processes of virtual team formation and development. This role is a much-expanded edition of the one-to-one coach–client role of many coaching models.

Leaders in a virtual environment must give attention to facilitating empowerment of their dispersed charges (Kirkman 2004). GVT team members will have to be, at times, completely self-sufficient and self-motivated and able to take responsibility for task completion and the other responsibilities of team membership. Particularly when there is little or no face-to-face contact, the GVT leadership should promote engagement in specialized empowerment build-ing activities. This is a significant leadership challenge. Empowerment is a key element of many coaching interventions. Coaches encourage individuals and teams to take responsibility and to be accountable for actions. In the GVT context, coaching approaches can play an important role in raising awareness about the need for empowerment and for encouraging discussions on generating contextually appropriate activities that can build empowerment in the absence of face-to-face interaction.

CULTURE

Considerable attention is given to cultural orientations and preferences of team members in the GVT literature. Most studies make reference to the importance of exploring the cultural background of team members and to pay attention to any potential cultural barriers early on in the team-forming process. A study of a GVT in the manufacturing sector found that cultural differences appeared to lead to coordination difficulties, and create obstacles to effective communication (Dani et al. 2006: 82). Leaders and managers in GVTs are encouraged to take account of culture and to manage differences. Cross-cultural communication can be put forward as a competency for facilitating creativity in GVTs (Nemiro 2004). Cultural diversity within international companies provides a source of different cultural perspectives: each perspective is potentially a different problem-solving approach. At the same time, there are difficulties in making use of this cultural resource in a GVT environment where time and distance barriers add to the existing challenges of cross-cultural communication (Elron and Vigoda-Gadot 2006).

In practice, culture is interwoven through all aspects of GVT life. The influence of culture should not be (but often is) underestimated. How coaches, leaders, team members and others involved with GVTs make sense of the information in this chapter will be colored and shaped by their cultural interactions and identities. An expanded view of culture is required for GVTs that gives attention to individual cultural identities, team culture, local culture, national culture, organizational culture, and so on, in a global context. An holistic global coaching approach that incorporates different approaches including culture is likely to have impact with GVTs. A powerful coaching intervention in the GVT estab-lishment phase is to engage team members in an exploration of cultural orientations and for the team to be fully aware of the cultural resources (i.e. problem-solving potentials) that are available in the group. Rosinski's global coaching model is an example of an approach that can extend perspectives for leaders and team members to take advantage of cultural differ-ences rather than to see them as barriers or obstacles (Abbott and Rosinski 2007; Rosinski 2003). Cultural measurement can be done online through tools such as those mentioned in Chapters 10 and 11. If at all possible the results should be debriefed in a face-to-face workshop as part of the communication and trust-building process.

COMMUNICATION

Communication is a make or break element of GVTs. Often, it is mistakenly taken to equate with excellent information and communication technologies (ICTs). However, a focus on technology can sometimes, paradoxically, be at the expense of excellent communications in the virtual environment. An expanded view of communication is more instructive. The amount of communication seems to be a crucial element. To compensate for a lack of physical proximity, most studies suggest that leaders promote over-communication using different kinds of communication. In practice, there is a risk of people tuning out in the face of copious emails, teleconferences, Skype chats, and so. A coaching strategy is to periodically promote feedback on what is and is not working. As mentioned earlier, there is general agreement that face-to-face communication is valuable if it can be arranged. If people get to know one another in the early phase in face-to-face meetings, then virtual communication should flow more smoothly.

An outcome of better communication is better collaboration. Fostering collaboration in the face of technological, distance and other challenges is a major hurdle for GVTs. Nemiro et al. (2008b: 1) give primacy to the collaborative nature of work in international companies. They apply a definition of collaboration as follows: 'the collective work of two or more individuals where the work is undertaken with a sense of shared purpose and direction that is attentive, responsive, and adaptive to the environment'. The collaborative nature of work is therefore dependent on a common purpose (see next section) and for attention to the context of work.

Coaching works from an assumption that collaboration is an essential element of how people work together. It is, with awareness, one of the two underpinning core principles of coaching by Stober and Grant (noted earlier). A coaching approach moves away from linear and directive work processes and practices into reflective practice including interaction with colleagues and connections across shared visions and practices. Coaching practices are therefore entirely consistent with the collaborative essence of successful GVTs.

There are various strategies for embedding and enhancing communication and collaboration. Establishing a virtual team charter is sound practice. Agreeing communication etiquette and sharing team profiles, and having an agreed format for reporting and evaluating team performance are other suggestions. Coping with time zone differences is awkward but not impossible. One idea is to establish meeting blackout periods (Combs and Peacocke 2007). A coaching approach can assist in each of these areas through generating creative dialogue about the establishment of practices that match team goals, team composition (including cultural orientations) and any other contextually relevant factors.

The challenge of working across time zones is a common issue in any truly global GVT. There is no easy solution to the difficulties of setting up real time regular telephone or web-based communications in truly global VTs. Someone has to be up early, someone has to be up late. Yet, discussions around protocols and procedures (facilitated through coaching approaches) may assist teams and individuals to reach workable and even attractive timetabling for effective interaction.

Coaching focuses on communication; highly skilled coaches are highly skilled communicators. By modeling and promoting creative dialogue and introducing ideas on how to foster better communication in a virtual team, a coaching approach can facilitate more effective GVT relationships and effectiveness. Coaching can assist GVTs to develop communications protocols that are appropriate to the demographics, task, timing and environment of the team.

Communication via technology is a defining feature of a GVT. As noted earlier, a focus on technology can reduce the effectiveness of GVTs. Teams can get into ongoing experimentation with the latest and greatest in technology (spurred on by well-intentioned techies and perhaps not-so-well-intentioned technology providers) and forget why they are even together in the first place (Dewar 2006: 22). MacPhail, in reporting in a GVT in the medical education sector, concluded that effective virtual team functioning means attending to group content and process with a minor focus on technology (MacPhail 2007: 569). Most studies suggest that more face-to-face contact enhances GVT effectiveness (e.g. Grove and Hallowell 1998), reinforcing a view that technology may not be the key. Nevertheless, technology needs to be effective or it can damage productivity and relationships. More recent technologies have smoothed the process of communication via technology. Internationally, many people use Skype for a cheap and easy audio and video link. At the top end, Cisco Systems has developed TelePresence which can link people in virtual reality environments around the world in a way that gives the look and even the feel of face-to-face communication. Real time sharing of documents, high quality video, and so on, are all valuable aids to virtual communication. All of the major texts on GVTs contain advice on the use of technology (see, for example, Lipnack and Stamps 2000; Nemiro et al. 2008a; Nemiro 2004;).

A comprehensive study of virtual teaming at Intel found that one of the biggest barriers to effective team functioning was the use of different ICTs and work practices. They concluded that:

> team distribution alone, e.g., collaborating with people in different time zones or who speak different native languages, is not perceived to have a significant influence on team performance in Intel. However, members of teams who perceive greater variety in work practices also perceive significant negative influences on a number of aspects of performance, including communication, trust in team members, and the ability to meet commitments and complete projects on time.
>
> (Lu et al. 2006: 5)

The role of the coach here would mainly be to ask questions around current practice – to raise awareness in the action learning mode. If there were problems, the coaching task would be to get team members to seek out information about technologies that might help them to be more efficient in collaboration and performance. They would then be given opportunities to explore options and implement approaches that worked in their context. An informed coach might also make suggestions based on other successful ICT solutions.

An outside coach might be very useful in asking the questions about technology that in-group GVT team members may not be able to ask. A 'friendly outsider' view might be very valuable when a single-minded leader of a GVT is driving the technological direction and may have 'lost the woods for the trees' (or the network for the cables). A friendly outsider might notice that a GVT is getting tangled in a technological web and could generate a discussion with a challenge such as, 'On a scale of 1 to 10, how effective is your current way of working across distance via technology?' The GVT might then have a window to discuss other ways of communicating that are contextually appropriate.

COMMON PURPOSE

Effective GVTs require an articulated common purpose to engender motivation and action. Lipnack and Stamps (2000: 82) suggest that a common purpose holds groups together. For virtual teams, the consequence of an articulated purpose can be a better focus on tasks – work progressing from goals to results. The articulation of purpose will reflect the nature of the team itself. Edwards and Wilson (2004) identify three kinds of GVTs – service, project and process. Service teams are set up by organizations to monitor and maintain some kind of service. A global information technology expert support team is a good example. Project teams have set objectives – such as the team of writers putting together this *Companion to International Business Coaching*. A process team is more concerned with running an ongoing element of business. A team of country managers responsible for the ongoing sales of a product line (say a motor vehicle) is an example.

No matter how small or large the task, early and focused attention is needed to ensure a shared understanding of why the group of people is working together. That nature of the task will have a strong impact on how a GVT is managed and the development of appropriate structures and processes.

A coaching approach (by a manager, external/internal coach, facilitator, etc.) can be to generate conversations about purpose quite early in the establishment process – preferably face-to-face. This may happen at various levels. At a team level, a coach may facilitate an exploration of the common purpose through task articulation and conceptualize to encourage shared meanings. Individually, coaching conversations might go deeper in looking at a leader or team member's broader purposes in work and life and examining connections with the GVT purpose.

TRUST

All of the literature on GVTs emphasizes that trust is an essential element of effective GVT functioning. Nemiro et al. point to a dilemma: 'Virtual teams depend on trust but find it more difficult to develop' (Nemiro et al. 2008b: 9). Various studies have found that trust reduces the need to document and formalize every aspect of work or to impose checks which slows down activity. Increased trust allows for work to be organized more quickly, with more creativity and more belief. When things go wrong, it allows higher levels of empathy in tackling cooperational problems (for further studies relating to trust in virtual teams refer to Crossman and Lee-Kelley 2004; Dani et al. 2006; Greenberg et al. 2007; Rosencrance, 2005; Ross 2006). Lipnack and Stamps conclude that high trust is essential to effective virtual teaming and is dependent upon people's networks and interactions: 'Trust, reciprocity, and networks all are mutually reinforcing, whether on the rise or on the wane. Trust is at the personal core; reciprocity is at the interface; and networks tie it all together' (Lipnack and Stamps 2000: 82).

A study of trust at mobile communications company Orange looked at this issue in one context where levels of trust had dropped (Lawley 2006). More detail is provided in the Orange case study which follows. They used coaching and action learning strategies to build trust and thus GVT effectiveness. They recognized that innovation was born from the quality of conversations that people are able to have and that quality is impacted by difficulties in the level of trust and collaboration (Lawley 2006:17). Face-to-face contact was listed as a key ingredient in trust building. This raises an issue for many GVTs that do not have the luxury of face-to-face contact, thereby requiring other strategies for trust building.

Coaching is a high trust relational process. A trusting relationship between the coach and the client is pivotal in allowing a robust and productive coaching intervention. Coaching approaches within GVTs are therefore likely to build levels of trust and thus enhance performance and satisfaction. Encouraging team members to value respect and to listen with empathy are two strategies that are likely to have impact. Drawing in a cultural perspective, discussions of respect would explore what that word means to different members of the group. Coaches often work with clients to encourage them to have crucial or difficult conversations, drawing on strategies in texts such as Patterson et al. (2002) and Stone et al. (1999). Trust frameworks such as that provided by Solomon and Flores (2001) would be extremely valuable additions to any GVT environment where trust building is seen as desirable. They outline the ingredients and strategies towards building sustainable and authentic trust by way of encouraging calculative risk taking and the keeping of commitments. External coaches or managers working with coaching models can introduce such approaches and have considerable positive impact.

ACTION LEARNING CASE STUDY: THE ORANGE EXPERIENCE

Debbie Lawley (2006), an external consultant, has described a knowledge management (KM) program at the mobile communications company Orange, which followed coaching and action learning approaches to revamp the operations of virtual teams. A summary follows.

By 1999, Orange had grown from its UK base to become a largely pan-European organization with a new owner in France, Telecome, and a presence in Africa and the Middle East. The KM (knowledge management) team was asked to assist the Orange product marketing and development teams in enhancing product delivery and innovation. Most people were working in virtual teams, with teams having established team leaders. The teams were originally instituted as enablers of innovation. However, low trust was causing less than effective cooperation.

The KM approach was to adopt action learning principles, including partnership with the Warwick Business School. Research with virtual team members was done through a questionnaire, reporting and coaching. An action-learning workshop led the intervention, including giving emphasis to the role of informal conversations and early investment in team building. Even so, trust building proved difficult with team members finding it hard to sustain trust without face-to-face contact. The KM team assisted in providing advice on how trust could be built through team design, activities and other approaches. An exhaustive 2004 literature review was accessed from Henley Management College in the UK. This review confirmed that virtual team performance is positively correlated with levels of trust through quicker work organization, higher levels of creativity, more belief, and higher levels of empathy in tackling cooperational problems (Lawley 2006: 13). The KM team summarized the components of trust in virtual teams to include perceived ability, benevolence, and feeling positive about people in the group and the group's integrity.

As a team design intervention, smaller teams were established. The literature and the experience on the ground was that large, dispersed virtual teams (often of 30 or 40 people) did not function well and experienced difficulties in trust and collaboration, or as described by Lawley, 'managing the relationships can be an unwarranted nightmare' (Lawley 2006: 13). They endeavored to keep team sizes to a maximum of ten. They also determined that good leadership was vital to trust development. The initial task of leaders was to draw people away from merely local concerns to identify with broader team and organizational priorities. This was done at initial face-to-face meetings. As noted earlier, the use of face-to-face meetings early in the GVT life cycle is often recommended as a trust-building mechanism, particularly when diversity is high (Ross 2006).

The other key leadership task was to establish a common team framework which was appropriate to the context of the team. They avoided pushing a 'one-size-fits-all' GVT model. Initial strategies included team assessment. One such assessment brought out the fact that British attempts at using humor had a profoundly negative impact on members in Paris, due apparently to the lack of facial expressions and different senses of humor. The Orange experience highlighted the need for leaders and teams to manage a wider range of stakeholders, including the local line managers of the virtual team members. They found that trust was best established early and with people who had been selected due to a higher capacity to trust and for independent working. A common finding was that the team leader should take on the task of establishing, in a purposeful way, the strengths, past successes, roles and responsibilities of team members. This had the effect of swiftly building trust based on personal reputation and credibility.

Workshops were run focusing on collaborative approaches. Trust building was embedded throughout the virtual team processes. It was enhanced through team coaching combined with team assessments and team-building material. A community style of working was encouraged which included sharing stories of best practice. At the time that the report was written, the change process was still in progress. Improvements were beginning to be seen in a shift from a climate described as 'a little bit antagonistic' (Lawley 2006: 17) to a far more up-beat and collaborative environment. Staff surveys revealed much higher levels of satisfaction with working practices. The collaborative working program proved popular and was rolled out from pilot studies in the UK to all operating companies.

A TOOL FOR COACHES: THE ORANGE FRAMEWORK

Orange developed a model for working with virtual teams that is useful for coaches and leaders working with teams more generally. The model is similar in its components to the series of themes identified in this chapter. It is a useful tool for coaches to offer to managers as a way of conceptualizing and teasing out the complexities of the GVT environment.

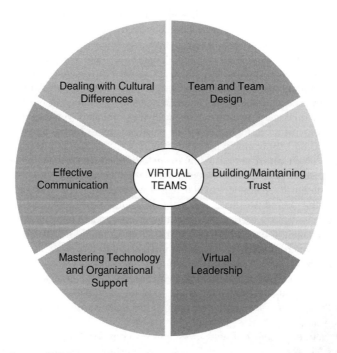

Figure 18.1 The Orange GVT Framework

Source: Lawley (2006)

A coach could work with the GVT leader to design exploration, awareness, action and reflection cycles for each of the segments and also to generate discussion around the interrelation of each. Further, additional segments could be added to the model (or segments removed) to reflect the challenges of the individual GVT.

CONCLUSION: A POSITIVE VIEW OF GVTs

There is great potential for external coaches, as friendly and informed outsiders – carrying theoretical and experiential knowledge – to work in partnership with GVTs in an action learning and action research mode, working from a position of insatiable curiosity to explore and research issues hand-in-hand with team members. External coaches can assist leaders and teams to contextually apply knowledge that has been learned in other situations – as occurred at Orange. Coaches need to build trust-based relationships with the leader(s) and team members, and to inform themselves with knowledge from different GVTs. From this position, they can ask informed questions and facilitate powerful action learning processes in-the-moment and in-the-mode of each unique GVT.

It is important to keep in mind that solutions which work in one context may not work in another, though the general framework for questioning and exploration is likely to be similar. The skill of the external coach working with the leader is to learn through rigorous and structured interventions that are collaboratively conducted with team members. The way in which the coaching is done has to be consistent with the very principles being advanced for effective GVT functioning around cultural sensitivity, high quality communication, articulation of purpose and trust building.

Much of the work with GVTs that is referred to above covers an assumption, perhaps not explicitly, that working in a GVT may somehow be less rewarding or less rich than face-to-face interactions. An assumption in international business coaching is that there are multiple realities, all of which have validity. External coaches can challenge negative dynamics by taking a solution- rather than problem-centered approach. They can encourage the embracing of an alternative assumption or reality regarding GVTs, i.e., working in GVTs offers experiences, opportunities, possibilities and potentials over and above geographically bound work in traditional organizations settings.

By taking GVTs through solution-focused discussion and action learning exercises related to the themes discussed above, leaders and coaches may be able to set the stage for a new GVT, or lift engagement levels and add cohesion in environments where the virtual teaming exercise may be struggling. The attitudes of the leaders and coaches that work with GVTs are going to determine the level of effectiveness of interventions. Positive psychology is informative in this regard. Mihaly Csikszentmihayli, a leading positive psychology and happiness researcher, concludes that happiness and good business go hand in hand: 'It may seem counterintuitive to argue that happiness and business have anything to do with each other, since for most people work is at best a necessary evil, and at worst, a burden. Yet the two are inextricably linked' (Csikszentmihayli 2004: 21). From this perspective, membership of a GVT should not be viewed as a necessarily evil but a possibility to find engagement, meaning, purpose and happiness. Similarly, a possibilities approach to GVTs is consistent with recent appreciative inquiry change processes, defined by Cooperrider and Whitney as, 'the cooperative, co-evolutionary search for the best in people, their organizations, and the world around them. It involves the systematic discovery of what gives life to an organization or a community when it is most effective and most capable in economic, ecological, and human terms' (Cooperrider and

Whitney 2005: 8). Solution-focused coaching approaches can help build richness and meaning in GVT community life through questioning around, 'What is possible?', and 'What is important?' and viewing everything as a gift.

Global virtual teams are real and their use will expand. Their use enables companies to address complex global issues in manageable ways. This form of collaborative working has great possibilities if done with due attention to the people involved. Coaching in various forms – including the use of the 'friendly outsider' – may help to foster collaboration, happiness, meaning and purpose in GVTs and in so doing, make a contribution to global society.

The virtual world of work is complex, uncertain and ambiguous. Paradoxically, working in a GVT creates further complexity and challenges. All the challenges of locally bound work are there – and then some. Leading such teams has added complexity but also the possibility of great reward. In the pace and pressure, there is a risk of individuals and teams becoming alienated and disconnected from each other and also their organizations and even societies. Friendly outsiders can help. Often, an outsider can see things that are blind to insiders – such as important themes, events, trends and relational issues. Kevin Rudd, the Australian Prime Minister, went back to the seventh century Chinese Tang dynasty to introduce the concept of Australia being a 'true friend' of China. In his speech to students in Beijing, Rudd was reported as saying, 'A true friend is one who can be a *zhengyou*, a partner who sees beyond immediate benefit' and who can 'engage in a direct, frank and ongoing dialogue about our fundamental interests and future vision' (*Sydney Morning Herald*, 12 April 2008). A *zhengyou* acts as a mirror – reflecting the good and the bad. GVTs can make use of friendly outsiders – their *zhengyous* – to support leaders in maximizing advantage from culture, communicating within and without, focusing on vision and purpose and to maintain powerful and trusting relationships.

Bibliography

Abbott, G. N. and Grant, A. M. (2005) 'Evidence-based executive coaching and action research: A natural fit', in I. F. Stein, F. Campone and L. J. Page (eds), *Proceedings of the Second ICF Coaching Research Symposium: November 3, 2004, Quebec City, Canada*. Washington, DC: International Coach Federation.

Abbott, G. N. and Rosinski, P. (2007) 'Global coaching and evidence based coaching: Multiple perspectives operating in a process of pragmatic humanism', *International Journal of Evidence Based Coaching and Mentoring*, 5: 58–77.

Bethanis, S. J. (2004) *Leadership Chronicles of a Corporate Sage: Five Keys to Becoming a More Effective Leader*, Chicago: Dearborn Trade Publishing.

Block, P. (2000) *Flawless Consulting: A Guide to Getting Your Expertise Used*, New York: Jossey-Bass/Pfeiffer.

Brake, T. (2006) 'Leading global virtual teams', *Industrial and Commercial Training*, 38: 116–21.

Combs, W. and Peacocke, S. (2007) 'Leading virtual teams', *T&D*, February 2007: 27–8.

Cooperrider, D. L. and Whitney, D. (2005) *Appreciate Inquiry: A Positive Revolution in Change*, San Francisco: Berrett-Koehler Publishers Inc.

Crossman, A. and Lee-Kelley, L. (2004) 'Trust, commitment and team working: The paradox of virtual organizations', *Global Networks*, 4: 375–90.

Csikszentmihayli, M. (2004) *Good Business: Leadership, Flow, and the Making of Meaning*, London: Penguin Books.

Dani, S. S., Burns, N. D., Backhouse, C. J. and Kochhar, A. (2006) 'The implications of organizational culture and trust in the working of virtual teams', *Journal of Engineering Manufacture*, 220b: 951–60.

Dewar, T. (2006) 'Virtual teams: Virtually impossible?', *Performance Improvement*, 45 (4): 22–6.

Edwards, A. and Wilson, J. R. (2004) *Implementing Virtual Teams: A Guide to Organizational and Human Factors*, Aldershot: Gower Publishing.

Elron, E. and Vigoda-Gadot, E. (2006) 'Influence and political processes in cyberspace: The case of global virtual teams', *International Journal of Cross Cultural Management*, 6: 295–317.

Goleman, D. (2000) 'Leadership that gets results', *Harvard Business Review*, March/April 2000: 78–90.

Grant, A. M. and Stober, D. R. (2006) 'Introduction', in D.R. Stober and A.M. Grant, (eds), *Evidence Based Coaching Handbook: Putting Best Practices to Work for Your Clients*, Hoboken: John Wiley & Sons Inc.

Greenberg, P. S., Greenberg, R. H. and Antonucci, Y. L. (2007) 'Creating and sustaining trust in virtual teams', *Business Horizons*, 50: 325–33.

Greene, J. and Grant, A. M. (2003) *Solution-Focused Coaching: A Manager's Guide to Getting the Best from People*, London: Pearson Education Limited.

Greenwood, D. J. and Levin, M. (1998) *Introduction to Action Research: Social Research for Social Change*, London: Sage.

Grove, C. and Hallowell, W. (1998) 'Spinning your wheels? 'Successful global teams know how to gain traction', *HR Magazine Focus*, 43 (5): 24–8.

Kirkman, B. L. (2004) 'The impact of team empowerment on virtual team performance: The moderating role of face-to-face interaction', *Academy of Management Journal*, 47: 175–92.

Lawley, D. (2006) 'Creating trust in virtual teams at Orange: Overcoming barriers to collaboration', *KM Review*, 9: 12–17.

Lewin, K. (1946) 'Action research and minority problems', *Journal of Social Issues*, 2: 34–46.

Lipnack, J. and Stamps, J. (2000) *Virtual Teams: People Working across Boundaries with Technology*, Toronto: John Wiley & Sons Inc.

Lu, M., Watson-Manheim, M. B., Chudoba, K. M. and Wynn, E. (2006) 'Virtuality and team performance: Understanding the impact of variety of practices', *Journal of Global Information Technology Management*, 9: 4–23.

MacPhail, J. (2007) 'Virtual teams: Secrets of a successful long-distance research relationship: A Canadian perspective', *Annals of Family Medicine*, 5: 568–9.

Nemiro, J. E. (2004) *Creativity in Virtual Teams: Key Components for Success*, San Francisco: Pfeiffer.

Nemiro, J. E., Beyerlein, M., Bradley, L. and Beyerlein, S. (eds) (2008a) *The Handbook of High-Performance Virtual Teams*, San Francisco: Jossey-Bass.

Nemiro, J. E., Bradley, L., Beyerlein, M. and Beyerlein, S. (2008b) 'The challenges of virtual teaming', in J.E. Nemiro, L. Bradley, M.Beyerlein, and S. Beyerlein, (eds), *The Handbook of High-Performance Virtual Teams: A Toolkit for Collaboration across Boundaries*, San Francisco: Jossey-Bass.

Patterson, K., Grenny, J., McMillan, R. and Switzler, A. (2002) *Crucial Conversations: Tools for Talking when Stakes are High*, New York: McGraw-Hill.

Rosencrance, L. (2005) 'Meet me in cyberspace', *Computerworld*, 21 February 2005: 23–4.

Rosinski, P. (2003) *Coaching across Cultures: New Tools for Leveraging National, Corporate and Professional Differences*, London: Nicholas Brealey Publishing.

Ross, J. A. (2006) 'Trust makes the team go "round" ', *Harvard Management Update*, June 2006: 1–6.

Seligman, M. E. P. and Csikszentmihayli, M. (2000) 'Positive psychology: An introduction', *American Psychologist*, 55: 5–14.

Solomon, R. C. and Flores, F. (2001) *Building Trust in Business, Politics, Relationships, and Life*, New York: Oxford University Press.

Stober, D. R. and Grant, A. M. (2006) 'Towards a contextual approach to coaching models', in D.R. Stober, and A.M. Grant (eds), *Evidence Based Coaching Handbook: Putting Best Practices to Work for Your Clients*, Hoboken: John Wiley & Sons Inc.

Stone, D., Patton, B. and Heen, S. (1999) *Difficult Conversations: How to Discuss What Matters Most*, New York: Penguin.

19

INTERACTIVE COACHING WITH CORPORATE VENTURES

Jean-Marc Loeser and Katrina Burrus

BIG, STRONG . . . AND FAST: THE SEARCH FOR AGILITY

In today's turbulent and unpredictable environment, traditional 'linear' approaches to change management are losing in efficiency and relevance and many organizations acknowledge that the nature of the context in which they operate requires new models of organizational flexibility. Creating a separate entity with a mandate to innovate is a way to foster and develop an entrepreneurial spirit which can help tackle such a challenge. We refer to such a *structure* (or 'in-group') inside a corporation (also called matrix or 'out-group') – as a 'corporate venture'. We term the *process* of developing and operating a corporate venture as 'internal corporate venturing' (ICV). Many examples of such hybrid structures exist, including action labs (cross-company projects giving people large amounts of power, and time with permission to be creative and to challenge the status quo), or skunk works (small and loosely structured units or subsidiaries, often undertaken in quasi-secret, and operating completely independently until the innovation is ready for commercialization). The *individuals* who drive and thrive in these structures and processes we term 'corporate venturers'. Coaching with corporate venturers is the focus of this chapter.

Internal corporate venturers are risk takers and opportunity seekers, and ideal catalysts of change. Their innovative skills and knowledge can fuse with broader organizational firepower and facilitate the emergence of a group capacity to innovate. From a practical standpoint, the corporate venture operates as a self-contained entity, which bypasses the bureaucratic, time-consuming planning practices of most large organizations, and thus makes possible a rapid reaction to shifts in the external (global) business environment which by nature has become unpredictable. ICV encourages the break-away from established norms, values, standards and practices. It relies, at the extreme, on:

- Individual leadership rather than hierarchical authority;
- Intuition rather than strategic planning; and
- Adaptability and creativity rather than operational compliance.

Our assumption is that the success of the corporate venture resides in the successful interpersonal interaction between the various parties to the venture, and that – given its hybrid nature – the intervention of an external coach is more relevant to supporting the process than some semi-hierarchical mentoring from the out-group. Our purpose is to explore here the key stages for the deployment of ICV inside the large corporation, and the resulting key drivers of a coach's intervention to successfully develop the corporate venture and leverage its contribution to the out-group.

ICV AS A CHANGE STRATEGY

Change dynamics

ICV leads organizations to proactively create a 'laboratory' where changes and challenges for the wider organization can be mapped. It opens up the exploration of new territories – both uncomfortable and unpredictable – where new modalities have to be designed, and provides a hands-on practice ground for the related skills to staff and managers involved. Such a gradual cultural transformation requires seeing the opportunity in any change situation, and accepting taking the risks that go with it.

Seminal work on ICV has concluded that such initiatives are often developed deep in the hierarchy with an in-group operating 'at the coal face', and subsequently given impetus by the out-group, resulting in a three-stage process (Burgelman 1983; Burgelman and Sayles 1988; Basso 2004; Govindarajan and Trimble 2005):

1   Forget – during the creation of the venture, the in-group is expected to 'forget', to or break away from the out-group's values and norms, in order to create its own sense of purpose. It is an individual cognitive process where rational strategic planning is often replaced by the corporate venturer's intuitive developments. The entrepreneurial strategy has therefore been described as, 'seeing rather than thinking' (Mintzberg et al. 1998: 259);

2   Borrow – when stabilizing the corporate venture, the in-group should 'borrow', i.e. leverage on the out-group's existing resources and structures – in order to establish its domination. This is a relational process where 'top-down' execution is replaced by a collaborative construction of the strategic deployment. ICV thus offers a modality which leaves an opening for idea generation and learning from the field rather than a prescribed approach to change. It is a step-by-step approach which encourages constructed change, or the 'bottom-up' design of change initiatives, providing for the early involvement of a large number of players; and

3   Learn – when the corporate venture reaches operational maturity, our focus is to study how the out-group can 'learn' from the in-group. Provided the corporate venture has reached its own legitimacy – the role it plays and which is accepted by the out-group – ICV is not simply a tactical modality, but also a potential vehicle for change management. It is a systemic problem-solving and innovating mechanism which fosters the development of regular and collective practices for organizational learning.

ICV is therefore a practical framework for a flexible dispersed change process. It potentially influences the change strategy in three ways:

1   From implementation to anticipation – ICV allows organizations to be trained to constantly monitor change patterns in their environment, and develop a sense of flexibility

and 'collective play' which enables them to rapidly adjust configurations (processes, behaviors, systems) in response to external discontinuities and opportunities;

2 From constraint to construction – ICV shifts the spatial design of change management from a perspective of dealing with administration and structures to a focus on groups and processes, allowing global businesses to address fragmented geographies with different local contexts; and

3 From analysis to (re)action – change is no longer 'implemented' or 'driven' in the ICV model but in many cases 'dealt with'. It thus better addresses the increasing number and visibility of stakeholders – traditional (customers, financial shareholders, employees, etc.) or emerging (environment protection, corporate governance, etc.) – which have transformed change management from a deterministic concept to the enactment of the best operational trade-off between situational contingencies and strategic choices.

Intervention framework

ICV can on one hand be considered as an essentially managerial and corporate process, with the coach working first and foremost for the larger organization. On the other hand, we can look at it as an individual and relational process with organizational consequences. From this viewpoint, the change process will concern an awareness of alternative behaviors, cognitive mechanisms and values, and is then open to a coaching intervention. The overall intervention process is then best positioned away from a mechanistic (and often management-driven) expert intervention, geared at delivering 'value' or 'performance' and on a continuum towards a relational posture, with three basic requirements (Heckscher, Maccoby, Ramirez and Tixier 2003):

1 It is socio-dynamic; i.e. it acknowledges the fact that group identities and memories produce resistances and 'irrational' behaviors;

2 It is interactive; consultants must work with the clients in helping them define their own problems and develop their capacities for dialogue and problem-solving; and

3 It is systemic; crossing all the major divides among stakeholders.

In other words, the coach's role in the corporate venture is to develop 'clock builders' with a contribution to an overall visionary organization, rather than 'time tellers' with a single individual vision (Collins and Porras 1994). Its overall framework is summarized in Figure 19.1.

PRESENT STATE	TRANSITION	DESIRED FUTURE
Hierarchical Authority Operational Compliance HQ's values and norms	Risk/Opportunity Reactivity to Change Particularism vs Universalism Trial & error vs Determinism	• **FORGET**: revamped Leadership: vision; intuition, adaptability ... • **BORROW**: Collaborative construction with HQ • **LEARN**: Improved Organization

Figure 19.1 The Coaching Framework

284

Searching for purpose

The creation of the corporate venture requires that the in-group define its purpose, i.e. its contextual role and meaning. This will include offering a shared visibility on its objectives, its environment and its strategic (and possibly operational) alignment to the out-group. In a rationalist approach; the typical deliverable would be a strategic business plan. In the ICV model, however, a loosely formulated plan can provide the initial structure for a corporate venturer's desired future and intuitive developments. The entrepreneur's vision replaces the chartered plan: it is a mental image of a possible and desirable future state of the organization; it operates on the individual emotional and cognitive resources of its constituents (values, commitment, aspirations, and so on) rather than on its physical resources (such as capital, human skills, and technology).

The out-group, on the other hand, is likely to rely on its legitimacy and on an historic continuity of purpose and operation ('We've always done it this way'). Such an attitude will be reinforced by avoidance or denial of the challenge confronted by the corporate venture ('Why do we need this anyway?'), and will lead it to either ignore or strongly criticize the initiative ('This is a waste of money, energy and my time!'). In other words, the in-group's dilemma can be defined as belonging vs achieving. For example, there may be a conflict between a predefined corporate strategy and the immediate situation of the ICV in the field. In order to successfully create team cohesion and purpose, the internal corporate venturer must make sure he or she is outward-looking, beyond the larger organization into the processes and forces at work in the external environment, while at the same time keeping channels open with the organization so that the work of the corporate venture is not blocked. This balancing act means that internal corporate venturers are often operating on the brink of what the headquarters will tolerate.

Coaching to 'forget'

We shall illustrate the coaching approach with the case of 'Peter', general manager of a multinational consumer product company.

> In Peter's case, the coaching process was instrumental in accelerating the development of a purpose, and a plan that integrated the vision, values, intuitions and meaning for both the venturer and the corporate venture. Instead of the linear framework outlined above, 'creative tension' (Senge 1994: 150–2) – energy for change – was generated from the interplay between the 'vision' of what Peter wanted to obtain and the truth about the 'current reality' in the in-group and out-group. The coach's role was to tap into the ICV's intrinsic motivation for change and hold a picture of what might be, making it more compelling to Peter than the present state. It also was to accompany Peter between the images of a 'present state' and of a 'desired future', and to support the corporate venture in a creative trial and error process during the transition:
>
> Coach: What do you think and feel about the opportunities and challenges of your new role in your company?
> Peter: I have just taken over the position of general manager in Hong Kong, Asia. I came from headquarters where everything seemed heavy, slow and laborious. Taking care of a subsidiary leaves me with a feeling of lightness. It is exhilarating. I know I am a high potential and selected to take the 'C' suite position of my multinational company in the next few

years, but I am not sure I want it. Being general manager away from headquarters and responsible for a country, I have a direct impact on the business. I am learning so much.

Peter is so excited by the newfound freedom and space to create that he wants to further separate from the out-group. He is expressing his sense of freedom in a separate entity. At this point, he is ready to forgo his next promotion for the pleasure of being a corporate venturer. Coaching can help channel this enthusiastic energy into a personal and intuitive plan.

Coach: For the next two to three years that you will be posted here, what do you want to contribute to the organization? What will be your legacy? How do you see the people in your organization developing? What behaviors/commitments do they portray?
Peter: (pauses, then answers enthusiastically) I want the company to increase market performance by changing employees' focus from being inward looking to being client oriented. My team's mindset is focused on what headquarters want and not on what the client wants. My objective is to have employees in the Hong Kong affiliate reconnect with consumers and pay less attention to what HQ would think.

These types of coaching questions are aimed at projecting Peter into the desired future. The corporate venture is moving away from an historical business model and established standards of business performance, all of which are probably reinforced by a solidly rooted culture. The corporate venture leader is expected early on to part with what was most likely his or her traditional toolbox. In ICV detailed analysis and forecasting are unavailable, execution cannot be formalized in carefully sequenced steps, and critical decision making is a lot more than a mere allocation of resources. Ultimately, the overall process borrows more inspiration from guerrilla warfare than from Roman legions.

As we have seen, one of the coach's key roles is also to monitor this potential dichotomy between the corporate venturer and his or her boss(es) at headquarters. In Peter's case, this relationship was discussed with Peter and his direct supervisor 'Sam':

Coach: How do you handle the possible contradictions between headquarters and the field?
Sam: When I feel strongly about representing the field, I argue it out passionately at headquarters.
Peter: My people have to be totally customer oriented and disregard what the bosses at headquarters want.

The coach can thus serve as a sounding board to develop the corporate venturer's purpose and to help him or her feel less constrained by the out-group ('forget'). Meanwhile, the coach can also help Peter balance his desire to create a team of corporate venturers with the interest of a collaborative relationship with the out-group which will provide resources and deter resistance (see 'Borrow' below). Maintaining a bond with headquarters also later enhances the transfer of learning from the corporate venture to headquarters (see 'Learn' below). While very sequential in theory, these stages are much more intertwined in actual facts. In Peter's case, a borrowing/learning process helped dissipate some apprehension when taking on his new role:

Coach: How are you going to tackle this position?
Peter: I don't know exactly how I am but I am asking key leaders that have been in my or similar positions what I need to be aware of.

Peter, with a sharp intellect and charismatic personality, could tap into the organization's knowledge. The learning from his network and the reflection time during the coaching process accelerated the transition from initial apprehension of finding himself in a totally new position to developing his purpose more rapidly. He leveraged the knowledge within his organization by actively interviewing leaders with experience of the field and headquarters and by maintaining a network of mentors.

At the same time, if the corporate venture cannot leave behind the out-group's formula for success, it will not find its own. The coach supports Peter to 'forget' the relative predictability of its earlier environment, and the only way to erase memory is to overhaul its organizational design. Such a process implies breaking from the values, norms and habits of the out-group and creating its own frame of reference. This, in turn, implies overcoming the fear of loss associated with a functional and possibly physical separation from the matrix, and the fear of failure associated with such a novel enterprise at its inception.

ICV is dependent on an initial intuitive balance between a risk-taking action and the associated potential retribution. The corporate venturer is usually driven by a higher-than-average need for achievement, and has an opportunity-focused, results-driven and self-motivated personality. He or she will work collaboratively but expect flexibility, autonomy, and rewards commensurate with the level of responsibility being undertaken and the results being achieved.

In Peter's case, personal visions integrating these strategic focuses can be exemplified by any of the following quotes:

> My legacy would be based on making the organization consumer-focused, helping employees transition from being inward looking and conforming to bosses' opinions within the matrix – to the detriment of consumers' interests – to integrating consumer feedback.
>
> We need to legitimize innovation and make it relevant by putting it in front of our door. I'd like our business unit to create successful, innovative, new products from customer feedback, rather than incremental changes of existing products instigated from within the company. Further on, I'd like to borrow this innovative mindset from the in-group and use it as a catalyst for more 'out-of-the-box' thinking in other categories and services.
>
> We have to develop local talent. Instead of being top-down and instruction-driven, we need to have local personnel holding key positions first within the in-group and then within the organization at large.

Although these desired achievements and opportunities are typical of many consumer companies, it is in the transition period within discontinuous change that the art of the corporate venturer is at play. A coach can be a sparring partner with the client as to how it can be done, what are the probable challenges and how to overcome them, while, above all, holding to the corporate venturer's compelling vision.

At a team level, the in-group has to develop a degree of cohesion between team members which supports their creative assignment, i.e. constructively designing plans and solving problems, without trying to avoid embarrassing issues (Moingeon 2004). Orientations towards short-term stability and predictability will thus migrate to risk-taking and opportunity-focus during the creation of the corporate venture. The coach thus will work with the group in order to revisit and reframe previous goals, roles and loyalties in the organization. Meta-communication on how their representations motivate their behaviors to satisfy needs or solve problems will allow team members to privilege innovative and creative developments, e.g. by dealing with the anxiety resulting from a necessary initial ambiguity (which may lead to sticking to established practices), or increasing tolerance for uncertainty on doubt and tasks, roles or procedures, which otherwise lay the ground for interpersonal friction and defensive behavior. This can be facilitated by (Basso 2005):

1   Legitimizing new viewpoints, trial balloons, tactical shifts and partial solutions and creating broad support to such initiatives, including championing, visible symbolic change actions, and overcoming opposition;
2   Catalyzing 'the normality of change', i.e. the fact that the only way a dynamic social system can survive is to generate new ideas, behaviors and patterns. Recognizing strategy as a non-linear, on-going process and institutionalizing change, i.e. seeing it as a permanent factor of improvement; and
3   Monitoring the 'permeability' of the out-group, i.e. the nature of its reactive adjustments in terms of structures, processes or systems and how much it allows an operational margin for complexity. This degree of tolerance for 'deviants' and rule-bending (as opposed to rule-breaking) will decide whether the corporate venturer runs into a wall and wastes physical and psychological energy. It will prove crucial in practical terms when reaching the 'Borrow' stage described in the following chapter.

STABILIZATION OF THE CORPORATE VENTURE

Networking for domination

The stabilization of the corporate venture requires the in-group to achieve domination, or a time-effective control of its operational resources. As the corporate venture does not have a large operational footprint yet, it must 'Borrow' what the out-group can provide: navigational guidance (i.e. information, 'sanity checks' on strategic alignment) and operational support in terms of people and services (e.g. staff, facilities, IT).

Peter was described by a member of the multinational's executive team as, 'a high-potential and therefore, closely monitored and visible to headquarters'. The coach can ensure that the corporate venturer maintains communication with headquarters by maintaining a link with key stakeholders throughout the corporate venture's process. Networking into the matrix will indeed be the in-group's operative modality for ensuring its successful development. It will foster organizational flexibility, collective responsibility and the development of emergent collaboration. This is a delicate transitional stage, which relies on an adequate understanding of the corporate venture's purpose and objectives and as such leverages on the work done at the previous stage (see above).

The requirement – along the lines of many cross-functional collaboration and project management examples – is here for both groups to integrate a large diversity of interests and perspectives, and work towards joint ownership of mutually agreed solutions. It will also lay the foundation for a viral mode of dissemination. Multidisciplinary teams will offer a framework for integrative knowledge-sharing, possibly the most intensive and valuable route to both individual and organizational learning (see below) in today's organizations.

The in-group must be aware of its impact (in terms of operations and information) on the out-group, as it channels new challenges into it, and balance its requirement of 'Forgetting' with its need of 'Borrowing', i.e. rely on the out-group only when it can gain a decisive competitive advantage. Incremental cost reductions, in particular, are never sufficient justifications for borrowing.

In the out-group, risk will most likely be managed by committing resources in a stepwise manner, continually monitoring the progress of the corporate venture, and being ready to reduce the resources allocated at the first sign of deviation. Resistance to support the in-group may develop, triggered by a fear of chaos or of the unknown. Yet, there are potential pitfalls in merely trying to keep key stakeholders in head offices informed of events and of eventual difficulties as they arise:

> *Coach:* How will you maintain your own focus and not merely attempt to comply with headquarters' pressure or demands?
>
> *Peter:* I will have key stakeholders at headquarters come out to us and spend a day sorting out our differences. This is much more effective than continually going to headquarters to maintain contact and communication.

Domination is a matter of being 'street-smart', rather than creative or analytical intelligence. When the corporate venture starts taking off, it is expected to leverage on the functional and operational systems of the out-group. The corporate venture has to 'manage the outside' and overcome the development of 'us vs them' situations, which otherwise lead to a collective under-structuring – detrimental to the in-group's stabilization in the short term and to the creation of a meta-culture for the out-group in the long term. Essentially, both groups share the dilemma of cooperation vs competition.

In Peter's case, this showed in both wanting to compete with the out-group for key talent, while cooperating with headquarters for product innovations needed by the corporate venture:

> Headquarters is currently launching new products and I want to use this as a catalyst for more innovative thinking in other categories and services. The initiatives in other markets are happening in different product categories and we will use these developments to stimulate our own thinking by opening up our organization to the voice of the consumer. This might be scary for most of our employees. I need to make my organization comfortable with this period of uncertainty, but also by legitimizing innovation and making it relevant.

Coaching to 'Borrow'

In order to better connect the various parts of the organization, the coach's challenge is here to facilitate the development of a collaborative support by getting the groups to:

- Be explicit about their concerns and issues (advocating) and explore each other's interests (inquiring);
- Tolerate the diversity of their power and/or resources (including information and know-how), and possibly the conflicting nature of their interests; and
- Accept the complexity of ill-defined problems and overcome, where possible, adversarial relationships (e.g. by defining appropriate 'rewards' to the out-group for the corporate venture's success).

Practical barriers may include stereotyping from either party, a high-level practice differentiation and – often – lack of information. Shared, unconsciously held, or basic assumptions (Bion 1961) will also prevent either group from engaging effectively in the borrowing process. Potential difficulties can arise from dependence on the corporate venturer inside the corporate venture, or 'fight-flight' attitudes in the out-group if it perceives the corporate venture as a threat (e.g. in terms of cannibalization of its existing business or assets). Such situations of uncertainty and anxiety typically lead to a search for status quo by the out-group (still perceived as dominant or privileged), and formal or informal pressure on resources. These include economic (including information), but also social, e.g. authority (rule-making) or the threat of ostracism.

Failing to acknowledge the diversity of interests and perspectives will usually result in response in terms of denial ('forcing' cohesion) or segregation (clustering people into more homogeneous categories) and will see the parties running for a common ground which allows them to escape confrontation. A classic avoidance is a 'coordination' that assigns tasks to sub-groups, where more time is spent looking for agreements (deal-making) than sharing perspectives. Rather, the coach should ensure that diversity is recognized, and trust developed so that members are emotionally free to be open about themselves and share appreciation (Vansina and Taillieu 1997). Only then can the proverbial common ground (or the ideal state of 'superordinate' goals) be dealt with.

Other forms of defensive reasoning should be addressed by raising the group members' awareness of their ladder of inference, or how context, assumptions and values lead them – all the more under threatening situations – to draw conclusions and take actions based on the interpretation of selected data (Putnam 1999). Naturally, the corporate venturer remains at the heart of this inter-group process. He or she can usefully work with the coach at:

- Reviewing interests and values of the various parties to the networking process, and monitoring the early impact of his initiatives on the out-group;
- Evaluating the 'viral' progress of the corporate venture so far (its strengths and weaknesses), and outline a plan of work for improving the inter-group overall performance; and
- Taking a personal step back from the corporate venture and assessing its overall consistence with other aspects of life, thereby balancing the significance of the ICV initiative with other constituents of the corporate venturer's identity and perceived self-worth.

It is essential for the corporate venturer to be able to smoothly 'let go' of the corporate venture. The challenge is to achieve a balance between commitment and distance at the 'Learn' stage described in the following chapter (Basso 2005).

To this end, the coaching process will naturally help the corporate venturer to take a distance and see what the corporate venture represents to the organization at large, and subsequently envision its next challenge:

> *Coach:* How do you see your organization's role and contribution to the matrix in the future?
>
> *Peter:* My vision for Hong-Kong is that we become a breeding ground and a talent pool for future leaders in our company. Although a small team, all the right ingredients are present today to achieve this goal. Hong-Kong has an excellent education system, a very strong, achievement-oriented mentality in society, and we can provide many opportunities for talent to develop multifunctional skills across business functions. It is my objective for the coming years that local Hong-Kong talent will become recognized by HQ and will be given opportunities to take up leadership positions outside.

MATURITY OF THE CORPORATE VENTURE

Reaching legitimacy

The maturity and legitimacy of the corporate venture signal its ability to balance creativity and subject mastery, and start to 'Learn'. This process takes place at two levels:

1 Within the in-group, as it discovers new ways of engaging into its future. This learning phase will serve to simplify processes, analyze actions through a new lens, and focus on resolving unknowns; and
2 Within the out-group, as it engages into intellectual cross-pollination, internalizes the practices and behaviors of the corporate venture and, having developed self-enabling and self-correcting models, performs rapid, rigorous and candid analysis of disparities between their predictions and outcome.

In this second aspect, ICV becomes a modality for organizational learning, and builds into the out-group a mindset that sustains more flexibility to continuous adaptation. Change and ambiguity then become accepted as features of the operating environment, and in a cyclical fashion, the organization is constantly ready to reassess its competitive environment and adapt to its next challenge.

From this standpoint, the groups' dilemma can be defined as blending-in vs breaking-out. For the in-group, which has acquired a new set of perspectives and practices, it means overcoming the temptation to avoid its parent organization, or deny the benefits and interest of knowledge sharing ('It will be wasted, these guys don't understand us'). For the out-group, it implies going beyond its own fear of loss of an 'old' system and of failure in a 'new' one. Anxieties over judgment, complexity, ownership of ideas and recognition may lead both groups at this stage to over-structuring and entrenched power.

Dealing with these paradoxes is essential to the development of a learning culture inside the out-group. Whatever the corporate venture has to offer in terms of operational know-how will be useless if there is no 'attention' being paid (or desire to improve) inside the rest of the organization, or if there is no formal or informal feedback mechanism.

Coaching to 'learn'

As a consequence, while the intervention's process will keep an inter-group scope, its objective is now to facilitate the out-group's learning of the in-group's experience. Peter, for example, is being groomed to take on a leading executive position at headquarters of this multinational. The learning from the corporate venture will naturally be transferred to headquarters when he will be reassigned there. The question, however, remains whether he will be satisfied as a leader in a more mature and regulated environment, whether he will be able to leverage high entrepreneurial spirit durably in that context, and for how long.

Such a dissemination of knowledge cannot efficiently rely on 'combination', or the formal passing of codified explicit knowledge, but rather needs to be built around three other modes (Nonaka and Takeuchi 1995):

1 Internalization – or 'learning by doing'; taking explicit knowledge back to tacit form;

2 Socialization – or sharing of 'implicit' (tacit) knowledge, e.g. through common experience; and

3 Externalization – or converting tacit to 'explicit' (formal) knowledge, e.g. use of intuition, metaphors and analysis.

The essence of such an integrative – or learning – behavior is the capacity to exercise one's curiosity, and to derive positive satisfactions from the expression of one's skills and powers. In other words, significant learning will occur in situations where the 'learner' defines the problem. Conversely, behavior which would be only directed at reducing anxiety would be adaptive not integrative (for the out-group, this would be engaging in the proverbial 'talk the talk' but not 'walk the talk').

The intervention should thus facilitate the identification of emotions and confusions associated with such a process (and provide appropriate ways of dealing with them); being able to recognize imperfections through appropriate awareness and informal information channels, accepting to learn from failure, designing mechanisms for sharing resources in a rapid and flexible way, sustaining improvement in the organization, or more generally 'doing things right' rather than 'doing the right thing'.

The coach should encourage formal and informal interaction between the groups, and stimulate imitation, diffusion, or cultural borrowing. The in-group should be a resource finder for the out-group, neither offer a carrot or a stick, and rely on the assumption that individuals who are in direct contact with problems and challenges desire to learn, create, master and grow (Rogers 1961).

The coach will lead the out-group to question how productive collective and repetitive strategies and behaviors are, e.g. by clarifying time and energy spent in obtaining 'input' (resources) vs attention paid to 'output' (results). He will also assist the out-group to uncover and alter collective frames of reference ('self-confirming' beliefs) which would hinder the successful interaction with the in-group (Cardon 2003).

In parallel, by correcting misperceptions and limiting the premature seeking of concurrence, the coaching process will minimize the in-group's risk of 'groupthink' (Janis 1982) or 'Nut Island' syndrome (Levy 2001). Under isolation, closed leadership and stress, a dedicated team of self-starters is likely to engage in an 'heroic' struggle for cohesiveness (or zero tolerance for non-conformity) and consensus (bordering self-censorship). Under growing illusions of invulnerability (and morality), the team loses sight of its own failures and flaws and develops a completely biased perception of the out-group.

TOWARDS AN INTERVENTION MODEL

The role of the coach

As mentioned earlier, ICV will require from the coach a systemic intervention with clients tackling the strategic, operational and relational aspects of the creation of an innovative nomadic unit; its operational integration into the rest of the organization, and finally the design of appropriate 'leverage' mechanisms by which the learning gained from successful ventures can rapidly transform processes, structures or behaviors for the future.

It will further rely on an interactive intervention ranging on a continuum from the individual to the group and the organization, a process which can be summarized under a single unifying framework of organizational learning (adapted from Crossan, Lane and White 1999) outlined in Figure 19.2.

Finally, from a socio-dynamic standpoint, the successful ICV process also relies on a clear understanding, in an anthropological sense, of the backgrounds and histories of the organization, so that a form of continuity with the past is acknowledged as a foundation to motivation and meaning.

The persistence of past organizational patterns of group behavior and emotion into the present is too often perceived as 'politics' by consultants providing such processes. It is dealt with through 'facilitated problem solving' or 'win-win' methods, with a strong cognitive focus on the present and the future. It often leads to oversimplifying issues (relations among groups in particular, where the meeting of visible needs may conceal threats to identity and solidarity) and precludes an appropriate reframing of 'irrational' group emotions.

Limitations: transference and counter-transference

As in all coaching interventions, the ICV consultation bears the risk of transference and counter-transference. The major patterns for transference will originate in the fact that organizations (and clients) will tend to make sense of the coach by fitting him or her into a predetermined pattern, or inventing a new one. The coach, wanting to be appreciated, and impatient to accomplish something, is then in danger of slipping into 'counter-transference' by playing into the projections of the parties and acting out roles in the existing system, i.e. not maintaining enough emotional distance with the client's organization and being drawn into the moral universe of one party or another.

There are many ways for resolving transference issues, including supervision (from peers and business partners at entry level), and being explicit about perceived projections to ourselves (idealizing the client, being impatient with inaction) and to others ('I think you are seeing me as some kind of magician').

Introductory language also plays an important aspect in the definition of the change intervention. It should not be intended to 'help' but rather to support a process of client-initiated

Level	Process	Inputs
Individual	Intuiting	Experiences Images/Metaphors
	Interpreting	Cognitive maps Conversation/Dialogue
Group	Integrating	Shared understandings Mutual adjustments
Organization	Institutionalizing	Plans/rules/procedures Values/norms

Figure 19.2 A unifying framework of organizational learning

Source: adapted from Crossan, Lane and White (1997)

changes and the associated autonomy/responsibility which will generate action towards non-feeling based results.

TOOLS FOR INDIVIDUAL AND COLLECTIVE CHANGE

Organizational cultures

An organizational culture encompasses the values and beliefs that have become accepted de facto inside an organization. It is,

> the pattern of basic assumptions that a given group has invented, discovered, or developed in learning to cope with its problems of external adaptation and internal integration, and that have worked well enough to be considered valid and to be taught to new members as the correct way to perceive, think and feel in relation to these problems.
>
> (Schein 1992: 9)

Clearly, the successful dissemination of the learning from ICV is bound to interact with the assumptions and solutions which are considered valid inside the out-group, and also influence and potentially transform the organization's culture going forward. A synthetic overview of culture (Moral 2004) can be applied to the organizational environment and indicate why cultural diversity between the corporate venture and the rest of the organization will play a significant role:

- On the one hand, individualistic cultures are oriented toward action in the present and the future. They are bound to be egalitarian and informal. Tasks are synchronized and defined by goal setting. Communication is factual and direct; and
- On the other hand, collectivist cultures will be more hierarchical and formal, less time focused with a respect for the past. Tasks are sequential and structured, and communication is highly contextual and often indirect.

In collective action, individualistic and collectivist cultures contribute to differentiating organizational values such as sociability (people) and solidarity (task). This classification allows mapping the influence of such values on the wider corporate cultures.

Socio-technical structures

Socio-technical structures reflect how an organization's processes and practices are oriented towards its goals. Working from a general assumption that an organization's structure will primarily develop as an adaptation to its environment, the coach should be aware of how perceptions of the out-group's environment (e.g. in terms of complexity, degree of risk or pace of change, and so on) will lay the foundations for its organization.

In keeping with a systemic approach, we believe that these structures also relate strongly with cultures in the way they influence key drivers such as tasks, roles, power or people. The coach should help the corporate venturer and the in-group to be aware of how these values, manifested in both structures and cultures, thrust or hinder the ICV deployment at its various stages:

- At the creation stage, in determining the autonomy and freedom available for creating the corporate venture. For example, results-oriented cultures will most likely provide a facilitating context for the creation of the corporate venture, while consensus-based cultures will have a hard time seeing a new entity and identity emerge in the organization;
- At the stabilization stage, in determining the ease and efficiency of operational support for the corporate venture. Structures where people and roles are core values may in fact prove to provide more efficient support than other structures; and
- At the maturity stage, in making sure that change 'sticks' to the out-group, rather than taking an institutionalized form of avoidance and selling or 'spinning-off' the corporate venture. Localized structures, where status is not being challenged, may accept the learning of the corporate venture more easily on the basis of its contribution to the group's mission.

Organizational systems

While cultures and structures provide an adequate reading grid for charting the individual and collective dimensions of the ICV process, our systemic approach should use other devices to keep the larger context of the corporate venture on its radar screen. Systems are particularly relevant to the intervention on relational and organizational level. They can be defined as the set of established standards, practices and procedures in place inside a group or an organization, and broken down into four categories (adapted from Simons 2000):

1 *Belief systems* are explicit sets of values, purpose, and direction, including how value is created, level of desired performance, and human relationships. A clear subset of organizational culture, their aim is to provide momentum and guidance to opportunity-seeking behaviors;

2 *Boundary systems* are formally stated rules, limits and proscriptions tied to defined sanctions and credible threat of punishment. Intended for the short-term stability of the organization, they also serve to allow individual creativity within defined limits of freedom;

3 *Interactive systems* are control systems that managers use to involve themselves regularly and personally in the decision activities of subordinates. They are used to focus organizational attention on strategic uncertainties and provoke the emergence of new initiatives and strategies; and

4 *Diagnostic systems* are feedback systems that monitor organizational outcomes and correct deviations from preset standards of performance. Their initial aim is to define goals, allow effective resource allocation and/or corrective action. They turn out to be helpful in providing motivation.

When creating the corporate venture at the 'forget' stage, the creativity expected from the in-group will challenge established belief and boundary systems. At the 'Borrow' stage, when stabilizing the corporate venture, the collaboration required between both groups will leverage on the wider organization's interactive systems. Through learning-by-doing and socialization, it will spread to the out-group the need to challenge the organization's boundary systems. Finally, at the 'Learn' stage, the out-group will also leverage on interactive systems and practices or processes for execution and control will be formally modified (diagnostic systems). This cannot take place efficiently without the corporate venture's purpose and strategy eventually transforming the out-group's collective values and representations.

Along this path, the coach will also monitor and adjust the possibility that these transformations will take place more easily – or are resorted to more frequently – depending on the entities' socio-styles (see above). Groups with a controlling style will for example tend to deal head-on with diagnostic and boundary systems, while facilitating types will spend (and possibly waste) more time 'evangelizing' on belief and interactive systems.

Symbolic management of cultural change

The coach can now participate in a process of viral dissemination of the entrepreneurial mindset, by encouraging the learning by the out-group and coaching more candidates for ICV through the creation and stabilization of their ventures. Change rituals are powerful levers to accelerate this development at a meta-level, and rapidly create cohesion and empower action (adapted from Trice and Beyer 1985: 186). The coach should help the corporate venturer recognize and create these signs of symbolic change – or emulate them from the out-group:

Transition rituals are intended to consolidate or change social roles (passage rituals), recognize priorities and the associated systems of power (renewal rituals), and recognize socially the values of the organization (distinction rituals). They will include:

- At the 'forget' stage, recruiting new skills to reinforce the momentum of the corporate venture (passage), or setting up task forces and appointing consultants, which will signal a shift in the balance of power (renewal); and
- At the 'borrow' and 'learn' stages, awards ceremonies acknowledging the achievements of the corporate venture, and even more so its contribution to the out-group (distinction).

Social rituals will be called for in order to signal public acknowledgement of problems (degradation rituals), maintain balance in social relations or compartmentalize disagreements (conflict reduction rituals) or revive commitment to the organization as a social system (integration rituals). Here are a few practical examples:

- Dismissal of those who – directly or indirectly – undermine the corporate venture, both in the in- and out-groups, will clearly communicate the strategic importance of, and organizational commitment to, the ICV process. While they play a role throughout the process, these rituals are key to establishing new 'rules of engagement' and develop alliances and partnerships at the 'forget' and 'borrow' stages (degradation);
- Not being fully invested in the negotiation and keeping a personal network into the out-group will allow the corporate venturer, at the 'borrow' stage, to provide an appeal system in the integration phase (conflict reduction); and
- Social and business events, such as Christmas parties or performance reviews, will be essential for maintaining social unity between the in- and out- groups, a much-needed action on the environment at the 'learn' stage (integration).

CONCLUSION

Our analysis of the ICV process and the related intervention from a coach has taken three successive angles:

1   *An individual focus* on the corporate venturer and the in-group, where issues and solutions are perceived and intuited. Mental representations and behaviors support the purpose creation and are transformed by the creation of the corporate venture;

2   *A relational focus* on inter-group transactions between the nomadic corporate venture and the matrix, where change issues are shared and collaboratively resolved. Systems (and structures) are transformed by the ICV process, while rituals (and cultures) support the domination of the corporate venture; and

3   *An organizational* focus on the out-group, where solutions for change are designed. Rituals (and cultures) are transformed by the ICV process, while systems (and structures) support the legitimacy of the corporate venture.

The relevance of the process to change management appears when we 'look at the dance, not at the dancer' (Gartner 1988). ICV is a practical contribution towards organizational learning, and offers the advantages of a 'positive deviance' approach to change (Pascale and Sternin 2005):

- It is bottom-up (not top-down). It relies on discovery rather than imposing, and on the practical solving of problems 'in the trenches';
- It is an 'outside-in', as opposed to an (expert-driven) 'inside-out' change and therefore is potentially less vulnerable to transplant rejection; and
- It is asset-based and concrete (i.e. the solution emerges from the group) rather than deficit-based (or resulting from a negative benchmarking to the outside world).

Bibliography

Basso, O. (2004) '*L'intrapreneuriat*', Paris: Economica.

Basso, O. (2005) 'La face obscure de l'intrapreneuriat: Héroïsme et sacrifice de soi dans l'entreprise', *Gestion 2000*, July/August 2005: 179–82.

Bion, W.R. (1961) *Experiences in Groups*, New York: Basic Books.

Burgelman, R. (1983) 'A process model of corporate venturing in the diversified major firm', *Administrative Science Quarterly*, 28(2): 223–44.

Burgelman, R.A. and Sayles, L.R. (1988) *Corporate Innovation: Strategy, Structure and Managerial Skills*, New York: The Free Press.

Cardon, A. (2003) *Le Coaching d'equipe*, Paris: Editions d'Organisation.

Collins, J.C. and Porras, J.I. (1994) *Built to Last*, New York: Harper Collins.

Crossan, M., Lane, H. and White, R. (1999) 'An organizational learning framework: From intuition to institution', *Academy of Management Review*, 24 (3): 522–37.

Gartner, W.B. (1988) ' "Who is an entrepreneur?" is the wrong question', *American Journal of Small Business*, 12 (4): 11–31.

Govindarajan, V. and Trimble, C. (2005) 'Building breakthrough businesses within established organizations', *Harvard Business Review*, May 2005: 58–68.

Heckscher, C., Maccoby, M., Ramirez, R. and Tixier, P. (2003) *Agents of Change: Crossing the Post-Industrial Divide*, Oxford: Oxford University Press.

Janis, I. (1982) 'Psychological studies of policy decisions and fiascos', in D.R. Forsyth, (ed.) (2006) *Group Dynamics* (4th edn), Belmont: Thomson Wadsworth.

Levy, P. (2001) 'When good teams go wrong: The Nut Island effect', *Harvard Business Review*, March 2001: 5–12.

Mintzberg, H., Ahlstrand, B. and Lampel, J. (1998) *Strategy Safari*, Englewood Cliffs, NJ: Prentice-Hall.

Moingeon, B. (2004) 'Le "learning mix": Un modèle pour l'entreprise apprenante', *Les echos l'art du management*, 2: 11.

Moral, M. (2004) *Le manager global*, Paris: Dunod.

Nonaka, I. and Takeuchi, H. (1995) *The Knowledge Creating Company*, Oxford: Oxford University Press.

Pascale, R. and Sternin, J. (2005) 'Your company's secret change agents', *Harvard Business Review*, May 2005: 72–81.

Putnam, R. (1999) 'Transforming social practice: An action science perspective', *Management Learning*, 30 (2): 177–87.

Rogers, C. (1961) *On Becoming a Person: A Therapist's View of Psychotherapy*, London: Constable.

Schein, E.H. (1992) *Organisational Culture and Leadership*, San Francisco: Jossey-Bass.

Senge, P.M. (1994) *The Fifth Discipline: The Art and Practice of the Learning Organization*, New York: Currency Doubleday.

Simons, R. (2000) *Performance and Control Systems for Implementing Strategy*, Engelwood Cliffs, NJ: Prentice–Hall.

Trice, H. and Beyer, J. (1985) 'Using six organizational rites to change cultures', in G. Johnson and J. Scholes (eds) (1988) *Exploring Corporate Strategy*, Englewood Cliffs, NJ: Prentice-Hall.

Vansina, L. and Taillieu, T. (1997) 'Diversity in collaborative task-systems', *European Journal of Work and Organisational Psychology*, 6 (2): 183–99.

EXECUTIVE COACHING THROUGH CROSS-BORDER MERGERS AND ACQUISITIONS

A powerful yet under-utilized intervention

Geoffrey Abbott

Organizational growth is generally considered by companies to be necessary for survival in the global marketplace. While there are various ways that growth can occur (organic, alliance, merger, acquisition), the most common method is by way of a merger or acquisition (noting that many so-called 'mergers' usually have a dominant partner). This chapter makes a case for the use of executive coaching as a way of enhancing and managing the challenges through the various phases of mergers and acquisitions (M&As). There are four characteristics of M&As which have implications for the applicability of coaching services:

1   The M&A environment is typically fast-paced and highly pressured;
2   Each M&A is different;
3   The people who set up and 'sign off' on M&A deals are usually not the ones who have to make them work; and
4   M&As invariably don't meet the expectations of those who engage in them.

Currently, the use of coaching in M&As is haphazard and most likely to occur in the 'mopping up' process when the pain meter in the new organization is in the red zone. Coaching is not often used in supporting the early stages of the M&A process, probably due to the pace of the process and also because the deal-making is often shrouded in secrecy. Also, it may be that coaches are not presenting as (or perceived as) being able to add value in such an environment where financial and business savvy are valued over the 'soft science' practices generally associated with coaching. Coaches are advised to give attention to playing different and appropriate roles through separate phases of the deals, accepting that most of the work that they do is likely to be in the final stage; that of post-deal integration. Also, if they want to be involved in the early stages, they need to have strong credentials in the M&A field and have established very high levels of trust with the players. If they are not M&A practitioners, they might also give attention to aligning with M&A consultancy specialists who have complementary skills.

This chapter gives particular attention to how coaching might be of value in M&As. The sheer variety of contexts and processes makes it virtually mandatory that coaches explore the context and operate pragmatically, flexibly and creatively – avoiding overly structured interventions. An extended case study is attached which may be useful to stimulate thinking about M&As and how coaches might add value.

I propose a role for the coach as a 'bricoleur'. Denzin and Lincoln (1994: 2–3), in the context of qualitative research, draw on the ideas of Claude Lévi-Strauss (1996/1962) to describe the bricoleur. The bricoleur is pragmatic, and works within and across the stories of each situation. He or she moves between and within competing and overlapping perspectives and paradigms, working with different methodologies depending on context. The bricoleur is a 'jack of all trades' who can piece together a set of practices that can be effective in a concrete situation. In the M&A environment, the coach's tool box should include some experiences and approaches that have worked in previous M&As. The choice of practice is strategic, pragmatic and self-reflexive, and if new tools have to be invented then the coach-bricoleur can do this. The point made often in this *Companion* is that the global marketplace (where M&A activity takes place) is complex and changing. If coaches wish to add value in the M&A environment, they need to be flexible, savvy and adaptable.

Thomson Financial reported that in 2006 alone, M&A transactions worldwide hit $US3.6 trillion, a 30 per cent increase over the previous year. 2007 moved closer to $US5 trillion. It is well known and documented that most deals do not meet pre-merger expectations. For example, Hofstede, Van Deusen et al. (2002) studied mergers across 15 countries and observed that, 'Mergers announced with great enthusiasm crash after some years, leaving a trail of broken careers and even ruined personal health of major proponents' (786). A paradox exists here. Analysts agree that an overwhelming majority of acquisitions fail to meet expectations – at least in the short term. But, to evolve into a global organization, it is almost impossible to do so through organic growth alone. Alliances with competitors are often problematic. That is why the M&A activity continues.

New trends have emerged in the global economy that have significant implications for business leaders and their coaches as they contemplate M&As. New global players have emerged from outside Europe and North America and the landscape is becoming increasingly complex – culturally, structurally, politically and economically. The IMF/Goldman Sachs (2008) recently forecast a list of the largest economies in 2050 (Figure 20.1). The trends suggest that the pattern of mergers and acquisitions is going to dramatically change.

	2007	2050
1	USA	China
2	Japan	USA
3	Germany	India
4	China	Brazil
5	UK	Mexico
6	France	Russia
7	Italy	Indonesia
8	Spain	Japan
9	Canada	UK
10	Brazil	Germany

Figure 20.1 World economies by GDP: 2007 (actual) and 2050 (predicted)

Source: Goldman Sachs (2007)

New players are already becoming significant. In Australia, for example, there is increasing investment activity from Indian and Chinese businesses. A hostile and successful takeover bid for Australian building materials company Rinker was recently completed by Mexican company Cemex. These kinds of acquisitions result in new international corporate entities with complex and hard-to-anticipate cultural and organizational challenges. It is unlikely that the success rate for these new entities is going to be any higher than for past M&A combinations (though early reports from Cemex are that the takeover has been an initial financial success). On the positive side, they provide opportunities for the coach-bricoleur who is skilled in navigating through turbulent waters.

There are multiple reasons for the past M&A failure rate. According to McKinsey & Co., managing the human side of change is the real key to maximizing the value of the deal. They suggest that the frequent failure to give attention to the human and cultural dimensions may explain why 50 per cent of all deals ultimately destroy shareholder wealth (Kempner 2005). Another reason for failure is the choice of formal merger and acquisitions instead of looser and more creative alliances (Dyer, Kale et al. 2004). Even the right deal is often wrongly handled, with rushed processes and skimping on due diligence (Lovallo, Viguerie, Uhlaner and Harn 2007). Also, when things do go wrong, companies will often push on over the waterfall; rather than walking away with a substantial but manageable loss (Cullinan, Le Roux and Weddigen 2004).

The fact is that the adrenalin pumps hard in the early stages. Once momentum is gained, and egos (usually male) are attached to outcomes, it is often virtually impossible to stop the deal going ahead no matter how obvious it might seem to outside parties that the outcome is likely to be less than successful. The problem is compounded when the senior manager driving the deal is distant and from a different culture. Assumptions are made about what is going on (work practices, market movements, and so on) and what people know, and these can often be incorrect for a variety of reasons.

In the end, the final entity is often in poor shape, not just in financial terms but also in morale and — even more fundamentally — in its capacity to function in line with original pre-deal expectations. This is the bad news. However, there are more positive aspects to this story. First, there is evidence that companies are beginning to be savvier in how they go about mergers and acquisitions, though less so in international deals than those in-country. More M&A deals are now financially successful, according to research across three phases of M&As between 1998 and 2004 conducted by London's Cass Business School, in conjunction with Towers Perrin (Moeller 2006). Better deal selection, better governance and more attention to integration were key reasons for better-performing deals. In the most recent phase, cultural synergies were taken much more seriously than they were in the previous two merger waves, with human resource issues being included much earlier in an M&A process. Professor Scott Moeller from Cass Business School, who led the research, summarized seven key lessons that companies have learned from the mistakes of the past that can serve as guidelines when considering future acquisitions:

1   Don't try to swallow too large a company;
2   Focus on deal governance;
3   Don't do too many deals at the same time;
4   Where possible, give attention to domestic companies;
5   Pay attention to due diligence issues and the role of HR;
6   Get well down the integration trail with one acquisition before trying the next one; and
7   Assume complete control of your target.

The challenging thing for coaches (and executives) to keep in mind is that there is ample evidence of 'exceptions' – success stories where opposite approaches have been followed; and certainly there is ongoing and growing interest in offshore deal-making. Nevertheless, if at least some of these lessons are learnt, then the paradox noted above may be resolvable. It may be possible to have your cake and eat it too: acquire and be successful. There are strong reasons to believe that coaching may assist in the cake preparation, presentation and digestion. Coaching could be particularly useful when the outcome is international gourmet fusion cuisine!

Another issue, and one that seems to be missing from the various studies of M&As, is the role of high-level strategic decision making in multinationals that result in the setting up of local deals that may fail. Companies seeking global success may engage in M&A deals that they know are not likely to meet hyped-up early expectations. That is, the short- or even medium-term failure of a merger or acquisition to meet original expectations may miss the point. In some cases, when the high-level strategy changes, a multinational company may simply dump an acquisition, take the loss (or profit – it may not matter in the big picture), and move on to greener pastures on the other side of the hill. As Hofstede et al. (2002: 768) note, 'The road to internationalization is lined with wrecks'. Coaches are often used to assist the survivors.

An example of how this high-level strategy works is to observe the multinational beer giant SABMiller's expansion into Latin America (from publicly available information). SABMiller began as South African Breweries based in South Africa. It moved its head office to London, and then merged with Miller in the US, all the time expanding its international operations. In 2002 SAB went into Central America with initial ventures in Honduras and El Salvador, taking over what were essentially local family businesses. The company centered its regional head-quarters in San Salvador and began to take a keen interest in other breweries in other Central and South American countries. The actual ventures in Honduras and El Salvador took some time to establish and in the first two or three years may or may not have met the expectations of SAB and the local partners. What is interesting is to observe this growth in relation to SABMiller's stated strategic priorities (2008, see www.sabmiller.com):

- Create a balanced and attractive global spread of businesses;
- Develop strong, relevant brand portfolios in local markets;
- Constantly raise the performance of local businesses; and
- Leverage global scale.

Viewed this way, this is a success story. SABMiller subsequently shifted its regional centre to Colombia and its brewing and beverage operations cover six countries – Colombia, El Salvador, Ecuador, Honduras, Panama and Peru.

The point of this example is that strategic decisions made for global reasons may result in individual deals that may not, initially, be spectacular successes – though obviously it would be nice for all concerned if they were! Global companies may be looking just for an entry point in a region. Also, the aim might be simply to eliminate as much competition as possible through multiple acquisitions of small ventures, thereby preventing multinational competitors doing the same. It is important to note, therefore, that the aim of coaching interventions is not to stop executives from pursuing individual M&A deals by pointing to statistics on M&A failure and stressing dangers and risks (though of course business coaches will always ask questions around risk assessment). The risks are often well known and the forces to close the deal are too strong. The coaching mindset instead needs to be to encourage the executive(s) to look ahead and consider all the issues ahead of time. They can then, ideally, work in partnership with the organization to add value at all stages of the process and assist all parties (local, head office, etc.) in reaching a successful outcome. This may include helping to facilitate effective termination of the deal if, that is, things go astray and that is the result that the executive wants. The coaching business challenge is to help individual executives and their local organizations to make the best of situations with pragmatic and appropriate interventions. The business structural and financial aspects are often well handled by the companies involved, though an astute coach might ask some useful questions and provide some valuable input. However, the particular value that coaching can add is in the human dimension and in planning for consequences of the merger or acquisition. Coaching can assist individuals and organizations to cope with what is essentially an accelerated change process.

There are so many potential ways for a coach to add value. The skilled coach-bricoleur is likely to be of high value in assisting with issues related to cultural change – particularly in M&As where the two entities are culturally poles apart. Getting across cultural issues as soon as possible is important so that culture can be leveraged as opportunity (Rosinski 2003) rather than become an obstacle that gets in the way of achieving success.

Executive coaching is gaining ground as an organizational intervention. This *Companion* traverses many different coaching approaches that have demonstrated success in organizational contexts. Anecdotally and from research, high quality coaching is valued because it:

- Provides executives with 'time out' for reflection;
- Builds self-confidence and efficacy;
- Assists individuals to consider consequences of actions (providing a credible external sounding board);
- Brings underlying issues to the surface (going deeper into areas of meaning and purpose, culture and hidden assumptions and mental models);
- Encourages accountability (turning attention to the executive's individual responsibilities and accountabilities in the role);
- Raises self-awareness (opening up discussions and strategies around blind spots);
- Assists individuals to manage the interplay of their thinking, feeling and behaving within and across different situations;
- Promotes effective goal setting (encouraging clarity and balancing short-, medium- and long-term thinking);
- Aids planning (checking for obvious omissions, timing, etc.);
- Helps executives to engage in difficult conversations (asking who else is key and how best to engage with them to achieve mutually beneficial outcomes);
- Encourages executives to face hard realities (i.e. high quality coaches will be experts in 'tough love');
- Sharpens decision making (exploring options, checking motivations, etc.);
- Supports team building and talent management;
- Helps executives to identify support needs (e.g. when to engage outside consultants, how to maximize the potential of internal human resources); and so on.

This is an extensive list – suggesting that coaching is perceived as having something to offer across diverse situations. In most international M&As, various forces come together to produce a highly pressured and emotionally charged change process. Coaching should be able to provide – in theory at least – the kind of support that may assist executives to (1) cope, (2) avoid major catastrophes, and (3) achieve sustainable success. The following sections gives attention to the different phases of M&As and how coaching might add value.

The *Harvard Business Review* recently published an article outlining some of the pitfalls of M&As through three stages (primary due diligence, bidding, and final due diligence) and proposing 'antidotes' (Lovallo et al. 2007). It focuses on the 'sexy' part of the process – from target identification through to the deal finalization. A summary follows, giving attention to the international dimension along with additional commentary including how, specifically, coaching of key personnel might make the process more effective. Also, a fourth stage is proposed which looks at the post-deal integration of the new acquisition in which the human element is given prime attention and where coaching has a potentially major role.

Stages one to three can be very rapid, meaning that early coaching interventions would most likely be in the form of condensed, pressured conversations rather than the more typical coaching style of reflective dialogue. Speed of the deal has been put forward as a key variable in Cisco Systems establishing a reputation as a success story in the M&A field (Gadiesh, Ormiston, Rovit and Critchlow 2001). Coaches need to operate flexibly to accommodate the M&A environment, including the fact that cross-border deals may require virtual conversations in hotel lobbies, airports, taxis, and so on. In these early stages, some of the survival coaching approaches described by Eddie Lievrouw in Chapter 9 may be appropriate.

Part of the attraction of the global M&A activity is the 'thrill of the chase'. Executives who choose careers in this field are usually people who are seeking adventure and challenge (Osland 1995). The driving metaphor is often the archetypal hero described in Joseph Campbell's classic work (Campbell 1968). Coaches must be prepared to run just as fast and in as many directions as the corporate players. At the same time, they need to work with those who perhaps don't have the same heroic enthusiasm. In this latter category might be the local executives (and their reports) in an acquisition, whose worlds have been turned upside down and who are facing 'management from across the seas' represented by a new arrival whose language may be foreign and whose style and approach may be in stark contrast to the local ways of operating. Put bluntly, being acquired is not as heroic as acquiring (drawing images of hammers and nails). That said, there are usually opportunities for most if not all players – in all areas of the deal landscape. Initial resistance, however, is likely to be a common element, perhaps even more prevalent in the international M&A environment than in most 'normal' homeland coaching engagements. In worst-case scenarios (which happen all too often), the home office, somewhere else in the world, may not actually be interested in what happens on the ground, operationally. They just want the subsidiary to establish a budget and to operate and report against it (positively) and not do anything that might affect the share price. On the ground, the local company might operationally be a disaster and be struggling to deliver from day one, all of which can be very demoralizing for the local people involved and highly stress-inducing for the expatriate manager who invariably is charged with making it all work.

STAGE 1: PRIMARY DUE DILIGENCE

Confirmation bias

A confirmation bias is when you seek out information that validates your initial interest in the target company. The suggested antidote is to seek evidence disconfirming your estimates of the deal's potential value, thereby providing a more balanced view. Individual coaching of the CEO or key decision makers could address this issue through awareness raising and direct questioning, perhaps initiating related actions from the deal support team to investigate disconfirming evidence.

Overconfidence

Overconfidence can be an issue when the deal relies solely on the key decision maker's overly optimistic estimates of synergies between his or her firm and the target. Another dimension of this issue is a tendency to place too much emphasis on the fact that the company in question comes from the region that is the strategic target. The suggested antidote is to examine numerous similar deals that the firm and others have done for a 'reality check'. A strong coaching relationship would be required to explore the connection of the executive's ego with the decision. A coach leading with such an issue may be shown the door quite quickly!

Underestimating cultural differences

Ignoring conflicts between merging firms' cultural orientations and preferences could (and often does) damage post-M&A performance. An interesting and consistent finding is that M&As tend to be more successful when risk levels are equivalent. That is, companies with cultures that encourage risk taking are potential matches for M&As – similarly medium with medium, low with low. Problems seem to occur with mismatches. It has been suggested that risk is significant because differences in the attitude towards risk are often symptomatic of a much wider range of differences between the two combining organizations (Ramaswamy 1997; Schoenberg 2005).

The proposed antidote is to identify potential problems related to culture and develop plans for addressing them. The measurement of cultural orientations and dimensions is possible, thanks to the work of researchers such as Geert Hofstede (2001). Frameworks such as Hofstede's five-dimensional model provide a mechanism for exploring cultural differences and similarities in the M&A environment. From Hofstede's work, there is comparative data on most countries that can inform broad country-level analyses of cultural differences and similarities. With regard to risk, Hofstede to some extent gets at this construct through the level of 'uncertainty avoidance' (Hofstede 2001: 145).

A coaching intervention may ideally extend into areas of the organization with some knowledge of the cultural issues that may be at play, for example with senior Learning and Development or Human Resources managers. Philippe Rosinski (2003), in his book *Coaching Across Cultures*, provides a coaching-specific framework, based on the work of Hofstede and others, that is useful for introducing new conversations about culture into organizations (see Chapter 10 of this *Companion*). This kind of approach would be very helpful in assessing and discussing cultural aspects of M&As. Cultural nuances may not be of immediate interest to the CEO and the financial drivers of the deal. Strong coaching relationships across the executive team, however, would potentially provide doors into the organizations for coaching conversations around cultural issues. Coaching can alert players to the dangers of possible cultural stereotyping in any assessment of cultural influences, noting for example that there are usually strong sub-cultures within countries, communities and organizations.

Underestimating time, money, and other resources needed for integration

Failure to accurately estimate the resources required for a successful integration is a common pitfall. The suggested antidote is to identify best practices for improving integration efforts. A coach is very useful in probing aspects of the deal that the initial team of deal makers may or may not have considered. Questions that investigate the accuracy of costing and other information provided by third parties in unfamiliar overseas countries may help to gain greater clarity on the challenges of integration.

STAGE 2: BIDDING

Bidding above the target's true value when multiple players enter the game

Once the heat rises and there is determination from various parties to secure a target, it is easy for the price to become inflated, thus reducing the chances of success. The antidote suggested is to set a maximum price for each deal and then walk away if competitors initiate a bidding war. The antidote here is easy to say, but not so easy to implement as anyone who has been a bidder at any kind of auction – and found something attractive – would understand. Certainly, a final conversation between a coach and the bidding team could harden resolve around the bidding price and at least ensure that there was a maximum price.

STAGE 3: FINAL DUE DILIGENCE

Anchoring

Anchoring is refusing to adjust an initial valuation even if new information about the target firm suggests the initial number is in error. Coaches working with highly pressured international executives can be useful in assisting individuals to 'un-stick' their thinking on key issues such as attachment to unrealistic valuations. This role can be important where the attachment is due to a binding of ego and valuation.

Sunk costs fallacy

The sunk costs fallacy is for the acquiring company to refuse to walk away from the deal, even if the costs are unrecoverable, because the players have invested so much time, money, effort, and reputations into making the deal happen. The suggested antidote is to hire fresh, dispassionate experts to examine relevant aspects of the deal – but without informing them of the initial company estimate of the deal's value. The recommendation is to entertain multiple M&A possibilities to reduce emotional attachment to one deal (which is contrary to Professor Moeller's advice noted earlier). Coaching that deals with the interaction of emotions, cognition and behavior is likely to assist players to gain awareness about this issue and therefore increase the likelihood that they will administer the antidote suggested above.

The emphasis of the *Harvard* article on the three key deal stages is on the nuts and bolts of the deal and little on the human elements. What is missing is a Stage 4 of 'integration' where coaching has a particular – but different – role.

STAGE 4: INTEGRATION

Lack of interest and support

The deal makers have done their stuff, shaken hands with the managers who are still stand-ing, and moved on to the next deal. The people left – who have to make it all work – are often disillusioned and confused. M&As are almost-instant, usually imposed and invariably intense organizational change processes. Often, there is little real attention given to the integration of the two entities (though, as noted earlier, recently there has been some change for the better). In the case of a hostile takeover or big/small takeover, the target employees are under intense pressure and face legitimate uncertainty. Even in a 'merger of equals', the real situation is that there is usually a 'winning' team and a 'losing' team – though the press releases won't say this (creating even more uncertainty). During many M&As, egos are bruised, and rumors abound; reputations are tarnished, relationships are soured (Kempner 2005).

The only known 'antidote' to the ills of a post-merger environment is a rigorous, com-prehensive and well-resourced change process. Kempner (2005) recommends that considerable attention be given to communications strategies as a way of safeguarding company and indi-vidual reputations, and increasing the chances for a positive transaction outcome. This is a common recommendation for any good change process. A good news message, however, is not always what is needed. Messages and assumptions that leadership is in complete control create a false sense of security and quickly turn the marriage made in heaven to the honeymoon from hell (Lee-Marks 2005).

Executive coaches who work in organizational contexts are change experts and are increas-ingly being directly involved in organizational change processes. Some of the coaching literature gives attention to organizational coaching interventions (some, strangely, does not). The Skiffington and Zeus behavioral coaching approach positions coaches as agents in organ-izational change processes who can address the behavior of individuals (Skiffington and Zeus 2003: 113). Coaches can assist change at the level of the individual, the team, and the organiza-tion, including engaging with the system to help facilitate organizational culture change. Harkins describes the role of an organizational coach as a 'free player' who can move around the field as the play requires – echoing the role of the bricoleur (Harkins 2005). The free player can be very useful in the complexity of the post-merger situation. For coaches to be useful in the international M&A arena, they must, however, have highly developed cross-cultural savvy.

Integrating too quickly

As noted above, deals move quickly through stages one to three. This 'need to speed' can send the whole deal off the rails if the players try to maintain it through stage four. The anti-dote – again – is the carefully planned change process begun (paradoxically) as soon as possible. Coaches can assist people to slow down, lick wounds, enter into a reflective process, and ensure that long-term processes are embedded that will facilitate sustainable success. There are many strategies for coaching interventions that may be appropriate in the integration phase. Team coaching (Chapter 17, Moral) has particular application as organizational players try to make sense of the new environment and create productive ways of working with new colleagues who were formerly the 'other'.

Conclusion

Every M&A deal is different – that is one reason why adventure-seeking executives love to be involved in the field! No one case study is going to give coaches any firm answers of how to assist executives in M&A processes. Coach-bricoleurs must be prepared to work pragmatically in the here-and-now to assist their clients to cope with what is happening, to make sense of it, and to build effective strategies for long-term success. This *Companion* provides many tools and methodologies for the coach-bricoleur. The art of the business coach is to construct an approach with the organizational clients that can lead to sustainable success and satisfaction.

What follows is a case which is the story of a cross-border alliance which has gone astray. It is a composite of several real cases in which the authors were involved in various coaching or advisory roles. It does not describe a coaching intervention; it presents an environment where a coach might be able to add value. The study, constructed by Geoffrey Abbott and Dina Zavrski-Makaric, comes with a series of activities in the style of a business school case study. It is designed to be used as a discussion generator in coach-training. It was successfully run as such within an Asia-Pacific *Coaching Across Cultures* seminar conducted by Geoffrey Abbott, Philippe Rosinski and Dina Zavrski-Makaric. It could also be useful for coaches working with managers who are involved in international M&A activities.

CASE STUDY

Murray Pharmaceuticals International Pty Ltd: A Chinese joint venture in crisis

Murray Pharmaceuticals, a medium-sized Australian pharmaceutical company was looking to expand its market into the Asia-Pacific region. In 2006, as part of this strategy, it began outsourcing production and research to a company in China (Hefei City Pharmaceuticals – HCP). But, all was not well – HCP seemed to have broken contractual agreements on pricing and competition, placing Murray Pharmaceuticals in a precarious financial position. How can the CEO make this work? Can a coach help?

Murray Pharmaceuticals: background

Murray Pharmaceuticals International is an Australian pharmaceutical company which has made a substantial impact in the Australian market. It specializes in the production and distribution of anti-arthritic drugs – most notably Reducin. The plan had always been to develop Reducin as a market leader for international distribution.

Established in 1987, Murray's head office and manufacturing plant were set up in Hobart in Southern Tasmania. Before outsourcing to China began, the Hobart manufacturing site was producing 50 million tablets per annum – mainly Reducin tablets and capsules. Additional products were manufactured for relief of asthma and general pain management. A chemical laboratory was also established to test and develop new products. More than 150 people worked at the site before the outsourcing move.

The founder is Dr Jane Murray. She is 68 years old. Originally from Bloomington, Minnesota, Jane migrated to Australia in 1976. She comes from a working-class family. Her father worked in a flour mill. She is tough and ambitious and has worked her way up in the face of considerable adversity.

Her doctoral research, at the University of Minnesota, was in the development of medications to treat chronic arthritis in the elderly and Jane has established a strong reputation among the global industrial and scientific community in this area. She was awarded the 1973 Sontag Foundation Fellowship of the Arthritis National Research Foundation. Both of her parents suffered from severe osteoarthritis. Jane has problems herself but keeps very active and uses her own products to good effect.

Jane has three daughters, all of whom have established professional careers unrelated to the business. One lives in Sydney, one in Singapore and the other in Minnesota. Jane's husband David Murray is a retired school principal, also from Minnesota. David is 77 and would like Jane to step back and enjoy retirement with travel to see their children and pursue other interests, including gardening and golf. Jane agreed to buy a house in Sydney and they have been based there since 2003. Jane flies down to Hobart every week at least once. David divides his time between Sydney, Minnesota, Hobart and Singapore.

Jane lived in Tasmania and worked at the University as a lecturer for many years until 1987 when she used all of her savings and David's retirement funds to set up a factory to research and produce Reducin. The factory and research facilities manager is Peter Smithers. Peter is Tasmanian and runs the factory like a family. Most employees have been with the company for over ten years. A third of the staff is from the Vietnamese community, whose families came to Tasmania after the fall of Saigon in the mid 1970s.

In 2004, it was clear to Jane that the Australian operation had reached its potential. Reducin sales were steady, with a slight decline in 2003 annual sales – for the first time in five years. Some overseas competitors were threatening Reducin's market position with some similar drugs. The Hobart factory was at full production and there was little scope for expansion on the site for logistical, cost and environmental reasons. Much of the technology and equipment was dated and the costs of production in Australia (skilled factory workers and good research scientists) were proving prohibitive. There were also problems with local residents complaining about the impact the plant was having on the environment.

A Chinese opportunity: the Hefei City pharmaceuticals deal

Jane looked overseas for cheaper options for larger-scale productions. Her search found an interesting possibility. A relatively unknown Chinese company Hefei City Pharmaceuticals (HCP) was having success with Anti-Ache, a cheaper product that was similar to Reducin – but not quite as sophisticated in chemical composition. Various studies had concluded that Reducin provided a more effective treatment long-term than Anti-Ache. HCP was also starting to build a range of other drugs that were similar to those being explored by Jane's company.

In February 2005, Jane decided to move aggressively. Jane travelled to Hefei City and met with Lee Keat Choon ('KC'), the President of HCP. Soon after, Jane entered into a contract with HCP with the aim of outsourcing production and research to Hefei City, thus saving costs and also removing a competitor.

Hefei is in the Anhui Province in China. Lying in the lower reaches of the Yangtze River and the central part of East China, Anhui is bounded by Jiangsu and Zhejiang on the east, Hunan and Hubei on the west, Jiangxi on the south and Shandong on the north. Hefei is the capital of Anhui and has a population of 4.3 million. It is an economic, political, cultural, transportation, tourism and information center of the province. Hefei is an ancient city with a history of more than 2,200 years.

The core elements of the contract between Murray and HCP were:

1 Agreement not to compete in any market;
2 Production of Reducin in China at an agreed price, with capped increases for five years; and

3   Development of research facilities engaging and training Chinese scientists.

Jane kept the plant running in Hobart but was aiming to close production in 2008 once Hefei City Pharmaceuticals was in full production. KC agreed to stay on to run the production in China. Research work would continue in Australia but also be extended in China, using associations with research institutes in Hefei (which were receiving increasing support from the Chinese government).

The purchase was made possible by Jane attracting an investor from the US. Patricia Jones, a former university colleague of Jane, invested heavily in the venture in 2005 and held 33 per cent of the Australian company. Patricia is American and lives in Atlanta where she is an Associate Professor specializing in aged care. She takes some interest in the company but rarely visits. Patricia and her family have considerable business interests in the USA and she doesn't need to see a rapid return. However, she is concerned about her Murray Pharmaceuticals investment.

Early promise then . . . production problems

The plan worked well through 2005. After the deal, Jane visited Hefei City once each two weeks for the first three months, in line with her understanding that face-to-face contact was important in China. Her routine was a one-hour update with KC in the morning, then a tour of the factory, a two-hour meeting with the management team, and then an evening flight out. The facilities were revamped and Jane hosted scientists from HCP in Australia to ensure they were familiar with the formula and production process for Reducin and able to take over production on a large scale in Hefei.

After three months, Jane placed two senior scientists in China on two-year assignment and stopped her regular visits. Graham Best and Roberta Palumbo had not had experience in China before and soon reported that they were having difficulty getting their Chinese counterparts to engage with them. Both worked with full-time interpreters. Roberta was a member of the senior management team in Hobart and had seven research scientists reporting to her directly.

Jane was getting good news from KC by phone, assumed all was well and embarked on an ambitious Asia-Pacific sales strategy. She appointed Stella Wong, a Singaporean-Chinese executive with experience in the industry, as International Sales and Marketing Manager. Stella was based in Singapore and had established an Asia-Pacific sales team. She had spent four years in Shanghai as marketing VP of a pharmaceuticals company.

Then, problems occurred. It was clear by early 2006 that the factory in Hefei City was not producing either the quality or quantity of Reducin that was expected. The new product lines had not eventuated. Graham and Roberta were clearly getting nowhere.

Another Chinese competitor had emerged – and Jane had heard rumors that the owners were in some way connected to KC and were associated with a European company. There had been an embarrassing and commercially damaging Australian government Commonwealth Scientific and Industrial Research Organisation (CSIRO) study which had revealed a gap between the stated and actual chemical composition of the Reducin coming in from China, resulting in a product recall and a regional PR damage control exercise.

KC had seemed happy with the idea of running the production at the time of the takeover. Now, Jane was not sure he was committed to the success of the new venture. She could not get a real sense of what was going on there. In advance of each phone call (often a conference call with both management teams), she emailed a set of questions to KC. All of the responses from KC and his team suggested that everything was fine but it was clear there were problems.

Jane had never publicly stated that she intended to close the Hobart factory. She knew that this was essential since the Hefei City venture soaked up a lot of capital and was only viable if the high-cost Hobart centre was shut down within three to five years. Her director of finance, Alison Wood, had been reminding her of this at each meeting. Alison was based in Hobart but aimed to relocate to Singapore or Hefei City once the Hobart plant closed.

July 2007: contact crisis – pricing and competition

In mid-2007, things got worse. Hefei City Pharmaceuticals announced that they were increasing prices for supply to Australia by more than 100 per cent, citing rising production costs. This was despite the Murray-HCP joint venture contract that set price rises at a maximum of 15 per cent per year over the first five years. Also, there were rumors that a Swedish company had a deal with HCP.

Jane received the pricing news via Alison Wood. She decided to send a delegation to Hefei City to sort out the problems. Jane had higher-priority meetings in the US and told Peter Smithers, Murray Pharmaceuticals' Australian production manager, to handle the situation with Alison. Graham and Roberta were also informed and were to join a delegation. Jane trusted Peter's knowledge of the production and contract issues and Alison's knowledge of the financial situation. She said she would be available by phone if needed.

Peter Smithers had handled the back-end production and contract logistics of the negotiations with HCP from the start. He was furious about the price rises and competition breaches. He had let go of 70 Australian employees only because of the certainty of long-term cheaper Chinese production and research and higher sales. His personal rationalization was that he could provide some employees with jobs in sales, marketing and distribution, and build the company's regional market by on-selling. Now the advantageous price margin was virtually gone and competition was increasing – placing the company in a high-risk environment.

Hefei City 26 July 2007: the meeting that wasn't

Peter and Alison arrived in Hefei City at 9am after an uncomfortable overnight flight via Shanghai. Even though their information was that the meeting had been agreed with the Chinese company, when they arrived at the hotel in Hefei they were not met by anyone from HCP – just Graham and Roberta (the two Australian scientists). Graham and Roberta were quite surprised, given the normal attention paid by the Chinese to arrival protocols.

Peter and Alison checked into the hotel and prepared for the arranged noon meeting which they had arranged in the hotel conference room. They knew that if they went to the factory they would get caught up in endless tours and greetings. They sat in the hotel for the afternoon. No HCP delegation turned up so they returned to Australia the next day – furious. Graham and Roberta were instructed to stay out of the plant until further notice.

Hefei City 12 August 2007: deepening crisis

Jane received the news of the meeting fiasco by email. She called Peter and they decided to have another go at meeting – but only if KC gave his direct agreement to Jane. She talked with him by phone and he apologized for the problem on 26 July, explaining that there had been a misunderstanding about timing. He agreed to meet the delegation personally but was not forthcoming about his views of what might transpire. Jane sensed that the 100 per cent price increase was very flexible and other things were going on – exactly what, she didn't know.

311

Jane's judgment was that the same team should go – not wanting to escalate tensions by attending herself.

Peter and Alison flew back into Hefei on the morning of 12 August ready to sort out what had become a crisis situation. The strategy was for them to follow up a Letter of Agreement that affirmed the validity of the contract. They also had scope to negotiate an annual capped price increase of 20 per cent (5 per cent above the agreed cap in the contract) through to 2011, reflecting increased production costs in China and world price movements in high end anti-arthritis drugs.

This time, they went to the factory and met in the main boardroom. It was clear to Peter from the start that there was not going to be much progress. To him, the Chinese just did not look enthusiastic. The Murray Pharmaceuticals delegation of four sat opposite the twelve HCP managers and scientists, who were polite but non-committal. Peter could barely hold back his annoyance and began to clash with KC, the HCP President.

Peter reported that the conversation went as follows:

Peter Smithers: I believe you received our Letter of Agreement. Have you had a chance to look at it? The main things concern the pricing and non-competition clauses. We want HCP to recommit to the original pricing cap and agree not to enter agreements with international competitors.

President KC: Yes, thank you. We received and read your email with great interest. I have spoken to your Dr Jane and we would very much like to resume our association with your company. We understand she has important business in the USA.

Peter Smithers: So you are ready to sign on it today?

President KC: My colleagues and I have spoken about it in great detail.

Peter Smithers: That's good. If there are no pressing difficulties, can we sign the agreement today? In fact, we have to leave first thing tomorrow morning. Ideally we would like to take a signed copy with us. There is nothing new in it – it reaffirms our original deal. With great respect, we would appreciate your giving it urgent attention.

President KC: We still need to show your agreement to our superior, Chairman Jiang.

Peter Smithers: I appreciate this, but you said you had already discussed it with your colleagues in detail. Are there things we need to know that have changed the situation since the original agreement?

President KC: Chairman Jiang will have a look at it very soon. He takes a personal interest in the relationship with Australia.

Peter Smithers: But I don't quite see the problem. At no point have we heard from Chairman Jiang or anyone else that the original agreement cannot be honored. That is why we are here. But you seem to be saying that you cannot sign the agreement today?

President KC: My colleagues and I will present our view to Chairman Jiang and make him aware of our views. I assure you he is very affectionate towards our alliance.

Alison Wood: Is there anything else we can do or clarify for you so that you can sign the agreement today?

President KC: (Addressing Peter Smithers) We will explain the situation and ask Chairman Jiang for his advice.

After an hour of similar exchanges, Peter could not tolerate the lack of information or cooperation he was receiving. He found the forced politeness offensive in the circumstances. He announced, 'You will either continue to sell it to us at the agreed contact price, or we are walking out of the room. He added, "And we don't expect to hear about other deals you are doing with the Swedish".'

The Chinese did not make any obvious effort to keep the meeting going. KC nodded and Peter motioned to the other Australians and they left the meeting. They convened back at the hotel and waited for several hours for some kind of approach from the Chinese delegation.

Nothing eventuated, so Peter had his secretary in Hobart cancel the arranged dinner and organized an early plane home the next day. Graham and Roberta made arrangements to relocate back to Australia but it was decided to leave them in China for another month or two as representatives of Murray Pharmaceuticals and to look for other opportunities.

Murray Pharmaceuticals stopped orders from HCP almost immediately, although there was no formal cessation of the contract. The Australian plant was moving into virtual shut down mode and Peter Smithers did what he could to generate production again, including re-employing 15 production staff. The loss of the Hefei factory started to significantly reflect on the company's sales and distribution in Australia.

After two months without communication with Hefei management, Jane Murray decided that she needed to take action. Not only was the Asia-Pacific expansion at risk, but Murray Pharmaceuticals might go under. She held a meeting with her top management team and also held a series of meetings and phone calls with trusted business associates in Australia, China and the USA.

Her conclusion was that there was no going backwards. Further, the only sources of cheap production and research capacity were outside Australia – most notably China. Also, she had invested considerable time and money in Hefei and was not going to abandon that deal unless she was absolutely forced to.

Jane had had an uncomfortable conversation with Dr Hian Xiaoming, the President of the Australian China Business Council. Dr Hian stressed that to do business in China, it was necessary to build relationships in China – not just with your main contact but with an extended network. He also gave her some alarming figures and examples of the high failure rates of M&A activity in China, citing poor relationship management as the main problem. Jane decided to take his advice and that of others and try to re-establish the Murray Pharmaceutical presence in Hefei and get a different outcome.

A different tactic: a new joint venture

Jane decided to pursue an opportunity that she had been sitting on to enter as a minor player (5 per cent stake) in a joint venture (JV) with another Chinese pharmaceuticals company in Anhui Province and a New Zealand investment firm. The Chinese company was not in competition with Murray or HCP. Jane knew that the president of the company was KC's cousin and both companies came under the control of Chairman Jiang.

The JV gave Jane a role as a board member. Her plan was to attend the board meetings, but not get much involved with the business. She would attend the major meetings but send her Australian managers to represent her at regular board meetings so they would get some exposure to Chinese business practice. As Jane planned this strategy, she was aware that competitors from the US and Sweden were entering China, wanting to establish new factories or to purchase pharmaceuticals from existing manufacturers in China – including HCP.

Through her new contacts, Jane identified a senior Chinese-Australian businessman who also acted as professional mentor and who was known to KC. At Jane's suggestion and with KC's agreement he conducted informal interviews with Jane and KC to help them to make sense of what had happened and to design strategies that would help them move forward (individually if not together). The discussions revealed the depth of the problems being faced.

Jane Murray

This seemed such a good idea at the time. I went into Hefei City convinced that we had a golden opportunity to position the company for the next five to ten years of growth. They had experience in pharmaceuticals and had a plant that could easily be tailored to our needs. This was obvious from the start. Understandably I suppose, KC was a bit resistant when I first met him in China in 2005. He was the key player because he spoke English and was really in charge of everything. He introduced me to lots of other people on that first night. It was a bit of a laugh really. The interpreter was trying to keep up but in between toasts and speeches and the many courses of the dinner, I really couldn't keep track of who was who. But, I knew if I made an offer to KC he would be responsive because I was told by a Chinese contact that they were short of cash. The next day, I made what we considered a low to medium offer. He pushed it up a bit and I said yes on the spot. We signed the deal a week later. They seemed happy with the contract that we had pre-prepared in Hobart.

What has made it difficult was that the plant refurbishment was so expensive. And, I found that the Chinese were not that keen on discussing issues with us as they cropped up. I tried to implement some better management practices in the joint venture Australia–China leadership team, using stuff we were already doing in Hobart. This included some 360 degree feedback done through a US consultancy firm I had links with through Patricia. Nothing much came from it. We sent people over there – two of our best scientists – but they were given the run around.

I might be wrong, but some of the consultancy fees we ended up paying in China – on top of our budget for the plant – seemed to be heading to various government officials and contacts. KC handled that part of the deal. With him, things got worse and worse. I thought he was going to be my best ally since it was his family company name that was at risk in China, even though we were the biggest player.

Then the price rise came as a bolt out of the blue. I was absolutely shocked that they could break the contract so blatantly. Sending Peter and Alison over twice to sort it out (would you believe the first time they didn't even meet!) didn't seem to get us anywhere.

My conversation with Dr Hian has made me think that I could have done things a bit differently – though I am not too sure that going back into China is a smart move.

KC (Lee Keat Choon)

I am very frustrated by what has happened. I had great hopes for our joint venture. I set up HPC because I wanted to get some pharmaceutical development in China that was leading edge. Other factories were just producing stock standard materials without the flexibility being demanded by our expanding customer base. My mother was crippled with arthritis for over twenty years so I have a personal interest in pain relief.

I am also passionate about doing things correctly and get China a better reputation internationally in doing business. So I hired some of our best scientists to come up with something better that would compete on the world market. And we succeeded to some extent. Our problem was that the local Chinese market is not that keen on these kinds of synthetic medicines and sales were slow. And anyway, the other Chinese companies were saturating the market with the cheap clones of inferior US drugs – which could not be sold outside due to the patent breaches.

We hoped to make an impact offshore in the US. But, the US Food and Drug Agency would not allow us in. Australia and New Zealand were more accommodating when they saw what we were doing. It took a while to get permission to distribute in those countries and it was around the same time that Reducin came on the market that we entered with Anti-Ache. It was unfortunate timing. We were cheaper but the 'Made in China' label is not a good seller for medicine. Also, we did have some quality control issues because our employees were not well trained. And frankly, Reducin was a better drug.

So when Dr Jane came to China I was ready to talk about an alliance. Frankly, we were a bit desperate. Fortunately, the initial Australian investment figure was way over what we had discussed with some Chinese competitors a few months before.

I could see some value in getting some Australian expertise mixed with our innovative approaches in developing new medicines and our cheap facilities. We could use the Aussie name in Australia and maybe the US – and fix our quality issues. It surprised me when straight away she started to talk about what was virtually a takeover but under the guise of a joint venture.

I organized a dinner for Dr Jane to welcome her and give my two brothers and their families a chance to get to know her. We got interpreters and made sure it was a full banquet but with some Western style food. Dr Jane was there just with her finance manager and they didn't do much except talk with me. The next day she made a cash offer much higher than I expected. I added 15 per cent to what she said and she left. I was amazed to receive an email with a full contract the next day.

I felt that the Australians had essentially taken control. But I agreed to stay on because I really am attached to the idea of the company and making a difference to elderly people's standard of living.

After the deal was done, Jane visited a few times. But then she more or less left us alone to fix everything, though we had a stream of her managers visit us for short periods. Some of our scientists went over there too but it was very difficult for them. They sent over two people for an extended period but the two they sent had no experience in China and did not assist us much. Also, many of my top people were disillusioned and left to work for competitors.

I told Dr Jane about the difficulties but after the deal she didn't seem interested. We had a series of short phone conversations that did not demonstrate that she was committed to us. We were not getting any value from Australia and I could see our original objectives would not be met.

In the end, I could see all the initial profits being lost and my company being torn to pieces by Chinese competitors working with other foreign companies. The Swedish had been making offers to us but I have an agreement with Dr Jane that we would not do business with other countries.

At present it is difficult to see a way through that is going to keep my colleagues here happy and also continue the deal. I see a lot of American and foreign companies come into China and then just disappear without achieving much except losing money and causing ill feelings. Fortunately, we are getting much better at ensuring a good outcome for our companies.

Another option: India?

At the same time as Jane was getting involved in the new JV, she had a conversation with a venture capitalist in Sydney who was in touch with a wealthy Indian businessman (Roshan Singh). Mr Singh was looking to invest in an Australian pharmaceutical company. Further, Mr Singh had indicated that he could establish a plant near Chennai to support the investment. The claim was that an operation in India would cost about half what an equivalent facility would cost in China.

What next?

In total, Jane was now employing over 120 people in Australia plus a sales and marketing office of 10 people in Singapore. Technically, she was still in a joint venture with HCP. Alison had given Jane a detailed financial report indicating that the company would need a significant injection of cash if it was to last another 12 months. Sales were barely meeting running costs. There was pressure coming from every angle.

ACTIVITIES

Role play

Jane Murray has decided to engage an executive coach to assist her manage the various issues. You are an associate with a consultancy firm specializing in international business coaching. You have received the brief above and have been asked for a proposal which sets out a coaching strategy for 12 months. You and your colleagues have been asked to make a presentation to Jane's executive team in 10 days' time.

Step 1: Individual analysis (15 minutes)

Before discussing this with your coaching colleagues, give individual consideration to each of the following, drawing where possible on ideas from this and other chapters of the *Companion*:

- What cultural issues might be at play here, now and in the future?
- What cultural orientations might be particularly relevant?
- The brief presents several perspectives. What others might there be?
- Examine the leadership of the two companies. On a scale of '1' to '10', where '1' is completely ineffective and '10' is highly effective, rate the performance of Jane and KC.
- Make some observations about each.
  1   Jane Murray (/10)
  2   Lee Keat Choon (/10)
- What else came to mind as relevant as you read the story?

Step 2: Group discussion

Consider the coaching proposal. Get a group consensus on putting a proposal to Jane. 'Consensus' does not necessarily mean whole-hearted commitment from all participants but that everyone can 'live with' and support this decision. You might consider, inter alia:

- What issues might you raise as potentially relevant?
- Who would you propose to coach?
- How long would you coach for?
- What format would you use – 1 to 1, team, other?
- Examine your team, who would coach who?
- What other expertise might you need?
- What form(s) of communication would you use?
- Where would the coaching be?
- How and how much would you charge?

Bibliography

Campbell, J. (1968) *The Hero with a Thousand Faces*, Princeton: Princeton University Press.

Cullinan, G., Le Roux, J.M. and Weddigen, R.M. (2004) 'When to walk away from a deal', *Harvard Business Review*, April: 14–22.

Denzin, N.K. and Lincoln, Y.S. (1994) 'Introduction: Entering the field of qualitative research', in N.K. Denzin and Y.S. Lincoln (eds), *Handbook of Qualitative Research*, Thousand Oaks, CA: Sage.

Dyer, J. H., P. Kale, et al. (2004). 'When to ally and when to acquire', *Harvard Business Review*, June 2004: 24–33.

Gadiesh, O., Ormiston, C., Rovit, S. and Critchlow, J. (2001) 'The 'why' and 'how' of merger success', *European Business Journal*, 13 (4): 187–94.

Goldman Sachs Economic Group (2008) *BRICs and Beyond*, Goldman Sachs Group. Available online at <www2.goldmansachs.com/ideas/brics/book/BRIC-Full.pdf> (accessed 30 April 2008).

Harkins, P. (2005) 'Getting the organization to click', in H. Morgan, P. Harkins and M. Goldsmith (eds), *The Art and Practice of Leadership Coaching*, Hobokin: John Wiley and Sons.

Hofstede, G. (2001) *Culture's Consequences: Comparing Values, Behaviors, Institutions and Organizations across Nations*, Thousand Oaks, NJ: Sage.

Hofstede, G., Van Deusen, C.A., Mueller, C.B. and Charles, T.A. (2002) 'What goals do business leaders pursue? A study in fifteen countries', *Journal of International Business Studies*, 33 (4): 785–803.

Kempner, M. (2005) 'When rumors thrive your deal's in trouble', *Mergers and Acquisitions*, 40 (4): 42–50.

Lee-Marks, M. (2005) 'The destructive force of acquisition denial', *Mergers and Acquisitions*, 40 (4): 47–53.

Lévi-Strauss, C (1966/62) *The Savage Mind*, Chicago: The University of Chicago Press.

Lovallo, D., Viguerie, P., Uhlaner, R. and Harn, J. (2007) 'Deals without delusions', *Harvard Business Review*, December: 4–10.

Moeller, S. (2006) 'Almost every significant research study argues that acquiring companies lose value for their shareholders when they attempt takeovers', *Financial Times*, London, 6 October 2006: 2.

Osland, J. S. (1995) *The Adventure of Working Abroad: Hero Tales from the Global Frontier*, San Francisco: Jossey-Bass.

Ramaswamy, K. (1997) 'The performance impact of strategic similarity in horizontal mergers: Evidence from the U.S. banking industry', *Academy of Management Journal*, 40 (3): 697–715.

Rosinski, P. (2003) *Coaching across Cultures: New Tools for Leveraging National, Corporate and Professional Differences*, London: Nicholas Brealey Publishing.

Schoenberg, R. (2005) 'Dealing with a culture clash: Richard Schoenberg explains how risk orientation can determine the success of M&As', *Financial Times*, London, 23 September 2005: 3.

Skiffington, S. M. and Zeus, P. (2003) *Behavioral Coaching: How to Build Sustainable Personal and Organizational Strength*, Sydney: McGraw-Hill.

21

INTERNATIONAL COACHING

A global human resources perspective

Marie-Brigitte Bissen, Judith Chapman, Paul-Michael Schonenberg and Rita Knott

Executive coaches spend a great deal of time and effort with influential executives in potential and new international client organizations, educating them about the nature, purpose and process of coaching and convincing them of the benefits. This phase is recognized as crucial in many organizational coaching programs, for example by Skiffington and Zeus (2003: 129), who list education of client and coach as the essential first step in a seven-step process. Often, human resource (HR) departments (now often differently titled, such as 'people and culture') are a natural entry point for coaches. Increasingly, 'HR' is charged with the responsibility of selecting coaches for organizational coaching panels, assessing coaching proposals, rolling out manager/leader-as-coach programs, and so on.

Many individual and team development training programs provided to international executives are outsourced. Most companies have found that it is resource-efficient for HR to concentrate on core activities (sometimes limited to administration, payroll, benefits management and, to a lesser degree, recruitment). This leaves training, development, coaching and counseling as some areas of potential benefit from outsourcing to trusted business partners with the required time and, more importantly, significantly more experience than the HR department in the daily practice of these jobs at a very high quality level. In practice, what is emerging is a growing in-house capacity for middle management coaching and a reliance on external coaching service providers for senior executive and CEO-level coaching. There is a variety of other reasons why senior level executive coaching is not done by HR professionals in-house:

- Only a small number of HR professionals have had high-level coach training, and few would have experience in coaching in an international environment;
- External coaches are seen as having an independent view;
- The level of trust between executives and HR management is not always high;
- HR intervention is often viewed as remedial and therefore may not be attractive to high potential executives; and
- Particularly in international business, HR professionals are sometimes not viewed as being sufficiently experienced outside of head office or the HR field to be credible sounding boards for senior managers.

The results of externally delivered executive coaching services can be mutually beneficial, particularly when the coaches are internationally experienced and connected. The HR department gains the support of a highly skilled and experienced partner who can help the company enhance the productivity and happiness of the internal human capital of the company. Considering the potential loss of time and experience, not to mention the cost of replacing employees, this possibility to partner with skilled coaches is both cost-effective and productivity enhancing. The costs of replacing and/or repatriating expatriate executives are notoriously high. Coaching has been shown to be a potentially powerful intervention to facilitate the acculturation of expatriates (Abbott et al. 2006), thus reducing the potential for failure.

There is considerable variation in the reactions coaches and coaching proposals are likely to receive from HR departments, particularly in countries where executive coaching is not well established or has a reputation that might be unattractive to organizations. For example, anecdotal evidence from recent coaching research in Central America (Abbott et al. 2006) revealed that several large companies reported negative 'first taste' experiences of poorly delivered or culturally inappropriate executive coaching programs. The result was that HR became a gatekeeper with instructions to keep the gate shut on coaches!

If organizations that are working internationally wish to take advantage of executive coaching as a powerful intervention for facilitating individual and organizational change, then the role of the HR department in the process needs to be well defined. A variety of questions need to be considered by coaches in working with HR professionals:

- Are there underlying cultural tensions between international business coaching and HR that need to be addressed prior to the development of a beneficial relationship? International HR departments traditionally have been expected to play the role of 'head office' organizational enforcers, gatekeepers and problem-solvers. Executive coaching gives attention to the particular contexts that managers work in, as well as issues related to self-management, inclusion and solution-focused approaches.
- What is the best way to integrate coaching into a broader international HR development strategy?
- How can companies ensure that HR managers with decision-making power over management development programs are sufficiently knowledgeable about coaching to enable them to choose services that are going to be of benefit?
- How can international business coaching providers be best packaged to be attractive to HR managers faced with a bewildering number of choices for management development and support?
- What can coaches do to ensure the best chance of forging mutually beneficial relationships with HR departments?
- What alternative entry points exist that might be open for coaches in the event that HR departments are not willing to engage in dialogue about coaching. How might coaches find and utilize such entry points?
- Are there situations when coaching providers are better off targeting non-HR high level executives to gain entry into organizations, leaving HR in an implementation role rather than as initiators?
- What are the implications in an international context of the increasing incidence of coaching 'in-sourcing', that is, the growing number of HR professionals who are skilling up as coaches and delivering in-house programs in an effort to save organizational resources?

This chapter will provide some ideas and shared experiences in order to better 'bridge the worlds' and thus meet in a true common nexus of interest between HR and corporate decision makers, senior executives and coaches. The next section offers ideas and strategies on how executive coaches can better understand the variety of HR realities within international organizations. Two very different case studies are then provided of coaching in international contexts, followed by some reflections for coaches and HR professionals who are seeking mutually beneficial relationships. The final sections include a set of diagnostic questions that coaches might use to form a better understanding of the coaching context in consultation with HR.

TO PROFESSIONAL COACHES: UNDERSTANDING YOUR CUSTOMERS

Clearly the old adage about 'knowing your customer' applies to the relationship between professional coaches and their international corporate clients, and is particularly relevant to the growing domain of global coaching (Abbott and Rosinski 2007). The key to establishing a successful relationship with both new customers and maintaining the desired relationship with current customers lies in the ability of coaches to put themselves into the others' shoes, to see the world from their point of view and to understand their perspectives and problems. Only by giving the customers what they want will the coach have success. Studies suggest that HR professionals and the coachees themselves are fast increasing their knowledge of coaching and how they can benefit from it (Turner 2006). At the same time, in an increasingly complex and fast-changing environment, HR professionals face competing demands and have little clarity on what their organizations either want or need. Coaches can be of value in the early stages simply by asking questions that might add clarity to HR's perception of their role.

Management theorists Bolman and Deal (2003) propose a 'four frame' model that is intended to help in understanding situations in the organizational world that appear to be complex, ambiguous or confusing. The four frames are:

1 Structural;
2 Psycho-social;
3 Political; and
4 Symbolic (cultural).

Coaching service providers might find this model useful when seeking to understand the perspective of their HR departmental customers (or other corporate stakeholders). The idea here is to use each frame (or lens) to highlight a particular aspect of the HR role and the way in which the HR department intersects with its host organization. To see the world of HR from the perspective offered by only one frame would be incomplete, and lead the coaching provider to either misread the situation or overlook factors that might prove crucial. An application of all four frames increases the likelihood of forming a robust picture of the HR role and the organization, thus increasing the chances of building a successful relationship immeasurably. For HR professionals, the frames might also provide a way of planning how best to position coaching services in the organization, and to avoid wasting valuable resources through coaching programs that do not hit the mark for various reasons. Bolman and Deal (2003) provide descriptions of each frame in both words and metaphors. We can add to these by drawing out some of the issues that relate to coaching.

The structural frame

This frame covers the architecture of the organization, including the design of departments and groups, formal roles and relationships, coordination, quality control, and communicating messages about the organization's mission and objectives. The metaphor here is of the organization as the factory or machine. When thinking from within the structural frame, our attention is drawn to the purpose of the coaching program from the sponsor's perspective and the policies and formal systems within which it is to be introduced: steps in the process, time frames, accountabilities and measurable outcomes.

Every organization needs structure to ensure that people and systems can work smoothly together but when we compare them, it is evident that the particular arrangements for doing so vary widely. Some organizations are, for example, very traditional, with tall hierarchies and a strong emphasis on the chain of command. They don't change or respond very quickly, and like things to be logically planned out. At the opposite extreme we find modern, streamlined and more spontaneous organizations that can quickly size up a good idea and decide whether or not to run with it. HR departments in traditional organizations are likely to expect a detailed plan from their coaching clients, and almost certainly in writing. The concrete nature of this will make a coaching proposal easier to analyze (because it is more likely to fit the organizational style and language) and therefore less likely to trigger resistance. HR departments (although likely to be named something more modern!) from the opposite kind of organization will still need to know what the coaching can offer. They are likely to want to connect the coach with the potential executive clients and their teams or units early on so that the process can be adjusted to suit everyone's schedules and time frames.

It is also important to understand where the client company is in time and in relation to its markets and objectives. Is the client small, mid-sized or large? Is it located in one place only, or in multiple locations across more than one country or continent? Is the client growing, stable in size and aspirations, or is it in decline? Is the company a provider of intellectual value-added services, a provider of finished goods, or a provider of low value services? Understanding these matters will also help to understand the challenges that a company faces, and the direction that the company is taking. Like people, companies change over time. They are both a product of where they have come from and where they are trying to go. Coaches who understand where the company is on its voyage through time and will better understand its needs and gain valuable clues on how to be an asset during the voyage.

Further, we recommend that HR professionals carefully examine the systems and structures behind any coach accreditation presented by external coaches. An example of a sound system is from the European Coaching Association of Luxembourg. The process and requirements include, inter alia:

- In-depth theoretical and practical training for a minimum of one year in one or more approved development tools or techniques;
- Demonstrated experience (life or professional coaching);
- Regular peer supervision by trained coaches;
- Teaching of coaching skills and attitudes (e.g. listening, respect, empathy, discretion, positive approach, open-mindedness);
- A demonstrated commitment to continuous personal development; and
- Adherence to a Code of Conduct (covering development/training, confidentiality, independence, responsibility for process facilitation, attitude towards third parties, respect of the person, obligations towards the contracting organization).

The psycho-social frame

This frame views an organization as a large extended family, emphasizing an understanding of people with their strengths, limitations, emotions, fears and desires. In particular, its focus is on the needs that people bring to their work, and how those needs are met or left unsatisfied. HR's role in bridging the gap between what individual coachees need for their personal and professional development, and the skills the organization desires in its executives, is vital information for coaches. HR departments will vary in this respect. On a continuum, some will tend more towards providing training and development opportunities that conform to a 'wish list' from employees, while others will be more strategically intent on building employee capacity to achieve specified organizational outcomes (of course, the two are not necessarily incompatible). It is important that coaches recognize the subtle differences when discussing the benefits of a coaching program with the HR department.

From a human resources perspective, it is also important to understand the attitudes of senior people in the company to their employees. This understanding will be useful in determining the 'fit' between the executives and the coaching services. Attitudes can range from viewing employees as replaceable commodities, in the worst case, to companies that view (and treat accordingly) their employees as strategic assets. Companies of the former kind hire and fire employees according to current needs, pay as little in salary and benefits as they can get away with, and use fear tactics and coercion to extract work from them. These companies concentrate decision making at the top and care little about what their employees think, only that they will do as they are told. On the other hand, companies that consider their employees to be strategic assets invest in training and development, ask them for their ideas and devolve decision making to the lowest possible level, building maximum amounts of trust and expecting staff to do the right thing. Obviously, the two extremes may react differently to different coaching programs (style, content, coach personality, structure, format, etc.)

For a professional coach, understanding the company from this perspective is absolutely essential. Clearly a professional coach will take a different approach when dealing with employees of a company that considers staff a commodity as opposed to dealing with staff in a company that consider employees a strategic asset. For most coaches, the dream is to work for companies of the latter kind, with all that implies, and to help them manage proactive diversity programs which unleash the full potential of each and every one of their employees. Unfortunately, this will not always (or even often!) be the case. But regardless, if the coach knows the company stance on these issues, he or she can make small steps towards that dream while helping them to solve the day-to-day problems. Another option is not to take a contract in the company.

The political frame

The Political Frame is a lens that sees the workplace as a jungle. This may not sound pretty but the reality is that 'it is a jungle out there'. Organizations are competitive environments characterized by limited resources, competing views and interests, and constant struggles for power, prestige and advantage. Who has power, and the influence of HR within the organization is of interest to coaching service providers as they seek to forge relationships. Sometimes key power relationships involve whole departments, and at other times individuals with the right connections. Those with power and influence are not always (or perhaps often) in the most senior positions. Traditionally, HR managers and departments have not been particularly influential:

but those with ideas that link developing managerial competencies through coaching programs and better organizational performance are more likely to attract the support of top management. Coaches can align themselves with their HR colleagues to press the benefits of coaching in the decision making forums that count in the organization.

It is worth considering where the decision making power is, where the coaching program is concerned:

- Who will have the ultimate choice in selecting the coaching program and the coaches?
- Will it be the HR department, a more senior manager, or the coachees themselves?
- Who controls the budget and expenditure for the program?
- Who has a vested interest in seeing the project succeed?
- How will this success help them?
- Who has a vested interest in seeing it fail?

Like any change process, those affected will always assess themselves as winners or losers, and the latter may seek to undermine the success of the project. For example, is there consensus over employing external coaches, or is there some resentment about this decision from within HR? Of course, there is no easy way to find answers to these questions: careful observation and indirect questions (framed in a positive way if possible) are more likely to provide insights than direct questions that could be too confronting.

It is also worth considering how the coaching program itself might become part of the political landscape of the organization, especially in relation to the power and prestige that participation might confer. Coaching is a relatively expensive human resource development initiative, and many companies provide it only to those who have reached a certain level or position. Further, coachees in more senior positions are generally allocated more hours. Having a coach may therefore be symbolic of power or success in the company, apart from the productively and skill development that it provides.

The symbolic (or cultural) frame

This frame is last but not least. The symbolic or cultural frame is often overlooked. It is a powerful window that builds on cultural and social anthropology and is vital when working in international business environments. It views organizations as carnivals, theatres or tribes. Organizations evolve unique cultures and sub-cultures built over time through stories, ceremonies, rituals and the behavior and achievements of employees set apart as 'heroes'. This is in contrast to an organization being driven by rules, authority and policies. When we see things from the symbolic frame, meanings that might be associated with coaching in the organization become very important. As coaches, we should be asking: what meanings do HR staff attribute to coaching and coaching programs? What do potential coachees in the organization make of coaching and coaching relationships? Of all the frames, the symbolic frame is perhaps the hardest to identify or explore, but arguably the most under-utilized in the international business context.

Every company has a unique culture which makes it special and which (either subtly or directly) molds the behaviors of its employees. Organizational culture often operates on several levels: there is the formal culture expressed through corporate values, sanctioned practices and the like, and the informal culture that becomes evident from observing how people actually think and behave. While the informal culture generally takes a longer time to know,

323

information about the formal culture is generally more readily accessible through web sites, annual reports, and so on. We recommend that coaches never go to a company to start or to develop a business plan with the company without first trying to understand the corporate culture from these (and other) sources.

When looking for pertinent issues along an international theme, it is important to ask questions such as:

- What languages are used to communicate?
- What themes and people are included in the photographs and other illustrations?
- Is there a dominant national culture in the multinational culture (French, Chinese, US and so on)?
- Are there strong sub-cultures?
- What is the demographic of the executive team (age, nationality, gender, class, etc.)?
- How does the demographic of the executive team compare to that of the workforce as a whole?
- Are women prominent in roles which imply equality, leadership, or only in subordinate roles?

Culture has been measured and studied in many ways. One of the best-known researchers in the area of organizational and national culture is Geert Hofstede. Hofstede's work (e.g., 1993, 2001) identifies five dimensions (presented as dichotomies) that distinguish national cultures and their influence on corporate culture. His work on 'individualism and collectivism' has been of particular value in organizational contexts. The 'individualism–collectivism' dichotomy distinguishes cultures according to whether people tend to seek individual achievement and recognition, or value harmony and participation in a well-functioning group. Japan and the USA represent two cultures at the opposite ends of this dimension. Another dimension which has proven useful in conceptualizing organizations is 'power distance'. This is the extent to which employees are comfortable with differences in status and expect to defer to the authority of those in positions of superiority. Australia, for example, has a low power distance culture, while most cultures in the Asian region have the opposite. Clearly, these factors will affect relationships involving the coach, coachee and their manager. For example, in a high power distance culture, executive coaches may need to have worked in a high-level executive position if they wish to gain credibility with senior executives. Also, in organizations with collectivist cultures, in some instances group coaching may be preferred over individual coaching.

It can also be the case in larger companies that, in addition to the corporate culture, there are sub-cultures which are dominant in different areas of a company. (Cross-border mergers and acquisitions are notorious for leaving multiple sub-cultures operating within one company structure with unresolved and ongoing tensions.) Many executives do not have high awareness of how the internal sub-cultures operate within the organization. This is not problematic if the internal variations are not great, as occurs if the companies hire employees from only similar cultural backgrounds (including cultural commonalities across national, social, educational, industry and class criteria). In these cases, the resultant homogeneity and efficiency of the common culture may even allow for rapid shorthand communications because of both shared symbols and shared values. However, when international companies include people from diverse backgrounds, distinct sub-cultures may emerge that set up and reinforce internal silos. The common organizational culture and values are likely to have relatively weak influences. It may take longer for the communication to be effective, and staff morale and productivity can suffer. Change processes can be impeded. People in the different sub-cultures are likely to make vastly different interpretations of cross-organizational initiatives managed by HR (such as organizational change processes and related coaching programs). Newcomers tend to find such environments particularly bewildering, with induction programs doing little to help them to make sense of what is going on. Clashes between sub-cultures or with the corporate culture add an extra layer of ambiguity for outsiders who are coming to terms with their new business partner. In general, things take longer to get done and nerves can be frayed during change processes.

Coaches also need to know if a company has a national or an international orientation. Simply assuming that a company that does business in many countries is an international company can be a mistake. Some companies are very nationalistic in their orientation, with all of the executives and key players coming from one national or social group even though they sell their goods and services in many countries. It is also worth noting situations where the executives are of one nationality while other nationalities make up the workforce in lower management and staff positions. So, an international outlook and orientation is more than just where one does business. It is fundamentally the culture of the board room and the key staff that principally determines the internationality of the corporate culture.

Knowing these details about the corporate culture will give the coach clues about how to handle coaching situations within the company and how, as well, to get aligned with the company in the first place. With cultural awareness, coaches can assist in improving the quality of communication in myriad ways, and in navigating around what can be very sensitive and difficult internal cultural terrain. As indicated earlier, unless underlying organizational cultural issues are sensitively and creatively managed, differences in cultural orientation can be the cause of considerable miscommunications, conflict and resentment. Coaching programs and coaches can become problems rather than solutions!

There are some final cultural considerations for both the coach and HR:

1   What is the culture of HR?
2   How does it fit within the organizational culture and sub-cultures?
3   What kind of cultural fit is coaching likely to have within the organization?

Regardless of the difficulties outlined above, there are considerable opportunities for both coaches and HR in companies where there is high cultural diversity. Culturally attuned coaching service providers can present innovative coaching approaches that can assist organizations to manage issues that have foundations in culture. One such approach is the 'global coaching' framework as proposed by Rosinski (2003) which proposes 'leveraging cultural differences' for advantage. In the international business environments, HR departments can add value by seeking out coaches who can assist their organizations in shifting from a 'cultural difference as a problem' to a 'cultural difference as opportunity' perspective.

THE CASE STUDIES

We reiterate that the factors included in the four frames are drivers of the corporate mindset and keys to understanding how coaching clients will react in different situations. Understand how these frames form part of the reality of HR and the coach will be better able to know how to make the business relationship a success. We cannot emphasize enough the importance for a coach of 'knowing your customer' in order to build an effective, long-term working relationship with an organizational coaching client. In the international business environment, that is particularly important – and particularly challenging. We offer the following contrasting case studies to draw out some observations and lessons for coaches who want to establish relationships that are of benefit to coach and client alike.

Case study 1: a new culture for a small banking company

With the arrival of a new CEO, the European affiliate of an Israeli Bank employing 50 people had to adapt to a new management style. Unlike his rather distant and autocratic predecessor, the new CEO was a firm believer in consultation, sharing of information and empowerment. He quickly discerned that his senior team was not used to putting forward their own views or accepting personal responsibility for the bank's results, nor were they adept at including their own direct reports in discussions about strategy and important operational matters. A review of the company's organizational chart revealed a very narrow span of control, with some managers having only one direct report. As a consequence, the bank had a tall hierarchy with several management and staff levels. On reflection, it was easy for the new CEO to see how this structure and culture were stifling the life out of the company and undermining relationships with key customers.

A change in the way that managers related to each other, their staff and customers was long overdue, but did they have the necessary skills and competencies to carry this through? The CEO had used coaching when in a different role, and thought that coaching might work here. His discussions with the HR manager revealed that the latter had previously introduced an executive coaching initiative for one senior manager and two department heads. He had chosen a male executive coach with extensive business experience in the banking sector and 15 years of experience in executive coaching. The HR manager was also convinced that the coach understood the links between developing certain managerial competencies and obtaining a cultural shift. The coach was fluent in the three languages spoken in the Bank and he had sound experience in cross-cultural organizations.

After a three-way meeting with the HR manager and the coach, the new CEO could see that the previous project had been well accepted by those involved and was more than satisfied with the HR manager's choice of coach. His confidence in the HR manager's judgment increased with the knowledge that the HR manager himself had recently completed extensive coaching studies. The decision was made to extend the coaching program to all in the management team.

His background helped the HR manager understand the importance of defining the goals of the coaching sessions with the coachee. The program provided for two one-hour coaching sessions per coachee and, depending on their needs, further sessions once per month or every second month. In order to ensure that the coachee focused on the development of skills relevant to the new culture and management style that the new CEO wanted for the bank, the HR manager put considerable time into clarifying development needs with the coach and each coachee, prior to the start of the process.

A process of blocking one day per month for between one and four sessions depending on demand turned out to be most efficient. Although no formal contract was signed, the coach indicated his hourly rate and agreed with the organization that the invoices would be sent on a monthly basis according to the actual number of sessions completed. Coaching sessions were held in the conference room of the Bank, or if the coachee opted for a quieter setting, in the premises of the coach. Two weeks in advance, HR staff coordinated the time schedule for the coaching days in order to match the coachees' availabilities during the predefined days.

The implementation of the coaching program facilitated the integration of the new leadership style by increasing each manager's awareness and involvement in the senior team in a smooth, effective and culturally sensitive way. The return on investment hasn't been estimated, but the excellent business results – 20 to 30 per cent increase in net profit compared to previous years and the evident satisfaction of the new CEO with his team – speaks for itself.

Case study 2: building leadership competencies in a large company

A South African Bank employing several thousand people in more than 15 African countries decided to act upon a major leadership enhancement commitment. In 2005, its leaders agreed to transform their training college into a Global Leadership Center while supporting its goals through ongoing executive coaching and mentoring activities, underpinning one of the company's nine strategic goals, 'To be an employer of choice, renowned for attracting, growing, empowering, rewarding and retaining talent, and being a leader in managing people across cultures'.

A decision was made not to hire coaches from one single coaching company and not to favor any specific coaching methodology in order to create a diverse framework from which the company's managers could choose. The company was more interested in employing coaches with the requisite level of cultural sensitivity to work with managers from diverse ethnic and national groups. In addition, criteria were developed based on years of coaching experience and the number of executive coaching assignments (10 was set as the minimum). In addition, an assessment day to determine the suitability of the participating coaches was held and included:

- A briefing on the Bank's leadership development strategy;
- 30 minutes of presentation by each coach;
- Coaching role plays (50 minutes), where each applicant participated in turn as coach, coachee and observer; and
- Individual debriefings with the panel members.

The selected coaches were not guaranteed they would have an assignment since the final decision regarding the chosen coach was made by the coachee, based on professional profiles prepared by the coach and cleared by the HR department.

An additional key decision was to include only coaches who were willing to involve the line manager in meetings at the beginning of the assignment to define outcomes, at mid term for a progress update and at the end for evaluation of the outcomes. Provisions were made so that meetings respected the coachee's predefined confidentiality parameters.

An independent research group was contracted by the company to evaluate the outcomes of the coaching intervention. Data were collected through a quantitative data collection instrument administered electronically, and qualitative assessments using telephone interviews with coaches and coachees. The entire process included almost 300 coach data questionnaires over 18 months and numerous interviews. Feedback was provided to coaches and areas for improvement were identified for each. While expensive in time and money, this was considered worthwhile given the several hundreds of executives who might potentially seek coaching support and the importance of the global leadership strategy to the success of the bank.

USING THE FOUR FRAMES APPROACH TO REFLECT ON THE CASES

Clearly, the relationship between the coach and the organization was very different in each case. From the structural frame, it is evident that the contracting arrangements and process in the case of the European Bank were rather informal and the 'evaluation' was rather impressionistic in nature. A potential problem with this level of informality is that it could lead to misunderstandings at some later point. From the psycho-social frame, the coach in this case had already forged a good relationship with the HR manager, who had initiated the earlier program, but with the change of leadership he had to convince the new CEO that he had relevant experience as well. The coach was fortunate that the CEO had confidence in the capabilities of his HR manager and agreed with his choice. However, he also needed to understand how the CEO saw the situation, that is, to realize that the CEO wanted to modernize the structure to improve levels of accountability and customer service, and that to do so a change of culture and new attitudes on the part of senior managers towards their staff were needed. Therefore, the coach also needed to be attuned to the cultural considerations (relating to the symbolic frame) so that he could communicate effectively with both the CEO and the HR manager. Overall, this was an interesting assignment for the coach and allowed him to use his language skills to considerable advantage.

The other case involving a large multinational bank is, we believe, more typical of the coaching assignments that are becoming more prevalent around the world. In this situation, the HR department was firmly in control of the selection of coaches, and used a multifaceted, formalized process to do this. What counted most here was not any personal relationship with HR or senior management (although we know that the value of such connections should not be underestimated!) but the capacity of the coaches to convince the selection panel of (a) their coaching credentials and skills and (b) their understanding of the organization and its context. In this, we see an increasing emphasis on issues arising from the structural frame, and that coaches hoping to win such assignments need to cover the formalities of timeframes, processes and outcomes very thoroughly. They also need to satisfy potential clients that they have the qualifications and experience to deliver on developmental outcomes for both coachee and organization (considerations from the psychosocial frame). This is not to diminish the importance of covering relevant issues from the symbolic and political frames from the earliest stages in the scoping phase, and in particular, relevant cultural considerations that arise in relation to the international and global context of business strategy and operations.

'FRAMING' THE COACH-HR RELATIONSHIP

Drawing on the four frames suggested by Bolman and Deal (2003), we now suggest a set of questions that may assist coaches in developing a well-rounded understanding of the organizational context, and in forming a constructive and successful relationship with the HR department. These are set out in Figure 21.1.

CONCLUDING REMARKS

Properly done, coaching can raise performance levels and increase the happiness and job satisfaction of both executives and working-level employees. External coaches have both the time and the experience to bring these activities to a successful outcome when compared with

From the structural frame	From the psychosocial frame
• What outcome is the company seeking from a coaching program?	• How will the coaching program meet the personal and professional needs of coachees?
• How will coaching make the company more successful and sustainable?	• How will the coaching program fit with other management development initiatives in the company?
• Have any recent structural changes affected the company (e.g., a merger, downsizing)?	• What prior experience do employees in this company have with coaching?
• What are the international dimensions of the company's structure?	• What experience and knowledge does the HR department have of coaching?
• At what level in the organization is the coaching program's sponsor?	• How do you think most employees will respond to an opportunity for coaching?
• Who will be included as coachees, and what is the basis for their selection?	• What are they looking for in a coach?
• What are the time frames for the program?	• Have there been any recent changes affecting morale or employee satisfaction?
• Who will make the key decisions about it?	• Will coachees be comfortable if their managers are included in planning the outcomes of the coaching sessions?
• What reporting arrangements are required?	
• How will results be measured and evaluated?	
From the political frame	**From the symbolic (cultural) frame**
• Tell me about the person(s) sponsoring the coaching program.	• How would you describe the corporate culture in this company?
• Which people and groups would expect to benefit from having a coaching program in this company?	• Are there strong subcultures?
• Who still needs to be convinced of the value of a coaching program?	• What events in the past have made the culture what it is?
• What arguments are likely to interest them?	• Who and what are the main influences today?
• What benefits will the HR department gain from implementing coaching?	• How does coaching fit with the corporate culture (or does it seem out of place)?
• Who is represented on the project/implementation committee (and who is not)?	• How do you think coaching will be received across different parts of the organization?
• To what extent will HR oversee the coaching process?	• What are the favored ways to communicate here (languages, degree of formality, etc.)?
• How important is it for employees to have a say in who will be their coach?	• How culturally diverse is this company?
• In what way will line managers be involved?	• Do you think that coaching will work equally well across the different cultural groups?
	• Would team coaching be more appropriate than individual coaching in some cases?
	• What is the HR culture and what implications might there be for running coaching programs?

Figure 21.1 Four frames: coaching questions

internal HR professionals who may be overburdened by day-to-day work and less skilled or experienced in coaching.

The successful employment of external coaches requires a clear understanding by the company and the chosen coach of the company culture, with particular attention to the cross-cultural and international aspects of that culture. Chapter 22, Abbott and McFarlane (p. 331) provides further guidance on choosing a coach. We have also suggested that an understanding of the organizational context necessitates the inclusion of other factors as well. Using the four frames as a guide, these concern structural characteristics, the company's orientation to its employees, and internal politics. If our contention that the selection of coaching companies will be increasingly formalized and managed through the HR department (particularly in larger, international firms) is true, then coaching providers must be prepared for a tough selection process. By using the above set of questions as a guide, coaching providers can put themselves ahead of the competition by using the scoping stages of the project to their best advantage. This includes both finding out, and then demonstrating their understanding of the context within which the project will be conducted, or on the other hand, deciding that the project is not appropriate and withdrawing.

Bibliography

Abbott, G. N. (2006) 'Exploring evidence-based executive coaching as an intervention to facilitate expatriate acculturation: Fifteen case studies', unpublished doctoral dissertation, Canberra, Australian National University.

Abbott, G.N. and Rosinski, P. (2007) 'Global coaching and evidence based coaching: Multiple perspectives operating in a process of pragmatic humanism', *International Journal of Evidence Based Coaching and Mentoring*, 5 (1): 58–77.

Bolman, L. G. and Deal, T. E. (2003) *Reframing Organizations: Artistry, Choice, and Leadership* (3rd edn), San Francisco: Jossey–Bass.

Hofstede, G. (1993) 'Cultural constraints in management theories', *Academy of Management Executive*, 7 (1): 81–94.

Hofstede, G. (2001) *Culture's Consequences Comparing Values, Behaviors, Institutions and Organizations across Nations* (2nd edn), Thousand Oaks, CA: Sage.

Rosinski, P. (2003) *Coaching across Cultures: New Tools for Leveraging National, Corporate and Professional Differences*, London: Nicholas Brealey Publishing.

Skiffington, S. M. and Zeus, P. (2003) *Behavioral Coaching: How to Build Sustainable Personal and Organizational Strength*, Sydney: McGraw-Hill Australia.

Turner, C. (2006) 'Ungagged: Executives on executive coaching', *Ivey Business Journal Online*, May/June. Available online at <www.iveybusinessjournal.com> (accessed 28 April 2008).

CHOOSING COACHES FOR INTERNATIONAL BUSINESS LEADERS?

Qualities and characteristics

Geoffrey Abbott and Chip McFarlane

International business coaches work with global executives and executive teams – the leaders in international business environments – across cultures and across borders. The role is demanding and not for the faint-hearted. The coach's remit covers support for the pursuit of multiple clients' business, personal and societal objectives within dynamic cultural and organizational contexts. This chapter is in three sections. In this first section we examine what characteristics and competencies might be desirable for an international business coach. We suggest that these should largely be a match with those needed for global leadership more generally (though a coach may even require some further capacities). Accordingly, we propose that international business coaches would ideally (though not necessarily) have experience in senior leadership and executive roles in international contexts. The second section is an interview with a leading international business coach, Chip McFarlane. Chip shares his experiences and makes some comments on the selection of coaches for complex international assignments. The final section contains a set of questions which might provide a useful basis for those selecting a coach for international executives.

Consultancy company Development Dimensions International (DDI) recently interviewed executives in multinational companies around the world and identified five characteristics of a successful global executive – i.e., business leaders:

1 Intellectual grunt;
2 Energy and resilience;
3 Cultural adaptation;
4 Emotional intelligence; and
5 Exploration/inquisitiveness (Tandukar 2006).

We agree that each of these is important for international business leaders and their coaches – but the story is not that simple as there are various layers of complexity, many stemming from vastly different contextual variables. Many academics and practitioners have proposed different qualities and competencies for international leaders and executives and we will examine some of these in the following sections.

We give particular attention to culture because it has such a major influence in all aspects of international business and coaching, a point made repeatedly through this *Companion*. For global leaders, cultural awareness, flexibility and adaptation are essential. Intercultural researchers Fons Trompenaars and Charles Hampden-Turner (1998), for example, have found vast differences in how leaders are perceived across cultures and organizations. Similarly, a 12-country study (Kowske and Kshanika 2007) found considerable variation both across and within countries in what was considered to be desirable as leadership competencies. *Analytical ability* and *a capacity to foster teamwork* were rated in the top six across the responses. Otherwise, there were considerable differences and some countries had distinct and unique profiles. They concluded that the research highlights the error in generalizing across countries and regions. They stressed the necessity for managers and HRD practitioners to be well versed in other countries' specific cultures (Kowske and Kshanika 2007: 38). They commented, 'Generalizing the interaction between leadership roles and culture by region may be, at best, insufficient, but at worst, may be harmful to at-work relationships and work practices' (Kowske and Kshanika 2007: 39). It therefore follows that different cultural business contexts are likely to require different qualities in a coach.

The GLOBE project, a major international research project into management, leadership and values, investigated the diversity of attitudes and practices in management. Global coach Cornelius Grove (2007) has selected nine findings which are instructive when considering what skills and abilities are needed to coach internationally:

1   Thirty-five personal attributes of leaders are viewed in some societies as contributing to good leadership, and in other societies as inhibiting good leadership. Among the 35 are 'cunning', 'provocateur', and 'sensitive';

2   'Charismatic leadership' is often said by businesspeople to be highly effective. The GLOBE research confirms that, worldwide, 'Charismatic/Value-Based' leadership is indeed effective; it also specifies the attributes of such leadership;

3   The United States emerges as the only culture in which participative leadership has a positive influence on employee performance;

4   Most managers around the world wish that their companies and supervisors would focus more heavily on high performance than actually is the case;

5   'Team Oriented' leadership is seen by business people in all cultures as moderately or highly desirable and as contributing to good leadership;

6   Managers in the Middle East were less likely than managers anywhere else to view leadership that is 'Charismatic/Value-Based,' 'Team Oriented,' and 'Participative' as substantially contributing to good leadership. On average, they viewed these three characteristics as having only a mildly positive effect;

7   Concern for gender egalitarianism is positively associated with good leadership in the great majority of societies; this finding is notable because fully three-quarters of the 17,300 respondents worldwide were male;

8   'In-Group Collectivism' is the degree to which people express pride, loyalty, and cohesiveness in their organizations. Contrary to the individualistic ethic of the US, American managers value (desire) In-Group Collectivism to the same extent as managers in Russia, Spain, Zambia, Turkey, and Thailand; and

9   Overall, the GLOBE findings suggest that leaders are seen as the embodiment of an ideal state of affairs, and thus as the society's instruments for change.

These findings confirm a variety of leadership practice around the world; the field is embedded with contradictions and paradoxes. They suggest that business executives — and their coaches – who are working in multiple countries and organizational environments, will need to be mindful of and adaptable to what constitutes effective leadership practice in each context. Given that effective leadership varies internationally, it is reasonable to anticipate similar differences in the practices and characteristics of executive coaches.

Executive coaches in any situation clearly need a high level of skill in order to be effective. Chapman, Best and Casteren (2003: 272) provide a description of the necessary attributes for a 'capable coach', including:

1   Self-management;
2   Communication skills;
3   Coaching craft (for example, goal-setting, action planning, capacity to support, exploring options);
4   Interpersonal skills; and
5   Breadth of experience and technical skills.

Abbott, Stening et al. (2006: 306) suggest that when working with expatriate managers (i.e. those working on overseas assignments), these attributes could usefully be supplemented with:

1   Sound appreciation of the cultures of the client and the host country;
2   Self-awareness of the coach's own cultural background;
3   Personal experience in cultural adaptation and acculturation; and
4   Familiarity with cross-disciplinary intercultural theory and research.

Taken together, these nine criteria provide a base set of qualities and competencies for international business coaches. However, we propose that if the coach is looking to work with senior leaders – the so-called 'C-Suite' – the bar has to be raised higher. The qualities and competencies need to match those (current and aspired) of the international executive being coached, noting a preference by many very senior executives to be coached only by someone who has been successful in high-level leadership roles. The DDI qualities noted earlier offer a starting point, but not the end point. Recent writings in leadership and coaching have offered various approaches that are informative as we contemplate qualities of a high-impact, high-level international business coach. We will consider the views of some of the leading researchers and practitioners in the coaching and leadership field.

Goldsmith, Greenberg, Robertson and Hu-Chan (2003) interviewed 200 leaders from around the world and identified five emerging characteristics of global leadership:

1   Thinking globally;
2   Appreciating cultural diversity;
3   Developing technological savvy;
4   Building partnerships and alliances; and
5   Sharing leadership.

These five qualities are notably different from the DDI list, illustrating the diversity of thinking around the issue of leadership. Returning to the influence of culture, global cross-cultural management company TMC proposes leadership development that highlights:

1   Cultural self- and other awareness;
2   Global learning;

333

3   Listening observation and inquiry skills; and
4   The skill of cultural style switching (Walker, Walker and Schmitz 2003: 311).

Earley and Ang (2003) (academic researchers in the field of international cross-cultural management and organizational behavior) argue that effective global executives must be high in cultural intelligence – or CQ. There are three facets that CQ encompasses:

1   Cognitive – Do I know about the cultural nuances and practices here?
2   Behavioral – Given (1), do I have the skills and abilities to respond appropriately and effectively?
3   Motivational – Even if I know what will work in this cultural context, and can change if I want to, am I really motivated to act (in other words, am I prepared to let go of my old ways of operating that are culturally bound)?

High CQ means answering 'yes' to all three Earley and Ang (2003: 59) questions.

Black, Morrison and Gregersen (1999: xii) found through their extensive and long-term research of expatriate management and through interviewing over 130 leaders worldwide that global leaders are consistently competent in four areas:

1   Inquisitiveness, 'They love to learn and are driven to understand and master the complexities of the global business environment';
2   Perspective, 'Global leaders relish the challenge of balancing the ever-present tensions between global integration and local adaptation';
3   Character, 'Character is exhibited through the leader's ability to connect emotionally with people of different backgrounds and cultures and through the consistent demonstration of personal integrity in a world full of ethical conflicts'; and
4   Savvy, 'Highly skilled at both identifying market opportunities and applying international resources to make the most of those opportunities'.

American futurist Gary Hamel (2007) envisages a totally new leadership and management landscape that more reflects the development of the internet than traditional management approaches. He suggests that new leadership will require qualities such as courage, experimentation, conversation, inclusiveness and passion, concluding that society needs a leadership model that, 'truly elicits, honors, and cherishes human initiative, creativity, and passion – these tender, essential ingredients for business success in the new millennium' (Hamel 2007: 255).

Organizational consultant Peter Block (2000), whose book *Flawless Consulting* has considerable application to international business coaching, observes that a 'consciousness of their own limitations' was a shared quality of great leaders such as Gandhi, Lincoln, Martin Luther King, and Confucius. He suggests that humility is a key ingredient of leadership and consulting (Block 2000: 341); similarly, we suggest, for international coaching.

Nancy Adler, a leading writer, researcher and theorist in international organizational behavior, draws attention to the tension between one's immediate national and organizational concerns and the broader interests of humanity and the future (Adler 2002: 66). She quotes *The Way of Lao Tzu* in capturing a traditional vision of leadership from the sixth century which is beginning to be echoed in leadership thinking in this century:

I have three treasures. Guard and keep them.
The first is deep love,
The second is frugality,
And the third is not to dare to be ahead of the world.
Because of deep love, one is courageous.
Because of frugality, one is generous.
Because of not daring to be ahead of the world,
One becomes the leader of the world.

(Adler 2002: 284)

Adler poses three powerful coaching questions for global executives (Adler 2005):

1 What am I good at?
2 What am I passionate about?
3 What is the world's greatest need?

Further, she invites a new vocabulary of leadership that sheds antiquated images based on the military, hierarchy, and production line concepts. Adler proposes the use of art and artistic processes to invoke new images. Global coach Philippe Rosinski gives prominence to art as a medium in his global coaching model (Rosinski 2003: 190).

Manfred Kets De Vries, an internationally recognized expert in the psychodynamics of leadership and management, makes a case for coaching for *authentizotic* organizations where leaders are authentic in fostering trust and reliance, and can invigorate people with values of exploration and learning (Kets de Vries 2007: 345). He argues that capacities of a leader in such an organization include:

• Building trust and trusting relationships;
• Long-term thinking;
• Genuineness (alignment of the public and personal);
• Willingness to face harsh realities;
• An interest beyond performance to meaning and purpose;
• Storytelling and sharing; and
• Being present.

For coaches to be able to work with leaders in this mode, they need to have undertaken their own development process and achieved a degree of self-actualization that includes a strong values base and capacity to be present.

Leading Australian management academic Amanda Sinclair in *Leadership for the Disillusioned* challenges traditional models of charismatic and heroic leadership and proposes a new leadership that is spiritual, reflective with less ego, in touch with the breath and body, concerned with identity, connected and freeing or liberating (Sinclair 2007: 165). She notes a paradox that, 'leadership is adulated as a remedy to all sorts of societal problems but routinely disappoints us' (Sinclair 2007: 186). Once again, for coaches to be able to work with leaders in challenging the status quo and encouraging expanded models of leadership as proposed by Sinclair, they need to have reached a high level of self- and professional development.

Researchers from two global business consulting companies (Rosen, Digh, Singer and Phillips 2000: 29) provide a comprehensive list of 'global literacies'. The list was based on a worldwide survey of 1,000 senior executives and interviews with CEOs of 78 companies:

335

1 Personal literacy (aggressive insight, confident humility, authentic flexibility, reflective decisiveness, realistic optimism);
2 Social literacy (pragmatic trust, urgent listening, constructive impatience, connective teaching, collaborative individualism);
3 Business literacy (chaos navigator, business geographer, historical futurist, leadership liberator, economic integrator); and
4 Cultural literacy (proud ancestor, inquisitive internationalist, respectful modernizer, cultural bridger, global capitalist).

These literacies make good sense for any coach wishing to work in high-level international business settings.

We propose that all of the above perspectives have potential applicability in international business coaching. If you are a coach, we suggest you use these various lists and criteria to examine your current preparedness to take on major international work. Executives might consider the material as they consider their future leadership development. Those who are selecting coaches might consider the information as they develop and run selection processes.

Our observation of global coaching is that like high impact leadership (Goleman 2000), high impact coaching requires a situational approach. Some competencies, literacies, personal characteristics, and so on will be more important than others depending on context and the challenges of the leadership and associated coaching challenges. Flexibility, adaptability and cultural awareness are valuable attributes for coaches as they find creative ways of working with a diversity of executive clients in a diversity of locations.

An item missing from the above perspectives is curiosity. We argue that because each assignment is so different, coaches need to have an insatiable curiosity about what is going on with their clients in the world. Curiosity fuels insightful coaching questions. This questioning assists clients to reach higher levels of awareness about the subtleties and nuances of their challenges. Clients are then better positioned to take actions that will lead to more productive and satisfying work and personal lives.

The scope and challenges of international business coaching are expanding. First, leaders and companies are expected to engage more with issues of sustainability and corporate responsibility. Bottom-line results and performance of course remain central to all international business activities. However, there is willingness by individuals and companies to go further and to look at societal and global issues. Secondly, traditional management approaches are being questioned and more attention is being devoted by leaders to consideration of meaning and purpose. Male-dominated charismatic leadership models don't seem to be offering the necessary long-term solutions. Thirdly, there is a growing awareness that culture has a major influence on personal and organizational success (i.e., the interplay between personal identity and different levels of culture including national, organizational, team, local, head office, community, and so on). The consequence of these and other developments are that executive coaches must be prepared and able to guide and to engage in different kinds of conversations and in so doing increase the potential for the reality of globalization to have positive impacts in many different ways.

CASE STUDY: CHIP MCFARLANE

The following is a discussion between Geoffrey Abbott and international leadership coach Chip McFarlane. Chip was born in Panama, grew up and began his business career in the USA, and has since managed and coached at executive level in Europe, the Americas, Asia and Australia. Chip is currently based in Sydney as a master coach and business owner/director with the Institute of Executive Coaching (Australia):

Geoff: Chip, you are well-traveled and have coached in many parts of the world. Can you give an overview of where you have been and what you have done in international coaching and leadership – the short edition!

Chip: I was born in Panama and raised in New York. I found in management roles that I was naturally drawn to coaching. I had a role with a French multinational as Director of Operations. I was having an impact in developing the people who worked for me and that made a difference in terms of profitability and their growth. That inclination was the strongest. I began to identify this thing called coaching, including with my peers, and moved more formally into coaching executives. I coached in New York. Then, individuals in the US I had coached moved overseas and my services were in demand internationally. I have coached just about everywhere except in Africa. I have coached in the Middle East, Israel, and Saudi Arabia.

Geoff: Are there variations in how you coach in Singapore, New York, Australia, etc.?

Chip: A key common element is to explore the executive and learn from them from the stories they tell about themselves – their stories of success, their stories of power – stories that include elements of their personal values. Whether they share their values explicitly or not, their stories and how they tell them give me a sense of the individual. How does power appear to them in their stories – when it works well for them, and when it doesn't? It gives me a stronger idea of the individual and also the cultural context they are in. These are global stories from individuals – how they are in the world and how they tell their stories from their local perspectives. That is a common piece of all my coaching. Beyond that, the brief that I am given by the company determines the specific elements. It is transitioning into a chief executive officer role from chief financial officer, or is it a role on the Board – or maybe a new assignment as a country manager. There will be a different flavor each time. The nature of the task determines the shape and content of the coaching intervention but I never lose sight of the individual's values and what shapes and drives them.

Geoff: What about your own identity in terms of culture and nationality etc., how does that play out in the coaching?

Chip: It is interesting. I find that it loses importance very quickly. Initially they have this view of me from my profile that I am American and a manager, especially when they hear my accent. They will assume things, particularly if they have not seen a photo. They assume a very Western leadership and management approach – American centric. While my formative years were in America and it is part of my fabric that I carry with me, there is more to it. I was a midshipman in the US naval academy and that affects the way I am – my experiences of leadership. I can look at leadership through the eyes of someone in the US military and also the Society of Friends. I incorporate Buddhist and Eastern approaches as well. I have Panamanian heritage, and Samoan, so for me it has been a journey of understanding many systems. Self and leadership work together in different ways in different contexts for me and they help me to work with executives who have a variety of stories and leadership experiences and practices.

Geoff: You are a leader yourself – as a company director. Do you have a set leadership style yourself that you articulate?

Chip: There are overt and covert elements of how I lead and influence. Sometimes there is the upfront, charismatic and sometimes loud individual who is passionate about how our culture and organization is. Also, there is the need to support and have side conversations that are more social so that people get a spectrum rather than a one dimensional leadership approach. Being approachable but at times not accessible – making unilateral decisions but also being consultative.

Geoff: From what you have observed, is leadership different in different places? Is there a common set of leadership qualities? What have you observed in your executive clients?

Chip: There are some leadership qualities – and leaders are not necessarily those holding the power positions in organizations – with those who take on the mantle of leadership there are some commonalities. A level of self awareness is a core element. The effective leader who builds great teams and organizations uses this awareness of self-in-context to great effect. I observe others who have a level of awareness about their impact and power – but also cause a degree of collateral damage by their actions. They in a sense act independent of their deeper awareness. They disconnect their actions from awareness – they don't have what I refer to as a moral or ethical compass. This is the other side of true leadership – to tap into the set of core values and to act with a sound ethical and moral framework. With international business so full of ambiguity and complexity, that moral compass is essential if the leader is to stay on track and focused on getting a sustainable outcome that does not cause damage locally, nationally or globally. Inside there needs to be internal guidance – a sense of self – through the maelstrom. The complexity is across business issues, cultural issues, political and so on.

Geoff: What else seems to lead to success?

Chip: Those who can identify themselves not just to one culture but to many. There is a spectrum at one end of almost arrogance, and at the other humility. So they are capable of moving to a variety of situations and can hold the paradox. There is arrogance around self belief but a high level of humility at the same time. They can lead in new situations with that wonderful balance of self confidence and humility – confidence in their capacity to succeed but also understanding that they are novices in the culture and can learn from those around them.

Geoff: A key question Chip – do you think international business coaches have to have the same or similar qualities to the executive they are coaching?

Chip: I would say yes. Having those qualities and preferably some comparable experiences can be invaluable. One other key ingredient is an insatiable curiosity. As a coach I have to be genuinely interested in the client and the client's world. In cross cultural work this is essential. It is also, of course, essential for leaders working internationally. But there is more to it. As a coach working with an expat, the demands are different. You are not as a coach being asked to identify so closely with the local culture and you find that many coaches working internationally are connected to expat communities and are effective in working in that space. However, if you want to coach host nationals, then there are new challenges. Say, if you want to be successful in coaching Japanese or Salvadorian nationals, perhaps over a local coach, one of the elements you need is self-understanding that is sufficiently strong to allow a temporary 'letting go' of self in order to understand the story of the other from the point of view of the other. This is not easily done. It is also not possible to do completely. You can never understand a different culture in the same way as someone from that culture. It is another paradox of letting go of self but not losing self as you work from someone else's cultural and personal worldview. I have to be open to the individual but maintaining an awareness of self.

Geoff: So the balance is between keeping yourself safe and centered but also letting go to move to a position of empathy – in the shoes of the other?

Chip: Yes. If I use the analogy of the pendulum on the end of a swing – the further it travels out from the center, the tighter the center has to be – otherwise the circular orbit is distorted. To stretch into new cultures and perspectives, I have to rely on the strength of my center so that I can stay with the client at my full capacity. The stronger the center the further I can go and still have impact in supporting the client.

Geoff: Have you run into any startlingly unsuccessful international coaching assignments (or been involved in any!)? What happened?

338

Chip: I have come in behind some where the coaches involved have fallen over. The coach has not been able to reach out sufficiently to work with the host national executive from their way of seeing the world. While the coach has been very high caliber working within more familiar territory, they have not been sufficiently centered to operate effectively at the full extension of the pendulum. They were using the cookie cutter approach – the 'seven-steps-of-whatever' coaching model – and there seemed to be no genuine connection between two people. The coach had not been able to see the world from the point of view of the other. Essentially a truly powerful coaching relationship was not possible. It fell down at the start – there was no exploration of the person's story and potential for growth.

Geoff: How important is that first meeting?

Chip: Very. It is interesting because sometimes it has to be done by telephone so you don't have the nuances of face-to-face. You have to convey your presence through your voice and insightful questions and the space you give the person for their story – all through the telephone.

Geoff: Some coaches say they don't like the telephone. Others use it all the time. With international work there is a need sometimes for telephone work. How do you view it when working across cultures?

Chip: I have a personal preference for a combination. Face-to-face is very important in establishing the relationship. In a business environment, any important engagement or negotiation has to be done face-to-face. You can do the groundwork electronically – the buildup. But typically the key work is done face-to-face. So I can do the first meeting by phone but once I have met the person it takes on new and deeper dimension. The relation-ship builds to a new level. It is then possible to challenge and add tension in a different way. They understand more about me and my presence and the level of trust is much higher. I can ask different kinds of questions.

Geoff: Building trust seems essential in international business relationships generally and in coaching – yet it is not given much attention – it is sort of assumed? Do you have any particular strategies for building trust in the coaching relationship?

Chip: For me, there is a certain level established by my track record – often by word of mouth. The executive will hear from someone they already trust that I am someone that can add value and can be challenging. This is of great value when the executive is from a different cultural background and may have some hesitation working with a foreigner. They will have a list of rational reasons to engage with me – plus the relational advantage I get from being referred by a trusted colleague. It then comes down to me to build on that swift trust through demonstrating empathy, support and value in the first and subsequent sessions.

Geoff: You have mentioned a couple of times the challenge of working with someone who is a host national – that is, you are the foreigner coaching in someone's own culture. Can you say more about that?

Chip: Yes, there are challenges of coaching host nationals – it is not just about language or even cultural knowledge as is sometimes assumed. Success comes from having a strong sense of self where the moral and ethical compass is accurate – to go back to the earlier metaphor. You can then relax into the task of identifying with the person's unique story. This raises a point – metaphors can be very powerful tools in international coaching. Effective international business coaches know that metaphors need to be contextually appropriate. Using clumsy metaphors can torpedo the relationship.

Geoff: You have mentioned the importance of being centered, having a moral compass and being able to operate from an empathetic perspective, is there anything else that makes a coach effective internationally?

Chip: An appreciation for the business environment of the person they are coaching is crucial. Another is an understanding of what structurally is important in the organizational environment. This includes the connection of the company to the local community, economy, environment – the coach needs to be savvy about what is really going on in the situation, and not just be culturally aware and adaptable. Many executives I coach have a very strong national identity. One of the individuals in Japan stated from the beginning that he wanted to make a difference for Japan. The same in Singapore – she said 'I want to make a difference to Singapore', even though the assignment was here in Australia – same in Malaysia.

Geoff: I found the same in El Salvador where many of the executives could have headed to an easier and successful life in the USA but had chosen to stay because of their deep affection for the Salvadorian people and concern about the future.

Chip: It is common and something that we as coaches need to be very aware of – this strong cultural and national identity, within a multinational company environment. And we have our own identities and affiliations that we need to be aware of as we work in these complex corporate and cultural environments.

Geoff: Are there other elements where leadership and coaching qualities tend to overlap?

Chip: The idea that there is a culture – we are not all the same. This is not something that everyone in international business necessarily gives genuine attention to. There is an overlap of culture and business. As a leader in international companies and as a coach, the challenge is to see the business and other issues in connection with rather than separate from the culture. Where I see disconnect, I see lack of effectiveness in both coaching and leadership.

Geoff: What you are saying is consistent with your Institute's approach of giving attention to Ken Wilber's Integral Model with its four quadrants – the self, behavior, culture and the broader structural and systemic issues: and, most importantly, how they all relate.

Chip: Yes.

Geoff: Let's look at the positive side. What would be your Rolls Royce international coaching assignment? What qualities were particularly important and how were these deployed to good effect?

Chip: Coaching a CEO of a funds management business. His results before coaching were great – exceeding targets by over 120 per cent. He was originally from India and operating in Singapore running a regional business with huge success. But his story to himself was dissatisfaction with living a provincial life. Results were not the issue. This was more along the lines of him making a shift in consciousness from a regional to global consciousness. He is now in a position which has a global reach. The coaching challenge was to allow him to take his story and his perspective to a global level. I still get cards and calls from him – he says, 'What you challenged me on and how I grew in tying in things is what brought me to this point.' For me, making the leap from local to regional to a global view was a Rolls Royce coaching experience.

Geoff: I heard Sir John Whitmore talk at a conference recently in Sydney. He talked a lot about the potential for coaching to make a significant impact for good at a global level – for example in finding ways of connecting people with very disparate political and religious viewpoints and where there are seemingly intractable problems. What do you think of that – the bigger picture?

Chip: Yes. Increasingly, there is a global role for coaching. Very good coaches are able to sometimes add in perspective without agenda. I am engaged by an organization to work on a person's growth. I do this with a high degree of care for that individual. With that degree of support and safety, the conversation can expand into challenging areas of how they see the world and what responsibilities they have to society beyond their immediate role. These kinds of challenging conversations – if they are happening around the world among leaders of all persuasions – can make a big impact in hitting some of the harder issues we are facing. I find that the more support I give to executives and connect with them on a fundamental level, the more they tend to reach out in their thinking to these global perspectives.

Geoff: Do you think that just asking questions about people's ethics can draw people's attention to their own values? Maybe just raising issues in coaching conversations that are otherwise not considered – that in itself leads to more ethical leadership practices?

Chip: More than just throwing around ideas of ethics but putting someone through the experience of exploring their ethics in the context of their current leadership challenges. This grounds the conversation and links it to what people are actually doing – not just saying.

Geoff: So we are like Trojan horses with our soldiers being conversations?

Chip: Something like that. It takes me back to helping them strengthen their moral and ethical compass so they are not overwhelmed by the complexity and ambiguities that surround them. So it has a very practical side – raising the level of leadership higher and giving people greater resilience in the face of what can be massive challenges in some of these international assignments conducted under duress and sometimes physical danger.

Geoff: This is almost a philosophical point about the nature of humans. Do you think that fundamentally people will behave ethically if given a choice? Meaning that if you ask questions about ethics you can make the assumption by and large that it is going to result in people connecting with some strong value sets. You have a minute to answer that one!

Chip: If someone says 'behave ethically' there is always a judgment about what that means in practice – particularly when you are talking about cross cultural work. Everyone is ethical – but how do they define that in the context. What is ethical behavior for them as they grow their organizations, grow high performance teams, increase shareholder value and so on? What we explore is how their ethics play out in the situation.

Geoff: As an executive coach then, what you are saying is that if you want to be effective with high level executives in multinationals and in international contexts you must be able to go into these kinds of areas. This sounds well beyond results focused goal setting processes that many coaching programs are teaching.

Chip: Sooner or later it does have to go there. Some of the more powerful coaching happens around values and ethics.

Geoff: How about the spiritual dimension – even beyond the societal and ethical issues – does that play a part in your coaching? Should a coach be able to introduce conversations about spirituality?

Chip: Yes, even helping people to understand what that means. For me personally, it is that which is greater than myself in this moment. So my values are actually part of my spiritual development because they form something greater than what I am right now. They allow me to aspire to something bigger beyond the moment. For some individuals it is religion and an understanding of their religion. Working with and understanding those religious and spiritual dimensions is important for the coach because many international executives don't live in an atheist environment or culture. They will be guided in their context some-how by some relationship to divinity. For a coach not to go there is to avoid a central part of who the person is and how their reality is constructed. That is not to say a coach has to be religious – but he or she has to be able to have deep conversations that can support the executive in all aspects of development.

Geoff: How about gender? Is it a factor in coach effectiveness internationally do you think?

Chip: Some individuals find it difficult to work with a woman. In most cases though there is no issue. Culturally, in strong patriarchal societies, it can be an issue. Senior male execu-tives may be unwilling to share their thoughts and be challenged by a woman – regardless of how personally or professionally powerful the coach may be. It may cause major resist-ance and I have seen this happen with some exceptional coaches in an international context.

Geoff: Looking ahead Chip, can you see any emerging trends in international business that are going to require new or different qualities and competencies in coaching?

341

Chip: Some multinationals are seeing the need to acknowledge the local culture and environments much more than in the past. This puts an equal pressure on coaches working with those companies across different locations – to engage much more personally and directly with local issues, people and cultures. Mining and pharmaceuticals – many are not only transnational, they also have to pay attention to the local community. Who is running what, who are the significant players? What issues are facing local communities that the company needs to engage with? This localization goes side-by-side with globalization. It is another paradox – the greater the forces of globalization, the more attention has to be paid locally. This is a very positive development for the health of society more generally. For coaches, we have to pay more attention to the context to be able to ask insightful questions on how executives engage locally.

Geoff: What about accreditation Chip? If I am an international executive and looking for a coach, should I ask about certification?

Chip: Big question. Some of the exceptional coaches internationally do not have accreditation. They may get accreditation afterwards. The trouble is that accreditation and coach training programs vary so much. In the Institute here, we make a point of only using very experienced and high quality coaches to train other coaches. They are not just getting theory and models and the '7 steps' to this and that. This is not always the case with coach training. Anyone looking for a coach should look beyond just the accreditation issue to the quality of the coach. And when looking at accreditation, find out what the training and accreditation was all about. You will also find that very few coach training programs give much attention to international business. Your accredited 'master coach' may or may not have, for example, business acumen that can equip them to ask insightful questions to a leader in a multinational. It is a difficult area and one we are very engaged with.

Geoff: Chip, it seems that to coach internationally you have to be some kind of super human being. Is it too much to expect of anyone?

Chip: Yes and No. I am Libran. We are setting the bar high – but not too high. Being effective in this kind of space does require a range of experiences and qualities so that you can keep your sense of self.

Geoff: What is ahead Chip? Is demand for international coaching of this kind going to grow?

Chip: It is, as the challenges grow and the support offered by peers and mentors is not enough. Leaders need support – there is a space for a good coach. The coach offers something different. I become the centre of their existence for a moment. None of their other relationships have that gift to offer. I am the centre of their world for the time I am coaching them. They can go back to self-in-context in a very profound way that otherwise is rarely if ever possible. They know – as I ask them the questions and challenge them – that all that I care about is their development and their issues.

Geoff: What you are saying is that the high care you give to individuals then allows them to explore further out into their organizational and even global responsibilities? It is all about me but it is all about the world.

Chip: Me, the chief executive and the person spinning around the globe.

Geoff: Do you find a gap there – between the public and private persona?

Chip: Sometimes. They are not allowed to let down the public face of confidence – even with close advisors. Coaching can provide an outlet for them to explore their doubts and fears and strengthen their resolve as they tackle the various challenges. The coaching conversation is often one they can't have with anyone else. For coaches to provide that kind of support we have to be there for the person and to help them to traverse the personal, the local, the organizational and the global. As a coach, to do that you have to challenge yourself – to move perspectives and to push into uncomfortable places.

TOOL: SELECTING A COACH – USEFUL QUESTIONS

These questions are not in a set order. They may be useful as a basis for designing a structured interview to select coaches for assignments in international business. Coaches seeking international assignments might use these as a checklist and in preparing for interviews.

1 What is your coaching experience?
2 What did you do before you were a coach?
3 What different kinds of management or leadership experience have you had?
4 What are your beliefs about leadership and being an executive?
5 Have you lived and worked in different countries? How was that experience for you?
6 How much do you consider that culture plays a part in leadership? Can you give some illustrations from your experience?
7 When has your curiosity got you into trouble?
8 When has your curiosity worked for you?
9 How would you describe your coaching approach when dealing with senior international executives?
10 Where did you learn about coaching? Have you had coaching-specific training? What did that entail?
11 In which companies have you conducted coaching programs before? What specifically did you do and what was the outcome?
12 What is your 'worst' experience in coaching internationally?
13 What is your 'best' experience in coaching internationally?
14 What do you consider to be the most important qualities of an international executive, particularly one with cross-border leadership responsibility?
15 How important is culture as an influence in international business?
16 Do you speak any other languages? How do you feel about coaching someone in a language that is not the client's first language?
17 Can you give some examples where culture has been an important issue in a coaching assignment? How did you work with the cultural issues? What was the outcome?
18 The clients you are dealing with are mostly from an X cultural background. What do you know about X?
19 Can you provide the names of two executives who you have coached who would be prepared to be referees?
20 Have you had experience either managing or coaching using the phone or different technologies? Provide details.
21 What kinds of personal and professional development do you do for yourself? Can you share some experiences with us?
22 If you were to list four of your key qualities that make you a successful coach, what would they be?
23 What is 'culture shock'? Have you experienced it yourself?
24 How might you coach someone who is experiencing difficulties adjusting to a new culture?
25 How would you describe or rate your international business savvy or acumen?

Bibliography

Abbott, G. N., Stening, B. W. et al. (2006) 'Coaching expatriate managers for success: Adding value beyond training and mentoring', *Asia Pacific Journal of Human Resources*, 44 (3): 295–317.

Adler, N. J. (2002) *International Dimensions of Organizational Behavior*, Cincinnati: South-Western.

Adler, N. J. (2005) 'The art of leadership: Coaching in the twenty-first century', in H. Morgan, P. Harkins and M. Goldsmith (eds), *The Art and Practice of Leadership Coaching*, Hoboken, NJ: John Wiley and Sons.

Black, J. S., Morrison, A. J. and Gregersen, H. B. (1999) *Global Explorers: The Next Generation of Leaders*, New York: Routledge.

Block, P. (2000) *Flawless Consulting: A Guide to Getting Your Expertise Used*, New York: Jossey-Bass/Pfeiffer.

Chapman, T., Best, B. and Casteren, P. V. (2003) *Executive Coaching: Exploding the Myths*, New York: Palgrave Macmillan.

Earley, P. C. and Ang, S. (2003) *Cultural Intelligence: Individual Interactions across Cultures*, Stanford: Stanford University Press.

Goldsmith, M., Greenberg, C. L., Robertson, A. and Hu-Chan, M. (2003) *Global Leadership: The Next Generation*, Upper Saddle River: Prentice-Hall.

Grove, C. (2007) 'Nine highlights from the GLOBE project's findings'. Available online at <www.grovewell.com/pub-GLOBE-highlights.html> (accessed 30 April 2008).

Goleman, D. (2000) 'Leadership that gets results', *Harvard Business Review*, March 2000: 78–90.

Hamel, G. (2007) *The Future of Management*, Boston, MA: Harvard Business School Press.

Kets de Vries, M. (2007) 'Conclusion: Towards authentizotic organizations', in M. Kets de Vries, M. K. Korotov and E. Florent-Treacy (eds), *Coaching and Couch: The Psychology of Making Better Leaders*, Basingstoke: Palgrave Macmillan.

Kowske, B. J. and Kshanika, A. (2007) 'Towards defining leadership: What mid-level managers need to know in twelve countries', *Human Resource Development International*, 10 (1): 21–41.

Rosen, R., Digh, P., Singer, M. R. and Phillips, C. (2000) *Global Literacies: Lessons on Business Leadership and National Cultures*, New York: Simon & Schuster.

Rosinski, P. (2003) *Coaching across Cultures: New Tools for Leveraging National, Corporate and Professional Differences*, London: Nicholas Brealey Publishing.

Sinclair, A. (2007) *Leadership for the Disillusioned: Moving Beyond Myths and Heroes to Leading that Liberates*, Crows Nest: Allen and Unwin.

Tandukar, A. (2006) 'Global powers', *Business Review Weekly*, 2–8 November: 36–8.

Trompenaars, F. and Hampden-Turner, C. (1998). *Riding the Waves of Culture: Understanding Cultural Diversity in Global Business*, New York: McGraw-Hill.

Walker, D., Walker, T. and Schmitz, J. (2003) *Doing Business Internationally: The Guide to Cross-Cultural Success*, New York: McGraw-Hill.

CONCLUSION

Michel C. Moral and Geoffrey Abbott

Before you close the book and store it in your library, let's take a few minutes to think about what it said.

As editors, to be explicit, we created this book with our colleagues because we passionately believe that international business coaching offers possibilities for invigorating the spirit and practice of global business. For good or for bad, globalization has given enormous influence to corporations and to those who run them, with corporate assets of major multinationals easily outstripping national GDPs of many developing nations. Our gift is a *Companion* to those who are seeking, through coaching, to take advantage of the opportunities and possibilities being presented by economic, social, and political change. We see coaching, based on action learning principles and ethical behavior, as a way of (1) exploring more efficient business practices and (2) bringing the best out of people by way of more satisfying relationships and stronger communities. (Regarding the latter, we see healthy organizations as 'communities'.)

Underlying beliefs around international business coaching are deeply embedded in issues relating to culture and the future of global societies. Richard Nisbett, in the epilogue to his book *The Geography of Thought* published in 2003, gives his opinion on the current debate on the future of the cultural values in international companies. One view (Fukuyama 1992) assumes domination of western 'natural' values while an alternative view (Huntington, 1996) predicts that irreconcilable differences between East and West will prevail. Richard finally considers the possibility of a convergence and the emergence of new cognitive forms based on 'the blending of social systems and values', at least within the upper part of the management system of global companies.

In fact, about three-quarters of the literature related to management has been written by US Americans and most concepts (motivation, leadership, satisfaction, cohesion, etc.) were invented and developed during the period 1950–1980. Individualism, with a taste of Protestantism, saying that the human being can drive his or her (usually his) destiny, is dominant in the management and coaching paradigms. Facts will show an increasing number of global executives born in countries considered a few years ago as 'emerging'. Despite these people having been trained in Oxford or Harvard, they are basically Indian (Lakshmi Mittal, Ratan Tata, Tulsi Tanti, Anand Mahinda, Azim Hasham Preji, etc.), Chinese (Li Ka-Shing, etc.) or Mexican (Carlos Slim Helú, probably the richest person in the world). We know from experience that

(1) values can spread from one world to another over time and that (2) acculturation assists in bringing out the potential of a person. For instance, each succeeding decade, French executives are considered less and less arrogant and more and more pragmatic. This is due to the diffusion of the inductive way of thinking among the population of top global managers. Hyper-deductive French high potential managers had to adapt or be rejected. These high fliers were then teaching in business schools that Descartes' view of knowledge ends at the French border.

We can anticipate that similar mechanisms will function over time. For instance, we have noted in David Drake's chapter (Chapter 4) the idea of a 'third space' involved in the development of a multicultural personality or identity. According to Richard Nisbett (2003), Chinese have no need of a 'third space' to reconcile contradiction, and according to Sigmund Freud, our unconscious is capable of accepting at the same time something and its contrary. Just as the French executive learned from Americans the virtues of inductive thinking over time, Americans may learn from Chinese the virtues of holistic reasoning or the virtues of a different management of time. 'It is not useful to pull the shoot off the tree to make it grow faster', says a Chinese proverb.

We have seen in the past that different cultural ways of doing things are slowly but surely spreading. For instance, the very Japanese approach in Toyota developed into concepts like 'lean production' (or just 'lean') which is now used all over the world. No doubt Indian and Chinese values in business will generate some new management concepts which will dramatically change the way of doing business. The history of 'lean' demonstrates that a concept is modified when it is exported from a given culture to the world. The same will occur with 'Chindian' concepts and it is difficult to predict what will be the future of business and, consequently, the future of coaching.

Our view is that coaching – done with a global mindset and with attention to the opportunities that cultural differences offer – has a role to play in encouraging deep and creative dialogue among leaders and followers about how the business world should look in the future. Even more powerfully, this kind of dialogue, supported by rigorous coaching practice, can lead to actions that support fundamental change for the good in the face of stark global challenges across financial, environmental, political, social and spiritual frontiers.

Some new trends in international coaching are already visible and we have tried to anticipate directions and add to the knowledge through the different chapters. For instance, collective forms of coaching are developing and our book has given attention to team and organizational coaching. Also, inter-cultural issues are becoming more prevalent – a theme interwoven through the chapters. The contributors share a multiple realities view of the world and social constructivism underlies the thinking through many chapters. Along these lines, diversity in general, gender diversity, as well as professional diversity or corporate culture diversity, will need some deeper investigations. We live in a global virtual world and coaches are increasingly being drawn into technological delivery forms that make the task more complex yet potentially more creative and dynamic. Remote, 'virtual' and transverse management will have to be addressed through coaching with more solid concepts and we have given some attention to this topic. Collective intelligence, which assembles all these issues, still lacks tools. We think that coaching might offer a starting point generating change through surfacing and mobilizing collective intelligence.

We have a wide area of potential research and practice in front of us. We are part of a multidisciplinary pursuit of knowledge where theory interacts with practice across multiple contexts. A lot of scholars, coaches, and consultants are accumulating and sharing knowledge and related skills but this gold mine has not yet been properly exploited. Our offering is to start a conversation and to bring together some ideas and tools that might help. We encourage you as coaches, consultants, CEOs, human resource professionals – whatever your current role – to engage with the possibilities and potential of international business coaching.

Michel C. Moral, Paris
Geoffrey Abbott, Sydney

Bibliography

Fukuyama, F. (1992) *The End of History and the Last Man*, New York: Free Press.
Huntington, S.P. (1996) *The Clash of Civilizations and the Remaking of World Order*, New York: Simon and Schuster.
Nisbett, R.E. (2003) *The Geography of Thought: How Asians and Westerners Think Differently . . . and Why*, New York: The Free Press.

Subject Index

Author Index